高校转型发展系列教材

实用英语口译实训教程

黄 岩 主编

隋丹妮 关明孚 符 蕊 赵唱白 副主编

A Coursebook of Practical Interpreting

清华大学出版社

北京

图书在版编目(CIP)数据

实用英语口译实训教程 / 黄岩 主编. —北京：清华大学出版社，2018（2024.1重印）
(高校转型发展系列教材)
ISBN 978-7-302-49635-9

Ⅰ．①实… Ⅱ．①黄… Ⅲ．①英语—口译—高等学校—教材 Ⅳ．①H319.9

中国版本图书馆 CIP 数据核字(2018)第 031742 号

责任编辑：陈 莉 高 妍
封面设计：常雪影
版式设计：方加青
责任校对：曹 阳
责任印制：沈 露

出版发行：清华大学出版社
   网 址：https://www.tup.com.cn, https://www.wqxuetang.com
   地 址：北京清华大学学研大厦 A 座   邮 编：100084
   社 总 机：010- 83470000   邮 购：010-62786544
   投稿与读者服务：010-62776969，c-service@tup.tsinghua.edu.cn
   质 量 反 馈：010-62772015，zhiliang@tup.tsinghua.edu.cn
   课 件 下 载：https://www.tup.com.cn，010-62781730
印 装 者：三河市君旺印务有限公司
经 销：全国新华书店
开 本：185mm×260mm   印 张：22.75   字 数：525 千字
版 次：2018 年 4 月第 1 版   印 次：2024 年 1 月第 4 次印刷
定 价：58.00 元

产品编号：074662-01

前　言

　　《实用英语口译实训教程》是沈阳大学外国语学院校级精品网络课程"英语口译"课程体系的一部分，本教材将口译基本理论、口译技巧和口译技能训练相结合，旨在培养学生的话语分析能力，拓宽学生的知识面，提高学生的逻辑思维能力、语言组织能力和双语表达能力及学生的跨文化交际能力，以使学生能担任一般外事活动的交替传译工作。

　　本教程以英语口译技能的培养为重点，体现能力与知识并重的编写原则，具有以下特点。

　　1. 教材结构新颖、系统性强

　　不同于其他同类教材，本教材在对话和篇章之前增加了单句口译环节，以减轻学生负担，在篇章口译后增加巩固练习部分，有利于检测学生的学习成果，最后的专题词汇部分，有利于扩充学生的专题词汇量，为各个主题口译打下坚实的基础。每单元最后整理了自2013年习近平主席提出"一带一路"倡议以来，在多个场合对该倡议做的阐述，为学生把握时代脉搏、了解中国发展提供全新资源。本教材介绍口译技能时力求全面，涵盖了演讲、记忆、笔记、语言转换、数字、跨文化、综述、翻译准备、应急技巧等。

　　2. 技能训练与主题相关联、难度有渐进性

　　本书将口译主题需要的口译技巧编排在一起，突出了章节的关联性，如经济、贸易主题与数字口译关联，文化主题与文化交际技巧关联。每个单元都是从难度较小的句子口译、段落口译渐进到难度较大的篇章口译。话题从简到难，从学生熟悉的趣味强的话题渐进到陌生的难度较大的话题。

　　3. 材料真实多样、话题全面时效

　　本书话题范围广泛，涵盖旅游、体育、教育、美容、家庭、科技、经济、外贸、环保、文化、外交、国际关系等。同时，本书尽可能地选择最新讲话，兼顾国际性，将全国性和地方性、经典与时事相结合。

　　4. 教材使用方便、与网络课程平台有机结合

　　本教材的参考口译材料已放在网络课程平台上(http://www.tupwk.com.cn/)，学生可自行下载使用。

　　本教材共14单元，按基础篇、提高篇两大部分教学，每章都设有口译技巧讲解。基础篇每单元的具体模块分为：(1)技能讲解；(2)主题口译；(3)参考译文；(4)主题词汇；(5)扩展练习；(6)口译点滴。提高篇的具体模块分为：(1)技能讲解；(2)主题口译；(3)参考译文；(4)主题词汇；(5)扩展练习；(6)延伸口译。

授课教师可根据口译课程开课年级和学生具体情况，在一个学期之内完成本教材的学习，每学期授课18周，每周授课2～4学时。本教材可供普通高等院校英语专业学生使用，也可供国际经贸、国际关系、工商管理等专业的学生作为复合型专业英语教材使用，并可为从事英语翻译工作者及社会各界人士提供参考。

由于编写时间仓促，本教程难免存在不足之处，望有关专家和各位读者见谅，并提出宝贵意见。

目 录

第一篇 基础篇

第二篇　提高篇

第一篇　基础篇

第1单元　口译简介(Brief Introduction)

口译主题：迎来送往

单元学习目的(Unit Goals) 💡

➢ 掌握口译的概念、种类、历史及口译人员的基本素质等。

➢ 学习迎来送往所涉及的常用词语和表达。

导入(Lead -in)

1. 你自己有过口译的经历吗？感受如何？
2. 口译和笔译，你觉得哪个更难？
3. 这些口译之间是什么关系？
   - 交传
   - 同传
   - 政务口译
   - 商务口译
   - 视译
   - 法庭口译
   - 会议口译
   - 联络陪同口译
4. 你认为联络陪同口译员需要具备哪些素质？

1.1　技能讲解(Skill Introduction)

■ 1.1.1　中西方口译简史(Brief History of Interpreting)

在西方，最早以某种方式记录下来的口译活动出现在公元前3000多年的古埃及法老(Pharaoh)统治时代；而到了金字塔时期末年(公元前3000年左右)，就有了有关译员的史料记载(参见Alfred Hermann，1956/2002:15~16)。在我国，与周边各国的交往可追溯至夏商时期。公元前11世纪的周朝也已有了通过"重译"(多重口译) 而进行交流的史实，而史料对于"象胥"(古代对翻译官的称呼)的记录距今已有3000年的历史(陈福康，2000:2~3)。

口译作为一种专门职业，在我国已有2000多年的历史。从事口译职业的人被称之为"译""寄""象""狄银""通事"或"通译"。《礼记·王制》中记载："五方之民言语不通，嗜欲不同。达其志，通其欲，东方曰寄，南方曰象，西方曰狄鞮，北方曰译。"《癸辛杂识后集·译者》做了这样的解释："译，陈也；陈说内外之言皆立此传语之人以通其志，今北方谓之通事。"《后汉和帝纪》提到了当时对译者的需求："都护西指，则通译四方。"

在人类社会的发展史上，口译活动成了推动人类社会的车轮滚动的润滑剂。人类的口译活动忠实地记录了千百年来世界各族人民之间的政治、经济、军事、文化、科技、卫生和教育的交往活动。人类历史上的各大事记无不烙有口译的印记，如佛教、基督教、儒教和伊斯兰教的向外传播，文成公主婚嫁西域，马可·波罗东游华夏，哥伦布发现新大陆，郑和下西洋，鉴真东渡扶桑，近代社会西方世界与中国之间在政治、军事、经济、文化诸方面的风风雨雨，现代社会两次世界大战的爆发，"联合国"的建立，"世贸组织"的形成，当代社会中国全方位的对外开放，经济持续高速发展，今日信息时代"地球村"的发展，欧元区的创建，亚太经合组织的成立，欧亚峰会的召开……显然，在人类的跨文化、跨民族的交往中，口译起着一种催化剂的作用。

口译在国际上被认定为正式专门职业，始于20世纪初。第一次世界大战结束后的1919年，"巴黎和会"的组织者招募了一大批专职译员，他们以正式译员的身份为"巴黎和会"做"接续翻译"(或被称为"连续翻译")。从此，口译的职业性得到了认可，口译基本方法和技能的训练开始受到重视。第二次世界大战结束后，纽伦堡战犯审判的口译工作采用了原、译语近乎同步的方法。以"同声传译"为标志的新的口译形式的出现使人们对高级口译的职业独特性刮目相看。

1957年巴黎索邦大学高等翻译学校成立。他们于20世纪60年代初步建立了口译的方法论，又于20世纪80年代正式创建了世界上第一套系统的口译理论，即口译的"释意理论"。

1953年国际会议口译员协会(International Association of Conference Interpreters，简称AIIC)成立，是会议口译这一专门职业唯一的全球性专业协会，负责审查、认定会议口译员的专业资格和语言组合，制定其职业规则、工作条件、道德规范和专业培训标准，推广会议口译最佳实践，并与联合国、欧盟等国际组织开展集体谈判以确定会议口译员的待遇，等等。随着联合国的创立，各类全球性和地区性组织的出现，国际交往日趋频繁，世界的多边和双边舞台上演了一幕幕生动的现代剧，口译人员在这些剧目中扮演了独特的角色。半个世纪以来，高级口译人才一直受到各类国际机构、各国政府、各种跨文化机构和组织的青睐。专业口译已成为倍受尊敬的高尚职业，尤其是高级国际会议译员，他们既是聪慧的语言工作者，也是博学的国际外交家。20世纪70年代初，中国重返联合国，自此我国的国际地位快速上升。今天，历史的车轮已把我们带入了一个新的世纪。这是我国全面振兴的世纪，重铸辉煌的世纪，是中华文化同世界各族文化广泛交流、共同繁荣的世纪，这也是口译职业的黄金时代。这些年来，我国同世界各国开展了全方位、多层次的交流，让我们更好地了解世界，也让世界更好地了解我们。涉外口译工作者作为中外交往的一支必不可缺的中介力量，肩负着历史的重任。今日的中国比以往任何时期更需要一大批合格的专职或兼职译员来共同构筑和加固对外交往的桥梁。

■ 1.1.2 口译的定义、标准和过程(What Interpreting Means)

口译的字义

口译是翻译的一种形式，指将一种语言所表述的内容用另一种语言即时、准确地用口头表达出来。Interpret来自拉丁语，表示"to explain"。从广义来说，口译泛指对晦涩难解之语的理解诠释或是不同语言之间的传译。从狭义来说，口译指通过口头方式在不同语言之间实现意义转换和重新表达的跨语言跨文化的交际行为。

国内外研究者对口译概念的界定

巴黎释意学派口译理论家塞莱斯科维奇(Seleskovitch)在谈及口译性质时说，口译就是交流。口译是通过口头表达的方式，准确、流利地为听众解释和说明讲话人的意思(黄为忻、钱慧杰译，1992:8)。

口译是以口头形式用一种语言将另一种语言即时地再现出来，它不是单纯意义上的言语行为，而是一种涉及诸多知识层面的跨文化的交际行为(钟述孔，1991:1)。

口译是一种高智能的思维科学形式和艺术再创造的活动。口译思维从主体上说属于抽象思维，更注重逻辑推理和分析；如果说翻译是艺术，那么它离不开形象思维，离不开感知(刘和平，2001:10)。

口译是语际间的解释行为，是一种即时性的活动(张文、韩常惠，2006:9)。

口译是一种通过口头表达形式，将所感知和理解的信息准确、快速地由一种语言形式转换成另一种语言，进而达到传递与交流信息之目的的交际行为，是现代社会跨文化、跨民族交往的一种基本沟通方式(梅德明，2007:1)。

口译是这样一种活动：译员在听取源语后，通过口头表达的方式以目的语向听众传达讲话人的意思，在语言上无法互通的异语双方或多方之间通过译员的传译能够进行交流沟通(仲伟合、王斌华：2009)。

口译标准

衡量口译优劣有两条基本标准：一是准确，二是流利。自从严复提出了"信""达""雅"翻译三标准之后，翻译界尽管对"信、达、雅"的解释各有不同，但是大部分学者对这些标准所持的态度是肯定的。翻译能做到"信、达、雅"固然不错，问题在于翻译不是照相业的复制行当，难以做到"信、达、雅"三全。基于不同文化的各族语言在翻译过程中难保原汁原味、原形原貌，因而"信、达、雅"只能是相对的。有时"信"虽然达标，而"达"和"雅"却有所不达，有所不雅。于是便出现了"信、达、雅"三标准之主从关系的争论。时至今日，争论仍在延续，焦点无非集中在翻译究竟应以"直译"还是"意译"为本的问题上。至于口译的标准，套用笔译的"信、达、雅"三原则是恰当的。口译不同于笔译，口译的"现时""现场""限时"的特点决定了口译的标准有别于笔译的标准。衡量口译质量的基本标准应该是"准确"和"流利"。

首先，口译必须"准确"。不准确的口译可能是"胡译"，可能是"篡译"，也可能是"误译"，这是不能容忍的。准确是口译的灵魂，是口译的生命线。"准确"要求译员将原语这一方的信息完整无误地传达给目标语的那一方。具体说来，口译的准确涉及口译时的主题准确、精神准确、论点准确、风格准确、词语准确、数字准确、表达准确、语速准确以及口吻准确等方面。准确的译语应该同时保持原语的意义和风格，准确的口译不仅是双语成功交际的保障，也是译员职业道德和专业水平的集中体现。准确的口译体现了译员对交际活动的尊重和负责，也体现了译员对交际双方的尊重和负责。必须指出，我们所讲的准确性并非是那种机械刻板的"模压式"口译或"盖章式"口译。例如，对原语者明显的口吃、口误或浓重的口音不可妄加模仿。其次，口译必须"流利"。译员在确保"准确"口译的前提下，应该迅速流畅地将一方的信息传译给另一方。如果说"准确"是口译的基本要求，那么"流利"则充分体现了口译的特点。口译的现场性、现时性、即席性、限时性、交互性等因素要求口译过程宜短不宜长，节奏宜紧不宜松。口译是交际工具，工具的价值在于效用和效率。那么，如何来衡量口译的流利程度呢？口译的流利程度包括译员对原语信息的感知速度和解析速度，以及用目标语进行编码和表达的速度。通常，口译时译员对母语信息的感知速度和解析速度快于对外语信息的感知速度和解析速度，同时，用母语编码和表达的速度也快于用外语编码和表达的速度。在口译场合，译员对信息的感知和解析受到"现时""限时"的制约，无法"自由自在"地调节速度，所以必须同步加工。一般说来，我们可以依据译员所用的口译时间是否同发言者的讲话时间大体相等来衡量口译是否流利。若以两倍于原语发言者的讲话时间进行口译，显然不能被视为流利。根据口译的目的是实现交际双方准确、有效、流畅的沟通，口译的标准可以总结为："快""准""整""顺"。"快"指的是说话者话音一落，译员就要开始把话中的重要信息传达给对方；"准"指的是准确地把最基本的、最实质性的内容译出，即说话者的观点、要点，包括数字、日期、地名、人名以及人的职务或职称等，而不是译出每一个字、每一句话；"整"指的是传译中应该尽量保持信息传达的完整度，即翻译的有效性；"顺"指的是语言通顺，表达流畅，层次分明，逻辑清晰。

口译思维

口译作为一项高智能的思维科学形式和艺术再创造活动，其思维也必定是一种抽象思维，需要精确的逻辑推理和分析。口译的过程实际上是一个语言间的信息传递过程，可以分解为：信息接受(reception)→信息解码(decoding)→信息记忆(memory)→信息编码(encoding)→信息表达(expression)。译员首先通过视、听接收到信息，然后将接收到的来源语的信息码进行理解，获得语言和非语言形式所包含的各种信息，然后将这些信息暂时储存下来，再通过思维将这些信息转换为目标语，最后用口头的形式表达给听众。这是一个极短暂而又极其复杂的过程。

■ 1.1.3 口译与笔译的异同(Interpreting and Translating)

口译与笔译虽然同属语言间的翻译活动，但两者之间也有显著的差异。

(1) 相同点：口译与笔译活动都需要将一种语言经过理解和重组用另一种语言表达出来；翻译者都必须精通两种语言、文化和转换技巧。

(2) 不同点：口译与笔译活动在语言输入、输出、内容、信息处理、互动方式及质量评价标准上有区别。

(1) 语言输入方式不同：在笔译过程中，译者可以反复地阅读理解原文；而口译源语输出是一次性的，一般没有机会再听一遍。

(2) 语言输出方式不同：在笔译过程中，译者整个过程都可以借助工具书等辅助工具，可以反复地修改译文。口译目的语输出是在时间压力下进行的，几乎没有机会进行修改。

(3) 互动形式不同：在笔译过程中，译者与原文作者和译文读者不在同一场合，只能推测场合的情景。口译译员一般与源语发言人和目标语接受者置身于同一现场，现场的各种言外信息和副语言信息有助于译员的理解和表达。

(4) 质量标准不同：如果衡量笔译的标准为"信""达""雅"，那么口译的质量标准可描述为"快""准""整""顺"。

▋ 1.1.4 口译的类型(Types of Interpreting)

根据时间工作模式，口译可分为交替传译和同声传译。

交替传译(consecutive interpreting，简称CI)，也称连续口译/传译、即席口译/传译、逐步口译(台湾用语)，简称"交传"或"连传"。讲话人说一段，译员翻译一段，然后循环往复、交替进行。3分钟以上即可称为长交传。交替传译常用于新闻发布会、外事会见、商务谈判、户外活动等。

同声传译(simultaneous interpreting，简称SI)，又称同步口译、即时传译(港台用语)，简称"同传"。讲话人的"说"与译员的"译"几乎同时进行。同声传译可分为常规会议同传和耳语同传两种。

常规会议同传(regular conference SI)，一般2~3人一组，在同传间/同传箱(booth)使用同传设备。一般译员每20分钟轮换一次，包括有稿同传和无稿同传两种形式。

耳语同传(whispered interpreting)，一般只有1~3人需要口译服务，无须同传设备。

根据空间工作模式，口译可分为现场口译和远程口译。

现场口译(live interpreting)，一般为当事双方和译员同时在场。

远程口译(remote interpreting)，一般为当事双方和译员不在一地，如电话、远程视频口译等。

根据活动场合和主题，可分为会议口译(conference interpreting)、陪同口译(escort interpreting)、外交口译(diplomatic interpreting)、商务口译(business interpreting)、媒体口译(media interpreting)、社区口译(community interpreting)、导游口译(guide interpreting)、医学口译(medical interpreting，国外有资格认证)、法庭/法律口译(court/legal/judicial interpreting，国外有资格认证)等，其中法庭译员被称为宣誓译员(sworn interpreter)。

根据活动的性质和正式程度，口译可分为会议口译(conference interpreting)和联络口译

(liaison interpreting)。

根据译语的流向，口译可分为单向口译和双向口译。对于单向口译(one-way interpreting)，译员只将A语译成B语。对于双向口译(two-way interpreting)，译员要将A语言和B语言进行交替互译。

根据源语到译语的直接性程度，口译可分为直接口译和接续口译。直接口译(direct interpreting)直接将一种语言译成另一种语言。接续口译(relay interpreting)，也叫接力口译，简称"接传"。译员甲将讲话人的A语言译成B语言，再由译员乙将B语言译成C语言给听者。

除此之外，还有视译(sight interpreting)、交传、同传、手语口译等形式。交传指译员将现场文字用目的语口译给听者，常见于导游讲解。同传指译员眼看讲话人发言稿或幻灯片，耳听发言人讲话，进行口译，常见于会议有稿同传。手语口译指在手语和口语间交替或同步翻译，主要为聋哑人服务。

■ 1.1.5　口译人员的素质(Qualifications of Interpreters)

口译是一门专业要求很高的职业。要成为一名合格的口译员，通常需要经过专门训练，培养和提炼职业译员所必需的素质。

(1) 扎实的双语知识(solid foundation in bilingual knowledge)，一名优秀的英汉口译员必须有扎实的语言功底，掌握英汉两种语言的特点，不仅通晓基本语言知识，还要具有自如运用语言知识的能力。

(2) 广博的非语言知识(extensive extralinguistic knowledge)，译员必须掌握丰富全面的百科知识。例如对百科知识(encyclopedic knowledge)、常识性知识(common sense / general knowledge)、文化知识(cultural knowledge)、主题知识(subject/domain knowledge)、语境/情景知识(contextual / situational knowledge)等都要略知一二，要努力做一个"杂家"。一名优秀的口译员，是能胜任各种口译工作的多面手。译员要具备快速学习新知识的能力。

(3) 娴熟的口译技能(unerring interpreting skills / techniques)，要想成为合格的口译员，熟练语言的输入及输出过程中涉及的口译技巧：例如听词取意(listening for sense)、记忆(memorization)、口译笔记 (note-taking)、公众演讲(public speaking)、语言转换(language transference)、数字转换(interpreting figures)、综述(summarization)、应急处理(coping tactics)、跨文化交际(cross-cultural communication)、译前准备(advance preparation)等是关键要素。

(4) 过硬的身体和心理素质(Sound physical and psychological quality)，口译工作是一项极其耗费脑力和体力的活动。译员首先要有健康的身体和充沛的精力，才能保证长时间的口译工作，同时译员良好的心理素质也是保证口译质量的要素。

(5) 良好的职业道德(Fine ethics-based professional conduct)，译员的活动属于外事活动，译员的一言一行都关系祖国的形象、民族的风貌、机构的利益。译员要洁身自好，不谋私利，不做有损国格和人格的事。译员要讲究外事礼仪、社交礼仪和口译规范。

1.2 主题口译(Topic Interpreting)

▌1.2.1 单句口译(Sentence Practice)

Please interpret the following sentences by using the techniques illustrated above. You may interpret to your partner first and then he/she comments on your performance.

(1) You must be our long-expected guest，Dr. Green from University of New York.

(2) Thank you very much for coming all the way to meet me in person.

(3) I'm delighted to make your acquaintance.

(4) I would like to show you our tentative itinerary.

(5) We appreciate very much that you have come to visit our university in spite of the long and tiring journey.

(6) 我谨向各位表示最热烈的欢迎！

(7) 您真好，专程来送别。

(8) 祝您访问圆满成功！

(9) 我们期待能有机会再次作为东道主接待您。

(10) 让我们保持联系！

▌1.2.2 对话口译(Dialogue Practice)

1. Vocabulary Work: Study the following words and phrases, and translate them into the target language.

国际贸易公司	to meet me at the airport
中国纺织品进出口公司	quite a nice flight
副总经理	baggage-claim area
设宴为您洗尘	a thoughtful arrangement

2. Read the following dialogue and interpret it into the target language.

接待外宾

A：请问，您是国际贸易公司的威尔逊先生吗？

B：Yes，I am. How do I address you？

A：我是李雯，中国纺织品进出口公司的副总经理。

B：How do you do. Miss Li.

A：您好，威尔逊先生，欢迎您来到中国。非常荣幸您能来我们公司。

B：Thank you. It's very kind of you to come to meet me at the airport，Miss Li.

A：乐意效劳。希望您在这儿过得愉快。

B：Thank you，I'm sure I will.

A：您路途上过得愉快吗？

B：Yes，quite a nice flight.

A：很高兴听您这么说。现在我们去看看您的行李好吗？

B：Yes. Where is the baggage-claim area?

A：在下面五号门。您有几件行李？

B：Two suitcase.

A：我们到了。您能认出它们吗？

B：Yes. This blue one，and that black one.

A：您已拿了行李，我们去进行海关检查吧。

B：All right.

A：我们将开车送您去香格里拉大酒店。酒店位于市中心，您一定会喜欢的。

B：That's wonderful. I love living in the region of prosperous. Do we have anything planned for this evening?

A：有，今天晚上7点设宴为您洗尘！这样安排可以吗？

B：Thank you so much.

A：别客气，那么我们6:50酒店大堂见。

B：That's fine. Thank you for such a thoughtful arrangement for me.

▌1.2.3 篇章口译[Passage Practice (E to C)]

1. Vocabulary Work: Study the following words and phrases, and translate them into the target language.

stiffly	Sherry
tipping	tuck
geometrically	chill
napkin	stem

2. Please interpret the following paragraph by using the techniques illustrated above.

The proper posture at dinner table is to sit straight，but not stiffly，against the back of the chair. Hands，when one is not actually eating，may be in the lap. Tipping one's chair is unforgivable.//There is one rule for a formal table and that is that everything must be geometrically spaced: the centre piece in the actual center，the places at equal distances with all table wares balanced.//Ordinarily，as soon as you are seated you put your napkin in your lap. At a formal dinner，however，you wait for your hostess to put hers on her lap first.//Remove the napkin from the table，place it on your lap，and unfold it as much as necessary with both hands. Never tuck it into your collar，belt，or between leg. // When the meal is finished，or if you leave the table during the meal，put the napkin on the left side of your place，or if the plate have been removed，in the center.// It is upon the host or hostess to ask guests to begin a hot course after three or four people have been served.// Sherry，which is served at room temperature，is poured into small，V-shape glass. White wine，which is served well chilled，is poured into round-bowled，stemmed glasses.

3. Please interpret the following passage by using the techniques illustrated above. Please pay attention to the underlined sentences as they require special treatment during interpreting.

① <u>Toast Speech by Richard Nixon</u>⁽¹⁾

② <u>Mr. Prime Minister and all of your distinguished guests</u>⁽²⁾ this evening: <u>On behalf of all of your American-guests，I wish to thank you for the incomparably hospitality for which the Chinese people are justly famous throughout the world. I particularly want to pay tribute，not only to those who prepared the magnificent dinner，but also to those who have provided the splendid music. Never have I heard American music played better in a foreign land.</u> ⁽³⁾

③ Mr. Prime Minister，I wish to thank you for your very gracious and eloquent remarks. At this very moment，through the wonder of telecommunications，more people are seeing and hearing what we say than on any other such occasion in the whole history of the world. Yet，what we say here will not be long remembered. What we do here can change the world.

④ As you said in your toast，the Chinese people are a great people，the American people are a great people. If our two peoples are enemies the future of this world we share，together is dark indeed. But if we can find common ground to work together，the chance for world peace is immeasurably increased.

⑤ In the spirit of frankness which I hope will characterize our talks this week，let us recognize at the outset these points: We have at times in the past been enemies. We have great differences today. What brings us together is that we have common interests which transcend those differences. As we discuss our differences，neither of us will compromise our principles. But while we cannot close the gulf between us，we can try to bridge it so that we may be able to talk across it.

⑥ So，let us，in these next five days，start a long march together，not in lockstep，but on different roads leading to the same goal，the goal of building a world structure of peace and justice in which all may stand together with equal dignity and in which each nation，large or small，has a right to determine its own form of government，free of outside interference or domination. The world watches. The world listens. The world waits to see what we will do. What is the world? In a personal sense，I think of my eldest daughter whose birthday is today. As I think of her，I think of all the children in the world，in Asia，in Africa，in Europe，in the Americas，most of whom were born since the date of the foundation of the People's Republic of China.

⑦ What legacy shall we leave our children? Are they destined to die for the hatreds which have plagued the old world，or are they destined to live because we had the vision to build a new world? There is no reason for us to be enemies. Neither of us seeks the territory of the other; neither of us seeks domination over the other; neither of us seeks to stretch out our hands and rule the world. Chairman Mao has written, <u>"So many deeds cry out to be done, and always urgently; The world rolls on, Time presses. Ten thousand years are too long, seize the day, seize the hour!"</u> [4]

⑧ This is the hour. This is the day for our two peoples to rise to the heights of greatness which can build a better world. <u>In that spirit, I ask all of you present to join me in raising your glasses to Chairman Mao, to Prime Minister Chou, and to the friendship of the Chinese and American people which can lead to friendship and peace for all people in the world.</u> [5] (A toast given by president Nixon on his first visit to China in 1972)

Notes on the text

(1) <u>Toast Speech by Richard Nixon</u>

尼克松访华祝酒词

1972年2月21日，美国总统尼克松飞越太平洋，在北京与中国总理周恩来完成了一次历史性的握手。这次震惊世界的握手，是双方克服了无数政治隔阂、跨越了巨大文化差异的结果。当天晚上，周恩来总理在人民大会堂举行了欢迎尼克松的宴会。

(2) <u>Mr. Prime Minister and all of your distinguished guests</u>

尊敬的总理先生，在座的各位贵宾

美国人士在讲话开始称呼主要嘉宾时，有时只简单地使用对方的头衔，比如：Mr. Prime Minister，在译成汉语时可以加上敬语"尊敬的总理先生"，以示尊重。

(3) <u>On behalf of all of your American-guests, I wish to thank you for the incomparably hospitality for which the Chinese people are justly famous throughout the world. I particularly want to pay tribute, not only to those who prepared the magnificent dinner, but also to those who have provided the splendid music. Never have I heard American music played better in a foreign land.</u>

我谨代表你们的所有美国客人向你们表示感谢，感谢你们的无可比拟的盛情款待。中国人民以这种盛情款待而闻名世界。我不仅要特别赞扬那些准备了这次盛大晚宴的人，还要赞扬那些给我们演奏这样美好的音乐的人。我在外国从来没有听到过演奏得这么好的美国音乐。

(4) <u>"So many deeds cry out to be done, and always urgently; The world rolls on, Time presses. Ten thousand years are too long, Seize the day, seize the hour!"</u>

"多少事，从来急；天地转，光阴迫。一万年太久，只争朝夕。"

(5) <u>In that spirit, I ask all of you present to join me in raising your glasses to Chairman Mao, to Prime Minister Chou, and to the friendship of the Chinese and American people which can lead to friendship and peace for all people in the world.</u>

本着这种精神，我请求诸位同我一起举杯，为毛主席，为周总理，为能够增进全世界所有人民的友谊与和平的中国人民和美国人民之间的友谊，干杯！

1.2.4　篇章口译[Passage Practice (C to E)]

1. Vocabulary Work: Study the following words and phrases, and translate them into the target language.

学术研讨会	筹委会
活动日程安排	复印机和投影设备
招待宴会	舒适如归

2. Please interpret the following paragraphs by using the techniques illustrated above.

　　您一定是来自澳大利亚的埃利斯教授吧。我叫王伟，是国际交流中心的主任。这是我的名片。// 自从我们收到您来访日期的电子邮件后就一直期待着您的到来。今天我为能够接待您而深感愉快。很高兴我们今后几天里合作共事。// 这是我们为您拟定的活动日程安排。如果对某些细节有意见的话，请提出来。我们真诚地希望您们在这里过得愉快。//埃利斯教授，我们的学术研讨会将如期在我中心举行，我很高兴地告诉您，先生已被筹委会选为研讨会的主要发言人。我们中心已经为您准备了复印机和投影设备，如果还有其他需要，请与我们中心联系。// 我们为您安排了我们中心的专家公寓。我们的公寓从设计到装潢都体现了中国古代的建筑风格，相信您一定会喜欢。您在我中心这段时间，我们会尽力为您服务，希望您在这里有舒适如归的感觉。// 今晚我们校长将设宴为您洗尘。长途旅行之后您应该好好休息一下。我告辞了，我们在今晚招待宴会上再见。//

3. Please interpret the following passage by using the techniques illustrated above. Please pay attention to the underlined sentences as they require special treatment during interpreting.

王毅部长在外交部2017年新年招待会上的致辞

　　① 尊敬的杨洁篪国务委员和夫人，
　　尊敬的各位使节、代表和夫人，(1)
　　女士们，先生们，朋友们：
　　② 一年一度的中国新春佳节即将到来(2)，我谨代表中国外交部，向今天出席招待会的各位嘉宾表示热烈欢迎，向过去一年为促进中外友好合作作出积极贡献的各位驻华使节和代表表示衷心感谢，向大力支持外交工作的各地方、各部门致以崇高敬意！(3)
　　③ 2016年是中华民族伟大复兴进程中不平凡的一年。中共中央召开十八届六中全会，明确了习近平同志在党中央和全党的核心地位，不仅得到中国人民一致拥护，在国际上也产生广泛、积极反响。以习近平同志为核心的党中央团结带领全国各族人民，统筹推进"五位一体"总体布局，协调推进"四个全面"战略布局，深化供给侧结构性改革，推动中国经济增长继续走在世界前列，实现全面建成小康社会决胜阶段的开门红。
　　④ 2016年，也是中国外交攻坚开拓之年。面对各种风险和挑战，我们以更加坚定、稳健的步伐，沿着和平发展道路不断前进，在国际形势的风云激荡中有力维护了国家的主

权、安全和发展利益；在国际格局的加速演进中显著提升了中国的话语权和影响力。

⑤ 我们积极参与全球治理体系变革。二十国集团领导人杭州峰会在推动创新增长、深化结构性改革、重振国际贸易和投资、促进可持续发展等领域取得一系列富有开创性、引领性、机制性的成果，为世界经济复苏注入生机活力，指明前进方向。在亚太经合组织领导人利马会议上，习近平主席高举构建开放型世界经济、反对保护主义旗帜，推动亚太自贸区建设迈出新的步伐。不久前在达沃斯和日内瓦，习主席进一步发出实现经济全球化进程再平衡、共同构建人类命运共同体的时代强音，起到了稳定人心、提振信心、凝聚共识的重要作用。中国率先提交《巴黎协定》批准书，率先发布落实2030年可持续发展议程国别方案，积极推动朝鲜半岛核、阿富汗、叙利亚、南苏丹等热点问题的政治解决，参与并加强国际反恐合作，为应对全球性挑战、维护世界和平与安全发挥建设性作用。

⑥ 我们同主要国家关系稳中有进。中美元首多次成功会晤，共同推动中美新型大国关系建设继续向前发展。中俄元首保持密切交往，全面战略协作伙伴关系迈向更高水平。我们成功主办第十八次中欧领导人会晤，中英继续致力于打造两国关系的"黄金时代"，中国—中东欧合作迈上新台阶。中国同金砖国家携手努力，保持了金砖合作发展的积极势头。

⑦ 我们着力维护周边睦邻友好大局。习主席热情接待菲律宾总统杜特尔特访华，中菲关系实现了华丽转身，为中国与东盟国家深化合作增添了动力。中国同缅甸、斯里兰卡等国的关系实现平稳过渡，开启了新的前景。同柬埔寨、孟加拉、巴基斯坦以及哈萨克斯坦等中亚国家的友好合作不断深化，相互信任更加巩固。澜沧江—湄公河合作全面启动并取得一系列务实成果，成为打造周边命运共同体的有益实践。

⑧ 我们深入拓展发展中国家朋友圈。过去一年，中国又同近20个国家新建或提升伙伴关系定位，其中绝大多数是发展中国家。习主席首次访问中东地区，提出面向中东和阿拉伯国家合作计划。习主席再访拉美，倡导铸就携手共进的中拉命运共同体。中非合作论坛约翰内斯堡峰会成果落实协调人会议在京成功举办，"中非十大合作计划"成效充分显现。中国同发展中国家合作风光正好，大有可为。

⑨ 我们推动"一带一路"建设取得新突破。在100多个国家和国际组织的积极支持和参与下，沿线各国战略对接、互联互通、产能合作、人文交流全面推进，一批标志性项目破土动工，亚洲基础设施投资银行开业运营，丝路基金启动首批投资项目。外交部为地方省区市举办全球推介活动，架起了中国地方和世界各国直接对接合作的便捷桥梁。

⑩ 我们坚定捍卫国家主权和安全。推动南海问题重新回到直接当事国对话协商解决的正确轨道，不仅维护了中国自身的正当合法权益，也维护了相关国际法及地区规则的公正性和权威性。我们旗帜鲜明地坚持一个中国原则，扎实开展涉台、涉藏、涉疆外交，反对外部势力干预港澳事务，有效维护了国家利益和民族尊严。

⑪ 女士们，先生们，朋友们！

2017年，中国共产党将召开第十九次全国代表大会，"十三五"规划进入全面深入推进阶段。我们将在以习近平同志为核心的党中央领导下，推动中国特色大国外交再上新台阶，为党的十九大召开营造稳定有利的外部环境，为实现中华民族伟大复兴的中国梦、推进世界和平与发展事业作出更大贡献。

⑫ 我们将精心办好"一带一路"国际合作高峰论坛，凝聚各方智慧，形成广泛合力，推动"一带一路"建设向更广领域、更深层次、更高水平发展。

⑬ 我们将履行好东道主职责，通过举办金砖国家领导人第九次会晤，打造南南合作重要平台，以合作共赢、联动发展的新思路，开辟世界经济和全球治理的新空间。

⑭ 我们将继续深化与世界各国友好合作。我们愿在尊重彼此核心利益的基础上，同美国新政府一道，聚焦合作，管控分歧，推动中美关系持续健康发展。

⑮ 我们愿继续全方位推进中俄高水平战略协作，切实发挥中俄关系的战略稳定作用。我们愿进一步构建中欧四大伙伴关系，从战略层面支持欧洲一体化进程。

⑯ 我们愿不断加强与周边国家睦邻友好，促进澜湄合作走深走实，坚持通过对话谈判解决南海问题的正确方向，积极探寻实现半岛无核化的可行路径。我们愿更好践行正确义利观，推动与新兴市场和广大发展中国家团结合作提质升级。

⑰ 我们将更好地服务国家发展。外交工作将紧紧围绕国内改革发展稳定大局，切实维护国家经济金融安全，维护中国不断拓展的海外利益。我们将进一步办好省区市全球推介活动，促进中国各地尤其是中西部地区同世界各国的交流合作。

⑱ 女士们，先生们，朋友们！

光阴荏苒，初心不忘。促进世界和平与发展是我们的共同愿望，增进中外交流与合作是我们的共同使命。各位使节和代表为中国与世界各国的友好往来不辞辛劳，我再次向大家表示衷心的感谢。外交部使团事务办公室成立以来，不断摸索搭建联系使团、服务使团的有效渠道。新的一年，外交部将继续提升对驻华使团服务水平，为使团人员履职提供更多便利。相信外交部与各位使节、代表的沟通交流将更加密切，同有关地方、部门的协调配合将更加顺畅，中国与世界各国友好合作将更加富有成效！

⑲ 现在，我提议：

为中国人民同各国人民的友谊，

为世界的持久和平与共同繁荣，

为各位来宾的健康，

干杯！

Notes on the text

(1) 尊敬的杨洁篪国务委员和夫人，尊敬的各位使节、代表和夫人

State Councilor Yang Jiechi and Madam Le Aimei, Your Excellencies Ambassadors

中国人致辞开始时往往会用"尊敬的XXX"来称呼在场的主要嘉宾。如果职位很高的嘉宾，可以采用"Your Excellency + 职衔 + 姓或姓名"的形式，"尊敬的各位使节"就可以译成 Your Excellencies Ambassadors，有时也可以用Respected 或 Honourable的形式。

(2) 一年一度的中国新春佳节即将到来

The Spring Festival is just a few days away

中国新春佳节，在中国，人们喜欢把春节或农历新年译成Spring Fesitival，但在国外人们一般都说Chinese New Year。

(3) 我谨代表中国外交部，向今天出席招待会的各位嘉宾表示热烈欢迎，向过去一年为促进中外友好合作作出积极贡献的各位驻华使节和代表表示衷心的感谢，向大力支持外交工作的各地方、各部门致以崇高敬意！

On behalf of the Ministry of Foreign Affairs，I would like to extend a warm welcome to all of you，and express my heartfelt thanks to all ambassadors，diplomatic envoys and representatives of international organizations for what you have done in the past year to strengthen friendship and cooperation between China and the world. I would also like to pay high tribute to all the localities and other government departments for your strong support to China's diplomacy.

(4) 为中国人民同各国人民的友谊，为世界的持久和平与共同繁荣，为各位来宾的健康，干杯！

To the friendship between people of China and people of all other countries，to lasting peace and shared prosperity of the world，and to the health of all distinguished guests present. Cheers!

1.3 参考译文(Reference Version)

1.3.1 单句口译(Sentence Practice)

Please interpret the following sentences by using the techniques illustrated above. You may interpret to your partner first and then he/she comments on your performance.

(1) 您一定是我们期盼已久的客人，从纽约大学来的格林博士吧！

(2) 谢谢您专程赶来接待我。

(3) 我很高兴能与您结识。

(4) 我想向您介绍一下我们初步拟定的活动日程。

(5) 我们十分感谢您们不辞辛劳远道来访我校。

(6) I would like to extend my warmest welcome to all of you

(7) It's very nice of you to come all the way to see me off.

(8) Wish your visit a complete success!

(9) We're looking forward to the opportunity of hosting you here again.

(10) Let's keep in touch.

1.3.2 对话口译(Dialogue Practice)

Read the following dialogue and interpret it into the target language.

A：Excuse me，are you Mr. Wilson from the International Trading Corporation？

B：是的，我是。您是哪位？

A：I'm Li Wen，the deputy managing director of China National Textiles Import & Export Corporation.

B：您好，李小姐。

A：How do you do，Mr. Wilson，Welcome to China，it's our great honor to invite you to visit our company.

B：谢谢，李小姐。您到机场来接我，真太客气了。

A：It's my pleasure，I hope you will enjoy your stay here.

B：谢谢，我相信会的。

A：Did you have a pleasant flight？

B：是的，愉快，这是一次非常愉快的旅行。

A：I'm glad to hear that，Now shall we go and see about your baggage？

B：好的，行李提取处在哪里？

A：It's down there at Gate No 5. How many pieces of baggage do you have？

B：两个小提箱。

A：Here we are. Could you point them out？

B：能，这个蓝色的，还有那个黑色的。

A：Since you have picked up your baggage. And now let's proceed through the customs.

B：好的。谢谢。

A：We'll drive you to the Shangri-La Hotel. It is located in the center of the city. I am sure you will like it.

B：好极了，我喜欢住在繁华地区。我们今天晚上有活动安排吗？

A：Yes，we will host a reception dinner in your honor at 7:00 this evening. Is that all right for you？

B：非常感谢。

A：It's my pleasure. Then we'll meet in the lobby at 6:50 this evening.

B：好的。感谢您为我们所作的如此精心的安排。

1.3.3　篇章口译[Passage Practice (E to C)]

1. Vocabulary Work: Study the following words and phrases and translate them into the target language.

直立	雪莉酒
翘起	塞进
整齐均匀的	冷藏
餐巾	柄

2. Please interpret the following paragraph by using the techniques illustrated above.

餐桌边理想的姿势是背靠椅子坐直，但不要僵硬。未进餐时可把手放在膝上。切记不要将椅子翘起。//正式餐桌的规则就是一切均按几何规则摆放：装饰品放在正中央，餐位间距离相等，餐具摆放对称。//通常情况下就座后就把餐巾放在腿上。但是正式宴会上等女主人首先把餐巾放在自己腿上后，客人接着照办。//把餐巾从桌上拿下来，放在腿上，用双手摊开至需要的大小。绝对不能把它卷起来插进你领口里、腰带上或两腿之间。//吃完饭或中途需要离开餐桌时，把餐巾放在餐位左边，如果盘子被拿走了就放在中间。//在三四位客人分到菜后主人应该请客人开始吃热菜，以免他们的菜变凉。//雪莉酒，室温下喝，装在V形小杯子里。白葡萄酒，冰凉时喝，装在圆碗形带柄的酒杯中。冰镇的茶或咖啡最好装在带垫或托的杯子里。如果盐罐里没有勺子，那就用干净的刀尖。如果咬了一口太烫的食物，迅速喝口水。//

3. Please interpret the following passage by using the techniques illustrated above. Please pay attention to the underlined sentences as they require special treatment during interpreting.

① 尼克松访华祝酒词

② 尊敬的总理先生，在座的各位贵宾：我谨代表你们的所有美国客人向你们表示感谢，感谢你们的无可比拟的盛情款待。中国人民以这种盛情款待而闻名世界。我不仅要特别赞扬那些准备了这次盛大晚宴的人，还要赞扬那些给我们演奏这样美好的音乐的人。我在外国从来没有听到过演奏得这么好的美国音乐。

③ 总理先生，我要感谢你的非常盛情和雄辩的讲话。就在这个时刻，通过电信的奇迹，看到和听到我们讲话的人比在整个世界历史上任何其他这样的场合都要多。不过，我在这里讲的话，人们不会长久记住。我们在这里所做的事却能改变世界。

④ 正如你在祝酒时讲的那样，中国人民是伟大的人民，美国人民是伟大的人民。我们两国人民不是敌人，否则我们共同居住的这个世界的前途就的确是黑暗的了。如果我们能够找到进行合作的共同点，那么实现世界和平的机会将无可估量地大大增加。

⑤ 我希望我们这个星期的会谈将是坦率的。本着这种坦率的精神，我们一开始就认识到这样几点：过去的一些时期我们曾是敌人；今天我们有巨大的分歧；使我们走到一起的，是我们有超过这些分歧的共同利益。在我们讨论我们的分歧的时候，我们哪一方都不会在我们的原则上妥协。但是，虽然我们不能弥合我们之间的鸿沟，却能够设法搭一座桥，以便我们能够越过它进行会谈。

⑥ 因此，让我们在今后的五天里在一起开始一次长征吧，不是在一起迈步，而是在不同的道路上向同一目标前进。这个目标就是建立一个和平和正义的世界结构，在这个世界结构中，所有的人都可以在一起享有同等的尊严；每个国家，不论大小，都有权利决定它自己的政府形式，而不受外来的干涉或统治。全世界在注视着，全世界在倾听着，全世界在等待着看我们将做些什么。这个世界是什么呢？就个人来讲，我想到我的大女儿，因为今天是她的生日。当我想到她的时候，我就想到全世界的儿童。亚洲、非洲、欧洲以及美洲的儿童，他们大多数都是在中华人民共和国成立以后出生的。

⑦ 我们将给我们的孩子们留下什么遗产呢？他们的命运是要为那些使旧世界受苦受

难的仇恨而死亡呢，还是他们的命运是由我们有缔造一个新世界的远见而活下去呢？我们没有理由要成为敌人。我们哪一方都不企图取得对方的领土，我们哪一方都不企图统治对方，我们哪一方都不企图伸出手去统治世界。毛主席写过："多少事，从来急；天地转，光阴迫。一万年太久，只争朝夕。"

⑧ 现在就是只争朝夕的时候了，是我们两国人民攀登那种可以缔造一个新的、更美好的世界的伟大境界的高峰的时候了。本着这种精神，我请求诸位同我一起举杯，为毛主席，为周总理，为能够增进全世界所有人民的友谊与和平的中国人民和美国人民之间的友谊，干杯！(美国尼克松总统1972年访华时的一次祝酒词)

1.3.4　篇章口译[Passage Practice (C to E)]

1. Please interpret the following paragraph by using the techniques illustrated above.

You must be Professor Rod Ellis from Australia. My name is Wang Wei. I'm director of the International Center for Cultural Exchanges. Here's my card.//We've been expecting you ever since we received your e-mail message informing us of your date of arrival. It gives me such a great pleasure to meet you. I'm glad that you will be working with us here for the next few days.//Here is a copy of itinerary we have worked out for you . If you have any questions on the details，feel free to ask. We really wish you'll have a pleasant stay here.// Professor Ellis，the Academic Symposium will be hold at our center as scheduled. I'm pleased to tell you that you have been chosen by the organizing committee as the keynote speaker for the symposium. We have prepared you a photocopier and an overhead projector for your presentation. If you need something else，do not hesitate to contact our Center.// We have reserved for you our Expert suite. It is a classic Chinese residence designed and decorated in the architectural style of China's ancient architecture. I'm sure you will like it. During your staying here，we'll do everything we can to accommodate you and make you comfortable.// Our president will host a reception banquet in your honor tonight. I'm sure you need a good rest after such a long flight. I suppose I'll have to go now. See you at the reception banquet tonight. //

2. Please interpret the following passage by using the techniques illustrated above. Please pay attention to the underlined sentences as they require special treatment during interpreting.

Remarks by Foreign Minister Wang Yi at 2017 New Year Reception Hosted by the Chinese Foreign Ministry

① State Councilor Yang Jiechi and Madam Le Aimei，

Your Excellencies Ambassadors，

Members of the Diplomatic Corps，

Representatives of International Organizations and Their Spouses，

Ladies and Gentlemen, Friends,

② The Spring Festival is just a few days away. On behalf of the Ministry of Foreign Affairs，I would like to extend a warm welcome to all of you，and express my heartfelt thanks to all ambassadors，diplomatic envoys and representatives of international organizations for what you have done in the past year to strengthen friendship and cooperation between China and the world. I would also like to pay high tribute to all the localities and other government departments for your strong support to China's diplomacy.

③ The year 2016 was a momentous year in the process of China's great national renewal. The Sixth Plenum of the 18th CPC Central Committee established Comrade Xi Jinping as the core of the CPC Central Committee and the whole Party. The decision was supported by all the Chinese people and received extensive and positive response abroad. The CPC Central Committee with Comrade Xi Jinping as its core led Chinese people of all ethnic groups in a concerted endeavor to pursue economic，political，cultural，social and ecological progress and the four-pronged comprehensive strategy in a well-coordinated way. Supply-side structural reform made further headway and China continued to lead the world in economic growth. We are off to a good start in the decisive phase of completing the building of a moderately prosperous society in all respects.

④ The year 2016 was also a year of tackling serious challenges and blazing new paths for China's diplomacy. In face of various risks and challenges，we continued to advance on the path of peaceful development with more determined and steady strides. Amid complex changes on the international landscape and fast evolution of global architecture，we firmly safeguarded our national sovereignty，security and development interests and significantly raised China's standing and influence in the world.

⑤ We took an active part in the reform of global governance system. The G20 Hangzhou Summit produced a series of visionary outcomes which will exert a far-reaching impact on promoting innovative growth，deepening structural reform，reenergizing international trade and investment，and promoting sustainable development. The Summit gave a strong impetus to global recovery and charted the way forward. At the APEC Economic Leaders'meeting in Lima，President Xi Jinping stressed the importance of building an open world economy and rejecting protectionism and pushed for new progress in realizing the FTAAP. Just a few days ago at Davos and Geneva，President Xi again called for rebalancing the process of economic globalization and jointly building a community of shared future for mankind. His remarks reflected the call of our times，sent a reassuring message to the world and boosted confidence and consensus in taking globalization forward. China was among the first group of countries to deposit its instrument of ratification of the Paris Agreement on climate change and release the national plan for the implementation of the 2030 Agenda for Sustainable Development. We worked hard for political settlement to the Korean Peninsula nuclear issue and hotspot issues in Afghanistan，Syria and

South Sudan. We took an increasingly active part in international counter-terrorism cooperation and played a constructive role in meeting global challenges and maintaining world peace and security.

⑥ We made steady progress in our relations with major countries. Heads of state of China and the US held a number of successful meetings and jointly pushed forward the building of a new model of major country relationship. Chinese and Russian presidents maintained close exchanges and China-Russia comprehensive strategic partnership of coordination was taken to a new high. We successfully hosted the 18th China-EU Summit. China and the UK expressed renewed commitment to opening a "Golden Era" of bilateral relations. Cooperation between China and Central and Eastern European countries entered a new phase. China and other BRICS countries worked hand in hand and sustained the sound momentum of BRICS cooperation.

⑦ We worked hard to promote friendly relations with our neighbors. President Xi warmly received President Duterte of the Philippines on his visit to China. The turnaround in China-Philippines relations added impetus to cooperation between China and ASEAN countries. Our relations with countries such as Myanmar and Sri Lanka went through a smooth transition and assumed new momentum of growth. Our friendship and cooperation with Cambodia，Bangladesh，Pakistan，Kazakhstan and other Central Asian countries continued to deepen with increased mutual trust. The Lancang-Mekong Cooperation Framework was fully established and produced concrete results. It marked a major step forward in our efforts to build a community of shared future in our neighborhood.

⑧ We further expanded our circle of friends with other developing countries. Over the past year，we established new partnerships and upgraded existing ones with nearly 20 countries，the majority of which are developing countries. President Xi paid his first visit to the Middle East，where he laid out plans for cooperation with the region and Arab States. He visited Latin America again and called for the building of a China-Latin America community of shared future. The Coordinators' meeting on the Implementation of the Follow-up Actions of the FOCAC Johannesburg Summit was successfully held in Beijing. The ten cooperation plans have brought significant benefits to China and Africa. Our cooperation with developing countries is booming with so much more to achieve.

⑨ We made new breakthroughs in building the Belt and Road. With the active support and participation of over 100 countries and international organizations，countries along the Belt and Road are synergizing their strategies and enhancing cooperation on connectivity，production capacity and people-to-people exchange. Construction kicked off on several landmark projects. The Asian Infrastructure Investment Bank is up and running. The Silk Road Fund launched its first batch of investment projects. The Foreign Ministry held promotion events for Chinese provinces，providing a bridge that links them directly with the rest of the world.

⑩ We firmly safeguarded sovereignty and national security. By bringing the South China

Sea issue back to the right track of seeking resolution through dialogue and consultation between countries directly concerned，we defended China's legitimate and lawful rights and interests and upheld the justice and authority of relevant international law and regional rules. We steadfastly upheld the one-China principle，conducted effective diplomacy on issues concerning Taiwan，Tibet and Xinjiang，fended off foreign interference in the affairs of Hong Kong and Macao，and successfully safeguarded our national interests and dignity.

⑪ Ladies and Gentlemen，Friends，

This year，the Communist Party of China will hold its 19th National Congress. And the implementation of the 13th Five-year Plan will enter an all-round and intensive stage. Under the leadership of the CPC Central Committee with Comrade Xi Jinping as the core，we will strive for new progress in conducting major-country diplomacy with Chinese characteristics，create a stable and favorable external environment for a successful CPC National Congress and contribute to the realization of the Chinese dream of great national renewal and to the cause of world peace and development.

⑫ We will make utmost efforts to host a successful Belt and Road Forum for International Cooperation to pool wisdom and strength from all parties for wider，deeper and better cooperation in building the Belt and Road.

⑬ We will play a good host to the ninth BRICS Summit and use the opportunity to build up the important platform of South-South cooperation，and break new ground for world economy and global governance with a new vision of win-win cooperation and interconnected development.

⑭ We will continue to deepen friendship and cooperation with countries across the world. We are ready to work with the new US administration on the basis of respect for each other's core interests to stay focused on cooperation，manage differences and promote sound and sustained growth of China-US relations.

⑮ We are ready to enhance high-level strategic coordination with Russia on all fronts and further exert the stabilizing role of China-Russia relations in the strategic arena. We will continue to foster the four partnerships with the EU and give strategic support to European integration.

⑯ We are ready to strengthen good relations and friendship with our neighbors，deepen and enrich Lancang-Mekong cooperation，keep to the right track of seeking settlement to the South China Sea issue through dialogue and negotiation，and actively explore a viable path towards denuclearization on the Korean Peninsula. We will uphold justice in the pursuit of interests and enhance solidarity and cooperation with other emerging markets and developing countries.

⑰ We will conduct diplomacy in better service of China's development. The diplomatic agenda will be closely aligned with the overall goal of China's reform，development and stability and serve to safeguard China's economic and financial security and its growing overseas interests.

We will continue to present Chinese provinces，regions and cities at the Foreign Ministry and bring all parts of China，especially the central and western regions，closer to the world.

⑱ Ladies and Gentlemen，Friends，

Time flies，yet we shall all stay true to our mission. Building a world enjoying peace and development and boosting China's exchange and cooperation with the world are the aspirations and tasks that we all share. As ambassadors，diplomatic envoys，and representatives of international organizations，you have worked tirelessly for the friendship between China and the rest of the world. Once again，I wish to express my heartfelt thanks to you all. Since its establishment，the MFA Office of Foreign Missions has been exploring effective ways to better communicate with and serve foreign missions in China. In the coming year，the Foreign Ministry will further improve its services to facilitate the work of foreign missions. This，I believe，will bring the Foreign Ministry closer to diplomatic envoys and representatives of international organizations，make our coordination with relevant provinces and departments more efficient，and open up new prospects for China's cooperation with the world.

⑲ Now，please join me in a toast:

To the friendship between people of China and people of all other countries,

To lasting peace and shared prosperity of the world，and

To the health of all distinguished guests present.

Cheers!

1.4　外事接待主题词汇汇总(Vocabulary Build-up)

schedule	日程安排
reserve	预订
upon ... request	根据……的要求
come all the way	专程造访
a thoughtful arrangement	精心安排
help out	排忧解难
terminal building	机场大楼
information/inquiry desk	问询处
waiting hall	候机大厅
departure/take-off time	起飞时间
arrival time	抵达时间
the Customs	海关
making a customs declaration	报关
round-trip ticket	往返票

(续表)

security check	安全检查
boarding pass	登记卡
entry/exit/tourist visa	入境/出境/旅游签证
duty-free shop	免税商店
luxury suite	豪华套房
single/double room	单/双人房
luggage claim	行李提取处
baggage depositary	行李寄存处
vaccination certificate	预防接种证书
foreign affairs office	外事办公室
buffet reception	冷餐招待会

1.5　扩展练习(Enhancement Practice)

Retelling.

Directions: Listen to the following passages once and then reproduce them in the same language at the end of each segment.

A. English Passage

A man was going to the house of some rich person. As he went along the road，he saw a box of good apples at the side of the road. He said，"I do not want to eat those apples；for the rich man will give me much food；he will give me very nice food to eat." Then he took the apples and threw them away into the dust.

He went on and came to a river. The river had become very big；so he could not go over it. He waited for some time；then he said，"I cannot go to the rich man's house today，for I cannot get over the river."

He began to go home. He had eaten no food that day. He began to want food. He came to the apples，and he was glad to take them out of the dust and eat them.

Do not throw good things away；you may be glad to have them at some other time.

B. Chinese Passage

康肃公陈尧咨，射箭技术举世无双，他本人也自命不凡。一天，他在自己的花园里射箭。有个卖油的老头儿正好路过这里，放下担子，站在一旁，斜着眼睛看了好久仍不离去。老头儿见他箭箭射中，并不喝彩，只是微微点头。康肃公问："你也懂得射箭吗？难道我的本领还不高明吗？"老头儿说："这没什么，只不过是手法熟练而已。"康肃公很恼火，大声斥责说："你怎么敢小看我的射箭技术!"老头儿不慌不忙地回答说：“我是通过打油得知的。” 说着，他拿了一只葫芦放在地下，又把一枚有孔的铜钱放在葫芦口上，然后用勺慢慢地往葫芦里灌油。只见油像一条细线一样，从铜钱眼里注入葫芦，铜钱却一点也没有沾油。老头儿笑了笑说：“我这也没什么，只是手法熟练罢了！”

1.6　口译点滴(Information Link)

■ 习近平主席在多个场合对“一带一路”倡议的阐述(一)

习近平主席在亚信峰会上的主旨发言

“亲望亲好、邻望邻好”。中国坚持与邻为善、与邻为伴，坚持睦邻、安邻、富邻，践行亲、诚、惠、容理念，努力使自身发展更好惠及亚洲国家。中国将同各国一道，加快推进丝绸之路经济带和21世纪海上丝绸之路建设，尽早启动亚洲基础设施投资银行，更加深入参与区域合作进程，推动亚洲发展和安全相互促进、相得益彰。

——2014年5月21日

"Neighbors wish each other well, just like family members do to each other." China always pursues friendship and partnership with its neighbors, and seeks to bring amity, security and common prosperity to its neighborhood. It practices the principles of amity, sincerity, mutual benefit and inclusiveness and works hard to make its development bring more benefits to countries in Asia. China will work with other countries to speed up the development of the Silk Road Economic Belt and the 21st Century Maritime Silk Road, and hopes that the Asian Infrastructure Investment Bank could be launched at an early date. China will get more deeply involved in the regional cooperation process, and play its due part to ensure that development and security in Asia facilitate each other and are mutually reinforcing.

——May 21st, 2014

第2单元　口译演讲(Public Speaking)

口译主题：礼仪祝词

单元学习目的(Unit Goals) 💡

➤ 掌握本课程所讲授的口译演讲技巧。
➤ 学习礼仪祝词专题所涉及的常用词语和表达。

导入(Lead-in)

1. 为会议发言人做口译时，口译人员在着装、面部表情等方面应该注意什么？
2. 口译过程中口译人员在音量和说话频率上应采取什么策略？

2.1　技能讲解(Skill Introduction)

在口译礼仪祝词的过程中，口译人员实际上向听众发表了一场公众演说，口译员除了注意译文的正确性外也要注意一些非语言因素。

■ 2.1.1　视觉表达(Visual Expression)

(1) 外表形象

口译者着装应适合特定场合，装扮不应分散听众注意力。在一些非正式场合，如旅行观光及日常交谈场合可搭配商务休闲风格衣着，而在商务谈判、会议、宴会等正式场合应着正装。

(2) 面部表情

口译者应保持温和的微笑，即使翻译过程中遇到困难也不应皱眉或表露出沮丧、失望的神情，同时注意不要有夸张虚假的表情。

(3) 眼神交流

口译者与说话人偶尔保持眼神交流是有效交流的保证。口译者还要同听众进行眼神交流，通过反馈做出合适的调整。但要注意，欧洲、美洲及阿拉伯国家的人往往直视交际者，而亚洲和非洲一些国家的人一般避免直接的眼神交流，尤其交流者是不同性别或不同社会地位时。

(4) 姿势仪态

口译者翻译过程中要仪态大方，身体放松，泰然自信，避免耸肩、歪站、交叉双臂等动作。当为旅游景点或名胜古迹当导游时，口译者可以使用一些姿势帮助听众理解；在正式场合应避免夸张不合适的姿势；在翻译室内进行口译时不用关注姿势，但要注意避免因移动桌椅及翻动纸张产生噪音。

▌2.1.2　声音表达(Voice Expression)

口译者必须说话频率适中，声音洪亮，确保在场的每一位听众都能听清。吐字清晰，避免发音不完整、误读、加多余音、口头语等。

▌2.1.3　常用句型(Useful Expressions)

(1) 欢迎词典型句型

我很荣幸地代表某某向来自某某地方的某某表示热烈的欢迎。

On behalf of sb., I have the honor/ I feel great honored to express/extend this warm welcome to sb. from sp.

请允许我向远道而来的贵宾表示热烈的欢迎和亲切的问候。

Permit me/ please allow me to express/extend these warm welcome and gracious greetings to our distinguished guests coming from afar.

我很愉快地以我个人的名义，向某某表示热烈的欢迎。

I am very delighted to extend/ express this personal warm welcome to... .

(2) 感谢词典型句型

我愿意借此机会，我谨代表……，对……的诚挚邀请和我们一踏上……便受到的友好款待，向……表示真诚的感谢。

On behalf of sb., I'd like to take this opportunity to express/extend our sincere thanks to sb. for their earnest invitation and gracious/incomparable hospitality we have received since we set foot on sp.

首先，请允许我感谢您的精心安排和热情好客。

First of all, permit me to say thank you for your extraordinary/ considerate/thoughtful arrangements and incomparable hospitality.

(3) 开幕词、闭幕词典型句型

宣布……开幕：

declare ... open / declare open ...

declare the commencement of...

预祝……取得圆满成功：

Wish ... a complete success!

宣布……闭幕：

declare the closing of ...

lower the curtain of ...

2.2　主题口译(Topic Interpreting)

▌2.2.1　单句口译(Sentence Practice)

Please interpret the following sentences by using the techniques illustrated above. You may interpret to your partner first and then he/she comments on your performance.

(1) It is a great pleasure today for me to attend this official dinner reception of the Asian-African Business Summit.

(2) I am looking forward with great expectation to visiting your country in the near future.

(3) I wish you a fruitful conference and I certainly wish the 9th Global Conference on Health Promotion a great success.

(4) First of all, I would like to express my heartfelt-thanks to our Chinese hosts for their extraordinary arrangements and gracious hospitality, although I know quite clearly that I can never thank them enough.

(5) For fifty years, International Literacy Day has celebrated literacy as an empowering force for women and men and for society as a whole.

(6) 本着友好合作、相互促进、共同繁荣的精神，我谨向您和代表团的全体成员表示最热烈的欢迎，并向您转达我石化集团全体员工最诚挚的问候。

(7) 我祝愿本届年会圆满成功，并祝各位在北京过得愉快。

(8) 我谨代表中国政府和人民，对本届论坛的召开表示热烈祝贺。

(9) 能有幸欢迎今晚在座诸位尊贵的客人，我感到十分荣幸。

(10) 这是根据《2030年可持续发展议程》举办的第一届健康促进大会，决心做到"不落下任何人"。

▌2.2.2　对话口译(Dialogue Practice)

1. Vocabulary Work: Study the following words and phrases and translate them into the target language.

建立业务关系	到岸价
让价	rock-bottom price
平等互利	barely cover production cost
各让一步	price sheet

2. Read the following dialogue and interpret it into the target language.

会谈与谈判

A：早上好，霍夫曼先生。

B：Good morning, Mr. Zhang, take a seat，please.

A：我们对贵公司生产的洗衣机非常感兴趣。事实上，我们正在考虑订货。我能看一下贵方的到岸价价目表吗？

B：Certainly, here is our price sheet. China is such an enormous market that nobody can afford to neglect. My company is willing to establish business relations with all interested Chinese parties.

A：谢谢。你这样说我很高兴。我们愿意同贵公司建立业务关系。

B：How do you like our price?

A：我认为价格毫无竞争力。

B：I should say that our price is reasonable. As you know, our products enjoy a high reputation and are always popular abroad. Comparing with the price of the other companies, I think our price is the most competitive.

A：你知道近几年在中国，大量的国产洗衣机已经上市。它们质量优良，价格却便宜得多。如果我们按照顾你们的报价进口你们的洗衣机，我可以肯定不会有多少顾客买它们的。

B：Our price might be higher than your homemade washing machines but our refrigerators are of better quality.

A：现在越来越多的顾客喜欢用国产洗衣机，因为它们价低质优，如果你们不想失去中国的市场，我认为你们最好让价5%。

B：To be frank with you, if we cut the price by 5%, it can barely cover our production cost. I should say a cut of 3% would be more realistic.

A：因为我们的目的是在平等互利的基础上做生意，因此我建议我们各让一半。

B：All right. In order to conclude the transaction, let's meet halfway. Though there is still a gap between your rock-bottom prices and my expectations, I'm willing to sign contracts with you.

A：我很高兴我们做成了这笔交易。

B：I believe this initial cooperation will lead to many more in the future.

3. Read the following dialogue and interpret it into the target language.

告别与送行

A：晚上好，约翰逊先生，我很高兴你来了。

B：Good evening, Mr. Yang, it's very kind of you to invite me to dinner tonight.

A：请坐。晚餐过几分钟就好。

B：Thank you for such a thoughtful arrangement.

A：今天晚上你穿着这一身衣服，真帅气，非常合身。

B：Thank you.

A：真遗憾，你明天就要离开我们了。

B：I'm sorry to leave you too.

A：希望你再次到我市来。

B：Sure.

A：晚餐已经准备好了，约翰逊先生，请入席吧。请这边坐。

B：Thanks. How delicious the food is!

A：约翰逊先生，为我们的友好合作干杯!

B：To your health and to your everlasting friendship.

A：谢谢。我非常感谢你为我所做的一切。但愿我能以某种方式回报你。

B：Don't mention it. I wish you a pleasant journey.

A：别忘了保持联系。但愿我们后会有期。

B：I hope so. I'll looking forward to it.

2.2.3　篇章口译[Passage Practice (E to C)]

1. Vocabulary Work: Study the following words and phrases and translate them into the target language.

Organizing Committee	cosmopolitan
boost	sportsmanship
fair play	gender equality

2. Please interpret the following paragraph by using the techniques illustrated above.

In just a few moments, the Olympic Games will officially return to London for the third time, setting an unmatched record for hosting the Games that spans more than a century. Thank you, London, for welcoming the world to this diverse, vibrant, cosmopolitan city yet again. // It has taken a lot of hard work by many people to get us to this point. I want to thank the entire team at the London Organizing Committee—superbly led by Lord Coe—for their excellent and hard work. I also want to thank all the public authorities who have helped ensure that these Games will leave a lasting positive legacy long after the closing ceremony.// And, of course, we are all grateful to the thousands of dedicated volunteers who are being so generous with their time, their energy and their welcoming smiles. // For the first time in Olympic history all the participating teams will have female athletes. This is a major boost for gender equality. // In a sense, the Olympic Games are coming home tonight. This great, sports-loving country is widely recognized as the birthplace of modern sport. It was here that the concepts of sportsmanship and fair play were first codified into clear rules and regulations. It was here that sport was included as an educational tool in the school curriculum.

3. Please interpret the following passage by using the techniques illustrated above. Please pay attention to the underlined sentences as they require special treatment during interpreting.

① Gary F. Locke's Remarks at Cascade Senior Living Opening Ceremony

② Thank you very much, James, for the introduction. It's really a pleasure to be here and quite an honor to be attending the Cascades Senior Living Apartment[1] opening ceremonies.

③ It's indeed a pleasure to share the podium with so many distinguished guests, especially Vice Minister of the Ministry of Civil Affairs, Mr. Do Yupei, but also Mr. Nathan McLemore who is Managing Director of Columbia Pacific Management and Mr. Granger Cobb who is the President and CEO of Emeritus Senior Living.[2] Both of the companies from my home state and my residence of Seattle, Washington.[3]

④ And of course this project would not be possible without the leadership and the vision of the Chinese companies, Sino Ocean Land, and the President Mr. Li Ming and also China Life Insurance Company Ltd. Mr. Yang.

⑤ China is really facing the challenges of taking care of a rapidly aging population because China now has almost 200 million people who are over the age of 60. But that number is increasing by almost nine million seniors a year, and by the year 2030 is expected to be almost 400 million seniors over the age of 60 years old. So this poses an enormous challenge for the people and the government of China.

⑥ The Chinese culture is known for emphasizing deep respect for one's parents and the elderly and of course taking care of our elderly. So it's only natural that China, we believe, will be a world leader in the quality of senior care services and in senior living communities.[4]

⑦ During a recent U.S.-China Dialogue, the Deputy Director General Peng of the National Development and Reform Commission indicated the desire of China for more cooperative exchanges with the United States in the area of health care and senior care services.[5] He encouraged U.S. companies to invest in the Chinese health care market and pledged China's support for both joint ventures and direct investments in health and senior care.

⑧ One of my priorities as U.S. Ambassador to China has been to foster closer cooperation between China and the United States in this area of health care and senior care, because both of our countries face the challenges of an aging population. So our Commercial Service has worked with the China Real Estate Chamber of Commerce[6] to coordinate Chinese government efforts to develop local senior care communities. We have facilitated a number of exchanges with U.S. experts to help the Chinese understand U.S. policy and actually help develop the first Chinese senior care standard for this industry.

⑨ In 2012 we led a trade mission focused on green hospital design and senior living, and the purpose of this mission was to introduce best practices of America to the Chinese government and to Chinese companies, and to introduce those U.S. companies on that trade mission to

Chinese enterprises.

⑩ Cascade Health Care, which was one of the partners of this project, was a delegate on that trade mission. <u>So we were also very pleased to arrange for Cascade Health Care and other U.S. companies to advise a task force of the State Council which is developing recommendations for Chinese national policy on senior living.</u>⁽⁷⁾

⑪ So it's a great pleasure to be here today to witness Cascade Health Care and Sino Ocean Land in celebrating the opening of their first major U.S.-China joint venture senior living project here in Beijing.

⑫ As I indicated, both China and the United States face the challenge of the rising numbers of seniors. I've had a chance to tour this facility. I must say it's absolutely beautiful. It has great support and medical services, talented, trained staff. The living units are very warm and friendly and I think the residents that will call this home will very much feel that it is a home.

⑬ Facilities like this really I think will be the model for the industry not just in China but also in the United States and indeed around the world.

⑭ I must confess, I have a personal interest in facilities like this because my mom suffers from a very advanced stage of Parkinson's Disease. She's still living at home. She wants to stay at home as long as possible. But now we're confronted with the need of providing almost 24 hour care to make sure that she's safe and gets the proper physical therapy, but also the medicine that she needs. All the members of the family are trying to provide care for her, but at some point we know she'll have to go into a more structured facility, hopefully a facility like this that offers 24 hour supervision, medical care, physical therapy and other support services.

⑮ We owe so much to our elders for all that they have done to raise us, their children, and for all of their sacrifices so that all of us could enjoy a better life. The least that we can do is ensure that our elders have quality care and quality living communities.

⑯ So it's a great pleasure to welcome partnerships between Chinese and U.S. senior living community companies like this, and to christen and cut the ribbon for facilities like this, because these facilities and these partnerships will not just to help meet the needs of our elderly generation, but really improve their quality of life.

⑰ So on behalf of the U.S. Embassy we wish all of you much success and a great future in serving the needs of the elderly here in China.

⑱ Thank you very much.

Notes on the text

(1) <u>Cascades Senior Living Apartment</u>
凯健老年生活公寓
(2) <u>Emeritus Senior Living</u>
荣休老年生活公司

(3) Seattle, Washington

此处的"华盛顿"并非指美国的首都华盛顿市，而指骆家辉家乡西雅图市的所在州华盛顿。

(4) So it's only natural that China, we believe, will be a world leader in the quality of senior care services and in senior living communities.

所以我们相信，中国将成为世界老年人护理服务质量和老年人居住社区的领军者，这是很自然的。

(5) ... the Deputy Director General Peng of the National Development and Reform Commission indicated the desire of China for more cooperative exchanges with the United States in the area of health care and senior care services.

……中国国家发展与改革委员会的彭副司长表明了中国愿在保健和老年人护理服务方面与美国进行更多的合作交流。

(6) the China Real Estate Chamber of Commerce

全国工商联房地产商会

(7) So we were also very pleased to arrange for Cascade Health Care and other U.S. companies to advise a task force of the State Council which is developing recommendations for Chinese national policy on senior living.

因此我们也非常愿意为凯健公司和其他美国公司进行安排，向正在制定中国养老服务业国家政策建议的国务院工作组建言献策。

▎2.2.4　篇章口译[Passage Practice (C to E)]

1. Vocabulary Work: Study the following words and phrases and translate them into the target language.

慈善音乐会	与时俱进
基金会	宏观
高速宽带网络	清谈馆
主席国	国情

2. Please interpret the following paragraph by using the techniques illustrated above.

很高兴再一次出席华为冬季音乐会。这已经是华为在伦敦连续第七年举办冬季慈善音乐会，也是华为成为英国王子基金会成员的第十个年头。//十年来，华为英国公司在践行企业社会责任、致力社会慈善事业的同时，更在英国高速宽带网络建设和研发领域取得了骄人的成绩，树立了在英中资企业的良好形象。//我希望华为继续秉承可持续发展理念，将业务做大做实，积极回馈当地社会，在英国取得更大发展，同时为构建更紧密的中英经贸关系作出更加积极的贡献！//我也希望更多的中国和英国企业加入到两国经贸合作的大潮，为中英关系黄金时代添砖加瓦，增光添彩！

3. Please interpret the following passage by using the techniques illustrated above. Please pay attention to the underlined sentences as they require special treatment during interpreting.

构建创新、活力、联动、包容的世界经济⁽¹⁾(节选)

习近平

① 各位同事：

② 我宣布，二十国集团领导人杭州峰会开幕！

③ 很高兴同大家相聚杭州。首先，我谨对各位同事的到来，表示热烈欢迎！

④ 去年，二十国集团领导人安塔利亚峰会开得很成功。我也愿借此机会，再次感谢去年主席国土耳其的出色工作和取得的积极成果。土耳其以"共同行动以实现包容和稳健增长"作为峰会主题，从"包容、落实、投资"三方面推动产生成果，中国一直积极评价土耳其在担任主席国期间开展的各项工作。⁽²⁾

⑤ 去年11月，我在安塔利亚向大家介绍，上有天堂，下有苏杭⁽³⁾，相信杭州峰会将给大家呈现一种历史和现实交汇的独特韵味⁽⁴⁾。今天，当时的邀请已经变成现实。在座的有老朋友，也有新朋友，大家齐聚杭州，共商世界经济发展大计。

⑥ 未来两天，我们将围绕峰会主题，就加强宏观政策协调、创新增长方式⁽⁵⁾，更高效的全球经济金融治理，强劲的国际贸易和投资，包容和联动式发展，影响世界经济的其他突出问题等议题展开讨论。

......

⑦ 二十国集团聚集了世界主要经济体，影响和作用举足轻重，也身处应对风险挑战、开拓增长空间的最前沿。国际社会对二十国集团充满期待，对这次峰会寄予厚望。我们需要通过各自行动和集体合力，直面问题，共寻答案。希望杭州峰会能够在以往的基础上，为世界经济开出一剂标本兼治、综合施策的药方，让世界经济走上强劲、可持续、平衡、包容增长之路。

......

⑧ 各位同事！

⑨ 二十国集团承载着世界各国期待，使命重大。我们要努力把二十国集团建设好，为世界经济繁荣稳定把握好大方向。

⑩ 第一，与时俱进，发挥引领作用⁽⁶⁾。二十国集团应该根据世界经济需要，调整自身发展方向，进一步从危机应对向长效治理机制转型⁽⁷⁾。面对重大突出问题，二十国集团有责任发挥领导作用，展现战略视野，为世界经济指明方向，开拓路径。

⑪ 第二，知行合一，采取务实行动⁽⁸⁾。承诺一千，不如落实一件。我们应该让二十国集团成为行动队，而不是清谈馆。今年，我们在可持续发展、绿色金融、提高能效、反腐败等诸多领域制定了行动计划，要把每一项行动落到实处。

⑫ 第三，共建共享，打造合作平台⁽⁹⁾。我们应该继续加强二十国集团机制建设，确保合作延续和深入。广纳良言，充分倾听世界各国特别是发展中国家声音，使二十国集团工

作更具包容性，更好地回应各国人民诉求。

⑬ 第四，同舟共济，发扬伙伴精神。伙伴精神是二十国集团最宝贵的财富。我们虽然国情不同、发展阶段不同、面临的现实挑战不同，但推动经济增长的愿望相同，应对危机挑战的利益相同，实现共同发展的憧憬相同。只要我们坚持同舟共济的伙伴精神，就能够克服世界经济的惊涛骇浪，开辟未来增长的崭新航程。

⑭ 各位同事！

⑮ 在杭州峰会筹备过程中，中国始终秉持开放、透明、包容的办会理念，同各成员保持密切沟通和协调。我们还举办了各种形式的外围对话，走进联合国，走进非盟总部，走进七十七国集团，走进最不发达国家、内陆国、小岛国，向世界各国，以及所有关心二十国集团的人们介绍杭州峰会筹备情况，倾听各方利益诉求。各方提出的意见和建议对这次峰会的筹备都发挥了重要作用。

⑯ 我期待在接下来两天的讨论中，我们能够集众智、聚合力，努力让杭州峰会实现促进世界经济增长、加强国际经济合作、推动二十国集团发展的目标。

⑰ 让我们以杭州为新起点，引领世界经济的航船，从钱塘江畔再次扬帆启航，驶向更加广阔的大海！

⑱ 谢谢大家。

Notes on the text

(1) 创新、活力、联动、包容的世界经济

an innovative, invigorated, interconnected and inclusive world economy

标题的翻译采用了英文押头韵的修辞手法，体现了音乐美和整齐美，更加铿锵有力，使标题更具感染力。

(2) 土耳其以"共同行动以实现包容和稳健增长"作为峰会主题，从"包容、落实、投资"三方面推动产生成果，中国一直积极评价土耳其在担任主席国期间开展的各项工作。

Under the theme "Collective Action for Inclusive and Robust Growth", Turkey brought about progress in inclusiveness, implementation and investment. China highly commends Turkey's efforts on various fronts during its G20 presidency.

(3) 上有天堂，下有苏杭

这句话有很多译法："Up in heaven, there is paradise; down on earth, there are Suzhou and Hangzhou"，"Just as there is paradise in heaven, there are Suzhou and Hangzhou on earth"，"Paradise above, Suzhou and Hangzhou below"，等等。

(4) 相信杭州峰会将给大家呈现一种历史和现实交汇的独特韵味。

And I said that I trust the Hangzhou Summit will be a unique setting where history is blended with modernity.

这句话及之前的"上有天堂，下有苏杭"都是习主席前一年在安塔利亚所说的话，因此翻译时补充"I said that"意思更确切。

(5) 宏观政策协调、创新增长方式

strengthening macro policy coordination, breaking a new path for growth.

(6) 发挥引领作用

lead the way forward

也可译为 "play a guiding role"，"take the lead role"。

(7) 进一步从危机应对向长效治理机制转型

further transform itself from a mechanism of crisis response to one of long-term governance.

(8) 知行合一，采取务实行动

这句话强调要把会议做出的承诺落到实处，因此译为 "honor its commitment" 较合适。

(9) 共建共享，打造合作平台

... the G20 should become a platform of cooperation built through joint efforts that delivers benefits to all

2.3　参考译文(Reference Version)

2.3.1　单句口译(Sentence Practice)

Please interpret the following sentences by using the techniques illustrated above. You may interpret to your partner first and then he/she comments on your performance.

(1) 今天我很高兴出席亚非工商界领导人的晚宴。

(2) 我期待着在不远的将来访问贵国。

(3) 我祝愿你们的会议富有成果，也衷心祝愿第九届全球健康促进大会圆满成功。

(4) 首先，我要对我的中国主人们表示衷心的感谢，感谢他们的精心安排和盛情款待，尽管我清楚地知道我对他们的感激是不尽的。

(5) 五十年来，国际扫盲日活动大力宣传扫盲工作，强调扫盲是增强女性、男性以及整个社会权能的重要力量。

(6) It is in the spirit of friendly cooperation, mutual promotion and common prosperity that I extend to you the warmest welcome and convey to you the most gracious greetings from all the employees of our petrol-chemical group corporation.

(7) I wish this annual meeting a complete success and wish all of you a pleasant stay in Beijing.

(8) I wish to extend, on behalf of the Chinese Government and people, warm congratulations on the convocation of the forum.

(9) It is a great privilege to be able to welcome the distinguished guests present here this evening.

(10) This is the first conference on health promotion being held under the Sustainable

Development Agenda 2030, leaving no one behind.

2.3.2　对话口译(Dialogue Practice)

1. Vocabulary Work: Study the following words and phrases and translate them into the target language.

enter into business relations with	C.I.F.
reduce your price	底价
equality and mutual benefit	不够成本费
meet each other halfway	报价单

2. Read the following dialogue and interpret it into the target language.

A：Good morning, Mr. Huffman

B：早上好，张先生。请坐。

A：We are quite interested in the Washing Machines made by your company. In fact, we're thinking of placing an order. May I look at your CIF price sheet ?

B：当然可以。这是我们的报价单。中国是一个无人敢忽视的巨大市场。我公司愿意同一切有兴趣的中国客户建立业务关系。

A：Thanks. I'm very glad to hear that. We wish to enter into business relations with your company.

B：你觉得我们的价格怎么样?

A：I think it's rather among the least competitive.

B：我认为我们的价格是合理的。你知道，我们的产品享有盛誉，并畅销海外。与其他公司的产品相比，我认为我们的产品是最具有竞争力的。

A：You know now in China large quantities of homemade washing machines have appeared on the local market in recent years. Their quality is good, but their price is much lower. If we import your washing machines at your price. I'm sure few customers will buy them.

B：我们的价格可能比你们国产冰箱的价格要高，但是我们的质量要好一些。

A：Now more and more customers like to use homemade washing machines because of its low price and a good quality. And if you don't want to lose the market in China, I think you'd better reduce your price by at least 5%.

B：坦率地说，如果我们让价5%，那几乎不够成本费。我认为让价3%是比较现实的。

A：Our purpose is to do business on the basis of equality and mutual benefit. So I suggest we meet each other halfway.

B：好吧，为了谈成这笔交易，我们各让一半。虽然贵方的底价与我方所希望得到的价格有差距，我还是愿意签合同。

A：I'm glad we have brought this transaction to a successful conclusion.

B：我相信我们这次合作仅仅是个开端，今后合作的机会将会更多。

3. Listen to the following dialogue and interpret it into the target language.

A：Good evening, Mr. Johnson, I'm glad you've come.

B：晚上好，杨先生。今晚您请我共进晚餐，真是太客气了。

A：Sit down, please, The dinner will be ready in a few minutes.

B：谢谢您所作的如此精心的安排。

A：You look really smart tonight in these clothes, It fits you perfectly.

B：谢谢。

A：It's a pity that you're leaving us to tomorrow.

B：要离开你们我也感到非常遗憾。

A：Hope you'll visit our city again.

B：一定。

A：Now the dinner is ready . Mr. Johnson, Please come to the table. Take a seat here, please.

B：谢谢。这菜真香。

A：Mr. Johnson here is to our friendly cooperation.

B：为您的健康以及我们的永恒友谊干杯。

A：Thanks, I appreciate everything you've done for me very much. I wish I could repay you somehow.

B：不用谢。我希望您旅途愉快。

A：And don't forget to keep in touch. May we meet again some day.

B：但愿如此。我盼望着这一天的到来。

2.3.3 篇章口译[Passage Practice (E to C)]

1. Vocabulary Work: Study the following words and phrases and translate them into the target language.

奥组委	国际化大都市
推动	运动精神
公平竞赛原则	性别平等

2. Please interpret the following paragraph by using the techniques illustrated above.

再过一会儿，奥运会将第三次来到伦敦，这是过去一个世纪中无可比拟的人类纪录。谢谢伦敦，再次将我们带到这个充满活力的国际化大都市。//为了实现这个目标，很多人付出了艰苦努力。我要感谢科勋爵士带领下的伦敦奥组委团队的出色工作，感谢他们做出了卓越的成绩。我还要感谢相关政府部门的合作，使得伦敦奥运会在闭幕之后能够留下一份持久有益的奥运遗产。//当然，对于数千名志愿者的辛苦付出，我们也心存感激，他们无私地付出时间、体能和微笑欢迎我们。//在奥运会历史上，第一次所有代表团都有女性运动员参赛，这是推动性别平等的重要一步。//在一定程度上，我们可以说，奥运会在今晚回家了。这个国家热爱体育，是现代体育的发源地。在这里，运动精神和公平竞赛原则首次得到了明确规定，在这里，体育进入了学校课程体系。

3. Please interpret the following passage by using the techniques illustrated above. Please pay attention to the underlined sentences as they require special treatment during interpreting.

① 骆家辉在凯健老年生活开幕典礼上的讲话

② 非常感谢詹姆斯的介绍。真的很高兴和荣幸来到这里，出席凯健老年生活公寓的开业典礼。

③ 真的很高兴与这么多尊贵的来宾分享同一张讲台，尤其是民政部副部长窦玉沛，还有哥伦比亚太平洋管理公司董事总经理南森·麦克勒莫尔先生，荣休老年生活公司总裁兼首席执行官格兰杰·柯布先生。这两家公司都来自我的家乡和我居住的地方——华盛顿州的西雅图。

④ 当然，如果没有中国公司，如远洋地产、李明总裁以及中国人寿保险股份有限公司的杨先生的领导和远见，这个项目就不会成为可能。

⑤ 中国的确正面临快速老龄化人口护理的挑战，因为中国目前有近两亿60岁以上的人口。而这一数字以每年将近900万的老年人口在增加，到2030年，将可能有近四亿60岁以上的老人。因此，这对中国人民和政府构成了巨大挑战。

⑥ 中国文化以强调对父母和老人的由衷尊重以及照顾我们的老人而著称。所以我们相信，中国将成为世界老年人护理服务质量和老年人居住社区的领军者，这是很自然的。

⑦ 在最近的一次美中对话期间，中国国家发展与改革委员会的彭副司长表明了中国愿在保健和老年人护理服务方面与美国进行更多的合作交流。他鼓励美国公司投资中国保健市场，并许诺中国为从事保健和老年人护理的合资企业和直接投资提供支持。

⑧ 作为美国驻华大使，我的优先事项之一就是促进中国和美国在卫生保健和老年人护理这方面更紧密的合作，因为我们两国都面临着人口老龄化的挑战。因此我们的商务服务局曾与全国工商联房地产商会配合，以协调中国政府发展地方老年人护理社区的努力。我们已经促成了与美国专家的多次交流，以帮助中国人了解美国的政策并真正帮助这个行业发展第一批中国老年人护理标准。

⑨ 2012年，我们组织了一个绿色医院设计与养老服务贸易代表团，目的就是向中国政府和企业介绍美国的成功经验，并将代表团中的美国企业介绍给中国企业。

⑩ 凯健医疗公司是这个项目的合作伙伴之一，也是那个代表团的成员之一。因此我们也非常愿意为凯健公司和其他美国公司进行安排，向正在制定中国养老服务业国家政策建议的国务院工作组建言献策。

⑪ 今天，我非常高兴能够在这里见证这个开业仪式。这是凯健公司和远洋地产在北京联手创办的第一个养老合作项目。

⑫ 正如我刚才说的，中国和美国都面临着老龄人口增长带来的挑战。我参观过这家养老机构，我得说，这里美极了。这里有非常好的支持和医疗服务，有聪明、训练有素的

员工。这里的居住单元非常温馨友好。我想，选择在这里安家的人会感觉这里就是家。

⑬ 我认为，这样的机构一定会成为养老服务业的典范，不仅是在中国，在美国和全世界都是如此。

⑭ 我必须承认，我对这样的机构有个人兴趣，因为我妈妈患有晚期帕金森氏症。她还住在家里。她希望尽可能久地住在家里。但是，现在我们面临提供近24小时监护的需要，以确保她的安全，确保她得到适当的物理治疗，以及她需要的药。所有的家庭成员都试图照顾她，但在某一刻，我们知道她将不得不住进一家更加功能化的机构，提供24小时监护、医疗护理、物理治疗和其他赡养服务。

⑮ 我们太亏欠我们的长辈，他们为了抚养我们，他们的孩子，做了很多牺牲，让我们都能享有更好的生活。我们至少要确保我们的长辈得到优质的护理服务和优质的生活社区环境。

⑯ 所以很高兴迎来这样的中国和美国老年社区企业之间的合作，并为这样的机构揭幕剪彩，因为这些机构和合作将不仅帮助满足老年人的需求，而且真正提高他们的生活质量。

⑰ 所以，我们代表美国驻华使馆祝福大家在服务这里的老年人的需求之际获得圆满成功、收获美好未来。

⑱ 非常感谢。

2.3.4 篇章口译[Passage Practice (C to E)]

1. Vocabulary Work: Study the following words and phrases and translate them into the target language.

charity concert	keep up with the changing times
Trust	macro
high-speed broadband network	talk shop
presidency	national conditions

2. Please interpret the following paragraph by using the techniques illustrated above.

It is a pleasure to join you again for the winter concert of Huawei Technologies UK. This is the seventh consecutive winter charity concert that Huawei has hosted in London. Ten years ago, Huawei UK became a member of the Prince's Trust.// Ten years on, Huawei UK is highly acclaimed for its devotion to charity and strong sense of corporate social responsibility. But much more than that. Huawei UK is also a proud leader in the construction, research and development of high-speed broadband network in Britain. In Huawei UK, we see a fine example of Chinese company doing business in this country.//I hope Huawei UK will continue to work for sustainable development. I hope your business will grow stronger and I hope you will continue to give back to the local community. I am sure your continued success in this country will help build stronger business relationship between China and the UK.// I want to encourage more Chinese and British companies to sign up for China-UK business cooperation and contribute your part to the "Golden

Era" of China-UK relations!

3. Please interpret the following passage by using the techniques illustrated above. Please pay attention to the underlined sentences as they require special treatment during interpreting.

Towards an Innovative, Invigorated, Interconnected and Inclusive World Economy
(Excerpts)
Xi Jinping

① Dear Colleagues,

② The G20 Hangzhou Summit now begins.

③ It gives me great pleasure to meet you here in Hangzhou, and I wish to extend a warm welcome to you all.

④ The G20 Summit in Antalya last year was a big success. I wish to use this opportunity to thank Turkey once again for its outstanding job and the positive outcomes achieved during its presidency. Under the theme "Collective Action for Inclusive and Robust Growth", Turkey brought about progress in inclusiveness, implementation and investment. China highly commends Turkey's efforts on various fronts during its G20 presidency.

⑤ Last November in Antalya, I talked to you about Hangzhou by quoting a Chinese saying, "Up in heaven, there is paradise; down onearth, there are Suzhou and Hangzhou." And I said that I trust the Hangzhou Summit will be a unique setting where history is blended with modernity. I am glad you have accepted my invitation and come to Hangzhou. Present here are old and new friends of mine, and we will discuss ways to sustain global growth.

⑥ In the next two days, under the theme of the Summit, we will have discussions on strengthening macro policy coordination, breaking a new path for growth, more effective and efficient global economic and financial governance, robust international trade and investment, inclusive and interconnected development, as well as other issues affecting the world economy.

...

⑦ The G20 consists of the world's major economies. Its critical role and impact place the G20 at the forefront of the global efforts to tackle risks and challenges and expand the space of growth. The international community has great expectation for the G20 and places high hopes on the Hangzhou Summit. In response, we should find solutions to the problems we face through both individual and collective efforts. I hope the Hangzhou Summit will build on previous progress to provide a solution that addresses both the symptoms and root causes of the global economic problems and achieve strong, sustainable, balanced and inclusive global growth.

...

⑧ Dear Colleagues,

⑨ The G20 carries high expectation of the international community and shoulders a heavy responsibility. We must ensure that the G20 fully plays its role of keeping the world economy on the track of prosperity and stability.

⑩ First, the G20 must keep up with the changing times and lead the way forward. The G20 should adapt itself to the needs of the global economy and further transform itself from a mechanism of crisis response to one of long-term governance. When major issues emerge, the G20 has the responsibility to play a leading role and, with strategic vision, set the direction and blaze the trail for global growth.

⑪ Second, the G20 should fully honor its commitment. As a Chinese saying puts it, one thousand promises do not count as much as one real action. We should make the G20 an action team instead of a talk shop. This year, we have formulated action plans for many areas such as sustainable development, green finance, energy efficiency and combating corruption, and each and every plan should be implemented.

⑫ Third, the G20 should become a platform of cooperation built through joint efforts that delivers benefits to all. We should continue to strengthen the institutional building of the G20 to sustain and deepen our cooperation. We should solicit proposals for improvement and heed the views of all countries, especially the developing countries, so as to make the G20 more inclusive and better respond to the demand of people of different countries.

⑬ Fourth, the G20 should stick together as partners in meeting challenges. Partnership is the most valuable asset of the G20. The G20 countries differ in national conditions, stages of development and face different challenges. But we all share a common goal of pursuing stronger growth, meeting challenges and achieving common development. So long as we stick together, we can navigate the heavy waves of the global economy and sail towards a future of growth.

⑭ Dear Colleagues,

⑮ In preparing for the Hangzhou Summit, China has followed the principle of openness, transparency and inclusiveness, and maintained close contact and coordination with all other members. We have also held dialogue of various forms with the United Nations, the African Union, the G77, the least developed countries, landlocked countries and small island states to brief them and all the people who show an interest in the G20 on our preparation. We have listened to the views and proposals of various parties and benefited greatly from them in making preparation for the Hangzhou Summit.

⑯ I hope that during discussions in the coming two days, we will pool our vision and create synergy so as to enable the Hangzhou Summit to fulfill its mandate of boosting global growth, strengthening international economic cooperation and promoting the future growth of the G20.

⑰ Let's make Hangzhou a new departure point and steer the giant ship of the global economy on a new voyage from the shore of the Qiantang River to the vast ocean.

⑱ Thank you!

2.4　礼仪祝词主题词汇汇总(Vocabulary Build-up)

deliver an opening/closing speech	致开/闭幕词
signing ceremony	签字仪式
goodwill visit	友好访问
declare ... open; declare the commencement/opening of	宣布……开幕
declare the conclusion/closing of ...	宣布……闭幕
distinguished/respected/respectable/honorable guests	尊敬的来宾
on the occasion of	值此……之际
heartfelt thanks	由衷的谢意
at the gracious invitation of ...	承蒙……的盛情邀请
look back on...; in retrospect	回顾过去
look ahead; look into the future	展望未来
propose a toast	提议祝酒
friends coming from a distant land/the other side of the Pacific	远道来访/来自大洋彼岸的朋友
with profound and amicable sentiments for your people	怀着对贵国人民的深厚感情
host country	东道国
take this opportunity to...	借此机会
in the spirit of	本着……精神
gracious hospitality	友好款待
His (Her, Your) Majesty	陛下
His (Her, Your) Royal Highness	殿下
His (Her, Your) Excellency	阁下

2.5　扩展练习(Enhancement Practice)

Retelling.

Directions: Listen to the following passages once and then reproduce them in the same language at the end of each segment.

A. English Passage

Over the past 40 years of international friendship cities activities, China has established 2,340 pairs of friendship city relations with more than 130 countries. Changsha city of Hunan province and the city of Entebbe in Uganda have had vibrant education and culture exchanges, and built together the "Entebbe-Changsha Demonstration Primary School". Nanjing city of Jiangsu province and Aichi prefecture of Japan have deepened their friendship through youth and art troupe exchanges. Ruili city in Yunnan province and City of Muse of Myanmar organize carnivals during China's National Day holiday week each year, which is quite popular among the local communities.

B. Chinese Passage

华盛顿州在中美贸易关系上扮演了具有历史性和相当重要的角色，为此我感到非常自豪。28年前的这个月，一艘飘扬着中华人民共和国国旗的货船抵达了西雅图港口。中国和美国的官员们都在海港迎候着它的到来。然而，这艘637英尺长、挪威造的船只却未装载任何货物。但是，当它离开西雅图时却满载了37 000公吨的美国中西部的玉米。这是30年来首次有中国船只进出美国港口。

2.6　口译点滴(Information Link)

■ 习近平主席在多个场合对"一带一路"倡议的阐述(二)

习近平主席在博鳌亚洲论坛2015年年会开幕式的主旨演讲

"一带一路"建设秉持的是共商、共建、共享原则，不是封闭的，而是开放包容的；不是中国一家的独奏，而是沿线国家的合唱。"一带一路"建设不是要替代现有地区合作机制和倡议，而是要在已有基础上，推动沿线国家实现发展战略相互对接、优势互补。

In promoting the Belt and Road Initiative, China will follow the principle of wide consultation, joint contribution and shared benefits. The programs of development will be open and inclusive, not exclusive. They will be a real chorus comprising all countries along the routes, not a solo for China itself. To develop the Belt and Road is not to replace existing mechanisms or initiatives for regional cooperation. Much to the contrary, we will build on the existing basis to help countries align their development strategies and form complementarity.

"一带一路"建设不是空洞的口号，而是看得见、摸得着的实际举措，将给地区国家带来实实在在的利益。在有关各方共同努力下，"一带一路"建设的愿景与行动文件已经制定，亚洲基础设施投资银行筹建工作迈出实质性步伐，丝路基金已经顺利启动，一批基础设施互联互通项目已在稳步推进。

——2015年3月28日

The Belt and Road Initiative is not meant as rhetoric. It represents real work that could be seen and felt to bring real benefits to countries in the region. Thanks to the concerted efforts of relevant parties, the vision and action paper of the initiative has been developed. Substantive progress has been made in the establishment of the AIIB. The Silk Road Fund has been launched, and constructions of a number of infrastructure connectivity projects are moving forward.

——March 28th,2015

第3单元 口译听辨(Listening Comprehension)

口译主题：体育

单元学习目的(Unit Goals) 💡

➢ 掌握本课程所讲授的听辨口译技巧。
➢ 学习体育专题所涉及的常用词语和表达。

导入(Lead -in)

1. 口译听辨中"听"的特点是什么？
2. 如何理解这句话：Listen for the ideas and not the words.
3. 如何有效提高口译听辨能力？
4. 口译的理解过程是什么？

3.1 技能讲解(Skill Introduction)

■ 3.1.1 口译听辨中听辨理解的特点(Features in Listening Comprehension)

(1) 以听懂为目标，以较高的效率完成传递源语信息的任务。听懂理解原文是口译的第一步，理解困难包括词汇、专业术语、议题内容、背景知识以及讲话者的语速、口音和语调。讲话者的口音、语速、节奏和长短变化对译员的听力能力有很高要求。

(2) 语音听辨、词义理解、句层意义理解以及语段或语篇意义理解同时完成。口译听辨中，从语音信息输入到目标语输出之间只有数秒到几分钟，这需要译员在短时间内完成对信息的理解并进行译入语加工。

(3) 译员的注意力集中在上下文、语篇逻辑、话语内容和意义上。信息的准确程度是判断口译质量的标准，听辨理解的准确是口译准确的前提。译员出现重要信息的理解错误可能会招致服务对象的重大损失。

(4) 口译听辨活动具有不可重复的特点，要求译员一次性理解所听内容，不可能重听或查阅资料后再听。

3.1.2 听辨过程与听力训练的区别(Differences between Listening Comprehension and Listening Training)

(1) 译员在听辨过程中注重意思以及讲话者的意图，并非具体的词句表达，在听到一段话后会在大脑里形成一个有逻辑关系的语意整体印象，不是简单的词句集合。听力训练注重语言层面，即语音、语调和语言的表达及用法。

(2) 听辨过程中要同时启动听觉系统、大脑中的分析理解机制和记忆机制，边听、边分析、边理解、边记忆。译员要具有一定的分析能力，学会一心多用。听力练习主要启动听觉系统，理解只是一个被动而附带的过程。

(3) 听辨过程需要译员积极主动的预测和判断，能同时调动非语言因素对所听内容进行分析、整理、补充和联想。而听力练习里对信息的接收是被动的和跟随性的，对信息的反映略显滞后。

(4) 听辨过程中，译员所处的信息环境是现场性的，具有较多不确定性因素；信息干扰、信息缺失也时有发生。而听力训练的材料中信息比较清晰，杂音干扰较少。

(5) 听辨过程比一般听力训练要复杂得多，要求也高得多。口译过程不是把信息背诵加字词翻译的过程，而是通过听辨将信息接收、理解，再用译入语将理解的信息加以表达的过程。

3.1.3 提高口译听辨能力(The Improvement of Listening Comprehension)

(1) 译员需要精神集中，主动对源语进行思维加工，分析源语的意义，综合源语的信息要点；力求预测所译内容，达到听辨理解与讲话者同步。

(2) 译员应充分运用语言能力，可以按照时间顺序、强调、解释、举例、转换话题、因果、递进、转折、假设和总结这十类话语标记辅助搜寻讲话要旨。

(3) 译员需要注意识别所听信息中的主题思想，从讲话者开口说话时就紧跟其思路，根据"意群"抓住内容要旨。

(4) 译员要不断提高自己的心理素质，克服现场紧张情绪，综合运用各种精力资源，并对各种资源进行最优化分配，以协调各个听辨认知过程。

(5) 在听辨过程中，译员可以运用联想、预测、推断、协调、表征以及存储等多种认知策略性技能辅助练习，以提高口译听辨能力。

▋ 3.1.4　口译听辨操作要点(Skill Focus on Listening Comprehension)

(1) 提取关键词，关注意群，合理断句，把重点放在对意思的理解上。关键词一般包括核心主语、主要动词、宾语、数字、表示时间地点的词和强调的词语等。意群是帮助译员切分和理解信息的较小翻译单位。

(2) 重视表示时态的词语，避免意义传达的错误和翻译的不准确。在关注关键词的同时不能忽略时态，因为时态在英语中是一项必不可少的表意工具，忽略时态会产生意义传递错误的严重后果。

(3) 关注句群之间的逻辑关系，句群之间的逻辑关系一般有以下几种：原因关系、转折关系、条件关系、让步关系、时间先后关系和结果关系。

(4) 处理好中文常见的四字词组和富含文化底蕴的表达。先理解意义，再传达意义，不能只做字面的翻译，让听者无法体会说话者的深意。然而对于有历史典故和文化内涵的表达，口译时可以直接传达实际含义。

(5) 关注讲话者的弦外之音，从表情、语气、语调和肢体语言判断所传达的真实情感和意义。译员需要在听的同时根据讲话者的副语言和肢体语言进行判断。

(6) 关注口译活动发生的现场、时间、地点、人物以及谈话内容的上下文，即具体语境。译员可以凭借对现场预警的观察来正确理解讲话者的意思。

▋ 3.1.5　训练听辨能力的方法(Ways of Training Listening Comprehension)

(1) 选择英文有声资料、现场讲话或模拟现场发言。听过一段话后，在不记笔记的情况下用源语(英文)进行复述。在听力过程中要把注意力从词句表达转移到专注于整段话的逻辑意思。复述时不必拘泥于原文词句，不用试图背原话。尽量把意思和逻辑关系复述得准确完整。

(2) 在听辨训练的初级阶段，由于不能完全掌握边听、边分析、边记忆的技能，可采取就所听内容进行提问的方式建立逻辑关系。可以先将注意力放在what、who、when、where、why、how等几个要素上，以增强逻辑分析意识，努力跟上讲话人的思路，从而正确理解所听语篇。

(3) 训练材料的长度可随熟练程度的增强而逐步增加，先听一小段，然后听一大段，再到听数段；听力材料可以尝试不同风格，选题也可以从熟悉的领域逐步扩展到陌生的领域，从而培养临场适应能力和综合分析能力。

(4) 训练材料可以从标准的英语视听资料开始，在对标准英文的听辨练到一定程度之后，逐渐引入带有各种口音的英文视听资料。真实环境中，会有很多讲话者带有地方口音，所以译员在平时的训练中不能只针对标准发音而忽视其他口音。

3.2 主题口译(Topic Interpreting)

▎3.2.1 单句口译(Sentence Practice)

Please interpret the following sentences by using the techniques illustrated above. You may interpret to your partner first and then he/she comments on your performance.

(1) I am not yet ready to give up on wearable devices but they need to do a lot more work if they are not to go the way of every other diet and exercise fad.

(2) The major "Electronic Competitive Sports and Management" is listed among 13 new majors for vocational schools in China, according to the Ministry of Education. The e-sports major will be launched in vocational collages nationwide from 2017.

(3) Cheers, tears and beers as first ever Games victory for Pacific nation sparks euphoria – with dancing in streets, work forgotten and schoolwork abandoned.

(4) Eating a diet rich in lean proteins will increase your metabolism because it takes more energy for your body to digest the protein.

(5) The researchers were "pretty confident" that the people with activity monitors would exercise more, eat better and lose more weight.

(6) 中国游泳运动员傅园慧搞笑的赛后采访和夸张的面部表情使她成为"网红"。里约奥运会前，其55万的新浪微博粉丝数量本已相当可观，本周这一数字已激增至500万。

(7) 当地时间周四上午，美国队通过申诉成功获得单独重赛的机会后，中国队无缘里约奥运会女子4×100米决赛。

(8) 郭川是首位创造了两项世界纪录的中国职业帆船手，即40英尺级帆船单人不间断环球航行世界纪录(2013年，历时138天)和北冰洋东北航道不间断航行世界纪录(2015年，12天零3个小时)。

(9) 托特纳姆热刺教练员还将和体育老师按照热刺专业教练员制定的培养计划，为超过6万名中小学生培训一年。

(10) 国家主席习近平号召践行奥林匹克精神，助力实现中华民族伟大复兴的中国梦。

▎3.2.2 对话口译(Dialogue Practice)

1. Vocabulary Work: Study the following words and phrases and translate them into the target language.

意志力	dribble
篮圈	observant
梯队	cheetah
合适的职业	relentless
重申	passionate
着迷的	resilient

2. Read the following dialogue and interpret it into the target language.

A：我想这一点就是我们今天的TED演讲中所要讲的，意志的力量。我想，你知道的，因为有很多运动员把NBA变成了世界上最高级别的职业篮球赛，有的运动员可以跳的像天空一样高，可以跑的和猎豹一样快，他们可以击打球框，他们可以做出反应，但是球员们比较特殊的一点就是，他们有那样的意志，有那种攻击模式，那种不屈不挠的模式，在最后几分钟也可以很冷静，你知道吗？我想那就是好球员和最佳球员之间的差别。

B：Yeah, you know, it's funny. To me, the mentality is a really simple one. In the sense that the confidence comes from preparation. So when the game is on the line, I'm not asking myself to do something that I haven't done thousands of times before. Right? So, when I prepare I know what I am capable of doing, I know what I'm comfortable doing and I know what I'm not comfortable doing. You know, right? So in those moments if it looks ice cold, or not nervous, it's because I've done it thousands of times before, so what's one more time?

A：那么我想说说今年科比在亚洲的巡回，我们重申曼巴精神。你可不可以稍微谈谈什么是曼巴精神，因为这已经发展了，我不是想说20年，它已经发展了35年，从你还是个小孩的时候就开始发展曼巴精神，因为你并不是从NBA开始工作的，你是从劳尔梅里恩高中开始的，当时你在意大利，只有5岁，那时你打的是内尔夫篮球，对吗？所以，来谈谈曼巴精神的发展，曼巴精神的五个支柱，然后我们来进行分解。

B：Well, overall, the idea is a very simple one. And the mamba mentality simply means trying to be the best version of yourself. That's what the mentality means. It means every day you're trying to became better. And it's a constant quest, it's an infinite quest. So starting at the age of two, when I first started playing the game and on and on and on, I always asked questions, I always tried to get better every day, learn more, learn more.

A：你在两岁就问问题了？

B：Oh, dude, I was asking questions all the time. You'd be surprised. Some people, like my kids, at two, could do a lot of things. At two I could dribble a basketball, I could shoot a basketball in a Nerf hoop at the house, and I could go to practice with my father, I would observe my father, I'd sit and watch games with him.

A：他是你第一个教练吗？

B：Yeah, I guess you could say that. A lot of things I learned just by being around the game. So by the age of six, I was already strategizing versus other six year olds, you know, at the age of six I figured out six year olds couldn't dribble with their left hand.

A：很多12岁的孩子也不能用左手运球。

B：Yeah, I could imagine six. So like when I was playing these six year old kids, I would make them dribble with their left, because I knew they couldn't, so they'd dribble off their foot, I'd pick it up, lay it up. Do it again, dribble off foot, pick it up, lay it up. So at six years old, I had 63 points. And I remember my dad.

A：所以6岁的你可以打败 38岁的你，他在最后一次比赛中只得了60分。

B：Yeah, no, but I can dribble with my left, though, so that's a problem. But, listen, I just constantly looked for things to learn from, and very observant.

A：所以今天在探讨曼巴精神的时候，你的展览业开始了。从上海开始的，对吗？另外，我们已经讨论了这个和5岁、10岁、15岁、20岁的年轻孩子一起的巡回。我们刚刚建立了一个科比学院，我们说了关于有激情、着迷、不屈不挠、有弹性而且无所畏惧。这些就是曼巴精神的五大支柱。

▌3.2.3　篇章口译[Passage Practice (E to C)]

1. Vocabulary Work: Study the following words and phrases and translate them into the target language.

motto	marathon
inexorably	sprinter
cinder	trowel
Biomechanical	synthetic track
gynecology	a performance-enhancing drug
somersault	diminutive
torso	democratization

2. A. Please interpret the following paragraph by using the techniques illustrated above.

　　Paris and Los Angeles are set to stage the 2024 and 2028 Olympic Games - provided they can agree which should go first, as both want to host in 2024. The International Olympic Committee has voted in favor of naming hosts for successive Games on 13 September with just Paris and Los Angeles bidding. // The IOC — which oversees the Olympic movement — wants the cities to reach an agreement on who hosts in 2028 by then. If there is no agreement, a vote to select just the 2024 host will be held. Budapest, Hamburg and Rome withdrew from the race for the 2024 event. //IOC president Thomas Bach told reporters after the meeting he hoped the agreement would be reached next month. And LA organizers said they were "thrilled" with the decision, adding: "We look forward to working with the IOC and Paris in the weeks ahead to turn this golden opportunity into a golden future together." //In June, Los Angeles bid chair Casey Wasserman appeared to concede to Paris when he said: "We have never been only about 2024." However, a spokesman later told BBC Sport: "LA is the ideal host city for 2024 and is not conceding anything in the race for the 2024 Games." //Paris has said it has to go first as the site it has earmarked for the Olympic Village will not be available for redevelopment after 2024. It took a while and it was a little confusing but Thomas Bach eventually got what he wanted - unanimous backing for Paris and Los Angeles to become Olympic hosts. //It's dependent on all parties reaching agreement but with the mayors of the two cities, who are friends, holding hands while thanking the IOC members for their approval, it would be a major surprise if a deal isn't struck. And there could be a quick decision. //Discussions will begin in the next few days – it's in no-ones' interest for any uncertainty to linger longer than is necessary. It's been dressed up as a win-win scenario. In truth one of them will be a bigger winner. Both cities started out bidding for 2024, now either Paris or Los Angeles will be asked to accept 2028 instead. //It's still better than losing. For the IOC it buys them time to revamp the bidding process, to encourage other potential contenders who have been scared off, especially in Western Europe. After years when competition was fierce to stage the prestigious event, there's been a declining number of cities that are interested. //Hamburg, Rome and Budapest pulled out of the current campaign, just two candidates competed for the right to host the 2022 Winter Games. The costs involved and a lack of public support were to blame.

3. Please interpret the following passage by using the techniques illustrated above. Please pay attention to the underlined sentences as they require special treatment during interpreting.

Are Athletes really Getting Faster, Better, and Stronger? (Excerpts)
David Epstein

① The Olympic motto is "Citius, Altius, Fortius." Faster, Higher, Stronger. And athletes have fulfilled that motto rapidly. The winner of the 2012 Olympic marathon ran two hours and eight minutes. Had he been racing against the winner of the 1904 Olympic marathon, he would have won by nearly an hour and a half. Now we all have this feeling that we're somehow just getting better as a human race, inexorably progressing, but it's not like we've evolved into a new species in a century. So what's going on here?

② I want to take a look at what's really behind this march of athletic progress. In 1936, Jesse Owens held the world record in the 100 meters. <u>Had Jesse Owens been racing last year in the world championships of the 100 meters, when Jamaican sprinter Usain Bolt finished, when would have still had 14 feet to go.</u> ⁽¹⁾ That's a lot in sprinter land. To give you a sense of how much it is, I want to share with you a demonstration conceived by sports scientist Ross Tucker.

③ Now picture the stadium last year at the world championships of the 100 meters: thousands of fans waiting with baited breath to see Usain Bolt, the fastest man in history; flashbulbs popping as the nine fastest men in the world coil themselves into their blocks. And I want you to pretend that Jesse Owens is in that race. Now close your eyes for a second and picture the race. Bang! The gun goes off. An American sprinter jumps out to the front. Usain Bolt starts to catch him, Usain Bolt passes him, and as the runners come to the finish, you'll hear a beep as each man crosses the line. That's the entire finish of the race. You can open your eyes now. That first beep was Usain Bolt. That last beep was Jesse Owens.

④ Listen to it again. When you think of it like that, it's not that big a difference, is it? <u>And then consider that Usain Bolt started by propelling himself out of blocks down a specially fabricated carpet designed to allow him to travel as fast as humanly possible. Jesse Owens, on the</u>

other hand, ran on cinders, the ash from burnt wood, and that soft surface stole far more energy from his legs as he ran.[2] Rather than blocks, Jesse Owens had a gardening trowel that he had to use to dig holes in the cinders to star from. Biomechanical analysis of the speed of Owens' joints show that had been running on the same surface as Bolt. He wouldn't have been 14 feet behind. He would have been within one stride. Rather than the last beep, Owens would have been the second beep. Listen to it again.

⑤ That's the difference track surface technology has made, and it's done it throughout the running world. Consider a longer event. In 1954, Sir roger Bannister became the first man to ran under four minutes in the mile. Nowadays, college kids do that every year. On rare occasions, a high school kid does it. And of the end of last year, 1 314 men had run under four minutes in the mile. But like Jesse Owens, Sir Roger Bannister ran on soft cinders that stole far more energy from his legs than the synthetic tracks of today. So I consulted biomechanics experts to find out how much slower it is to run on cinders than synthetic tracks, and their consensus that's one and a half percent slower. So if you apply a one and a half percent slowdown conversion to every man who ran his sub-for mile on a synthetic track. This is what happens.

⑥ Only 530 are left. If you look at from that perspective, fewer than ten new men per year have joined the sub-four mile club since Sir Roger Bannister. Now, 530 is a lot more than one, and that's part because there are many more people training today and they're training more intelligently. Even college kids are professional in their training compared to Sir Roger Bannister who trained for 45 minutes at a time while he ditched gynecology lectures in med school. And that guy who won the 1904 Olympic marathon in three in a half hour that guy was drinking rat poison and brandy while he ran along the course. That was his idea of a performance-enhancing drug. Clearly, athletes have gotten more savvy about performance-enhancing drug as well, and that's made a difference in some sports at some times, but technology has made a difference in all sports, from faster skis to lighter shoes.[3]

⑦ Take a look at the record for the 100-meter freestyle swim. The record is always trending downward, but it's punctuated these steep cliffs. This first cliff, in 1956, is the introduction of the flip turn. Rather than stopping and turning around, athletes could somersault under the water and get going right away in the opposite direction. This second cliff, the introduction of gutters on the side of the pool that allows water to splash off, rather than becoming turbulence that impedes the swimmers as they race. The final cliff, the introduction of full-body and low-friction swimsuits. Throughout sports technology has changed the face of performance.

⑧ In 1972, Eddy Merckx set the record for the longest distance cycled in one hour at 30 miles, 3 774 feet. Now that record improved and improved as bicycles improved and become more aerodynamic, all the way until 1996, when it was set at 35 mile, 1 531 feet nearly five miles farther than Eddy Merckx cycled in 1972. But then in 2000, the international Cycling Union decreed that anyone who wanted to hold that record had to do so with essentially the same equipment that Eddy Merckx used in 1972. Where does the record stand today? 30 miles, 4 657 feet, a grand total of 883 feet father than Eddy Merckx cycled more than four decades ago. Essentially the entire improvement in this record was due to technology.

⑨ Still, technology isn't the only thing pushing athletes forward. While indeed we haven't evolved into a new species in a century, the gene pool within competitive sports most certainly has changed. In the early half of 20th century, physical education instructors and coaches had the idea that the average body type was the best for all athletic endeavors; medium height, medium weight, no matter the sport. And this showed in athletes' bodies. In the 1920s, the average elite high-jumper and average elite shot-putter were the same exact size. But as that idea started to fade away, as sports scientists and coaches realized that rather than the average body type, you want highly specialized bodies that fit into certain athletic niches, a form of artificial selection took place, a self-sorting for bodied that fit certain sports, and athletes' bodies became more different from one another.

⑩ Today, rather than the same size as the average elite high jumper, the average elite shot-putter is two and a half inches taller and 130 pounds heavier. And this happened throughout the sports world. In sports where height is prized, like basketball, the tall athletes got taller. In 1983, the National Basketball Association, signed a groundbreaking agreement making players partners in the league, entitled to shares of ticket revenues and television contracts. Suddenly, anybody who could be an NBA player wanted to be, and teams started scouring the globe for the bodies that could help them win championships. Almost overnight, the proportion of men in the NBA who are at least seven feet tall doubled to 10 percent. Today, one in 10 men in the NBA is at least seven feet tall, but a seven-foot-tall man is incredibly rare in the general population—so rare that if you know an American man between the ages of 20 and 40 who is at least seven feet tall, there's a 17 percent chance he's in the NBA right now. That is, find six honest seven footers, one is in the NBA right now.

⑪ Conversely, in sports where diminutive stature is an advantage, the small athletes got smaller. <u>The average elite female gymnast shrunk from 5`3``to average 4`9`` on average over the last 30 years, all the better for their power-to-weight ratio and for spinning in the air.</u> [4] And while the large got larger and the small got smaller, the weird got weirder. The average length of the forearm of a water polo player in relation to their arm got longer, all the better for a forceful throwing whip. And as the large got larger, small got smaller, and the weird weirder.

⑫ In swimming, the ideal body type is a long torso and short legs. It's like the long hull of a canoe for speed over the water. And the opposite is advantageous in running. You want long legs and a short torso. And this shows in athletes' bodies today. Here you see Michael Phelps, the greatest swimming in history, standing next to Hicham El Guerroul the world record holder in the mile. These men are seven inches different in height, but because of the body types advantaged in their sports, they wear the same length pants. Seven inches difference in height, these men have the same length legs.

⑬ Changing technology, changing genes, and a changing mindset. Innovation in sports, whether that's new track surfaces or new swimming techniques, the democratization of sport, the spread to new bodies, and to new populations around the world, and imagination in sport, an understanding of what the human body is truly capable of, have conspired to make athletes stronger, faster, bolder, and better than ever. Thank you very much.

Notes on the text

(1) Had Jesse Owens been racing last year in the world championships of the 100 meters, when Jamaican sprinter Usain Bolt finished, when would have still had 14 feet to go. 如果让杰西·欧文与去年的百米世界冠军比赛，当牙买加短跑运动员尤塞恩·博尔特跑完时，欧文仍然还差14英尺。

注意体育口译中人名的译法。

(2) And then consider that Usain Bolt started by propelling himself out of blocks down a specially fabricated carpet designed to allow him to travel as fast as humanly possible. Jesse Owens, on the other hand, ran on cinders, the ash from burnt wood, and that soft surface stole far more energy from his legs as he ran. 接下来想：尤塞恩·博尔特从支架助推自己出发，支架下有特殊的弹性地毯，目的是让他在一瞬间跑出人类最高速度。可是杰西·欧文，在焚烧木头所产生的煤渣上跑步。他跑步时，柔软的地面会从他的腿上偷走更多的能量。

注意口译中体育用品的译法。

(3) Clearly, athletes have gotten more savvy about performance-enhancing drug as well, and that's made a difference in some sports at some times, but technology has made a difference in all sports, from faster skis to lighter shoes. 很明显，运动员们也已知道更多关于兴奋剂的知识，这有时会让某些运动不一样，但科技已让所有运动出现差异，从更快的滑雪板到更轻的鞋。

注意口译中体育词汇的译法。

(4) The average elite female gymnast shrunk from 5`3``to average 4`9`` on average over the last 30 years, all the better for their power-to-weight ratio and for spinning in the air. 女子体操的平均数据在过去30年中从5英尺3英寸缩小到4英尺9英寸，这有益于他们的能量-体重比率和在空气中旋转。

注意口译中体育术语的译法。

3.2.4 篇章口译[Passage Practice (C to E)]

1. **Vocabulary Work: Study the following words and phrases and translate them into the target language.**

球衣退役	历任教练
蓄势待发	义无反顾
不确定的因素	大学联赛
新秀赛季	预测

2. Please interpret the following paragraph by using the techniques illustrated above.

尽管中国足球队在赛场上屡屡失利，但去现场观看2018世界杯总决赛的中国球迷人数仍有望创下纪录。这主要是因为中国人对足球的兴趣与日俱增，而且中国与东道主俄罗斯关系友好。//中国队只打进过一次世界杯。但市场营销与活动公司盛开体育的首席执行官冯涛认为，即便如此，中国球迷还是会涌入俄罗斯。盛开体育已经与BH Hospitality签订了一项向中国市场出售世界杯旅游套餐的独家协议。//冯涛表示："我们相信，凭借着中俄两国的关系，我们可以将更多中国球迷带到俄罗斯。""这两个国家离得很近，去俄罗斯比去巴西容易得多。从中国到巴西要花24~25个小时，到南非要花14~15个小时，而到俄罗斯只需7个小时，这方便多了。"// 从历史上看，中俄两国关系友好，而当下足球已经走入中国人的精神世界。企业家、媒体和球迷都对世界杯表现出浓厚的兴趣。目前，大多数人只能在电视上观看世界杯，但他们现在将有机会亲临现场观赛。// 虽然这次的观众人数不太可能超过2002年赴韩观看中国队比赛的人数——据悉当时有10万国人在现场观看了中国队的世界杯首秀——盛开公司预计向中国球迷出售5万份套餐，交易额有望达到2500万美元。这一预估数字在中国队未打进的世界杯中是最高的一届，相比2014年世界杯决赛的销售数据出现显著提升，当时售出了3000份套餐。//

3. Please interpret the following passage by using the techniques illustrated above. Please pay attention to the underlined sentences as they require special treatment during interpreting.

姚明球衣退役演讲

① 谢谢，谢谢，火箭队的球迷们。

② 我有太多的感谢想送给火箭，社区和老板莱斯利-亚历山大，是你把我们凝聚在一起，谢谢你打造了这只球队和社区，非常感谢。

③ 首先，现在是中国的新年，我祝福大家新年快乐，万事如意，意思是希望你的梦想成真。当我踏进这个球馆看见球衣号码在那里挂着的时候，我想我的愿望不能够实现了，因为我希望能够再获得10天的合同。(1)但这个时候，我情不自禁地回想起我第一次看火箭的比赛是在1994年。那时NBA第一次在中国转播，同时也是大梦为火箭带来第一个总冠军的时候。我知道，我知道今天在座的许多人或者有些人见证过那个时刻，同样，在遥远的中国有个孩子通过电视也见证过那个时刻，那就是我梦开始的地方。

④ 谢谢你们给我的那些回忆。谢谢我的历任教练们，鲁迪·汤姆贾诺维奇，范甘地，里克·阿德尔曼。他们为我付出的努力，他们对我的信任让我相信休斯顿是我命之所归。

⑤ 曾经，我们站在球员通道入口蓄势待发。而走上球场后，一切有太多的不确定，也许是一场胜利，也许是一场失利，也许能创下生涯新高，也许是生涯最后一场比赛。(2)但是没有人会怀疑我们是否会为了休城的胜利义无反顾，因为我们不仅有最优秀的球员，还有伟大的休城粉丝支持我们。10年前，我们年轻又充满激情。我相信穆托姆博也是这么认为的。那会儿，我在转换进攻的时候会追着弗老大和莫布里跑，那场面就好像两辆小

坦克拖着一架又大又笨的波音777。之后麦迪来到休城，加入了我们的队伍。谢谢你来到这里。

⑥ 比赛中有很多不确定的因素，但你只需要记住，如果比赛只剩下35秒，把球传给麦迪就好了。⁽³⁾ 你知道那场比赛结束后，我回到家后和我的邻居是怎么说的吗？他在比赛还有几分钟的时候关掉了电视。我告诉他，我和麦迪在最后几分钟合砍了15分，逆转了马刺。

⑦ 那时候在更衣室里，肖恩-巴蒂尔整天拉着我们预测NCAA"疯狂三月"，啊，你懂的。我没打过大学联赛，所以并不了解。不过幸运的是，每次赌注结果出来之后，我从没有那种"天啊！我在想什么"的时候。怎么做到的呢，因为我都从电视上看总统选谁，然后跟着抄就行了。我是说，上一位总统。现在这位我不了解，他选谁我也不知道。

⑧ 我刚来的时候，休斯顿对我来说，和其他美国城市没什么不同。<u>但随着时光流逝，身边一张张面孔印入脑海。朋友、队友、教练、制服组、媒体，最重要的，是球迷。比如坐在那的索伊尔家族的球迷们，几十年来一直支持着火箭。谢谢你们。</u>⁽⁴⁾记住。休斯顿三字于我，已不只是一个简单的词语。每次他们说起这个词，你们大家的音容笑貌，便会在我记忆中、脑海中浮现。

⑨ 我想和大家讲个故事。那是我的新秀赛季。那年的现在这个时节。是我和家人第一次在海外、在异国过年。我被骗到康柏中心的一个更衣室(火箭当时主场)。所有的队友、总经理道森、教练以及工作人员在那里等我。史蒂芬，你也在那儿。他们祝我新年快乐。每个人都给了我红包。这是我们中国的习俗。

⑩ 谢谢你们为我做的一切，让我感觉像在家一样。等我打开那个红包，里面只有2美元。我和道森说：道森，你至少也应该放10美元在里面吧。<u>道森说：你知道我们有工资帽不能乱花钱吗？我把这红包里的其中1美元放在口袋里。从那时起，我就一直带着它。</u>⁽⁵⁾因为我知道无论去哪儿，无论走多远。只要带着那1美元，家就在我身边。谢谢，感谢大家的一路陪伴。谢谢!

Notes on the text

(1) 当我踏进这个球馆看见球衣号码在那里挂着的时候，我想我的愿望不能够实现了，因为我希望能够再获得10天的合同。

But when I walk in this room that I saw the number is up there, almost there, that I know my first wish in my year is already gone, because I wish I got a ten days contract.

(2) 而走上球场后，一切有太多的不确定，也许是一场胜利，也许是一场失利，也许能创下生涯新高，也许是生涯最后一场比赛。

It was out that there was so many unknowing maybe a victory, maybe a loss, maybe a career high, maybe a career ending.

(3) 比赛中有很多不确定的因素，但你只需要记住，如果比赛只剩下35秒，把球传给麦迪就好了。

You know there are so many unknowing, but just remember give the ball to him, when there's just 35 seconds left.

(4) 但随着时光流逝，身边一张张面孔印入脑海。朋友、队友、教练、制服组、媒体，最重要的，是球迷。比如坐在那的索伊尔家族的球迷们，几十年来一直支持着火箭。

But when time passed by, all the faces become into my memory. Friends, teammates, coaches, staff, medias and most important, fans. The fans like Ms. and Mr. Soyle family right there, the supporter for rockets for over decades.

(5) 道森说：你知道我们有工资帽，不能乱花钱嘛？我把这红包里的其中1美元放在口袋里。让从那时起，我就一直带着它。

Dason came back to me and said you know we have salary cap, right? I still have one of those 2 dollars in my pocket. And I carried it since then. Because I know, because I know where I go and how far I go. As long as that bill in my pocket, the home is with me.

3.3　参考译文(Reference Version)

■ 3.3.1　单句口译(Sentence Practice)

Please interpret the following sentences by using the techniques illustrated above. You may interpret to your partner first and then he/she comments on your performance.

(1) 我暂时不会放弃使用可穿戴设备，但是如果想让它们像某些节食计划或者运动一样仅仅成为一时的流行，你们还需要做更多的工作。

(2) 教育部近日公布了我国职业学校新增的13个专业，"电子竞技运动与管理"专业赫然在列。电子竞技专业将自2017年起在全国各职业院校开设。

(3) 这个太平洋岛国在奥运会取得的第一次胜利让整个国家欢欣鼓舞。人们欢呼、落泪、举杯畅饮，在街头巷尾手舞足蹈，全然把工作和学习丢在了一边。

(4) 富含精益蛋白质的饮食可加快新陈代谢，因为消耗蛋白质需要更多的能量。

(5) 研究人员原本深信不疑地认为，穿戴运动监测器的人们会做更多运动、吃得更健康、减掉更多体重。

(6) Chinese swimmer Fu Yuanhui's hilarious post-race interviews and exaggerated facial expressions have turned her into an online sensation, with her followers on Weibo rocketing from an already considerable 550 000 people before the Rio Olympics to a staggering 5m this week.

(7) China unfortunately lost the chance to enter the woman's 4×100m final at Rio Olympics after the US successfully appealed its chance to rerace alone on Thursday morning local time.

(8) Guo Chuan is the country's first-ever professional sailor with two world records: the 40ft solo non-stop circumnavigation world record (finished in 138 days in 2013) and Arctic Ocean Northeast Passage non-stop sailing world record (12 days 3 hrs in 2015).

(9) The Tottenham Hotspur Global Coaching Team will give guidance to 42 PE teachers on developing yearlong training plan to over 60,000 students.

(10) President Xi Jinping issued a rallying call on Thursday for the Olympic spirit to be practiced in helping to realize the "Chinese Dream" of national rejuvenation.

3.3.2 对话口译(Dialogue Practice)

1. Vocabulary Work: Study the following words and phrases and translate them into the target language.

mentality	运球
hoop	观察力敏锐的
echelon	猎豹
niche	无情的
reiterate	热爱的
obsessive	有弹力的

2. Read the following dialogue and interpret it into the target language.

A：I think that's what we're leading here to today in our Tedx talk, the power of the mind. And I think, because, you know, there's been so many athletes that have made the NBA the highest echelon of professional basketball in the world, and there's athletes that can jump as high as the sky, run as fast as, you know, a cheetah, they can hit buckets, they can react, but it's the special niche of players that have that mindfulness, that have that attacking mode, that relentless mode, that mode where they go ice cold last few minutes, you know? I think that makes a difference between the great ones and the greatest ones.

B：是的，你知道的，这挺有趣。对我来说，意志力这点真的很简单。在某种意义上说，自信来源于准备工作。所以当比赛要开始的时候，我要自己做的事情，在比赛之前就已经做过成千上万次了。对吧？所以，当我做准备工作的时候，我就知道我有能力做什么事情，我知道我做什么事情是很轻松的，我知道做什么事情我是不轻松的。你懂的，对吗？所以在那些时刻，看上去很冷静，或者说不紧张，那是因为之前我已经做过无数次了，所以再来一次又如何？

A：So that leads me to talk about, a lot of this Kobe tour this year in Asia is we reiterate the mamba mentality, you know, can you talk a little bit about what the mamba mentality is, because that's something that's been developing over, I don't want to say 20 years, it's been developing for 35 years, since you were a little kid, the mamba mentality, because you didn't start working when you go to the NBA, you started working when you were at Lower Merion, when you were in Italy, when you were five, when you were playing Nerf basketball, right? So talk about the development of the mamba mentality, the five pillars of this mamba mentality, and then we'll kind of break it down.

B：总体而言，这个理念是非常简单的。其实曼巴精神指的就是尝试做最好的自己。那就是意志的本意，它意味着每一天你都努力变得更好。这是一种不懈的追求，一种无止境的追求。所以从两岁开始，从我最早打篮球开始，然后一直这么打下去，我总是在问问题，我每天都想变得更好，学习更多的东西。

A：You were asking questions at two?

B：哦，兄弟，我一直都在问问题。你会很惊讶。有些人，比如我的孩子们，在两岁的时候可以做很多事。我在两岁的时候可以运球，我可以在室内投篮，我会和我的父亲一起练习，我会观察我的父亲，和他坐在一起看比赛。

A：Was he your first coach?

B：是的，我猜你会这么说。我通过比赛学到了很多东西。所以到6岁的时候，和其他6岁孩子对阵，我已经在制定战略了，要知道，我在6岁的时候发现，其他6岁孩子不能用左手运球。

A：A lot of 12 year olds can't dribble with their left hands.

B：是的，我可以猜到6岁的。所以当我和6岁孩子一起打球时，我会让他们用左手运球，因为我知道他们不行，所以球从他们的脚边掉下来，我就把球捡起来，上篮。再做一遍，从脚边掉下来，捡起来，上篮。所以6岁时，我就得过63分。我记得我爸爸。

A：So you 6 year old self could beat your 38 year old self, he only scored 60 in the last game.

B：是的，不，但是我可以用左手运球，所以那才是问题所在。但是，听着，我总是在寻找可以让我学习的东西，同时善于观察。

A：So when we talk about the mamba mentality, you have your exhibition today. Starting in Shanghai, right? Also we've been talking about this whole tour with young kids that are 5, 10, 15, and 20. We just did a Kobe Academy right now; we talk about being passionate, being obsessive, being relentless, being resilient and being fearless. These are the five pillars of the mamba mentality.

3.3.3　篇章口译[Passage Practice (E to C)]

1. Vocabulary Work: Study the following words and phrases and translate them into the target language.

格言	马拉松赛跑
不可阻挡地	短跑选手
煤渣	泥刀
生物医学的	合成跑道
妇科学	兴奋剂
翻筋斗	矮小的
躯干	民主化

2. Please interpret the following paragraph by using the techniques illustrated above.

巴黎和洛杉矶将承办2024年及2028年奥运会，不过在这之前，他们要就先后顺序达成一致，因为双方都希望主办2024年奥运会。国际奥委会已经投票决定于9月13日公布两届相邻奥运会的主办城市，申办城市只有巴黎和洛杉矶。//作为奥林匹克运动的管理机构，国际奥委会要求这两座城市到时就谁来承办2028年奥运会达成一致。如果届时双方无法取得共识，将投票选出2024年的举办城市。布达佩斯、汉堡以及罗马均已退出2024年奥运会申办角逐。//国际奥委会主席托马斯·巴赫会后告诉记者，他希望下个月能就此事达成协议。洛杉矶申奥组织者称，这个决定让他们感到"激动"，并称："我们期待在未来几周内与国际奥委会和巴黎合作，把握住这个千载难逢的好机，开辟美好的未来。"//今年6月，洛杉矶申奥主席凯西·沃瑟曼似乎对巴黎做出让步，他说："我们从没有想过只申办2024年奥运会。"不过，一位发言人随后告诉英国广播公司体育频道："洛杉矶是2024年奥运会东道主的理想选择，我们并没有在申奥中做出任何让步。"//巴黎方面称，他们必须承办2024年奥运会，因为作为奥运村的场地在2024年后将不能重新开发。"双城之争"持续了很久，情况有些混乱。但最终还是如托马斯·巴赫所愿，巴黎和洛杉矶获得一致支持，成为奥运会东道主。//事情最终还需各方达成协议，但巴黎和洛杉矶的市长是好朋友，他们手握着手，感谢国际奥委会成员的支持，如果双方没有达成协议，真的会让人大跌眼镜。双方可能很快就会做出决定。//他们将在接下来的几天展开讨论，让不确定因素继续拖延下去对"任何一方"都不利。现在已经促成了双赢的局面。事实上，巴黎和洛杉矶其中一方将成为更大的赢家。两座城市起初申办的都是2024年奥运会，现在有一方将被要求举办2028年奥运会。//但是这还是比申奥失败好。对于国际奥委会来说，这个结果为其改革申奥程序赢得了时间，且让其他望而却步的潜在申奥城市看到了希望，特别是西欧国家。数年前，申办奥运会是一场激烈的竞争，但现在对此感兴趣的城市越来越少。//汉堡、罗马和布达佩斯退出了这次竞争，只有两个候选城市争夺2022年冬奥会的主办权，原因在于经费问题和缺乏公众支持。

3. Please interpret the following passage by using the techniques illustrated above. Please pay attention to the underlined sentences as they require special treatment during interpreting.

运动员们真的在做到更高，更快，更强吗(节选)

大卫·桑德罗

① 奥林匹克精神是"高，快，强"，即更高，更快，更强。运动员们执行了这种精神。2012年奥运会马拉松冠军花费了2小时8分钟，他比1904年奥运会马拉松冠军要快近一个半小时。现在我们都有一种感觉：作为人类我们已有无可争议的进步，但这并不意味着我们在一个世纪内进化成了新物种。发生了什么？

② 我想要看看这种运动的巨大进步背后究竟存在着什么。在1936年，杰西·欧文保持了百米世界纪录。如果让杰西·欧文与去年的百米世界冠军比赛，当牙买加短跑运动员

尤塞恩·博尔特跑完时，欧文仍然还差14英尺。这在短跑上是一个很长的距离。为了给大家一个14英尺是多远的概念，我想要给大家分享一个运动科学家罗斯·塔克的研究结论。

③ 想象去年世锦赛百米比赛体育场：成千上万粉丝屏住呼吸等待观看尤塞恩·博尔特，史上跑得最快的人；如同闪光灯闪动一样，世界最快九个人在各自跑道上做好准备。我想让你们遐想杰西·欧文正在这个赛场上，现在你闭眼一秒钟想象一下这场比赛。砰，发令枪响了。一个美国短跑运动员领先。尤塞恩·博尔特开始赶上他，尤塞恩·博尔特超过了他，每个运动员跑完时，你会听到每个人跨越终点线的哔哔声，整个比赛结束。现在睁眼，第一名是尤塞恩·博尔特，最后一名是杰西·欧文。

④ 再听一下，与你的想象没有区别，是吗？接下来想：尤塞恩·博尔特从支架助推自己出发，支架下有特殊的弹性地毯，目的是让他在一瞬间跑出人类最高速度。可是杰西·欧文，在焚烧木头所产生的煤渣上跑步。他跑步时，柔软的地面会从他的腿上偷走更多的能量。谈到起跑支点，杰西·欧文有把园丁铲，他经常用来在煤渣跑道挖洞以支撑支架。从生物学上讲，杰西·欧文关节的速度显示他和尤塞恩·博尔特跑得一样远，他本不该落后14英尺，他应该已经往前一大步。杰西·欧文本应该跑第二而不是最后。现在再听一下。

⑤ 这就是不同的跑道表面科技所造成的差异，这种差异遍及整个田径世界。想一件更久的事。在1945年，罗杰·本尼斯特阁下成为了第一个在四分钟内跑完一英里的人，如今大学生每年如此。在极少的偶然下，高中生也可以做到。在去年末，1314人在四分钟内跑完了一英里。但就像杰西·欧文一样，罗杰·本尼斯特阁下在柔软的煤渣上跑步，这从他腿上偷去的能量要多于今日的塑胶跑道。所以我请生物力学专家找出在煤渣上跑步要比塑胶跑道多耗费多少能量，他们的一致意见是会慢1.5%。所以如果假设每个人在人工跑道跑四英里的时候会有1.5%的速度变化，这就是真相。

⑥ 还有530人，如果从这个角度看，从罗杰·本尼斯特阁下开始，每年只有不到10个人加入这个四分钟跑完一英里的行列。530人当然远大于一个人，部分原因在于现代更多的人可以接受训练，训练方法更加科学合理。罗杰·本尼斯特阁下在医药学校学习妇科医学时一次训练45分钟，甚至连大学生都要比他的训练更专业。有人用三个半小时赢得1904年马拉松冠军，他边沿着跑道跑步边喝老鼠药和白兰地。这是他认为的兴奋剂。很明显，运动员们也已知道更多关于兴奋剂的知识，这有时会让某些运动不一样，但科技已让所有运动出现差异，从更快的滑雪板到更轻的鞋。

⑦ 让我们看一下百米自由泳纪录。它们总是趋于下降，但总会被一些陡峭的"斜坡"打断。第一个陡坡是在1956年，普及翻转式跳水。相比于停下后转身，运动员可以翻转入水并在相反方向立即前进。第二个陡坡，是游泳池边排水沟的普及，这让水随意溅出，而不是变成比赛时阻碍运动员的漩涡。最后一个陡坡，是普及全身式低摩擦力泳衣。纵观运动史，科技已改变了其面貌。

⑧ 在1972年，埃迪·麦克莱斯打破了一小时骑行最远的记录，1小时骑30英里，3774英尺。现在该记录随自行车对空气动力学的发展一直在提升，直到1996年，记录是35英里，1531英尺，比埃迪·麦克莱斯在1972年取得的成绩多了将近5英里。但在2000年，国际自行车协会颁布条例：任何人想要打破纪录都要使用相同的基础设备，就像埃迪·麦

克莱斯在1972年使用的一样。今天的世界纪录呢？30英里，4657英尺，整整比40年前埃迪·麦克莱斯的记录多出883英尺。在世界纪录上取得的所有进步基本上都因为科技。

⑨ 但科技不是推动运动进步的唯一因素。我们确实没在一个世纪内进化成一个新物种，但竞技运动内的基因库大部分确实已改变。20世纪上半叶，体育教师和教练都认为匀称的体型对于所有运动来说是最好的；中等身高，中等体重，任何运动。这体现在运动员的身体上。在20世纪20年代，跳高运动员的平均身高和铅球运动员一样。但这种见解逐渐消失，运动学家和教练们了解到，不需要高度专业体型来吻合特定运动框架，普通身形也不用。现在有特定标准，一份适合某种运动的体型种类，某类运动员的体型就与其他种类运动员更不一样。

⑩ 如今，铅球运动员的平均体型要比于同规格跳高运动员高2.5英寸，重130磅。整个运动界都这样。在强调身高的运动里，如篮球，很高的运动员变得更高。1983年国家篮球协会签署了一个突破性的文件，运动员可以在联盟里合伙，分享门票所得和电视合约。突然，任何有潜力当球员的人都想进入NBA，球队走遍世界寻找能帮他们赢得冠军的球员。几乎一夜之间，NBA球员比例中身高七英尺的人翻了两倍，达到10%。今天，NBA里十人中至少有1个人七英尺高，但是一个七英尺高的人在普通人里是不可思议地稀少——稀少到如果你认识一个美国人，他的年龄在20岁到40岁，身高至少七英尺，那么有17%的几率他就在NBA里。所以如果有6个刚好身高七英尺的人，其中一个现在就在NBA。

⑪ 相反的是，在微小身材占优势的运动中，很矮的运动员变得更矮。女子体操的平均数据在过去30年中从5英尺3英寸缩小到4英尺9英寸，这有益于他们的能量-体重比率和在空气中旋转。在大的更大和小的更小的同时，奇怪的变得更奇怪。游泳运动员的平均前臂长度相对于他们的整个手臂变得更长了，这有益于强有力的划动。在大的更大的同时，小的更小，奇怪的更奇怪。

⑫ 在游泳中，理想体型是长躯干短腿。就像独木舟的长船身一样是为了水中的速度。与此相反就在跑步中占优势，你需要长腿短躯干。这是现在运动员的体型。这里你看到迈克·菲尔普斯，历史上最伟大的游泳运动员，站在希查姆·艾尔·奎罗伊旁边，一英里世界纪录保持者。他们身高差有七英寸，但由于在他们运动时的优势体型，他们都穿着一样长的裤子。这些人有七英寸的身高差和同样长的腿。

⑬ 这就是变化的科技，变化的基因，以及变化的精神状态。运动上的改革，无论是新的跑道表面或者新的游泳科技，亦或是运动的民主化，新体型和新的人口在世界上的传播，运动中的展望，对于人体极限的理解，将使运动员比以往更强、更快、更无畏，甚至对自身有更好的策划。非常感谢。

▊ 3.3.4 篇章口译[Passage Practice (C to E)]

1. Please interpret the following paragraph by using the techniques illustrated above.

Chinese fans are expected to travel to the 2018 World Cup finals in record numbers with the growing interest in soccer and a cordial relationship with hosts Russia seen as key factors, despite the national side's failings on the pitch. // China have only played at one World Cup, but Feng Tao, chief executive officer of marketing and events firm Shankai, believes fans will flock to Russia regardless. // "We are confident we can bring more fans to Russia because of the relationship between Russia and China," said Feng Tao, whose company has signed an exclusive deal with BH Hospitality to sell travel packages for the tournament to the Chinese market. "The countries are very close, it's much easier to go to Russia than it was to go to Brazil, which took 24 or 25 hours, or to South Africa, which took 14 or 15 hours. To go to Russia takes only seven hours from China, so it's easier." //Historically, there's a good relationship between China and Russia and now football has become part of the mentality of the Chinese people. Businessmen, the media and fans are showing strong interest in the World Cup. Until now, the majority has only been able to follow the World Cup on television but now there's going to be the opportunity for them to travel to watch and for them to see a World Cup.// While the figures are unlikely to eclipse the numbers who travelled to South Korea to watch China play in 2002 — as many as 100 000 were believed to have seen the side's World Cup debut — Shankai are expecting 50 000 packages to be sold to Chinese fans as part of the expected $25 million deal. The projected figure represents the most for a World Cup that does not feature the Chinese team, a significant upswing on the numbers sold for the 2014 World Cup finals, when 3 000 packages were sold. //

2. Please interpret the following passage by using the techniques illustrated above. Please pay attention to the underlined sentences as they require special treatment during interpreting.

The Jersey Retirement Ceremony of Yao Ming

① Thank you, thank you, Rockets fans.

② I like to ... there are so many thanks I want to send to Rockets, to city of Huston, the community, to Leslie who brought us together, thank you for build this team and this community, thank you very much.

③ First of all, you know, this is Chinese New Year, I wish everybody happy Chinese New Year, wanshiruyi, which means make your wish come true. But when I walk in this room that I saw the number is up there, almost there, that I know my first wish in my year is already gone, because I wish I got a ten days contract. Um, but at this moment, I can't help myself but thinking back when I first met rockets back to 1994 when NBA first time broadcast in china, that's when great Dream bring a championship cup back to Huston for the first time. I know, I know many of you, or some of you, today at here, witness that moment just remember there is a kid over ten thousand miles away seeing that too through a TV, that is where my dream started.

④ Thank you for the memory. Thanks to my coaches Rudy Tomjanovich，Jeff Van

Gundy，Rick Adelman. Their effort and their trust on me, make me believe that coming to Houston is my destination.

⑤ The every time when we were ready for the game at that tunnel, ready for getting to the court. It was out that there was so many unknowing maybe a victory, maybe a loss, maybe a career high, maybe a career ending. But no one doubt we will run out there and fight for the city not only because we are the greatest teammates around us, but also we have great fans here. We were a very passion and young team ten years ago. I believe the Dikembe Mutombo will agree that. Back then, I was chasing Steve Francis and Cuttino Mobley in a transition just like two mini tanks dragging a huge Boeing 777 plane on an airport. And after that, T-MAC came to the town joining us. Thank you for being here.

⑥ You know there are so many unknowing, but just remember give the ball to him, when there's just 35 seconds left. But you know what I tell my neighbor, after that match when I've driven home, because he turned off the TV minutes before the game over. I told him that, oh I, T-MAC and I scored 15 points in the last minutes which turned the game around.

⑦ Back to locker room Shane Battier always has us bet on the March Madness and you know. I'm not from NCAA I don't know much about it. But luckily I never win the "what the hell am I thinking" award. And how I did it is because I just simply took copy Mr. President's answer from the TV. I mean the last one not this one. I don't know about this one, how this one would do.

⑧ When I just came to town，Houston for me is no different than any other city in United States. But when time passed by, all the faces become into my memory. Friends, teammates, coaches, staff, medias and most important, fans. The fans like Ms. and Mr. Soyle family right there. The supporter for rockets for over decades. Thank you. Remember this. The Houston from now on for me is not just simply a word. Every time they mention it, your faces were in my memory, in my brain.

⑨ I would like to share a story with everybody to control my speech. That's at my rookie season. About the same time during the year. It's my first Chinese New Year for me and my family spent overseas outside my country. Well, I was tricked to a locker room in Compaq Center. All my teammates, Dason, and coach staffs were waiting there. Stephen, you there, too. They wished me a "happy new year". Every one of those and gave me those red envelopes. That's according to our traditions in Chinese.

⑩ Well, thanks for doing that to make me home over here that year. But I checked the red envelop there were only 2 dollars in there. So, I talked to Dason. I say, "Dason, you did well put at least 10 dollars instead of 2." Dason came back to me and said, "you know we have salary cap, right?" I still have one of those 2 dollars in my pocket. And I carried it since then. Because I know where I go and how far I go, as long as that bill in my pocket, the home is with me. Thank you, thank you for the journey. Thank you!

3.4 体育主题词汇汇总(Vocabulary Build-up)

competitive sports	竞技体育
recreational sports	休闲体育
Olympic events	奥运赛事
live broadcast	现场直播
real-time strategy game	即时战略游戏
multiplayer online battle arena/MOBA game	多人在线竞技游戏
e-sports competitions/events	电竞赛事
massively multiplayer online role-playing game, MMORPG	大型多人在线角色扮演游戏
shoutcaster	电竞解说员
Jumping Jack	开合跳
improve cardiovascular system	增强心肺系统
squat	下蹲
tone the legs	使下肢健美
lift the butts	提臀
knee high	高抬腿
flexibility	灵活性
plank	平板支撑
sculpt abs	塑造腹肌
superman	小燕飞
pushup	俯卧撑
improve arm strength	增强臂力
build pectoral muscles	锻炼胸肌
burpee	波比
burn fat	燃脂
Russian twist	俄式转体
glute bridge	臀桥
youth football development training	青少年足球人才的培养
English Premier League Clubs	英格兰超级联赛俱乐部
public fitness activities	全民健身活动
Olympic Truce Mural	奥林匹克休战墙
track and field	田径
decathlon	十项全能
the Court of Arbitration for Sport	国际体育仲裁法庭
Bull's-eye	靶心
firing range	射击靶场
skeet shooting	双向飞碟射击
sharpshooter	神枪手
springboard diving	跳板跳水

(续表)

platform diving	跳台跳水
twist	转体
somersault	翻腾
degree of difficulty	难度系数
starting position	站姿
position in height/in the air	空中姿势
steal the show/limelight	抢镜，出风头
catapult to fame	一举成名
preliminary, prelim	预赛
hurdles	跨栏
relay (race)	接力
record a personal best	创下个人最佳成绩
medalist	奖牌获得者
podium	领奖台
foul	犯规
performance-enhancing drugs	提高比赛成绩的药品
banned/prohibited substances	违禁药品
anti-doping campaign	反兴奋剂工作
doping ban	兴奋剂违规禁赛
doping scandal	兴奋剂丑闻
butterfinger	黄油手，是对经常扑球失误的足球守门员的戏称，意思是手上像抹了黄油一样，拿不稳球
underdog	比赛中不被看好者
melee	混战，格斗；互殴
hooliganism	流氓行为
bleacher	(运动场的)露天看台

3.5 扩展练习(Enhancement Practice)

Retelling.

Directions: Listen to the following passages once and then reproduce them in the same language at the end of each segment.

A. English Passage

The Duke and Duchess of Cambridge went head to head in a relay race this afternoon alongside Prince Harry as they turned out to support a training day for runners who are taking part in this year's London Marathon, although they won't be donning their trainers for the 25 mile course themselves. Competitive Kate tied her hair back as she pelted full throttle alongside her husband during the 100m sprint which took part at the Queen Elizabeth Olympic Park in London on Sunday. Despite her efforts the Duchess, 35, lost out to her brother in-law who came in first followed by Prince William who came second thanks to the encouragement of well-wishers from the sidelines.

B. Chinese Passage

女仆健身馆的各种细节还有待披露，但我们已知的是它不会是大多数人熟悉的那种拥挤的大型场所。据报道，这将是一个更具有私密性的健身馆，每个时段来健身馆的客人只能限制在三位，每个人都配有自己的女仆教练。穿着维多利亚女仆服装的年轻女孩不一定懂健身，但是漂亮的女教练一定知道如何使用各种健身器材以及如何教导客户来实现自己的健身目标。此外，这些女教练还会提供口头鼓励，如"别担心，有我在你不会跌倒的"或者"做得很棒，主人！你变得越来越强壮了"，她们还会在"主人"做仰卧推举的时候给他数数。

3.6 口译点滴(Information Link)

■ 习近平主席在多个场合对"一带一路"倡议的阐述(三)

习近平主席在新加坡国立大学发表题为《深化合作伙伴关系，共建亚洲美好家园》的重要演讲

两年前，我在访问中亚和东南亚时，提出建设"一带一路"的设想。这是发展的倡议、合作的倡议、开放的倡议，强调的是共商、共建、共享的平等互利方式。

——2015年11月7日

Two years ago, during my visit to Central Asia and Southeast Asia, I put forward the initiative of building the Silk Road Economic Belt and the 21st Century Maritime Silk Road. The Belt and Road Initiative, as it is now called, is about openness, development and cooperation, and it calls for pursuing joint development and sharing benefits on the basis of equality and mutual benefit.

——November 7th, 2015

第4单元 口译记忆 I (Memory in Interpreting I)

口译主题：旅游

单元学习目的(Unit Goals) 💡

➢ 掌握本课程所讲授的口译技巧：短时记忆，长期记忆，工作记忆。

➢ 学习旅游专题所涉及的常用词语和表达。

导入(Lead -in)

1. 什么是记忆？记忆可以分成几类？

2. 口译记忆困难的原因有哪些？

3. 译员的记忆力超群，对吗？

4. 你知道如何训练短期记忆吗？

5. 这个口诀能够帮助你提高记忆吗？

- I have six honest serving men. They taught me all I know.
- Their names were what and where and when. And why and how, and who.

4.1 技能讲解(Skill Introduction)

◼ 4.1.1 记忆的种类(The Classification of Memory)

记忆是人脑对经历过的事物的反映(鲍刚，2005:150)。心理学根据信息保持时间的长短将记忆分为三类：瞬时记忆、短期记忆和长期记忆。

(1) 瞬时记忆(instantaneous memory)，外界刺激结束后，受到注意的信息会转入瞬时记忆中。瞬时记忆持续的时间很短，只有0.25～2秒，但容量却很大。信息经过大脑过滤之后，值得注意的信息就会进入短期记忆。

(2) 短期记忆(short-term memory)，短期记忆是将少量信息贮存在脑中一定时间，并保持活跃状态的能力。它是连接瞬时记忆和长期记忆的桥梁，从瞬时记忆中接收有意义的信息，从长期记忆中筛选出与新信息相关的知识，并将新旧信息进行处理和贮存。它是整个记忆系统中至关重要的一环。短期记忆只能将信息保留几秒钟到一分钟的时间，容量大约为7±2个单位。短期记忆的容量可以通过"组块"(chunking)得到扩充。所谓"组块"就是把旧信息组成更多的信息单位来增大记忆容量。组块对于提升短期记忆容量是十分有效的且具有重要意义的。

(3) 长期记忆(long-term memory)，研究表明，长期记忆的容量是无限的，持续时间也可以是终身的。从心理学的角度来说，长期记忆中的信息是通过大脑CPU短期记忆筛选处理而来的，是一个人知识经验的总和。这些信息在脑中处于不活跃状态，只有在被调用时才会被激活。长期记忆在被激活后，会回到短期记忆中，参与对新信息的分析与处理。

■ 4.1.2　记忆与口译(Memory and Interpreting)

(1) 口译记忆的困难一般可归结为三个原因，一是短时记忆的局限性，二是长期记忆中存储的信息处于不活跃状态，三是心理压力大。

(2) 瞬时记忆在口译中的运用。在瞬时记忆阶段，译员为了更好地分析处理源语信息，必须更加专注于讲话人的话语。由于刻意进行了积极的听辨，译员能够更快地对信息进行推理和分析。心理学研究表明，记忆的效果与动机成正相关。

(3) 短期记忆在口译中的运用。心理学家认为，在口译中，短期记忆将源语转化为目标语，同时激活贮存在长期记忆中的与新信息相关的信息。一个译员短期记忆的好坏将决定他分析、理解和处理源语的速度。口译中短期记忆的重要性受到了极大的关注。短期记忆的持续时间为5～20秒，容量为7±2个字符。而心理学实验表明，人说话的平均正常语速为每秒10～15个音素(Moore，1977：218)。假设一个译员能将信息在短期记忆中贮存20秒，他每次就需要处理200~600个音素，这超过了短期记忆容量的几十倍。译员必须寻找途径扩充自己短期记忆的容量，并提高处理信息的速度。优秀的短期记忆是十分必要的，这也通过一些著名的EI译模型得到了证明。在系统意义理论中，核心思想就是"脱离语言外壳"(deverbalization)。在实际口译活动中，译员无法记住每个确切的词，只能抓取源语中的大意或关键信息，并将信息以非语言的形式储存起来。由于在脱离语言外壳的过程中发挥了重要作用，短期记忆在口译活动中是必不可少的。

(4) 长期记忆在口译中的作用。在一些特殊情况下，译员无法做笔记，只能借助已有的知识对听到的信息进行整合，并记住源语的大意。由于短期记忆的持续时间只有不到一分钟，译员在这种连续无笔记口译中借助的是长期记忆。在长时间巨大的工作压力下，许多优秀译员都会在口译时刻意忘掉一些信息，在工作压力之下，他们可以将源语信息留存较长的时间；但一旦压力消失，他们就会立刻忘掉源语信息，为新信息留出空间。

4.2 主题口译(Topic Interpreting)

4.2.1 单句口译(Sentence Practice)

Please interpret the following sentences by using the techniques illustrated above. You may interpret to your partner first and then he/she comments on your performance.

(1) Australia is a land of exceptional beauty. It is the world's smallest continent and largest island, and a relatively young nation established in an ancient land.

(2) Today visitors come by the thousands—the great and simple of the earth—all in a spirit of marvel.

(3) Though filled with an astonishing array of geologic wonders: geysers, hot springs, fumaroles, canyons, waterfalls, Yellowstone is perhaps most remarkable as a wilder life sanctuary.

(4) The Glacier Express is superb in all four seasons: shimmering peaks in summer, snow-covered, fair-tale scenery in winter, fabulous Alpine flowers in spring and a kaleidoscope of colour in autumn.

(5) Barcelona is king of Modernism architecture. From 1880 to 1910, architects used themes and shapes from nature in designing their buildings.

(6) 桂林位于广西壮族自治区的北部，面积565平方公里，人口100多万，是国内外旅游胜地之一。

(7) 湖南省位于长江中游南部，东经108度至114度，北纬24度至30度。因地处洞庭湖之南，所以叫做湖南。

(8) 云南有26个少数民族，是中国少数民族种类最多的省份。各民族的服饰、建筑、歌舞、饮食等形成了一幅美丽的风情画卷。

(9) 不允许自带食物进入园中，只能在里面的快餐店用餐。

(10) 有人说，沱江和古街是凤凰浓郁风情的代表，是一曲自然风景和风土人情融合出的最完美的和弦。

4.2.2 对话口译(Dialogue Practice)

1. Vocabulary Work: Study the following words and phrases and translate them into the target language.

行程单	大英博物馆
大本钟	沈阳故宫
议会大厦	福陵
西敏寺	昭陵
白金汉宫	独特的满族风格

2. Read the following dialogue and interpret it into the target language .

A：Ms. Li, I suppose you had already been informed of the arrangement of your whole trip before you came. But just in case, this is a copy of your itinerary. If you have any questions or seriously need any changes, do let me know.

B：谢谢您，亚历克斯。旅行社的人已经跟我解释得很清楚了，我也完全同意。今天我们去参观大本钟、议会大厦、西敏寺、白金汉宫、大英博物馆等景点是吧？

A：Yes，you must be hungry. Let have breakfast first.

B：我这次行程的第一顿是西餐啊！不过西餐是我们中国人的说法，相信实际上美式和英式食物肯定大有不同。想想看，光中国就有八大菜系呢，更不要说两个不同的国家了。

A：You're right! There are lots of differences between American and British food.

B：我比较喜欢健康食品，比如煮鸡蛋。

A：We like it, too. The proper way to eat a boiled egg in the UK is to soft boil it so that the yolk is still running. Three and a half to four minutes should do it. While doing the egg, we make toast.

B：吃鸡蛋也那么多讲究吗？ 英国人的生活还真精致。

A：English breakfast is big, the traditional one is called FEB. The Full English Breakfast consists of at least one slice of bacon, preferably two, one or two fried eggs, fried bread, sauté(fried) potatoes, fried mushrooms, tomatoes, or tinned ones heated, and baked beans. Many cafes serve the FEB all day.

B：要吃那么多东西，得用很长时间吧？

A：Yes. In many European countries it is normal to have a long break in the middle of the day when all members of the family are back home to eat together. This is not common in Britain because normally it is a long way from the place of work or school to the home. Consequently the British people tend to have a big breakfast before they go to work.

B：说的我都饿了。在国内忙着工作，早餐要么是面包牛奶，要不就是速冻食品。这次来一定要好好品尝一下英式早餐。

A：Ms. Li here we are. The best food for miles.

B：谢谢您给我介绍英国美食。

A：Enjoy your food!

B：再次感谢您！

3. Read the following dialogue and interpret it into the target language .

A：你好，我们有很多选择，不知您想去什么地方玩？

B：Please tell me about some interesting places in this city.

A：好的，您对什么感兴趣？

B：I want to visit some historic sites. What are the places of special interest here?

A：看一下这些照片：这是沈阳故宫、福陵、昭陵，还有新乐遗址、南关天主教堂、张氏帅府等。

B：From these pictures, it seems like the Shenyang Imperial Palace is well-preserved. I have been to the Forbidden Palace in Beijing, now I would like to visit the Shenyang Imperial Palace.

A：是啊，沈阳故宫是除北京故宫外，中国现存的第二大完整的宫殿建筑群，它独特的满族建筑风格使之区别于北京故宫。

B：I want to visit Shenyang Imperial Palace. I know in 1625 A.D., it was established by the first emperor of Qing Dynasty — Nuerhachi and the second emperor — Huangtaiji before they went into Shanhai Guan.

A：看来您对沈阳故宫有一些了解。沈阳故宫占地面积6万多平方米，有古建筑114座，是一处包含着丰富历史文化内涵的古代遗址。1961年，国务院将沈阳故宫列入"国家重点文物保护单位"。

B：Well，shall we go there today？ I want to take some shots there.

A：当然，如果您感兴趣的话，我明天开车带您去福陵、昭陵看看。福陵是清代开国皇帝清太祖努尔哈赤和他的后妃孝慈高皇后叶赫那拉氏的陵寝。昭陵是清太宗皇太极和孝慈高皇后博尔济吉特氏的陵墓。

B：That a wonderful! In that way, I have the chance to have a full picture of the most famous historical interest in this city！

4.2.3 篇章口译[Passage Practice(E to C)]

1. Vocabulary Work: Study the following words and phrases and translate them into the target language.

mysterious and exotic	Delta
the Assyrians	be absorbed into
hieroglyphic script	invade
mummification	acquired

2. Please interpret the following passage by using the techniques illustrated above. Please pay attention to the underlined sentences as they require special treatment during interpreting.

Ancient Egypt
Interpretire Panels of the Egyptian Galleries in the British Museum

Even in ancient times, the civilization of Egypt was famous for its great age and wisdom. Its distinctive culture made it seem mysterious and exotic to other people in the ancient world, including the Assyrians and the Greeks.

Egyptian religion, hieroglyphic script and buried customs, such as mummification, lasted for over 3000 years and have continued to fascinate the world in modern times.

The kingdom of Egypt occupied the Nile valley and Delta in north-east Africa from around 3000 BC. For much of its long history, Egypt was largely self-contained, but it acquired territory in Nubia(Sudan), to the South and in the Near East. The River Nile ensured Egypt's agricultural wealth, and the kingdom all had access to gold and other mineral resources.

Egypt was invaded by other powers, including the Assyrians, Persians and Greeks. Throughout its history, however, it retained its distinctive and sophisticated culture, even after the death of Queen Cleopetra in 30 BC, when it was absorbed into Roman Empire. The long tradition of ancient Egyptian art and culture finally ended when the Egyptian temples were closed in the early Christian era, in the fourth and fifth centuries AD.

3. Please interpret the following passage by using the techniques illustrated above. Please pay attention to the underlined sentences as they require special treatment during interpreting.

Romantic city – Paris[1]

① Ah, beautiful Paris. For centuries this city has attracted the admiration of the world. The allure and charm of Paris captivate all who visit there.

② Where can you discover the charm of Paris for yourself. Is it in the legacy of all the French rulers who worked to beautify their beloved city? Is it in the famous castles, palaces, statues and monuments? Can you it in the world-class museums, such as the Louvre? Perhaps Paris' allure lies in the zest and style of the Parisians.

③ When you visit Paris, you don't have to spend all of your time visiting museums and monuments. They are certainly worthy of your time, but ignore them for a day. First take some time to look around and experience life in Paris. You'll find it charming.

④ Take a stroll along the Seine River. Browse through the art vendors colorful paintings. Peek through delicate iron gates at the well kept gardens. Watch closely for the French attention to detail that has made France synonymous with good taste. You will see it in the design of a doorway or arch and in the little fountains and quaint balconies. No matter where you look, you will find everyday objects transformed into works by art.

⑤ Spend some time in a quiet park relaxing on an old bench. Lie on your back on the green grass. When you need refreshment, try coffee and pastries at a sidewalk cafe. Strike up a conversation with a Parisian. This isn't always easy, though. With such a large international population living in Paris, true natives are hard to find these days.

⑥ As evening comes to Paris, enchantment rises with the mist over the riverfront. You may hear music from an outdoor concert nearby classical, jazz, opera or chansons, those French folk songs. Parisians love their music. The starry sky is their auditorium. You can also hear concerts in the chateaux and cathedrals. In Paris the Music never ends.

⑦ Don't miss the highlight of Paris evening: eating out. Parisians are proud of their cuisine.

And rightly so; it's world famous. Gourmet dining is one of the indispensable joys of living. You need a special guidebook to help you choose one of the hundreds of excellent restaurants. The capital of France boasts every regional specialty, cheese and wine the country has to offer. If you don't know what to order, ask for the suggested menu. The chef likes to showcase his best dishes there. Remember, you haven't tasted the true flavor of France until you've dined at a French restaurant in Paris.

⑧ After your gourmet dinner, take a walking tour of the floodlit monuments. Cross the Pont Neuf[2], the oldest bridge in the city. The most famous landmark of Paris looms up in front of you the Notre Dame Cathedral[3](Cathedral of Our Lady). Stand in the square in front of the cathedral. Here, you are standing in the center of France. All distances are measured from the front of Notre Dame. Every road in France leads to her front door. All French kings and leaders have journeyed here to commemorate important occasions and give thanks. Notre Dame is the heart of Paris and the heart of France.

⑨ Your visit in Paris has only just begun. You've just started to discover the charm of this old city. May the rest of your journey be unforgettable. When it is time to leave, you will go reluctantly. You will say with the French, "A bientot, Paris, a bientot!" (See you again soon, Paris!)

Notes on the text

(1) Romantic city–Paris

巴黎——法国时尚之都

巴黎是法国的心脏、世界时尚之都、浪漫之乡、世界上最繁华的都市之一。在巴黎城市的各个社区中，到处可以看到博物馆、影剧院、花园、喷泉和雕塑，文化环境非常好。巴黎是艺术之都，也是鲜花之都。无论是在房间里、阳台上、院子中，还是在商店里、橱窗前和路边上，到处都有盛开的鲜花，到处都有迷人的芳香。至于那五彩缤纷的花店和花团锦簇的公园，更是常常让人驻足观赏，流连忘返。著名的凯旋门由罗马时期留存至今，它地处巴黎香榭丽舍大道尽头，戴高乐星形广场的中央，是欧洲100多座凯旋门中最大的一座。这一座是为纪念拿破仑远征军而建的，正面有四幅浮雕——《马赛曲》《胜利》《抵抗》《和平》。这其中最吸引人的是刻在右侧(面向田园大街)石柱上的"1792年志愿军出发远征"，即著名的《马赛曲》的浮雕，是世界美术史上占有重要的一席之地的不朽艺术杰作。

(2) the Pont Neuf

新桥(法语为Pont Neuf，英语为New Bridge)

新桥是巴黎横跨塞纳河(Rio Seine)的最古老的桥。它的名字，只是表明在排列在两岸宫殿建筑之间众多的旧桥中，它是最著名的一座。

(3) the Notre Dame Cathedral

巴黎圣母院

其因同名的经典小说和改编而成的歌剧为人们熟知。这座经典的哥特式教堂地处法国巴黎市中心，是西堤岛上的地标建筑，也是天主教巴黎总教区的主教座堂。去巴黎圣母院最好从教堂的北门步入，一进门就能撞见绚丽夺目的3个玫瑰画窗。巴黎圣母院两边的商店也很有名气，可以买到很多精美的纪念品，最受欢迎的是一种造币机：投进一个2欧元硬币，它就会吐出一个新的纪念币，其图案是圣母抱圣婴。巴黎圣母院卢浮宫也许是全世界最著名的博物馆和艺术殿堂，同时也是法国最古老的王宫。与卢浮宫有关的电影有《卢浮魅影》等。这里包含雕塑馆、绘画馆和古埃及艺术馆，最著名的镇馆之宝包括米诺斯维纳斯、胜利女神和《蒙娜丽莎》等。这里哺育出不少世界艺坛名家。当然更多的普通游客是把这里当作观赏世界艺术精品的殿堂。

■ 4.2.4 篇章口译[Passage Practice(C to E)]

1. Vocabulary Work: Study the following words and phrases and translate them into the target language.

中国民族文化特色	地方风味小吃
旅游线路	旅游的报价
中国戏剧和杂技表演	半价收费
中国烹调	全额退费

2. Please interpret the following paragraph by using the techniques illustrated above. Please pay attention to the underlined sentences as they require special treatment during interpreting.

中国国际旅行社为各位安排了富有中国民族文化特色的有趣的旅游线路。各位将要游览举世闻名的景点和名胜，参观雄伟的古建筑群，观赏珍贵的中国文物。你们还将有机会欣赏中国戏剧和杂技表演，品尝纯真的中国烹调和地方风味小吃。我国人民传统的热情和好客将使各位的访问愉快而又难忘。在各位做出选择之前，我想谈一下本旅行社有关团体旅游的报价问题。首先，对于参加团体旅游的个人，其报价均含交通费、住宿费、膳食费、观光费、导游服务费以及双程国际机票。其次，每位成人游客可以携带一名年龄在12岁以下的儿童，以半价收费。最后，如果发生某些不可预见的、使旅游无法正常进行的情况，本旅行社则保留修改原定计划的权利，包括全额退费。

3. Please interpret the following passage by using the techniques illustrated above. Please pay attention to the underlined sentences as they require special treatment during interpreting.

中国旅游资源简介

① 中国旅游资源丰富，拥有壮丽的山岳河流，丰富多彩的民俗民风，奇特的动植物和数不尽的名胜古迹(1)，加之独具特色的戏曲、音乐、舞蹈和享誉世界的美食，每年都吸引着大批的国内外旅游者。目前，中国已形成世界上规模最大、增速最快、潜力最强的旅

<u>游市场</u>⁽²⁾。

② 据世界旅游及旅行理事会(WTTC)初步测算，中国旅游及旅行业在未来十年有望实现10.4%的年增长率，中国将成为世界第四大旅游业发展经济体。另据世界旅游组织预测，到2020年，中国将成为世界第一大旅游目的地国家和第四大客源输出国。中国的旅游资源主要分为三部分：自然景观、历史人文景观和民风民俗。

③ 首先说一下自然景观。中国广袤的土地上有不胜枚举的奇山异水——高山、湖泊、峡谷、溶洞、瀑布，绚丽多姿。泰山、衡山、华山、恒山和嵩山自古以来被合称为"五岳"，乃中国名山。其中绵亘于山东省中部的泰山气势磅礴、拔地通天，素有"五岳之首"之称。位于安徽省南部的黄山则以奇松、怪石、云海和温泉组成奇幻的自然景观。

④ 九寨沟、黄果树瀑布和桂林山水均位于中国西南部。四川北部的九寨沟，是一条纵深40余公里的山沟谷地，总面积约620平方公里，兼有湖泊、瀑布、雪山和森林之美，被称为"童话世界"。贵州省的黄果树瀑布为一大瀑布群，由18个地面瀑布和4个地下瀑布组成，5公里之外就能听到轰鸣声。在广西境内，漓江从桂林至阳朔一段，长82公里，蜿蜒于岩溶峰林之间，江水清澈，风景如画，是著名的桂林山水所在地。

⑤ 长江三峡景色久负盛名，两岸众多的名胜古迹和优美动人的传说令人神往。瞿塘峡雄伟险峻；巫峡秀丽深幽；西陵峡滩多水急，礁石林立，更有小三峡葱郁苍翠，水清见底。修筑在此处的三峡大坝，为中国最大的水电枢纽工程。

⑥ 第二，说一下历史人文景观。中国漫长的历史为今天的旅游者留下了无数文化古迹。长城作为中华民族的象征，已经成为中国最著名的旅游景点，这个人类文明史上最伟大的建筑工程始建于2000多年前的春秋战国时期，其工程之浩繁，气势之雄伟，堪称世界奇迹。目前向游人开放的有八达岭、老龙头、嘉峪关等数十处地段及其所属的关隘、墩台和烽堡。

⑦ 石窟、岩画和雕塑艺术也是中国旅游资源中绚丽的瑰宝。石窟比较集中地分布在甘肃境内的丝绸之路古道上，最著名的是莫高窟，被称为"东方艺术宝库"。莫高窟现存的492个石窟分布在崖壁上三、四层不等，壁画总面积约45 000平方米，彩塑像2100多身，其艺术造诣精深，想象丰富，蔚为大观。石窟艺术在中国南方的杰作以四川的乐山大佛为代表，这座依山凿成的大佛，高71米，肩宽28米，乃中国最大的一尊石雕坐佛。它不仅体形巨大，而且结构匀称，显示出古代工匠高超的雕刻技艺。

⑧ 宗教文化圣地从南到北星罗棋布。中国佛教禅宗的发源地少林寺建于公元495年，以少林功夫而闻名于世。武当山风景区位于湖北省，方圆30公里之内有72个山峰，峰奇谷险，风景秀丽，是中国著名的道教圣地，也是中国现存最完整、规模最大、等级最高的道教古建筑群。群峰叠翠、苍翠欲滴、有"峨眉天下秀"之誉的峨眉山地处四川西部，是中国四大佛教名山之一，山上有不少佛教古建筑遗迹。

⑨ 中国有100座历史文化名城，大多已达上千年历史。长江以南的苏州、杭州两座城市，<u>河湖交错、水网纵横、小桥流水、田园村舍、如诗如画，自古就有"人间天堂"的美誉。</u>⁽³⁾建于明代、迄今仍保护完好的平遥古城位于山西省中部，这里陆续发现的新石器时期的仰韶文化和龙山文化类型遗址，证明五六千年前人类就已在此繁衍生息。云南丽江古

城既是纳西族东巴文化的中心，又是汉、藏、白等各族文化的交汇地，拥有丰富的历史人文景观。该城始建于宋代，城内有许多明、清时期的石桥、石牌坊和民居，为研究中国民居建筑史提供了宝贵的资料，堪称"活的古民居博物馆"。

⑩ 第三，说一下民风民俗。中国56个民族的不同文化和生活方式异彩纷呈，民族节日各具特色。藏族最大也最有趣的节日之一——雪顿节(即酸奶节)，又被定为藏戏节，每年藏历6月30日开始的五天中，西藏各地的藏戏主要流派会聚在拉萨罗布林卡进行表演比赛，热闹非凡。

⑪ 农历七月在草原举行的那达慕(娱乐、游艺)大会，乃蒙古族一年一度的盛大节日。蒙古族人在节日里唱歌跳舞，进行摔跤、赛马和射箭比赛，还有祭敖包和物资交流活动。

⑫ 云南西双版纳傣族人的泼水节在农历清明节后，水被傣族视为吉祥、美满、幸福的象征。在节日的首日，人们以花枝沾水互致祝福礼；翌日为泼水日，场面隆重热烈，众人以瓢、盆、桶盛水，互相追逐、泼洒。节日期间还举行赛龙舟、跳孔雀舞等活动。

⑬ 新近修建的道路使云南与四川交界处的高原湖泊——泸沽湖成为旅游热点。湖周围数百平方公里范围内居住着古老而神秘的3万摩梭人，至今仍保留着母系社会特点和"男不娶，女不嫁"的婚姻习俗，被称为地球上最后的女儿国。摩梭少女的风姿，独木轻舟的典雅和此起彼伏的渔歌被旅游者称为"湖上三绝"。

Notes on the text

(1) 拥有壮丽的山岳河流，丰富多彩的民俗民风，奇特的动植物和数不尽的名胜古迹

high mountains, elegant rivers, springs and waterfalls, rich and varied folk customs, rare species

(2) 中国已形成世界上规模最大、增速最快、潜力最强的旅游市场

China has become one of the world's largest tourist markets with the greatest potential and growing at a rate unequalled anywhere

(3) 河湖交错、水网纵横、小桥流水、田园村舍、如诗如画，自古就有"人间天堂"的美誉

long known as "paradise on earth", are crisscrossed with rivers, lakes, bridges, fields and villages, as beautiful as paintings.

4.3 参考译文(Reference Version)

■ 4.3.1 单句口译(Sentence Practice)

Please interpret the following sentences by using the techniques illustrated above. You may interpret to your partner first and then he/she comments on your performance.

(1) 澳大利亚是一个异常美丽的国家。它是世界上最小的州，也是最大的岛，是在古老的土地上建立起来的较为年轻的国家。

(2) 今天，数以千计的游客，不管是普通人还是大人物，都怀着一种好奇心来到这里。

(3) 黄石公园的奇观比比皆是，充满了各种各样的地理奇观，间歇泉、温泉、喷气孔四处可见，更有高峡深谷，飞瀑流泉，令人叹为观止。

(4) 一年四季，冰川快车都带给您无与伦比的旅游体验：春季，阿尔卑斯鲜花娇艳动人；夏季，千山万壑熠熠发光；秋季，各种色彩缤纷绚丽；冬季，整个世界粉妆玉砌。

(5) 巴塞罗那是现代主义建筑的王国。从1880到1910年，建筑师使用自然主题及造型设计他们的建筑物。

(6) Located in the north of Guangxi Zhuang Autonomous Region, Guilin is one of the tourist attractions famous both at home and abroad, with an area of 565 square kilometers and a population of more than 1 million.

(7) Hunan Province is located just south of the middle reaches of the Changjiang(Yangtze) River between 108° and 114° E longitude and 24° and 30° N latitude. Since it lies to the south of the Dongting Lake, it has its name Hunan, which means "south of the lake".

(8) Home to 26 ethnic groups — the largest number in China — Yunnan Province offers tourists a cultural feast of unique ethnic costumes, architectures, costumes, cuisines, songs, and dances.

(9) You're not permitted to bring your own food to the perk; you can only consume the fast food sold on the premises.

(10) It is said that Tuojiang River and the Ancient Street are embodiments of Fenghuang's glamour, a harmony between natural landscape and local customs.

■ 4.3.2 对话口译(Dialogue Practice)

1. Vocabulary Work: Study the following words and phrases and translate them into the target language.

itinerary	the British Museum
the Big Ben	the Shenyang Imperial Palace
the Houses of Parliament	Fuling
the Westminster Abbey	Zhaoling
the Buckingham Palace	distinctive Manchu features

2. Read the following dialogue and interpret it into the target language .

A：李女士，我想您来之前对于本次行程安排就已经很清楚了吧？以防万一，这是您的行程单。如果您有任何问题，或者确实需要做一些修改，请一定告诉我。

B：Thank you, Alex. The travel agency has explained it to me in detail. Today, we will visit the Big Ben, the Houses of Parliament, the Westminster Abbey, the Buckingham Palace, the British Museum and so on, right?

A：对，您肯定有点饿了吧？我们先吃早饭。

B：My first Western food of this trip! But I guess "Western" is too general, as there must be some differences between British food and American food. Look, there are at least eight major schools of cooking within China, let alone two countries.

A：对，美国和英国的食物大不相同，举不胜举。

B：I prefer something healthy, like boiled eggs.

A：我们也很爱吃鸡蛋。在英国我们只是把鸡蛋稍微煮一下，大概3分半到4分钟，这时蛋黄还是稀的。在煮鸡蛋的同时，我们一边做吐司。

B：What a dainty life you British people have!

A：英国早餐很丰盛。传统的英式早餐被称为FEB，也就是全套英式早餐，它包括：至少一片培根，最好有两片；一两个煎蛋；炸面包；炸土豆；炸蘑菇；加热后的西红柿罐头和烤豆子。很多咖啡店全天都供应这种早餐。

B：It must take a long time to finish them all.

A：对。在很多欧洲国家，午休时间都很长，所以人们有时间回家与家人共进午餐。但是在英国则不同。因为大家的工作地点或者学校通常离家很远，中午回家不方便，所以英国人习惯在早上饱餐一顿之后再去上班。

B：This conversation makes me hungry. When I was in China, I ate only instant frozen food or bread and milk for breakfast as I had to rush to the workplace. Now I'm here, I must try the FEB.

A：李女士，我们到了，这家是方圆几里内最好的咖啡馆了。

B：Thanks a lot for introducing so many delicious foods to me.

A：祝您用餐愉快！

B：Thanks again！

3. Read the following dialogue and interpret it into the target language.

A：Hi there! We have all kinds of choices here. What kinds of places would you like to visit?

B：请告诉我这座城市一些有趣的地方。

A：OK, what are you interested in?

B：我想参观一些历史名胜。这里有什么特别有趣的地方吗？

A：Look at these pictures：the Shenyang Imperial Palace，Fuling, Zhaoling, Nanguan Cathedral，Zhang Shuai Fu and son on.

B：从照片上看，沈阳故宫保存得很好。我去过北京的故宫，很想再看看沈阳故宫。

A：You see, In addition the Imperial Palace in Beijing, the Shenyang Imperial Palace is one of the only two well-preserved palaces of China. Its distinctive Manchu features made it have totally different styles with the Beijing Imperial Palace.

B：我想去沈阳故宫。我知道沈阳故宫始建于1625年，由清太祖努尔哈赤与皇太极入关之前建造而成。

A：It seems that you know something about the Shenyang Imperial Palace . It covers a total area of over 60 000 square meters, consisting of 114 buildings with more than 500 rooms and halls. It is an ancient sites with rich historical and cultural connotation and in 1961, the Shenyang Imperial Palace was entitled "Historic Culture Relics Preserved Buildings" by the State Council .

B：我们今天能去那里吧？ 我想拍些照片。

A：Sure, I'll drive you to Fuling and Zhaoling tomorrow if you like. Fu Tomb is the tomb of the first emperor of Qing Dynasty Nuerhachi and his empress Yehnala. Zhaoling is the tomb of the emperor Huangtaiji and his empress Boerjijite of Qing Dynasty.

B：太好了！这样的话我就有机会看全这个城市最著名的景点了！

4.3.3 篇章口译[Passage Practice(E to C)]

1. Vocabulary Work: Study the following words and phrases and translate them into the target language.

高深莫测	三角洲
亚述人	占领了
岩石壁画	侵略
木乃伊	被纳入

2. Please interpret the following passage by using the techniques illustrated above. Please pay attention to the underlined sentences as they require special treatment during interpreting.

古老的埃及

大英博物馆埃及馆的牌示解说

早在远古时期，埃及就以其悠久的历史和聪明智慧闻名于世。在古代其他民族，包括亚述人和希腊人的眼里，埃及独特的文化似乎高深莫测。

埃及的宗教仪式、岩石壁画和丧葬风俗，如木乃伊，延续了3000多年，直到今天，这些古老的文化仍让现代人着迷不已。

公元前3000年左右，埃及帝国就占领了尼罗河平原以及非洲东北部的三角洲地带。在漫长的历史长河中，埃及人基本上自给自足，但还是占领了努比亚(现在的苏丹)并吞并了近东地区。尼罗河孕育了埃及的农业，而埃及人也拥有大量的黄金和其他贵重金属资源。

埃及也曾遭受外族侵略，包括亚述族、波斯人和希腊人，但埃及人一直保留着自己独特、精湛的文化。即使在公元前30年古埃及女王克莉奥帕特拉去世，埃及被纳入罗马帝国的版图后，埃及人对自己的古老文化仍不离不弃。公元4至5世纪，随着基督教的诞生，古老的埃及文化和艺术也走到了尽头。(程尽能、吕和发，2008：306，有改动)

3. Please interpret the following passage by using the techniques illustrated above. Please pay attention to the underlined sentences as they require special treatment during interpreting.

浪漫之都——巴黎

① 啊，美丽的巴黎！几个世纪以来，这座城市赢得了整个世界的崇拜。巴黎的诱惑与魅力吸引了所有到此游玩的人。

② 你在哪里可以找到巴黎对你的吸引力呢？是在历任的法国统治者们在美化他们所钟爱的城市时所留下来的遗产里？还是在那些有名的城堡、皇宫、雕像和纪念碑里呢？你能否在世界一流的博物馆，例如卢浮宫中找到呢？或许巴黎的诱惑力在于巴黎人的特殊品味和风格。

③ 当你到巴黎游玩时，别把时间全都花在看博物馆和纪念碑上面。它们当然很值得你花时间去参观，但今天先忘掉它们。首先来四处看看，并体验一下巴黎的生活。你会在其中发现它的迷人之处。

④ 沿着塞纳河漫步吧。浏览艺术家们丰富色彩的绘画，透过那些精致的铁门，向内偷窥那些被精心照看的花园。仔细留心法国人对于细节的留意，这使得法国成为"好品味"的同义词。你可以在门廊或拱门以及小喷泉和古怪有趣的走廊的设计上发现这一点。不管你往哪里看，你都会觉得日常物品已经变成了艺术品。

⑤ 花些时间，在一个安静的公园里面的旧板凳上轻松地休息或是躺在青草地上。想吃点心的时候，尝尝路边咖啡店的咖啡及点心。你也可以找一个巴黎人展开一段会话，但这也不太容易，有这么大的国际人口居住在此地，要找到一个真正当地的巴黎人是很难的。

⑥ 到了傍晚时分，随着码头上雾气的升起，巴黎的诱惑力也随之而起。你会听到附近室外音乐会所演奏的乐曲，其中包括古典乐、爵士乐、歌剧或是香颂(即法国的民歌)。巴黎人热爱自己的音乐，繁星点缀的天空，就是他们演奏的大礼堂。你也可以在城堡或教堂里聆听音乐会。在巴黎，音乐是不会停止的。

⑦ 不要错过了巴黎的夜生活中最重要的一部分：下馆子。巴黎人对其烹饪非常骄傲，他们理当如此，因为它世界驰名。美食本来就是与生活享乐不可分割的。为了帮你从几百家绝佳的餐厅中做选择，你需要一本特别的指南。法国的首都以各地的特色风味、乳酪和酒著称于世，如果你不知道要点什么，可以拿"推荐菜单"来看。大厨喜欢在此将他最拿手的菜做一番橱窗展示。请记住，在你尚未在巴黎的法国餐厅里吃过饭之前，都不算尝过法国真正的风味。

⑧ 在你的美食晚餐之后，可以到被聚光灯照耀的纪念碑去走一趟。穿过(Pont Neuf)这个城市中最古老的桥——第九桥，你将到达城市之岛(Ile de la Cite)，此时巴黎最有名的标志——圣母院会隐约地呈现在你的面前。站在教堂前面的广场，此时你也正处于法国的正中心，因为所有的距离皆是以圣母院前门开始计算的，法国的每一条路都通往它的前门。所有的法国国王或统治者都曾经旅游到此来纪念重要的节日或感恩。圣母院是巴黎的中

心，也是法国的中心。

⑨ 你的巴黎之旅才刚刚开始，你才刚刚开始发现这个古老城市的魅力，希望你剩余的旅程令你难以忘怀。当你该起程回家时，你会依依不舍，然后用法文说："后会有期，巴黎！"

4.3.4 篇章口译[Passage Practice(C to E)]

1. Vocabulary Work: Study the following words and phrases and translate them into the target language.

characteristic of Chinese national culture	local delicacies.
tour program	quotation for each group tour
Chinese operas and acrobatic shows	calculated on a half-price basis
authentic Chinese food	a full refund

2. Please interpret the following passage by using the techniques illustrated above. Please pay attention to the underlined sentences as they require special treatment during interpreting.

China International Travel Service is offering you an interesting tour program that is characteristic of Chinese national culture. You will visit world-famous scenic spots, historical sites and magnificent ancient architectural complexes, and appreciate precious cultural relics. You will also have opportunities to enjoy Chinese operas and acrobatic shows, and taste authentic Chinese food and local delicacies. The traditional warmth and hospitality with which the Chinese people entertain their guests will make your visit a pleasant and memorable experience.

Before you make a decision on our tour, I'd like to make some remarks about the quotation policies regarding the group tours with this travel agency. First, and individual's quotation for each group tour includes the cost of transportation, accommodation, meals, sightseeing, tour-guide service and round-trip international airplane tickets.

Next, each adult can take a child under the age of twelve, whose quotation is calculated on a half-price basis. And finally, we reserve the right to make changes to the set itinerary should we encounter any unforeseeable circumstances which would prevent us from otherwise normal operations, including a full refund.

3. Please interpret the following passage by using the techniques illustrated above. Please pay attention to the underlined sentences as they require special treatment during interpreting.

A Brief Introduction of China's Tourist Resources

① Thanks to its rich tourist resources—high mountains, elegant rivers, springs and waterfalls, rich and varied folk customs, rare species, scenic spots and historical sites, distinctive opera, music and dance, and world-famous cuisine—China attracts a large number of domestic and foreign tourists every year. Today, China has become one of the world's largest tourist markets with the greatest potential and growing at a rate unequalled anywhere.

② According to the World Tourist and Travel Council(WTTC), China's travel industry may grow by 10.4 percent a year over the next 10 years, lifting China to fourth rank in terms of industry size. The World Tourism Organization predicts that by 2020 China will be the world's top tourist destination, and fourth in outbound tourist numbers with 100 million Chinese people traveling abroad every year. Tourist resources in China can be divided into three main groups: natural sites, historical and cultural sites and folk customs.

③ First, natural sites.

China has countless mountains, lakes, valleys, caves and waterfalls. Mount Tai in the east, Mount Heng in the south, Mount Hua in the west, Mount Heng in the north, and Mount Song in the center of China have been called the Five Sacred Mountains since antiquity. The magnificent Mount Tai, which snakes through central Shandong Province, is admired by Chinese as paramount among them. Another mountain celebrated for its beauty is Huangshan Mountain in southern Anhui Province, known for its graceful pines, unusual rocks, cloud seas and hot springs.

④ Jiuzhaigou, Huangguoshu Waterfalls, and Guilin are all located in southwestern China. Jiuzhaigou in northern Sichuan Province is a beautiful "fairyland" running over 40 km through snow-covered mountains, lakes, waterfalls, and forest, with a total area of 640 square km. The Huangguoshu Waterfalls in Guizhou Province are a group of waterfalls, 18 above-ground and four below, which can be heard from five km away. The Lijiang River in Guangxi Zhuang Autonomous Region winds its way through karst peaks for 82 km between Guilin and Yangshuo. It has clear water and picturesque landscape.

⑤ Along the renowned Three Gorges of the Yangtze River are many scenic spots and historical sites that have nurtured many beautiful legends. The Three Gorges Dam built here is China's biggest hydro-power project

⑥ Second, historical and cultural sites.

China's long history has left many cultural relics for today's tourists. The Great Wall, a symbol of the Chinese nation, is also a prime example of historical sites that have become major tourist attractions. As the greatest defence-structure project in the history of human civilization, it dates back more than 2 000 years ago to the Spring and Autumn and the Warring States periods—huge in its scale and grandeur,

⑦ It rating as a world wonder. Grottoes, murals and sculptures are treasures of China's tourist resources. They are concentrated along the ancient Silk Road in Gansu Province. The best known are the Mogao Caves, a "treasure house of oriental art". In the south, grotto art is represented in Sichuan Province by the Leshan Giant Buddha, carved into a cliff face. 71 meters high and 28 meters wide, it is the largest sitting Buddha in stone, showing the superb carving skill of ancient craftsmen.

⑧ The Shaolin Temple in Henan Province is the birthplace of Chinese Zen Buddhism and famous for its Shaolin kungfu martial arts. In central China's Hubei Province, beautiful Wudang Mountain, with 72 grotesque peaks in 30 sq km, is a sacred site of Taoism, which preserves China's most complete, largest-scale and ancient Taoist architecture. In western Sichuan Province, Mount Emei, dotted with ancient Buddhist temples and structures, is one of China's four holy Buddhist mountains.

⑨ Most of China's 100 cities classified as famous historical and cultural cities are over 1 000 years old. Located in the south of the Yangtze River, Suzhou and Hangzhou, long known as "paradise on earth", are crisscrossed with rivers, lakes, bridges, fields and villages, as beautiful as paintings. Ancient Lijiang in Yunnan Province is not only the center of Dongba culture of the Naxi ethnic group but also a meeting place for the cultures of Han, Tibetan and Bai ethnicities. Built in the Song Dynasty, this city has many stone bridges, stone memorial arches and dwelling houses, which provide precious materials for architectural history and can be called a "living museum of ancient dwelling houses".

⑩ Third, Folk Customs.

The diverse cultures and life-styles of China's 56 ethnic groups are relected in their festivals. The biggest Tibetan festival—Shoton(Yogurt) Festival—is also the setting for the Tibetan Theatrical Festival, when for ive days every summer Tibetan theatrical groups perform and compete in Norbulingka Palace.

⑪ Another summer festival is the Nadam Fair in the Mongolian grasslands, where attractions include wrestling, horse racing and archery competitions.

⑫ The Water-Sprinkling Festival of the Dai ethnic group in Xishuangbanna, Yunnan Province, is a lively occasion taking place after the Qing Ming Festival(Tomb-sweeping Day). People chase and pour water(a symbol of good luck and happiness) over each other, among other activities such as dragon boat racing and peacock dance.

⑬ Lugu Lake between Sichuan and Yunnan provinces has become a tourist destination. The matriarchal society of the 30 000 local Mosuo people is noted for its "no marriage" traditions and is called the last women's kingdom on the earth. Mosuo women, local dugout canoes and undulating singing style are considered unique to Lugu Lake.

4.4　旅游主题词汇汇总(Vocabulary Build-up)

backpacker	背包旅行者
outbound tourism	出境游
excursion	远足
outward journey	单程旅行

（续表）

return journey/round journey	往返旅行
business trip	商务旅行
off season/low season	淡季
shoulder period/season	平季
peak season	旺季
local tourist organization	当地旅游组织
local guide	地陪/当地导游
national guide	全陪/全程导游
electric guide	电子导游机
holiday resort	度假区
China's category A travel agency	一类社
China's category B travel agency	二类社
China's category C travel agency	三类社
circular tour	环程旅行
travelling expense	旅费
minimum tour price	最低旅游价格
tour route	旅行路线
receiving country	旅游接待国
World Tourism Day	世界旅游日
tourist destination	旅游目的地
tour group	旅游团
tour brochure	旅游小册子
Tourist association	旅游协会
Tourist council	旅游委员会
Municipal Tourism Administration	市旅游局
Provincial Tourism Administration	省旅游局
Autonomous Region Tourism Administration	自治区旅游局
Autonomous Prefecture Tourism Administration	自治州旅游局
Tourism Administration	中国旅游局
World Tourism Organization	世界旅游组织

4.5 扩展练习(Enhancement Practice)

Retelling.

Directions: Listen to the following passages once and then reproduce them in the same language at the end of each segment.

A. English Passage

The White House is the official residence and principal workplace of the President of the

United States. Located at 1600 Pennsylvania Avenue NW in Washington, D.C., the house was designed by Irish-born James Hoban, and built between 1792 and 1800 of white-painted Aquia sandstone in the Neoclassical style. It has been the residence of every U.S. President since John Adams. When Thomas Jefferson moved into the house in 1801, he(with architect Benjamin Henry Latrobe) expanded the building outward, creating two colonnades that were meant to conceal stables and storage.

In 1814, during the War of 1812, the mansion was set ablaze by the British Army in the Burning of Washington, destroying the interior and charring much of the exterior. Reconstruction began almost immediately, and President James Monroe moved into the partially reconstructed house in October 1817. Construction continued with the addition of the South Portico in 1824 and the North in 1829. Because of crowding within the executive mansion itself, President Theodore Roosevelt had all work offices relocated to the newly constructed West Wing in 1901. Eight years later, President William Howard Taft expanded the West Wing and created the first Oval Office which was eventually moved as the section was expanded. The third-floor attic was converted to living quarters in 1927 by augmenting the existing hip roof with long shed dormers. A newly constructed East Wing was used as a reception area for social events; Jefferson's colonnades connected the new wings. East Wing alterations were completed in 1946, creating additional office space. By 1948, the house's load-bearing exterior walls and internal wood beams were found to be close to failure. Under Harry S. Truman, the interior rooms were completely dismantled and a new internal load-bearing steel frame constructed inside the walls. Once this work was completed, the interior rooms were rebuilt.

Today, the White House Complex includes the Executive Residence, West Wing, Cabinet Room, Roosevelt Room, East Wing, and the Eisenhower Executive Office Building, which houses the executive offices of the President and Vice President.

The White House is made up of six stories—the Ground Floor, State Floor, Second Floor, and Third Floor, as well as a two-story basement. The term White House is regularly used as a metonym for the Executive Office of the President of the United States and for the president's administration and advisers in general. The property is a National Heritage Site owned by the National Park Service and is part of the President's Park. In 2007, it was ranked second on the American Institute of Architects list of "America's Favorite Architecture".

B. Chinese Passage

兵马俑，即秦始皇兵马俑，亦简称秦兵马俑或秦俑，位于今陕西省西安市临潼区秦始皇陵以东1.5公里处的兵马俑坑内。

兵马俑是古代墓葬雕塑的一个类别。古代实行人殉，奴隶是奴隶主生前的附属品，奴隶主死后奴隶要作为殉葬品为奴隶主陪葬。兵马俑即制成兵马(战车、战马、士兵)形状的殉葬品。

1974年3月，兵马俑被发现；1987年，秦始皇陵及兵马俑坑被联合国教科文组织批准列入《世界遗产名录》，并被誉为"世界第八大奇迹"。先后已有200多位国家领导人参观访问，成为中国古代辉煌文明的一张金字名片。

兵马俑从身份上区分，主要有士兵与军吏两大类，军吏又有低级、中级、高级之别。一般士兵不戴冠，而军吏戴冠，普通军吏的冠与将军的冠又不相同，甚至铠甲也有区别。其中的兵俑包括步兵、骑兵、车兵三类。根据实战需要，不同兵种的武士装备各异。

俑坑中最多的是武士俑，平均身高1.80米左右，最高的1.90米以上，陶马高1.72米，长2.03米。秦俑大部分手执青铜兵器，有弓、弩、箭镞、铍、矛、戈、殳、剑、弯刀和钺，身穿甲片细密的铠甲，胸前有彩线挽成的结穗。军吏头戴长冠，数量比武将多。秦俑的脸型、身材、表情、眉毛、眼睛和年龄都有不同之处。

4.6　口译点滴(Information Link)

■ 习近平主席在多个场合对"一带一路"倡议的阐述(四)

习近平主席在亚洲基础设施投资银行开业仪式上的致辞

中国开放的大门永远不会关上，欢迎各国搭乘中国发展的"顺风车"。中国愿意同各方一道，推动亚投行早日投入运营、发挥作用，为发展中国家经济增长和民生改善贡献力量。我们将继续欢迎包括亚投行在内的新老国际金融机构共同参与"一带一路"建设。

——2016年1月16日

The door of China's opening up will never shut and China welcomes all countries to ride on its development. China stands ready to work with other parties to make sure that the AIIB will start to operate and play its due role as soon as possible and contribute to economic growth and better livelihood in developing countries. And China continues to welcome AIIB and other international financial institutions to take part in the building of the Silk Road Economic Belt and 21st Century Maritime Silk Road.

——January 16th,2016

第5单元　口译记忆Ⅱ(Memory in Interpreting Ⅱ)

口译主题：教育

单元学习目的(Unit Goals) ☀

➢ 掌握本课程所讲授的口译记忆技巧。
➢ 学习教育专题所涉及的常用词语和表达。

导入(Lead -in)

1. 这个口诀能够帮助你提高记忆吗？

● I have six honest serving men. They taught me all I know.
● Their names were what and where and when. And why and how, and who.

2. 提高口译记忆效力的策略有哪些？

5.1　技能讲解(Skill Introduction)

对记忆类型和特点的研究为口译教学提高记忆力提供了有力的理论依据。实际上，通过科学合理的训练，译员的记忆技巧可以得到提高，记忆效果可以得到改善。因此，对译员记忆能力的训练是口译教学的重要内容之一。口译工作要求译员不仅具有几乎平行的双语水平，还必须具备深厚的专业知识、丰富的百科知识和个人社会文化积淀。因此，文化知识的积累是译员必须长期坚持的任务。这些知识一般储存在译员的长时记忆中，并会持续数周、数月，甚至终生。

■ 5.1.1　遵循遗忘曲线原理

根据德国心理学家Hermann Ebbinghaus(1885)的遗忘曲线，人们会在开始学习的20分钟后，忘记所学内容的42%，1个小时之后，则会忘记56%，9个小时之后是64%，1天之后67%，31天后则是所学内容的79%，也就是在学习后头几小时遗忘最快，随着时间的推延，材料遗忘越来越少。为了有效地掌握主题专业知识，译员可以遵循遗忘曲线原理，在学完之后的20分钟，1小时或1天之后分别复习回顾所学内容。每一次的复习都能保留90%，甚至更高的所学内容。

5.1.2　利用构词法

译员也可以运用构词法来帮助他们记住某一翻译主题的相关术语。由于英语属于印欧语系，很多英文单词可以被分解成前缀、后缀和词根。从词源学的角度来讲，很多英文单词都来源于拉丁语或希腊语，特别是一些专业术语。因此，了解一些拉丁语和希腊语词根对于理解和记忆这些术语是非常有帮助的。如果译员稍微熟悉构词法和词根变异，他就能准确定位多音节术语不同构成部分的意义及整个词的意义。以医学为例，大部分医学术语都来源于希腊语或拉丁语，希腊语kardia，意为"心脏"，因此我们就有英语词根cardi，vascular这个词意为管道或血管，所以复合词cardiovascular肯定就与心脏及血管有关，意为"心血管的"。拉丁语pulmo意为"肺"，因而就有词根pulm，英文单词pulmonary就指"肺的，肺动脉的"。又如epidemic这个词也是希腊语，epi意为"在……中间"，demic意为"民众"，合起来即意为"在民众间传播的"，后来就引申为传染病。

5.1.3　译前准备

即使译员通过长时间的知识积累可能已经掌握了广泛的百科知识和一定的专业知识，仍有必要针对特定的专业知识进行强化。勒代雷(Seles kovitch，D. &M. Lederer，1984)认为专业技术口译的准备其实就是"学会学习"的过程。根据释义派理论，专业技术口译的准备应该从学习专业知识开始，否则无法恰当使用专业术语。译员在收到某一特定翻译任务的专业资料后，如果可能的话，首先咨询专业人士，专家的讲解能让译员在很短的时间里以很高的效率理解某一专业知识，达到事半功倍的效果。如果无法得到专业人士的帮助，译员可以通过查询相关资料，了解所涉及专业或行业的相关背景，并记录可能有用的专业术语。这些术语可能不会进入译员的积极词汇库中，但他们已经进入了译员的长时记忆中，当收到语境提示时就会被激活和再现。

5.1.4　影子跟读

影子跟读是以落后几秒的速度用原语跟读发言人的讲话。这个练习方法的目的就是训练听说同步技巧和注意力的分配。刚开始学员只是依赖听觉记忆做语音跟读，复述所听到的每一个发音，而不是一个完整的意义单位或单词。一段时间练习后，学员可以开始短语跟读，尽量落后于发言人，直到和他达到一个意义单位的距离。在这个练习过程中学员不是被动地鹦鹉学舌，而是让所有器官都参与其中，耳朵负责接收原语，嘴巴负责复述，大脑负责处理信息，尽量抓住单词所表达的信息，而不是局限于单个的音节。当学员能够比较自在地同时进行听说并且不会遗漏太多信息时，即可开始双重任务练习，即一边做其他事情一边跟读。起初，一边跟读一边从1数到100，然后从100倒数到1。熟悉了之后，练习一边跟读一边写单词，开始写名字和地址，然后写诗歌或短文。以上练习需在长时间内反复操练才能达到效果。

▋5.1.5 原/译语概述

原/译语概述是在影子跟读基础上的进一步练习。原语概述是学员跟读完一段讲话内容以后，根据自己的记忆对刚刚跟读的内容用同种语言进行概述，总结该段讲话内容的主要思想。译语概述则是在原语概述训练一段时间以后对所跟读的内容用译语进行概述。学员先练习原语概述，刚开始跟读时内容可以稍微短一点，在掌握要领之后可逐步拉长。该练习的目的是训练学员边听、边说、边抓主要大意的能力。在熟练掌握了原语复述的技巧之后，学员即可开始译语概述的练习，通过该练习即可逐步过渡到同声传译。在进行原/译语概述时，学员无须过度强调句式结构和细节内容，而是学会用简练的语言传达原语的主要思想和核心信息。该练习有助于学员学会抓住所听讲话的层次和逻辑关系。

▋5.1.6 运用笔记技巧

同声传译中无须用到笔记，但在交替传译中笔记却发挥了不可或缺的作用。其重要性主要在于，它能有效地减轻译员大脑的信息负荷，弥补其短时记忆不足的缺陷。另外，做笔记的过程也是一个思维整理的过程，有助于译员把被动记忆转化为主动记忆，提高口译记忆的效率及质量。口译笔记不同于学生的课堂笔记，也不同于会议记录，更不同于使用一定的速记符号的"速记"。口译笔记只是译员为了完成某一特定的翻译任务，把精力集中在理解源语和抓住关键信息上，边听边思考，在本子上或纸上记下能辅助自己记忆的关键词或符号。

长期的知识积累和充分的译前准备对于提高译员的长时记忆效果比较有帮助，而有效的笔记、影子跟读练习和原/译语概述练习则有助于改善译员的短时记忆能力。总而言之，记忆是口译过程中非常关键的一部分。通过科学合理的训练方法，译员的记忆能力能够得到有效的提高。

其他方法还有复述电影故事、源语单句重复、目标语段落概述、听抄、模拟会议等。

5.2 主题口译(Topic Interpreting)

▋5.2.1 单句口译(Sentence Practice)

Please interpret the following sentences by using the techniques illustrated above. You may interpret to your partner first and then he/she comments on your performance.

(1) They are questions that require decisions and trade-offs from every part of the institution.

(2) I want to focus for a few minutes on three essential features of universities.

(3) Universities have long been regarded as engines of opportunity and excellence.

(4) It is undeniable that keeping higher education affordable is crucial to the nation and crucial to the universities.

(5) Just as we are committed to bringing the brightest minds to fill our classroom, so we must continue to invest in exceptional faculty to lead them and to pursue the work of discovery.

(6) 你们选择教育事业是明智的，这是一个充满无限可能的职业。

(7) 你们可以为这世上的小孩子、青少年、成年人的心智发展提供机会，于是他们可以用自己的力量使环境和社会变得更加人性化、更加公平。

(8) 我们需要开办一所接纳不同性别、不同种族、不同宗教信仰和不同社会背景的孩子的学校。

(9) 哈佛凭借其悠久的传统、标志性的声望和吸引无数优秀学子和教师的深厚内涵，在所有的大学里遥遥领先。

(10) 就算处在最艰难的环境中，你们还是有力量让明天变得更美好。

5.2.2　对话口译(Dialogue Practice)

1. Vocabulary Work: Study the following words and phrases and translate them into the target language.

disseminate	reaffirm
peer	undertake
accountability	magnify
architect	recession

2. Read the following dialogue and interpret it into the target language .

A：在您看来，大学所肩负的责任是什么？

B：knowledge – and people with knowledge – are critical to addressing the challenges that face us. This is what we do as a university and this is who we are.

A：该怎样做呢？

B：We produce knowledge, and we disseminate it – as we teach our students, as we share the fruits of our research.

A：的确如此。

B：But even as we reaffirm the importance of universities and their work, we have begun to see that we need to do this work differently.

A：具体怎么做呢？

B：As a university community we have spent a great deal of time this year focused on these difficult new realities – beginning to decide what we can and must live without.

A：这一点很重要。

B：Yes. For all this work, we are still at the outset of a process that will define our future and, as our peers undertake similar exercises, the future of higher education.

A：明确自身的责任至关重要啊！

B：Yes. I spoke about that accountability before – what we at universities owe one another as teachers, students, and scholars and what we as universities owe the world.

A：不同的情况下，我们的责任也不同。

B：You are right. These responsibilities, this accountability, have now been magnified by the times that confront us. We cannot simply serve as stewards or curators of our university's storied traditions and proud distinction. We must define and shape the purposes of universities for a changed future.

A：著名的中世纪历史学家卡洛琳·拜纳姆曾说："变化迫使我们询问自己的身份。"什么是转瞬即逝的？什么又是必不可少的？什么只不过是习惯？

B：These are good questions. Our accountability – to our university, to one another, and to higher education – means that we must ask these questions and we must seize the moment of change and opportunity before us.

A：变化可以发生在我们身上，也可以通过我们而发生。

B：Exactly. We must make sure we become its architects, not its victims. We must ask ourselves what it is we want to be on the other side of recession and crisis – when the world has reached what we might call "a new normal". How should we envision ourselves and our purposes?

5.2.3　篇章口译[Passage Practice(E to C)]

1. Vocabulary Work: Study the following words and phrases and translate them into the target language.

precious	resilience
personalization	accomplish
massive	adjust
emotional	permanence

2. Please interpret the following paragraph by using the techniques illustrated above.

There are so many moments of joy ahead of you. That trip you always wanted to take. A first kiss with someone you really like. The day you get a job doing something you truly believe in. All of these things will happen to you. Enjoy each and every one. // I hope that you live your life—each precious day of it—with joy and meaning. I hope that you walk without pain—and that you are grateful for each step. // And when the challenges come, I hope you remember that anchored deep within you is the ability to learn and grow. You are not born with a fixed amount of resilience. Like a muscle, you can build it up, draw on it when you need it. In that process you will figure out who you really are—and you just might become the very best version of yourself. // Build resilience in yourselves. When tragedy or disappointment strike, know that you have the ability to get through absolutely anything. I promise you do. As the saying goes, we are more vulnerable than we ever thought, but we are stronger than we ever imagined. // Build resilient organizations. If anyone can do it, you can, because Berkeley is filled with people who want to make the world a better place. Never stop working to do so—whether it's a boardroom that is not representative or a campus that's not safe. Speak up, especially at institutions like this one, which you hold so dear. When you see something that's broken, go fix it. // Build resilient communities. We find our humanity—our will to live and our ability to love—in our connections to one another. Be there for your family and friends.

3. Please interpret the following passage by using the techniques illustrated above. Please pay attention to the underlined sentences as they require special treatment during interpreting.

① Commencement Address by Sheryl Sandberg[1] (Excerpts)

② Today is a day of celebration. A day to celebrate all the hard work that got you to this moment.

③ Today is a day of thanks. A day to thank those who helped you get here—nurtured you, taught you, cheered you on, and dried your tears. Or at least the ones who didn't draw on you with a Sharpie when you fell asleep at a party.

④ Today is a day of reflection. Because today marks the end of one era of your life and the beginning of something new.

⑤ A commencement address is meant to be a dance between youth and wisdom. You have the youth. Someone comes in to be the voice of wisdom—that's supposed to be me. I stand up here and tell you all the things I have learned in life, you throw your cap in the air, you let your family take a million photos —don't forget to post them on Instagram[2]—and everyone goes home happy.

⑥ Today will be a bit different. We will still do the caps and you still have to do the photos. But I am not here to tell you all the things I've learned in life. Today I will try to tell you what I learned in death.

⑦ I have never spoken publicly about this before. It's hard. But I will do my very best not to blow my nose on this beautiful Berkeley robe.[3]

⑧ One year and thirteen days ago, I lost my husband, Dave[4]. His death was sudden and unexpected. We were at a friend's fiftieth birthday party in Mexico. I took a nap. Dave went to work out. What followed was the unthinkable—walking into a gym to find him lying on the floor.

Flying home to tell my children that their father was gone. Watching his casket being lowered into the ground.

⑨ For many months afterward, and at many times since, I was swallowed up in the deep fog of grief—what I think of as the void—an emptiness that fills your heart, your lungs, constricts your ability to think or even to breathe.

⑩ Dave's death changed me in very profound ways. I learned about the depths of sadness and the brutality of loss. But I also learned that when life sucks you under, you can kick against the bottom, break the surface, and breathe again. I learned that in the face of the void—or in the face of any challenge—you can choose joy and meaning.

⑪ I'm sharing this with you in the hopes that today you can learn the lessons that I only learned in death. Lessons about hope, strength, and the light within us that will not be extinguished.

⑫ You wanted an A but you got a B. OK, let's be honest—you got an A— but you're still mad. You applied for an internship at Facebook, but you only got one from Google.

⑬ Game of Thrones the show has diverged way too much from the books—and you bothered to read all four thousand three hundred and fifty-two pages.

⑭ You will almost certainly face more and deeper adversity. There's loss of opportunity: the job that doesn't work out, the illness or accident that changes everything in an instant. There's loss of dignity: the sharp sting of prejudice when it happens. There's loss of love: the broken relationships that can't be fixed. And sometimes there's loss of life itself.

⑮ Some of you have already experienced the kind of tragedy and hardship that leave an indelible mark. Last year, Radhika spoke so beautifully about the sudden loss of her mother.

⑯ The question is not if some of these things will happen to you. They will. Today I want to talk about what happens next. About the things you can do to overcome adversity, no matter what form it takes or when it hits you. The easy days ahead of you will be easy. It is the hard days—the times that challenge you to your very core—that will determine who you are. You will be defined not just by what you achieve, but by how you survive.

⑰ A few weeks after Dave died, I was talking to my friend Phil about a father-son activity that Dave was not here to do. We came up with a plan to fill in for Dave. I cried to him, "But I want Dave." Phil put his arm around me and said, "Option A is not available. So let's just kick the shit out of option B."

⑱ We all at some point live some form of option B. The question is: What do we do then?

⑲ As a representative of Silicon Valley, I'm pleased to tell you there is data to learn from. After spending decades studying how people deal with setbacks, psychologist Martin Seligman found that there are three P's—personalization, pervasiveness, and permanence—that are critical to how we bounce back from hardship. The seeds of resilience are planted in the way we process the negative events in our lives.

⑳ The first P is personalization—the belief that we are at fault. This is different from taking responsibility, which you should always do. This is the lesson that not everything that happens to us happens because of us.

㉑ When Dave died, I had a very common reaction, which was to blame myself. He died in seconds from a cardiac arrhythmia. I poured over his medical records asking what I could have—or should have—done. It wasn't until I learned about the three P's that I accepted that I could not have prevented his death. His doctors had not identified his coronary artery disease. I was an economics major; how could I have?

㉒ Studies sow that getting past personalization can actually make you stronger. Teachers who knew they could do better after students failed adjusted their methods and saw future classes go on to excel. College swimmers who underperformed but believed they were capable of swimming faster did. Not taking failures personally allows us to recover—and even to thrive.

㉓ The second P is pervasiveness—the belief that an event will affect all areas of your life. You know that song "Everything is awesome?" This is the flip: "Everything is awful." There's no place to run or hide from the all-consuming sadness.

㉔ The child psychologists I spoke to encouraged me to get my kids back to their routine as soon as possible. So ten days after Dave died, they went back to school and I went back to work. I remember sitting in my first Facebook meeting in a deep, deep haze. All I could think was, "What is everyone talking about and how could this possibly matter?" But then I got drawn into the discussion and for a second—a brief split second—I forgot about death.

㉕ That brief second helped me see that there were other things in my life that were not awful. My children and I were healthy. My friends and family were so loving and they carried us—quite literally at times.

㉖ The loss of a partner often has severe negative financial consequences, especially for women. So many single mothers—and fathers—struggle to make ends meet or have jobs that don't allow them the time they need to care for their children. I had financial security, the ability to take the time off I needed, and a job. Gradually, my children started sleeping through the night, crying less, playing more.

㉗ The third P is permanence—the belief that the sorrow will last forever. For months, no matter what I did, it felt like the crushing grief would always be there.

㉘ We often project our current feelings out indefinitely—and experience what I think of as the second derivative of those feelings. We feel anxious—and then we feel anxious that we're anxious. We feel sad—and then we feel sad that we're sad. Instead, we should accept our feelings—but recognize that they will not last forever. My rabbi told me that time would heal but for now I should "lean in to the suck." It was good advice, but not really what I meant by "lean in." (5)

㉙ None of you need me to explain the fourth P ... which is, of course, pizza from

Cheese Board.

㉚ But I wish I had known about the three P's when I was your age. There were so many times these lessons would have helped.

㉛ Day one of my first job out of college, my boss found out that I didn't know how to enter data into Lotus 1-2-3. That's a spreadsheet—ask your parents. His mouth dropped open and he said, 'I can't believe you got this job without knowing that"—and then walked out of the room. I went home convinced that I was going to be fired. I thought I was terrible at everything... but it turns out I was only terrible at spreadsheets. Understanding pervasiveness would have saved me a lot of anxiety that week.

㉜ I wish I had known about permanence when I broke up with boyfriends. It would've been a comfort to know that feeling was not going to last forever, and if I was being honest with myself... neither were any of those relationships.

㉝ And I wish I had understood personalization when boyfriends broke up with me. Sometimes it's not you—it really is them. I mean, that dude never showered.

㉞ And all three P's ganged up on me in my twenties after my first marriage ended in divorce. I thought at the time that no matter what I accomplished, I was a massive failure.

㉟ The three P's are common emotional reactions to so many things that happen to us—in our careers, our personal lives, and our relationships. You're probably feeling one of them right now about something in your life. But if you can recognize you are falling into these traps, you can catch yourself. Just as our bodies have a physiological immune system, our brains have a psychological immune system—and there are steps you can take to help kick it into gear.

㊱ One day my friend Adam Grant, a psychologist, suggested that I think about how much worse things could be. This was completely counterintuitive; it seemed like the way to recover was to try to find positive thoughts. "Worse?" I said. "Are you kidding me? How could things be worse?" His answer cut straight through me: "Dave could have had that same cardiac arrhythmia while he was driving your children." Wow. The moment he said it, I was overwhelmingly grateful that the rest of my family was alive and healthy. That gratitude overtook some of the grief.

㊲ Finding gratitude and appreciation is key to resilience. People who take the time to list things they are grateful for are happier and healthier. It turns out that counting your blessings can actually increase your blessings. My New Year's resolution this year is to write down three moments of joy before I go to bed each night. This simple practice has changed my life. Because no matter what happens each day, I go to sleep thinking of something cheerful. Try it.

㊳ Last month, eleven days before the anniversary of Dave's death, I broke down crying to a friend of mine. We were sitting—of all places—on a bathroom floor. I said: "Eleven days. One year ago, he had eleven days left. And we had no idea." We looked at each other through tears, and asked how we would live if we knew we had eleven days left.

㊴ As you graduate, can you ask yourselves to live as if you had eleven days left? I don't mean blow everything off and party all the time— although tonight is an exception. I mean live with the understanding of how precious every single day would be. How precious every day actually is.

㊵ A few years ago, my mom had to have her hip replaced. When she was younger, she always walked without pain. But as her hip disintegrated, each step became painful. Now, even years after her operation, she is grateful for every step she takes without pain—something that never would have occurred to her before.

㊶ As I stand here today, a year after the worst day of my life, two things are true. I have a huge reservoir of sadness that is with me always—right here where I can touch it. I never knew I could cry so often—or so much.

㊷ But I am also aware that I am walking without pain. For the first time, I am grateful for each breath in and out—grateful for the gift of life itself. I used to celebrate my birthday every five years and friends' birthdays sometimes. Now I celebrate always. I used to go to sleep worrying about all the things I messed up that day—and trust me that list was often quite long. Now I try really hard to focus on each day's moments of joy.

㊸ It is the greatest irony of my life that losing my husband helped me find deeper gratitude—gratitude for the kindness of my friends, the love of my family, the laughter of my children. My hope for you is that you can find that gratitude—not just on the good days, like today, but on the hard ones, when you will really need it.

㊹ Lift each other up, help each other kick the shit out of option B—and celebrate each and every moment of joy.

㊺ You have the whole world in front of you. I can't wait to see what you do with it.

㊻ Congratulations, and Go Bears!

Notes on the text

(1) <u>Sheryl Sandberg</u>

雪莉·桑德伯格是十足的商界女强人，脸书(Facebook)的二当家，执掌上千亿美元市值的商业帝国。然而正在她事业蓬勃之际，她的丈夫却撒手人寰，她又有着惊人的毅力克服悲痛。在丈夫去世一年后，脸书(Facebook)首席运营官雪莉·桑德伯格学会了如何更有韧性。她在周末加州大学伯克利分校的毕业典礼上分享了自己的经历，并有可能将其写入自己的第二本书中。在演讲过程中，她数度哽咽。马克·扎克伯格在桑德伯格这篇演讲的下面评论："如此美丽而又激励人心，谢谢你。"

(2) Instagram

Instagram是一款跨平台(iOS、Android、Windows Phone)的图片社交应用，以正方形照

片和个性的滤镜效果获得用户的青睐，搭配强大的社交分享功能，支持脸书(Facebook)、推特(Twitter)、新浪微博、轻博客(Tumblr)等社交网站，为用户搭建起快速分享生活瞬间的平台。Instagram 的创意来自于即时成像相机，命名取自"Instant(即时的)"与"-gram(记录)"，意为"像电报般即时分享照片"。

(3) But I will do my very best not to blow my nose on this beautiful Berkeley robe.

今天我会尽量不哭，不用漂亮的伯克利大学长袍来擦鼻子。

(4) Dave

戴夫•桑德伯格，雪莉•桑德伯格的丈夫，曾担任雅虎副总裁一职，创办了Yahoo! Music的前身Launch Media，然后于2009年加入了调查猴子公司(SurveyMonkey)。在他的管理下，调查猴子(SurveyMonkey)从一个员工数屈指可数的小公司壮大到员工数超过450人、用户超过2500万的大型企业，就连脸书(Facebook)联合创始人马克•扎克伯格(Mark Zuckerberg)都曾评价他是"一个了不起的人"。《财富》杂志高级编辑亚当•拉辛斯基(Adam Lashinsky)在《财富》上撰文对桑德伯格进行了一番缅怀，他写道："桑德伯格拥有着百科全书般的历史知识，且在硅谷和音乐领域有着非常广泛的人脉。桑德伯格可以将一件看似非常复杂的商业交易以通俗易懂的语言向他人解释清楚，且他一直以来都是多笔硅谷交易案背后的神秘天使投资人，同时也有许多投资公司和个人都希望能够得到他的投资建议以及人脉资源。总的来说，你或许一辈子都很难遇到这样一个富有天赋、成功、聪明、善良、谦虚以及被整个行业所广泛爱戴的人物。"

(5) It was good advice, but not really what I meant by "lean in."

这是个好建议，但并不是指的我写的那本书《向前一步》。

5.2.4 篇章口译[Passage Practice(C to E)]

1. Vocabulary Work: Study the following words and phrases and translate them into the target language.

受益者	辍学
教科文组织	梦想
女高音	教育资源
呼吁	倡议

2. Please interpret the following paragraph by using the techniques illustrated above.

当我还是个孩子时，我总是喜欢阅读那些英雄神话故事，他们往往与坏人战斗，必须要经历许多磨难，之后他或她才能从此过上幸福快乐的生活。// 正义总能战胜邪恶这种想法陪伴着我长大。好莱坞电影也是这样。无论在电影里发生什么，你都可以假定最后好人赢得胜利。// 嗯，即使这些故事并不真实，即使我们很少面临险境，从英雄的故事或电影当中我们分享到的是一些相同之处。我们每天都学习到经验教训。就像里面的人物，从我的每日冒险中可以学到东西。// 有时候冒险有点普通，但是你的经历却是……我们学习到经验和教训越多，我们越能汲取教训并使以后的冒险更容易，或者至少我们可以接受更大的挑战或至少避免犯同样的错误。

3. Please interpret the following passage by using the techniques illustrated above. Please pay attention to the underlined sentences as they require special treatment during interpreting.

彭丽媛在"教育第一"全球倡议高级别会议上的演讲

① 博科娃总干事女士们、先生们：

② 在联合国纪念成立70周年之际，我很荣幸能够参加这一重要倡议的相关活动。

③ 我对教育感念至深。我的父亲生长在中国一个非常小的村庄里。在那些岁月里，许多村民都不识字，因此我的父亲开办了一所夜校帮助他们识字。在他的帮助下，许多人学会了写自己的名字；在他的帮助下，许多人有生以来第一次读报；在他的帮助下，许多妇女开始有能力教自己的孩子读书写字。作为她的女儿，我知道教育对一个人来说意味着什么，特别是那些没有文化的人。

④ 经过几代人的努力，中国的教育取得了巨大的进步。我自己就是这一进步的受益者。否则，我不会成为一个女高音和一名声乐教授。我在中国音乐学院教书，沿着父亲的足迹，帮助复制中国的成功故事。(1)

⑤ 我要感谢教科文组织任命我为"促进女童和妇女教育特使"(2)。我对与联合国一道工作、为了全球教育做些工作感到由衷的荣幸。我访问了世界上的许多学校，我亲眼看到，我们在教育工作上还有很多的事情可以做。

⑥ 教育事关妇女和女童。女童入学非常重要，因为她们有一天会成为自己孩子的第一位老师。然而，妇女依然占世界贫穷人口的一半，她们中有六成成年人不识字。教育是解决此类不平等的关键。在中国，"春蕾计划"已经帮助300万女童重返校园。(3)许多人读完了大学，并在工作岗位上表现出色。

⑦ 教育事关平等。在贫穷国家和地区，辍学儿童的人数高得惊人。我们呼吁将更多的教育资源投入这些地方。

⑧ 教育事关年轻人。年轻人是我们的未来。教育之所以重要，是因为它不仅给年轻人带来知识，还帮助他们成为负责任的公民。

⑨ 作为教科文组织的"促进女童和妇女教育特使"和一名母亲，我对人人享有教育的承诺永不改变。许多年前，我的父亲使他的村庄发生了改变。团结起来，我们可以使这个世界得到巨大改变。

⑩ 我曾经被问道自己的梦想是什么。我说我希望所有的儿童，特别是女童，都可以接受良好的教育。这就是我的中国梦。我相信有一天"教育优先"将不再是一个梦想，它将变成这个星球上每一个妇女都能享有的现实。(4)谢谢大家。

Notes on the text

(1) 我在中国音乐学院教书，沿着父亲的足迹，帮助复制中国的成功故事。

I am following my father's footsteps by teaching at China's Conservatory of Music to help continue China's success story.

(2) 促进女童和妇女教育特使

the Special Envoy for Women and Girls Education

(3) 在中国，"春蕾计划"已经帮助300万女童重返校园。

In China，Spring Bud Education Program has helped over 3 million girls go back to school.

(4) 我相信有一天"教育优先"将不再是一个梦想，它将变成这个星球上每一个妇女都能享有的现实。

I believe one day education first will no longer be a dream，it will be a reality enjoyed by every young woman on this planet.

5.3　参考译文(Reference Version)

5.3.1　单句口译(Sentence Practice)

Please interpret the following sentences by using the techniques illustrated above. You may interpret to your partner first and then he/she comments on your performance.

(1) 这些问题也需要学校各部门进行决策和权衡。

(2) 接下来几分钟，我想集中谈谈大学的三个基本特征。

(3) 大学长期以来都被看成创造机会和卓越的发动机。

(4) 让学生读得起大学对我们国家和大学来说都是至关重要的。

(5) 既然我们矢志不移地将最聪明的学生吸收到我们的学校里来，我们就必须继续投入大量的师资来引导他们并从事探索的工作。

(6) You are very wise to have chosen a profession that will allow you to create spaces of possibility.

(7) You expand the opportunities for children, youth and adults around the world to develop their minds and their hearts, so they can work to make their communities and societies more humane and more just.

(8) We need to have a school that would welcome girls and boys, children of different races, of different religions, of different social backgrounds.

(9) With its great tradition, its iconic reputation and its unmatched capacity to attract brilliant students and faculty, Harvard stands out among universities.

(10) Even under the most challenging circumstances, you have the power to contribute to make a future that is better than the present.

5.3.2 对话口译(Dialogue Practice)

1. Vocabulary Work: Study the following words and phrases and translate them into the target language.

传播，扩散	重申
同行，同辈	从事
责任	放大
缔造者	经济衰退

2. Read the following dialogue and interpret it into the target language.

A：In your opinion, what's the responsibility of a university?

B：知识——以及有知识的人——对于应对我们目前面临的挑战是至关重要的。这正是我们大学该做的，是我们的身份。

A：How to do it, then ?

B：当我们教育学生、分享科研成果的时候，就生产并传播了知识。

A：That's right.

B：但是，即便我们重申大学及其工作的重要性，我们也已经看到我们必须用一种不同的方式来完成这项任务。

A：How?

B：作为一所大学，我们今年已经把大量的时间花在研究这些艰难的现实上，并渐渐开始明确为了生存我们可以和必须舍弃的东西是哪些。

A：It's very important.

B：是的，很重要。所有这些工作我们都还只是开了个头，但它们将决定我们的未来，并且随着我们的同行采取类似的措施，它们也将决定高等教育的未来。

A：It's necessary to clarify our responsibilities.

B：是的。以前我曾谈论过"责任"——在大学里，老师、学生或者是学者之间相互负有什么责任和义务，作为大学，我们对世界又负有什么责任和义务。

A：We have different responsibilities in different situations.

B：你说的很对。这些责任，这种义务现在被我们面临的这个时代放大了。我们不能只是简单地做我们大学举世闻名的传统或骄傲的荣誉的管理者。为了应对一个不同于往常的未来，我们必须定义并发展大学的目标。

A：The distinguished medieval historian Caroline Bynum once observed that "change is what forces us to ask who we are". What is ephemeral? What is essential? What is just habit?

B：问得好。我们对我们的大学、对彼此及对高等教育所担负的责任意味着我们必须思考这些问题，必须把握变化的瞬间及眼前的机会。

A：Change can happen to us – or through us.

B：完全正确。我们必须确保我们是变化的缔造者，而不是它的受害者。当世界达到了我们所谓的"新标准"时，我们必须问问自己，我们希望经济萧条和危机的另一面是什么？我们应当如何设想我们的未来及我们的目标？

5.3.3　篇章口译[Passage Practice(E to C)]

1. Vocabulary Work: Study the following words and phrases and translate them into the target language

珍奇的，珍贵的	恢复能力
个人化	完成
巨大的	调整，适应
感情的	持久性

2. Please interpret the following paragraph by using the techniques illustrated above.

未来你们会有很多快乐的时刻。你们一直想去的旅行。与你们超级喜欢的人第一次接吻。找到一份和你价值观相符且热爱的工作。这些事情都将会发生在你们身上。请尽情享受每一件事情。//我希望你们好好活着，快乐地、有意义地过好你们珍贵的每一天。我希望你们没有痛苦地行走，这意味着你们要好好珍惜你们所走的每一步。//然后，当挑战来临的时候，我希望你们能够记得，在你们内心深处牢牢稳固着的，是你们可以不断学习和成长的能力。你们并非天生具有从苦难中康复的能力，但是这种能力就像肌肉一样，是可以锻炼的，然后当你们需要时就可以用到它。在这个过程中，你们会明白你们自己是谁，你们也会知道你们可以成为最好的自己。//请在你们的内心建立起恢复能力。当你在生活中遇到不幸的时候，你们会懂得，实际上你们有能力战胜那些不幸。相信我，你们绝对有这个能力。就像俗话说的一样，我们比我们想象的更脆弱，但我们也比我们想象的更强大。//请建立互助的恢复组织。如果别人可以做到，你们也可以做到，因为伯克利大学充满了想要把这个世界变得更美好的人。永远不要放弃坚持做到这个，不管是在一个没有代表性的会议室，不管是在一个不安全的校园。请大声地说出来，尤其是在这样的一个大学，你们无比珍视的大学。当你们看到一件事情不对，请尝试修正它。//也请建立恢复团体。在我们与彼此联系中，我们发现了我们的人性——我们的生存意志和我们的爱的能力。请成为你们家人和朋友的依靠。

3. Please interpret the following passage by using the techniques illustrated above.

① 雪莉·桑德伯格在毕业典礼上的演讲(节选)

② 今天是值得庆祝的一天。庆祝你们为今天所付出的一切努力。

③ 今天是充满感谢的一天。感谢那些帮助你们的人，那些熏陶过你们，教导过你们，为你们欢呼，宽慰过你们的人。或者，你们至少得感谢那些当你们在派对上昏昏欲睡时，没有拿记号笔在你们脸上涂鸦的人。

④ 今天也是让你们反思的一天。因为今天意味着你们人生一个阶段的结束，也是你们下一段崭新冒险的起点。

⑤ 毕业演讲应该是青春和智慧的交汇。你们正值青春年少，而我作为毕业典礼的演讲人应该充满着智慧。我站在这里告诉你们我的人生经验，你们将你们的毕业帽抛在空

中，你们让你们的家人拍上万张纪念照(别忘了发在Instagram上)，最后所有人兴高采烈地各回各家。

⑥ 但是今天会有些不同寻常。我们还是会抛毕业帽，你们会照很多照片。可接下来我不会和你们说我的人生经验，我会试着和你们分享我从死亡中学到的领悟。

⑦ 我从未在公众场合谈过这个话题。对我来说，真的很难开口。今天我会尽量不哭，不用漂亮的伯克利大学长袍来擦鼻子。

⑧ 一年零十三天前，我失去了我的丈夫，戴夫。事情发生得非常突然和出人意料。我们当时在墨西哥参加一个朋友五十岁的生日聚会。我正在午睡，戴夫去做运动。之后发生的一切都是不堪回首的：比如我发现他躺在体育馆的地板上，停止了呼吸；比如我不得不独自飞回家，告诉我的孩子们他们父亲的死讯；比如我眼睁睁看着他的棺材渐渐地没入地面。

⑨ 在那之后的好几个月，在那之后的很多时候，我感觉我自己要被悲痛吞噬了。那是种填满你的心脏、你的肺、限制你思考，甚至让你无法呼吸的空虚。

⑩ 戴夫的离去深深地改变了我。我知道了悲伤的深度，痛失挚爱的残酷。但同时，我也领悟到，当你们的生活沉入谷底，你们可以反击，冲破表层的障碍，再次呼吸。我认识到，当你们面对无边无际的空虚，又或者当你们面临任何挑战，你们可以选择过快乐的和有意义的人生。

⑪ 今天，我希望你们可以学习到一些我对于死亡的体悟——那些关于希望，力量，以及我心中永不灭的光。

⑫ 你们渴望得到A，但你们只得到个B。好吧，咱实话实说，你们拿到A-却依然不开心。你们申请做脸书的实习生，但你们只拿到了谷歌的录用意向。

⑬ "权力的游戏"的电视剧版已经脱离原著太多了，你们也没有兴致去读四千三百五十二页的原著。

⑭ 你们肯定很快就会面临更多和更惨的不幸——你们有可能会错失机会，你们工作失利，一场疾病或事故会在一瞬间改变你们的一切。你们有可能会丧失尊严，尖锐的偏见会深深刺痛你们。你们有可能会痛失挚爱，破裂的感情无法修复。而有的时候是生命本身的失去。

⑮ 你们有些人或许已经经历过了以上的一些悲剧和困难，那些事情也给你们的人生烙上了深深的印记。去年，拉迪迦和你们分享了她痛失母亲的故事。

⑯ 问题不在于这些事情是否会在你们的身上发生。因为它们最终会的。因此，今天我想和你们说的是，当悲剧发生了之后，你们该如何应对？其实不论是哪种不幸，不管它发生在何时。该轻松的日子你仍旧会很轻松，至于那些承载着苦难的时光，那些从根本上挑战你每一份坚持的日子，将最终决定你会是一个怎样的人。最终被用以塑造你的是你所走过的那些艰难，而非浮名虚利。

⑰ 在戴夫离世后的几个星期后，我和朋友菲尔聊起一件本应该由戴夫去完成的一件父子间互动的事情。我们虽然找到了一个弥补方案，我还是哭着对他说："可我还是想要戴夫。"那时，菲尔搂着我，说："第一个选择不存在了，我们只好将就着用第二个

选择。"

⑱ 是的。在有些时候，我们除了第二个选择，别无他选。那么在这样的时候，我们该如何是好？

⑲ 作为硅谷的一员，我很高兴地告诉你们我这么说是有数据可参考的。在花费几十年的时间研究人们如何面对挫折之后，心理学家马丁·塞利格曼发现，三个P(后文总结为三个假象)——个人化(Personalization)、普遍性(Pervasiveness)和持久性(Permanence)——是我们从苦难中再次振作起来的关键。我们所经历的每一次挫折，都会在灵魂深处种下坚韧的种子。

⑳ 第一个假象是个人化：总以为是自己做错了什么才导致不幸的发生。这与承担责任不同，责任是你们该做的。你们要懂得的是，并非所有发生在你们身上的不幸都是由你们自身引起的。

㉑ 我的丈夫去世后，我有一个很常见的行为，就是会责怪自己。戴夫是在几秒钟内死于心脏病突发的。当我翻阅他的病历，我不停地责问自己：我本来可以做些什么的，那样或许戴夫就不会死了。直到我了解了三个P的假象，我才接受了我无法阻止他死亡。他的医生们没有发现他的冠心病。我是学经济学的，我怎么可能发现呢？

㉒ 研究显示，停止埋怨自己是可以逐渐让你变得更加强大的方法之一。一个有能力但是却无法令学生适应他教学方法的老师在走出自责之后，可以在未来的教学中做得更加出色。而学校的游泳运动员在原谅自己偶尔的发挥失常之后，也通常可以获得更加出色的成绩。不要总是将失败完全归咎于自己。这样你才能够快速走出失意，甚至做得更好。

㉓ 第二个假象是普遍性——以为某一件事会影响到你生活的全部。你们知道那首叫"一切都是极好的"的歌吗？那时的一切就是这首歌的反调："面对那吞噬一切的悲哀，我们无处逃避。"但实际上并不是这样的。

㉔ 一个儿童心理学家曾鼓励我尽快引导我的孩子们回到正常的生活轨道。所以，在戴夫去世的十天后，孩子们开始上学，我开始工作。我记得，那是在我丈夫去世之后第一次参加脸书的会议，我的精神十分恍惚。我心里想的是"他们所有人在讲些什么，这些和我有关系吗？"后来我被卷入了讨论，有那么一秒的时间我忘记了我丈夫的逝世。

㉕ 那短短的一秒钟让我看到我的生命中还有其他并不可怕的东西。我和我的孩子们都健健康康的。我的朋友和家人都深爱着我们，都陪伴支撑着我们。其实毫不夸张地说，很多时候都是这样的。

㉖ 失去伴侣往往会引发严重不利的经济后果，尤其是对女性而言。因此，许多单身母亲和父亲必须为生存而不懈奋斗，繁忙的工作往往不允许他们有足够的时间去照顾孩子。但我有经济保障，我有时间照顾孩子，我还有一份工作。渐渐地，我的孩子们开始在晚上安然入睡，他们越来越少哭闹，他们又能玩耍了。

㉗ 第三个假象是永久性——以为悲伤将永远持续下去。有那么好几个月，无论我做什么，我都感觉那令人窒息的悲伤将永远伴随着我。

㉘ 我们有时候觉得自己现在感受到的情感是会无限期地存在的，然后我们会经历由情感衍生来的其他情绪。我们首先会感到焦虑，然后会为自己的焦虑而焦虑。我们觉得伤心，然后又会为自己的伤心而伤心。实际上，我们应该接受自己的感情。但同时，也应该清楚地明白，它们并不会永远地持续下去。我的犹太教拉比告诉我，时间会治愈一切，但现在我需要向前一步去直面悲剧。这是个好建议，但并不是指我写的那本书《向前一步》。

㉙ 至于第四个P……就不需要我来解释了，你们都懂的，这自然是奶酪板上的披萨嘛。(有什么事儿一个披萨不能解决的，那就来两个！)

㉚ 话又说回来，我其实很希望我在你们这个年龄的时候，就能够了解到有关失败假象的这三个理论。现在回想起来，知晓这些事情，实际上可以从很大程度上帮助曾经的我。

㉛ 当我还在做大学毕业后的第一份工作时，我的老板发现我不懂操作Lotus 1-2-3表格。这是一个电子表格——去问问你们的父母就知道了。他张大着嘴惊讶地说："我简直不敢相信，你们连这个都不会，却能得到这份工作。"然后他走出了房间。我回家的时候深信我会被解雇。我以为我在所有事情上都很糟糕。但事实证明，我只不过是不太擅长做电子表格罢了。如果早些知道"普遍性"的假象，我当时就不会那样焦虑了。

㉜ 现在回忆起来曾经和男朋友分手的事，我也希望我那时可以理解"永久性"的假象。这样一来我就可以自我宽慰。因为我会早知道，那种感觉其实不会永远持续下去，如果我对自己诚实的话，我就会懂得任何关系都不是永远存在的。

㉝ 当我的男朋友和我分手时，我也希望已经理解了"个人化"的假象。有的事情，不是你的过错，真的是别人的过错。我的意思是说，那家伙从来不洗澡。

㉞ 在我20多岁时，我的第一次婚姻以离婚告终，那时所有的失败假象都在一同折磨着我。我当时认为无论我已经有了怎样的成就，我都是一个大写的失败。

㉟ 这三个假象是我们面对许多事情时会产生的常见反应，在事业上，在个人生活中，在人际关系上。你们或许会觉得你们现在就面对着它们中的一个。但是，如果你们能认清你们正落入了这些陷阱，你们就能自救。正如我们的身体有一个生理免疫系统，我们的大脑也有一个精神免疫系统，有一些步骤可以帮助你们开启你们的精神免疫系统。

㊱ 有一天，我的心理学家朋友亚当·格兰特建议我想象事情本可以更糟糕。这完全是反直觉的。"更糟糕？"我说，"你是在逗我吗？事情怎么可能会变得比现在还要糟糕呢？"他回答说："戴夫也很有可能在开车带着孩子们出去时突发心脏病。"意识到这一点的那一瞬，我很强烈地感激我家里的其他人都还安然无事地活着。这种感激之情在那一瞬间超越了我心中的苦楚。

㊲ 试着去寻找那些让你们觉得感恩的事情，这是从悲伤中复原的关键。那些能够花时间列出值得让自己感动的小事情的人，会变得越来越快乐和健康。事实证明，感恩你们的福分可以增加你们的福分。我今年的新年决心是每天晚上睡觉前写下这天的三个幸福时刻。这件简单的事情已经改变了我的生活。因为不管每一天发生什么，我都会想着快乐的事情入睡。你们也可以试试。

㊳ 上个月，也就是戴维逝世周年前的十一天，我在一个朋友面前失声痛哭，那时我们坐在浴室地板上。我说："十一天。一年前，他的生命只剩下十一天了，而我们却毫无察觉。"于是我泪眼朦胧地看着对方问道，如果我们知道我们还剩十一天了，我们将如何度过？

㊴ 在你们毕业之际，你们能够做到让自己过得就像生命只剩下最后十一天一样吗？我并不是让你们抛开所有事情，每天都去开派对(今晚例外)。我的意思是，我们应该明白每一天是多么珍贵。每一天真的都是那么珍贵。

㊵ 几年前，我的妈妈不得不做换髋手术。当她还年轻的时候，她走路并没有不舒服。但是，随着她髋部病情的恶化，每走一步都是痛苦的。现在，手术愈合已经好几年了，不过她仍在为能不觉痛苦而迈出的每一步心存感激——如果没有这些经历，恐怕她也不会有这种感恩的心。

㊶ 在我生命中最糟糕的事情发生一年之后的今天，我站在这里，有两件事情是确切存在的。我心里始终有一片望不到尽头的悲伤之海，它就在那里，我可以触摸到它。我从来不知道我可以哭得那么频繁，那么悲痛。

㊷ 但我也知道，我每天都可以正常行走。这是我第一次为我的每一个呼吸而感激，为我依然活着而感激。我过去是每五年庆祝一次我的生日，偶尔庆祝朋友们的生日。如今，我总在庆祝着。我曾经在睡前常常为当天搞砸的事情而揪心着，相信我，真的有好多糟心的事情。现在，我会努力去回顾每天的幸福瞬间。

㊸ 说来讽刺，我失去了丈夫，但这件事却帮我找到了更深的感激——感谢我朋友们的善意、家人们的爱和我的孩子们的欢声笑语。我希望当你们需要时，你们可以怀有那样的感激之情，不仅是为美好的日子感激，也要为艰难的日子而感激。

㊹ 治愈彼此，帮助彼此赶走那些关于第二选择的悲观想法。还有，要记得庆祝你们生命里的每一个小确幸。

㊺ 整个世界都在你们的面前。我迫不及待地想看到你们将做些什么。

㊻ 祝贺你们！加油！

5.3.4 篇章口译[Passage Practice(C to E)]

1. Vocabulary Work: Study the following words and phrases and translate them into the target language.

beneficiary	school dropouts
UNESCO	dream
soprano	educational resources
call for	initiative

2. Please interpret the following paragraphs by using the techniques illustrated above.

When I was a child, I always like reading fairy tales about heroes who were good, who had to go through many difficult situations often battling the bad guys before he or she lived happily ever after.// I grew up thinking that the good always trumped over the evil. Hollywood films are like that too. No matter what happens in the movie, you can assume at the end the good guys win.// Well, even though the stories are not so realistic and even though we rarely face and tasks, there are some similarities we share with the heroes of the stories or the movies. We learn lessons everyday. Just like the characters in, there are lessons to be learned from my daily adventures. // Sometimes the adventures are bit ordinary, but the experience is ... The more experience we have and lessons we learn, the better we can function and the adventures just can easier, or at least we can take on bigger challenges or at least avoid making the same mistakes.

3. Please interpret the following paragraphs by using the techniques illustrated above. Please pay attention to the underlined sentences as they require special treatment during interpreting.

Speech by PengLiyuan at Global Education First Conference

① Director General Bokova Ladies and gentlemen,

② It gives me a great pleasure to join you for this important initiative as the UN marks its 70th anniversary.

③ Education is very close in my heart. My father grew up in a very small village in China. In those days，not many villagers could read. So my father opened a night school to teach them how to read. With his help，many people learned to write their own names; with his help，many people learned to read newspapers for the first time; with his help，many women were able to teach their children how to read. As his daughter，I know what education means to the people，especially those without it.

④ After generations of hard work，China has come a long way in education. I myself am a beneficiary of that progress. Otherwise I would never become a soprano and a professor of musical. I am following my father's footsteps by teaching at China's Conservatory of Music to help continue China's success story.

⑤ I want to thank Director-general Bokova and UNESCO for naming me the Special Envoy for Women and Girls Education. I am truly honored to work with the UN and do something about Global Education. I have visited many schools around the world. I've seen first-hand on how much we can do for education.

⑥ Education is about women and the girls. It is important for girls to go to school because they will become their children's first teacher someday. But women still account for over half of the world's poor in population and 60% of adults who can't read. Education is crucial in addressing such inequalities. In China，Spring Bud Education Program has helped over 3 million girls go back to school. Many of them have finished university education and they are doing well at work.

⑦ Education is about equality. In poor countries and regions the number of school dropouts is astonishing. We call for more educational resources to these places.

⑧ Education is about the young people. Young people are the future. Education is important because it not only gave young people knowledge and skills but also help them become responsible citizens.

⑨ As the UNESCO special envoy and the mother myself my commitment to education for all will never change. Many years ago my father made a small difference in his village. Together we can make a big difference in the world.

⑩ I was once asked about my Chinese dream. I said I hope all children especially girls can have access to good education. This is my Chinese dream. I believe one day education first will no longer be a dream，it will be a reality enjoyed by every young woman on this planet. Thank you very much.

5.4　教育主题词汇汇总(Vocabulary Build-up)

correspondence school	函授学院
middle / high school affiliated to ...	附中
political and ideological education	政治思想教育
to become educated through independent study	自学成才
Ph.D candidate	博士生
post–doctoral	博士后
the national higher education exams for self-taught adults	成人高考/自学考试
college town	大学城
transcript	成绩单
internship; field work	实习
graduation ceremony; commencement	毕业典礼
certificate	毕业证书
higher education	高等教育
institution of higher education	高等学府
comprehensive university	综合性大学
colleges of(liberal) arts	文科院校
college / university of science and engineering	理工科大学
teachers' college / normal college	师范学院
institute of traditional Chinese medicine(TCM)	中医院
(university / college) entrance examination	高考
the college expansion plan	高校扩招

(续表)

visiting professor; guest professor	客座教授
assistant for political and ideological work	辅导员
pedagogy; teaching method	教学法
extracurricular activities	课外活动
class discussion	课堂讨论
required / compulsory course	必修课
elective / optional course	选修课
specialized course	专业课
basic course	基础课
school schedule	课程表
credit	学分

5.5 扩展练习(Enhancement Practice)

Retelling.

Directions: Listen to the following passages once and then reproduce them in the same language at the end of each segment.

A. English Passage

Through the wonders of modern technology, our world is more connected than ever before. Ideas can cross oceans with the click of a button. Companies can do business and compete with companies across the globe. And we can text, email, Skype with people on every continent. So studying abroad isn't just a fun way to spend a semester; it is quickly becoming the key to success in our global economy. Because getting ahead in today's workplaces isn't just about getting good grades or test scores in school, which are important. It's also about having real experience with the world beyond your borders — experience with languages, cultures and societies very different from your own. Or, as the Chinese saying goes: "It is better to travel ten thousand miles than to read ten thousand books." But let's be clear, studying abroad is about so much more than improving your own future. It's also about shaping the future of your countries and of the world we all share. Because when it comes to the defining challenges of our time—whether it's climate change or economic opportunity or the spread of nuclear weapons—these are shared challenges. And no one country can confront them alone. The only way forward is together.

B. Chinese Passage

中国被称为文明古国，经千年颠沛而魂魄不散，历万种灾厄而总能重生，就是因为我们重视教育，我们尊师重道。早在我们文化的源起，就已经将孔子这位伟大的教育家，立为我们这个文化的精神图腾。而对于教育的执念，即便在最困苦的岁月，最艰难的日子里，总有人不抛弃，总有人把教育重新拾起、擦拭，奉还于我们的神坛！曾经我们说，读书无用，才学与财富不成正比，造就了这个社会浮躁的状态，然而什么都可以浮躁，唯独教育不可以！教育是什么，教育是社会良心的底线，是人类灵魂的净土，是立国之本，是强国之基。教育有什么用？教育就是帮助我们个人认知自己，帮助这个民族认知自己。唯有这样，我们才有可能掌握个人的命运，并且创造这个国家的未来。我们作为教育者，作为受教育者，要始终谨记，教育、读书的终极目的：为天地立心，为生民立命，为往圣继绝学，为万世开太平！

5.6　口译点滴(Information Link)

■ 习近平主席在多个场合对"一带一路"倡议的阐述(五)

习近平主席在二十国集团工商峰会开幕式上的主旨演讲

中国的发展得益于国际社会，也愿为国际社会提供更多公共产品。我提出"一带一路"倡议，旨在同沿线各国分享中国发展机遇，实现共同繁荣。丝绸之路经济带一系列重点项目和经济走廊建设已经取得重要进展，21世纪海上丝绸之路建设正在同步推进。

——2016年9月3日

China's development has benefited from the international community, and we are ready to provide more public goods to the international community. I have proposed the initiative of building the Silk Road Economic Belt and the 21st Century Maritime Silk Road to share China's development opportunities with countries along the Belt and Road and achieve common prosperity. Major progress has been made in launching key projects and building the economic corridors of the Silk Road Economic Belt, and the building of the 21st Century Maritime Silk Road is well underway.

——September 3rd,2016

第6单元 口译笔记 I (Note-Taking in Interpreting I)

口译主题：社会

单元学习目的(Unit Goals) 💡

➢ 掌握本课程所讲授的口译笔记的作用与特点。
➢ 学习社会专题所涉及的常用词语和表达。

导入(Lead -in)

1. 口译过程中为什么需要做笔记？
2. 口译笔记的特点有哪些？

6.1 技能讲解(Skill Introduction)

■ 6.1.1 口译笔记的作用(Functions of Note-Taking in Interpreting)

在口译过程中，单纯依靠记忆很难把信息完整、准确地翻译出来。掌握口译笔记的记录方法和技巧，适当利用口译笔记，可以帮助译员更好地记住重要的细节，减轻记忆负担，确保工作质量，确保信息的完整与准确。

■ 6.1.2 使用口译笔记的注意事项(Tips for Note-Taking)

(1) 译员使用的笔记本最好是带活页圈的记录本，且最好是20厘米长、15厘米宽、上翻式的，约为手掌宽大小。通常情况下，译员需要站立在一旁一手拿着笔记本，一手用笔记录，进行翻译。如果笔记本过大，则不便于手拿；左右翻页的笔记本不便于翻页，会在翻译过程中造成很多不必要的麻烦。此外，笔记本的封底最好为厚硬的纸板，便于书写。

(2) 建议译员使用按压式的且不带笔帽的圆珠笔或是水性笔，可以有效避免遭遇到笔帽掉落、铅笔芯折断或是钢笔漏墨水的尴尬。

(3) 只使用笔记本纸张的正面，不用反面，便于译员翻动纸张。

(4) 即便口译笔记记得再成功，也不可能体现出全部的信息。笔记仅仅是口译的一个辅助工具，译员不能完全依赖口译笔记而忽略理解和记忆的主导地位，只有做到"脑记"和"手记"的有效结合，才能确保翻译的顺畅和准确。

■ 6.1.3 口译笔记的特点(Features of Interpreting Notes)

(1) 简洁。口译笔记要记得尽量简洁，实现用最少的纪录来表达最全面的内容。内容太多会浪费译员的过多时间和精力，也会使译员过度依赖笔记。

(2) 即时。口译笔记只适用于翻译的当下，即只需在翻译的当时能明白笔记所记的内容并用适当的目的语将之清楚地表达出来即可。翻译结束后，可能译员本人也不能清楚地解释出笔记内容了。

(3) 个性化。每个译员记录笔记的方法都不同，可以采用多种文字、缩略语、字母、各类符号、图形等进行记录，目的只有一个，那就是可以针对自己的记忆弱点有效、准确地提示自己所需的内容。

6.2 主题口译(Topic Interpreting)

■ 6.2.1 单句口译(Sentence Practice)

Please interpret the following sentences by using the techniques illustrated above. You may interpret to your partner first and then he/she comments on your performance.

(1) We have had a century of extraordinary scientific discovery about human health. But we have found ourselves with yawning gaps in our ability to provide it to people around the world.

(2) With an evidence base and an ethical underpinning, public health interventions are a powerful force for enlightened social transformation.

(3) At that time, I wanted to become a diplomat, serving our country.

(4) Pursuing the common good will require addressing many global challenges that hold the key to our common future.

(5) Those generous pledges now need to be kept, and all the new partnerships formed to achieve the goals need to forge ahead.

(6) 全球化指的是一系列进程，这一系列进程将随着人类之间依存关系的日益紧密而影响到世界上的每一个民族。

(7) 你们中的每一位，都像已经播下的种子——注定都会成为富有创造性的研究者，明智的决策者，或是公共卫生机构的专业医生，注定都将对社会的发展产生重要的影响。

(8) 我们需要认真讨论一下诸如全球金融危机、气候变化、全球健康以及裁军等问题。

(9) 飘升的粮食与燃料价格、气候变化以及发展中的突发状况，所有这三大危机都因全球金融危机而加剧。

(10) 随着旅游、移民与城市化的增加，在我们看待全球健康的问题上，模式发生了转变。

6.2.2 对话口译(Dialogue Practice)

1. Vocabulary Work: Study the following words and phrases and translate them into the target language.

approach	resolution
promise	cultivate
harmony	privilege
original	stroke

2. Read the following dialogue and interpret it into the target language .

A：新年即将来临，在你们的家乡，通常都会做些什么？

B：As we approach the final day of the year, it is the tradition in my homeland to do two things.

A：哪两件事呢？

B：First we look back over the past year and second we make resolutions, that is, promises to ourselves, for the coming year, promises to get rid of some old habits and cultivate certain new ones to improve our lives and life all around us.

A：你的新年决心是什么呢？

B：My resolution for the coming year is to do what I can do to promote harmony in my own environment.

A：太棒了。

B：The desire of so many of us is that the cycle of violence can be broken and that my country, along with the rest of the planet Earth, may find peace by showing love and goodwill to all the people everywhere.

A：目前你住在青岛，将要在这里度过你的新年了。

B：Yes. This year 2016, was my first full year of living in Qingdao. It has been my great privilege to be in this clean, green city by the sea, enjoying the health air.

A：你喜欢青岛吗？

B：Yes. Qingdao is clearly what we may all a "work in progress" with the city's leaders acting as artists painting an original piece of modern art. We move in and around each stroke of the artists' brushes in our daily lives, happy that they love the color green.

A：非常感谢。

B：Thank you all for your attention and for giving me this chance to share my feelings with you. Thank you.

6.2.3　篇章口译[Passage Practice(E to C)]

1. Vocabulary Work: Study the following words and phrases and translate them into the target language.

budget	deficit
mental health problems	injustice
working-class	prioritize
challenge	mission

2. Please interpret the following paragraph by using the techniques illustrated above.

The New Year is a time to reflect on what has passed and look ahead to the opportunities to come. And this year，as I consider all that 2017 has in store，I believe those opportunities are greater than ever. For we have made a momentous decision and set ourselves on a new direction. // And if 2016 was the year you voted for that change. This is the year we start to make it happen. I know that the referendum last June was divisive at times. I know，of course，that not everyone shared the same point of view or voted in the same way. But I know too that，as we face the opportunities ahead of us，our shared interests and ambitions can bring us together. //We all want to see a Britain that is stronger than it is today. We all want a country that is fairer so that everyone has the chance to succeed. We all want a nation that is safe and secure for our children and grandchildren. These ambitions unite us so that we are no longer the 52% who voted Leave and the 48% who voted Remain，but one great union of people and nations with a proud history and a bright future.//So when I sit around the negotiating table in Europe this year，it will be with that in mind：the knowledge that I am there to get the right deal，not just for those who voted to Leave，but for every single person in this country.// Of course, the referendum laid bare some further divisions in our country between those who are prospering and those who are not；those who can easily buy their own home，send their children to a great school，find a secure job and those who cannot；in short，those for whom our country works well and those for whom it does not.

3. Please interpret the following passage by using the techniques illustrated above. Please pay attention to the underlined sentences as they require special treatment during interpreting.

Inaugural Address by Theresa May

① I have just been to Buckingham Palace where Her Majesty the Queen has asked me to form a new government, and I accepted.

② In <u>David Cameron,</u>⁽¹⁾ I follow in the footsteps of a great, modern prime minister. Under David's leadership, the government stabilized the economy, reduced the budget deficit, and helped more people into work than ever before.

③ But David's true legacy is not about the economy, but about social justice. From the introduction of same-sex marriage, to taking people on low wages out of income tax altogether.

④ David Cameron has led a one nation government and it is in that spirit that I also plan to lead. Because not everybody knows this, but the full title of my party is the Conservative and Unionist Party. And that word Unionist is very important to me. It means we believe in the Union. That precious, precious bond between England, Scotland, Wales and Northern Ireland.

⑤ But it means something else that is just as important. <u>It means that we believe in a Union not just of the nations of the United Kingdom, but between all of our citizens.</u>⁽²⁾Every one of us, whoever we are and wherever we are from.

⑥ That means fighting against the burning injustice that if you are born poor, you will die on average nine years earlier than others. If you're black, you're treated more harshly by the criminal justice system than if you are white.

⑦ If you're a white, working-class boy, you're less likely than anyone else in Britain to go to university. If you're at a state school, you're less likely to reach the top professions than if you were educated privately.

⑧ If you are a woman, you will earn less than a man. If you suffer from mental health problems, there's not enough help to hand. If you're young, you'll find it harder than ever before to own your own home.

⑨ But the mission to make Britain a country that works for everyone means more than just fighting these injustices.

⑩ <u>If you're from an ordinary working-class family, life is much harder than many people in Westminster realize.</u>⁽³⁾You have the job, but you don't always have the job security.

⑪ You have your own home, but you worry about paying the mortgage. You can just about manage, but you worry about the cost of living and getting your kids into a good school.

⑫ If you're one of those families. If you're just managing. I want to address you directly. I know you're working around the clock, I know you're doing your best, and I know that sometimes, life can be a struggle. The government I lead will be driven not by the interests of a privileged few, but by yours.

⑬ We will do everything we can to give you more control over your lives. When we take the big calls, we'll think not of the powerful but you. <u>When we pass new laws, we'll listen not to the mighty, but you.</u>⁽⁴⁾ When it comes to taxes we'll prioritize not the wealthy, but you. When it comes to opportunity, we won't entrench the advantages of the fortunate few.

⑭ We will do everything we can to help anybody, whatever your background, to go as far as your talents will take you.

⑮ We are living through an important moment in our country's history. Following the referendum we face a time of great national change. And I know because we're Great Britain, we will rise to the challenge.

⑯ As we leave the European Union, we will forge a bold, new positive role for ourselves in the world. And we will make Britain a country that works not for a privileged few, but for every one of us.

⑰ That will be the mission of the government I lead, and together, we will build a better Britain.

Notes on the text

(1) David Cameron

戴维·威廉·唐纳德·卡梅伦(David William Donald Cameron)，1966年10月9日生，具有纯正的英国王室血统，父亲曾是一位股票经纪人，母亲是一位男爵的女儿。卡梅伦家族源自苏格兰高地的印威内斯，在英国金融界有很长的历史，祖辈有很多成员担任股票经纪或金融投资工作。戴维·卡梅伦是英国保守党的政治明星，2001年成为英国下议院议员，2005年在年仅39岁时成为英国保守党领袖，2010年5月11日起成为英国第53任首相，是英国自1812年以来最年轻的首相。2015年5月8日，英国大选计票完毕，执政保守党大获全胜，赢得过半议会席位，首相卡梅伦成功连任。2016年7月13日，卡梅伦正式卸任，其职位由特蕾莎·梅接替。2016年9月12日，卡梅伦宣布辞去英国议会下议院议员职务，彻底退出英国政坛。

(2) It means that we believe in a Union not just of the nations of the United Kingdom, but between all of our citizens.

它意味着我们不仅相信联合王国的统一，还相信所有公民的统一。

(3) If you're from an ordinary working-class family, life is much harder than many people in Westminster realize.

如果你来自普通工人阶级家庭，生活比政府里许多人知道的更艰难。

(4) When we pass new laws, we'll listen not to the mighty, but you.

我们做重大决定时，我们想的不是那些有权之人，而是你们。

■ 6.2.4　篇章口译[Passage Practice(C to E)]

1. Vocabulary Work: Study the following words and phrases and translate them into the target language.

改革举措		无私奉献	
形式主义		官僚主义	
保障人民权益		深化改革	
集思广益		给予支援	

2. Please interpret the following paragraph by using the techniques illustrated above.

历史，总是在一些重要时间节点上更能勾起人们的回忆和反思。今年是世界反法西斯战争暨中国人民抗日战争胜利70周年，联合国成立70周年，万隆会议召开60周年，东盟共同体建成之年。//这是值得人们纪念的重要年份，也是激发人们铭记历史、鉴往知来的重要时刻。//70年来，世界发生了前所未有的深刻变化，历史性地改变了人类的命运。全球殖民体系土崩瓦解，冷战对峙不复存在，各国相互联系、相互依存日益加深，和平、发展、合作、共赢的时代潮流滚滚向前，国际力量对比朝着有利于维护世界和平的方向发展，保持国际形势总体稳定、促进各国共同发展具备更多有利条件。//70年来，亚洲形势也发生了前所未有的变化。地区各国实现了民族独立、掌握了自己的命运，壮大了维护地区和世界和平的力量。亚洲国家率先倡导和平共处五项原则，并同非洲国家一道，在万隆会议上提出处理国家间关系的十项原则。//冷战结束后，亚洲国家在推进区域合作实践中逐步形成相互尊重、协商一致、照顾各方舒适度的亚洲方式。这些都为正确处理国家关系、推动建立新型国际关系作出了历史性贡献。

3. Please interpret the following passage by using the techniques illustrated above. Please pay attention to the underlined sentences as they require special treatment during interpreting.

习近平主席2015年新年贺词

① 同志们，朋友们，女士们，先生们：

② 时间过得真快，2014年就要过去了，2015年正在向我们走来。在这辞旧迎新的时刻，我向全国各族人民，向香港特别行政区同胞和澳门特别行政区同胞，向台湾同胞和海外侨胞，向世界各国和各地区的朋友们，致以新年的祝福！(1)

③ 2014年是令人难忘的。这一年，我们锐意推进改革，啃下了不少硬骨头，出台了一系列重大改革举措，许多改革举措同老百姓的利益密切相关。我们适应经济发展新常态，积极推动经济社会发展，人民生活有了新的改善。12月12日，南水北调中线一期工程正式通水，沿线40多万人移民搬迁，为这个工程作出了无私奉献，我们要向他们表示敬意，希望他们在新的家园生活幸福。(2)这一年，我们着力正风肃纪，重点反对形式主义、官僚主义、享乐主义和奢靡之风，情况有了很大改观。我们加大反腐败斗争力度，以零容忍的态度严惩腐败分子，显示了反腐惩恶的坚定决心。这一年，我们加强同世界各国的合作交往，主办了北京亚太经合组织领导人非正式会议，我国领导人多次出访，外国领导人也大量来访，这些活动让世界更好地认识了中国。

④ 为了做好这些工作，我们的各级干部也是蛮拼的。当然，没有人民支持，这些工作是难以做好的，我要为我们伟大的人民点赞。

⑤ 这一年，我们通过立法确定了中国人民抗日战争胜利纪念日、烈士纪念日、南京大屠杀死难者国家公祭日，举行了隆重活动。(3)对一切为国家、为民族、为和平付出宝贵生命的人们，不管时代怎样变化，我们都要永远铭记他们的牺牲和奉献。

⑥ 这一年，我们也经历了一些令人悲伤的时刻。马航MH370航班失踪，150多名同胞下落不明，我们没有忘记他们，我们一定要持续努力、想方设法找到他们。这一年，我国发生了一些重大自然灾害和安全事故，不少同胞不幸离开了我们，云南鲁甸地震就造成了600多人遇难，我们怀念他们，祝愿他们的亲人们都安好。

⑦ 新年的钟声即将敲响。我们要继续努力，把人民的期待变成我们的行动，把人民的希望变成生活的现实。我们要继续全面深化改革，开弓没有回头箭，改革关头勇者胜。<u>我们要全面推进依法治国，用法治保障人民权益、维护社会公平正义、促进国家发展。</u>⁽⁴⁾我们要让全面深化改革、全面推进依法治国如鸟之两翼、车之双轮，推动全面建成小康社会的目标如期实现。

⑧ 我国人民生活总体越来越好，但我们时刻都要想着那些生活中还有难处的群众。我们要满腔热情做好民生工作，特别是要做好扶贫开发和基本生活保障工作，让农村贫困人口、城市困难群众等所有需要帮助的人们都能生活得到保障、心灵充满温暖。

⑨ 我们要继续全面推进从严治党，毫不动摇转变作风，高举反腐的利剑，扎牢制度的笼子，在中国共产党领导的社会主义国家里，腐败分子发现一个就要查处一个，有腐必惩，有贪必肃。

⑩ 我们正在从事的事业是伟大的，坚忍不拔才能胜利，半途而废必将一事无成。我们的蓝图是宏伟的，我们的奋斗必将是艰巨的。<u>全党全国各族人民要团结一心，集思广益用好机遇，众志成城应对挑战，立行立改破解难题，奋发有为进行创新，让国家发展和人民生活一年比一年好。</u>⁽⁵⁾

⑪ 中国人民关注自己国家的前途，也关注世界的前途。非洲发生了埃博拉疫情，我们给予帮助；马尔代夫首都遭遇断水，我们给予支援，许许多多这样的行动展示了中国人民同各国人民同呼吸、共命运的情怀。当前世界仍很不安宁。我们呼唤和平，我真诚希望，世界各国人民共同努力，让所有的人民免于饥寒的煎熬，让所有的家庭免于战火的威胁，让所有的孩子都能在和平的阳光下茁壮成长。

⑫ 谢谢大家。

Notes on the text

(1) <u>在这辞旧迎新的时刻，我向全国各族人民，向香港特别行政区同胞和澳门特别行政区同胞，向台湾同胞和海外侨胞，向世界各国和各地区的朋友们，致以新年的祝福。</u>

At this turn of the year, I now extend my best wishes to people of all ethnic groups in China, to our compatriots from Hong Kong and Macau Special Administrative Regions, to compatriots in Taiwan and overseas Chinese, as well as to friends in other countries and regions in the world.

(2) <u>12月12日，南水北调中线一期工程正式通水，沿线40多万人移民搬迁，为这个工程作出了无私奉献，我们要向他们表示敬意，希望他们在新的家园生活幸福。</u>

On December 12, the first phase of the central route of Water Diversion Project from South to North was officially completed. More than 400 thousand residents along the route were relocated. We pay our sincere tributes to them for their sacrifice, and wish them a happy life in their new homes.

(3) 这一年，我们通过立法确定了中国人民抗日战争胜利纪念日、烈士纪念日、南京大屠杀死难者国家公祭日，举行了隆重活动。

In the past year, through legislation we established the Commemorative Day to mark the victory of Chinese People's War of Resistance against Japanese Aggression, the Commemorative Day of Martyrs, and the National Memorial Day to commemorate victims in the Nanjing Massacre. Solemn ceremonies were held on these days.

(4) 我们要全面推进依法治国，用法治保障人民权益、维护社会公平正义、促进国家发展。

We will push forward the rule of law in an all-round way, safeguard the rights of people in line with law, maintain social justice and promote national development.

(5) 全党全国各族人民要团结一心，集思广益用好机遇，众志成城应对挑战，立行立改破解难题，奋发有为进行创新，让国家发展和人民生活一年比一年好。

All party members and people of all ethnic groups in the country must be united as one, draw on collective wisdom and useful ideas to grasp opportunities, jointly face challenges with united strength, conquer problems with quick action, be bold to carry on innovation, making China a better country year by year and constantly improving people's lives.

6.3　参考译文(Reference Version)

6.3.1　单句口译(Sentence Practice)

Please interpret the following sentences by using the techniques illustrated above. You may interpret to your partner first and then he/she comments on your performance.

(1) 这个世纪，我们在人类健康方面有很多卓越的科学发现，但是我们也看到，要把这些发现用来为全球的人民谋福利，我们还有很多不足。

(2) 有事实为基础，道德为支撑，公共卫生的介入会是开启社会转型的一股强大力量。

(3) 那时，我想成为一名外交官，报效祖国。

(4) 追求共同利益要求我们应对许多全球性挑战，因为这些挑战关系到我们共同的未来。

(5) 这些慷慨的承诺现在需要大家遵守，并且所有为实现目标而建立的新的伙伴关系需要大家共同开拓进取。

(6) Globalization refers to processes that affect every population in the world through our growing interdependence.

(7) In each one of you, a seed has been planted—to be an inspired researcher, an illuminated policymaker, a devoted practitioner of public health, and to have an important impact on the

society.

(8) We need to have a serious discussion on such major issues as the global financial crisis, climate change, global health issues and disarmament.

(9) Now, all these triple crises—soaring food and fuel prices, climate change, and also development emergencies—have been compounded by the global financial crisis.

(10) With increased travel, migration and urbanization, a paradigm shift has occurred in the way we look at global health.

6.3.2　对话口译(Dialogue Practice)

1. Vocabulary Work: Study the following words and phrases and translate them into the target language.

接近	决心
承诺	培养
和谐	荣幸
首创的	笔画

2. Read the following dialogue and interpret it into the target language.

A：The New Year's Day is coming, what do you usually do in your homeland?

B：明天是今年的最后一天。按照我家乡的传统，年终岁尾人们要做两件事。

A：What are they?

B：一件事是对过去的一年进行回顾，另一件事是对新的一年进行筹划，并决心在新年中丢掉坏习惯，养成好习惯，从而改善自己和身边人的生活。

A：What is your resolution for the coming year?

B：我的新年决心是努力创造和谐的环境。

A：That's great!

B：我们大家的愿望就是这种暴力循环能被打碎，希望我的祖国和地球上其他国家一道，友爱亲善，共享和平。

A：Now you are living in Qingdao, and you will have your New Year's Day here.

B：是的，2016年，我第一次完整地经历了青岛的四季。能在这样一座绿色的海滨城市里尽享清新的空气真是一大幸事。

A：Do you like Qingdao?

B：当然。青岛好比一幅正在创作中的美术作品，而城市的领导者就是那正浓墨重彩地描绘这幅原创现代画作的艺术家。在我们的生活中，每天都能感受到艺术家们的笔触，并且为他们对绿色的偏爱而喜悦。

A：Thank you very much.

B：感谢各位给我这个机会与你们分享我的感受。谢谢。

6.3.3 篇章口译[Passage Practice(E to C)]

1. Vocabulary Work: Study the following words and phrases and translate them into the target language.

预算	赤字
精神疾病	不公正
工人阶级	优先处理
挑战	使命

2. Please interpret the following paragraph by using the techniques illustrated above.

　　新年正是这样一个时刻，我们既要反思过去，也要放眼未来，展望机遇。而今年，当我考虑到2017年将面临的各种状况，我坚信我们迎来了比以往更加千载难逢的机遇。我们做出了一项重要的抉择，它带领我们朝着新方向一路前行。//如果说，2016年是你投票选择想做出改变。那么今年，我们则要开始实现改变。我知道，去年6月的公投可以说是具有分裂性的。当然我也知道，不是所有人都有着相同的观点投票做出一致决定。但我也同样知道，当我们面对未来这些机遇时，我们共同的利益和雄心将使我们联合起来。//我们都希望看到一个比现在更强大的英国。我们都想要一个更为公平公正的国家，这样才能让每个人都有成功的机会。为了子孙后代，我们都希望国家变得更加安全稳定。这些雄心将我们联合起来，我们不再是52%支持脱欧的选民，也不再是48%支持留欧的选民，而是一个由人民和构成国组成的伟大联盟，我们拥有光荣的历史和光明的前途。//因此，今年当我坐在谈判桌前与欧盟继续协商时，我会将此铭记于心：我在这里是要为英国争取最佳利益，不只是为投票脱欧的人争取，而是为这个国家的每个人争取。//确实，脱欧公投进一步加剧了我们国家的分化程度，在富裕阶层和并不富裕的人之间产生分化；那些可以轻而易举购置房产，将子女送进最好的学校，轻易找到一份稳定工作的人和做不到这些的人也产生了分化；总之，分化就在这些国家利益既得者和国家利益缺失者之间产生。

3. Please interpret the following passage by using the techniques illustrated above. Please pay attention to the underlined sentences as they require special treatment during interpreting.

特蕾莎·梅就职演讲

　　① 我刚去过白金汉宫，女王陛下要我组建新政府，我接受了。

　　② 我沿戴维·卡梅伦的足迹前行，他是一位伟大、现代的首相。在卡梅伦的领导下，政府稳定了经济，降低了财政赤字，帮助比以往更多的人找到工作。

　　③ 但戴维真正留下的并非是经济成果，而是社会公正。他认可同性婚姻，让低收入人群彻底免交所得税。

　　④ 卡梅伦领导了一国政府，我将本着这种精神执政。不是所有人都清楚，我所在的党的全称是保守和统一党。统一一词对我而言至关重要。这表明我相信统一，这是英格

兰、苏格兰、威尔士和北爱尔兰之间十分珍贵的结合。

⑤ 可它还意味着同样重要的东西，它意味着我们不仅相信联合王国的统一，还相信所有公民的统一，每个人，不论我们是谁，我们从哪里来。

⑥ 那意味着要反对亟待解决的不公正。如果你出身贫穷，就比其他人少活九年；如果你是黑人，相比于白人会受到司法体系更严厉的惩罚。

⑦ 如果你是白人工人阶级的男孩，在英国上大学的机会会更低。如果你上国立学校，相比接受私立教育的人获得顶尖工作的机会要少。

⑧ 如果你是一个妇女，你赚的比男人少。如果你有精神疾病，会很无助。如果你是年轻人，会发现想要拥有自己的住房简直难于登天。

⑨ 可让英国践行为所有人服务这一使命不仅意味着要应对这些不公。

⑩ 如果你来自普通工人阶级家庭，生活比政府里许多人知道的更艰难。你有工作，可往往并不稳定。

⑪ 你有房子，可担心付不起月供。你还能凑合活，却担心生活费增加，没法把孩子送进好学校。

⑫ 如果你来自这些家庭，如果你也凑合活着，我想要直接和你说：我知道你起早贪黑，我知道你竭尽全力，我知道生活有时是一种挣扎。我领导的政府不会被一小撮特权群体的利益驱使，而会为你的利益而奔走。

⑬ 我们将尽一切所能让你更好地掌控自己的生活。我们做重大决定时，我们想的不是那些有权之人，而是你们。我们通过新法时，我们所听的不是那些有势之人，而是你们的心声。在收税时，我们不会优先考虑那些有钱之人，而是你们。当提供机会时，我们不会只给予那些少数幸运之人。

⑭ 我们将尽一切所能帮助所有人，不论你背景如何，都让你能发挥所长。

⑮ 我们经历着国家历史上一个重要时刻。公投后我们面临着国家重大变革的时代。我知道因为我们是大不列颠，我们将迎接挑战。

⑯ 我们离开了欧盟，我们会在世界上打造一个勇敢、积极的新角色。我们要让英国成为不为少数特权阶级服务的国家，一个为每个人服务的国家。

⑰ 这是我领导政府的使命，我们一起努力，就会建成一个更美好的英国。

6.3.4　篇章口译[Passage Practice(C to E)]

1. Vocabulary Work: Study the following words and phrases and translate them into the target language.

reform measures	sacrifice
formalism	bureaucracy
safeguard the rights of people	deepen the reforms
draw on collective wisdom and useful ideas	assist

2. Please interpret the following paragraph by using the techniques illustrated above. Please pay attention to the underlined sentences as they require special treatment during interpreting.

There are certain historic occasions that are likely to remind people of what happened in the past and set people reflecting on them. This year marks the 70th anniversary of the end of the World Anti-Fascist War, the victory of the Chinese People's War of Resistance Against Japanese Aggression and the founding of the United Nations. This year is also the 60th anniversary of the Bandung Conference and will witness the completion of the ASEAN Community.// As such, it is an important year to be commemorated as well as a historic juncture to reflect on the past and look to the future.// Over the past 70 years, the world has experienced profound changes as never before, making a difference to the destiny of mankind. With the days of global colonialism and the Cold War long gone, countries are now increasingly interconnected and interdependent. Peace, development and win-win cooperation have become the prevailing trend of our times. The international forces are shifting in a way that is more favorable to maintaining world peace. Countries are now in a better position to uphold general stability in the world and seek common development.// Over the past 70 years, Asia has also gone through unprecedented changes. After gaining national independence, Asian countries took their destiny in their own hands and strengthened the force for regional and world peace. Asian countries were the first to advocate the Five Principles of Peaceful Co-existence and, together with African countries, put forward the Ten Principles on handling state-to-state relations at the Bandung Conference.// Since the end of the Cold War, Asian countries have gradually come up with an Asian way of cooperation in the course of advancing regional cooperation, which features mutual respect, consensus-building and accommodation of each other's comfort levels. All this has contributed to a proper approach to state-to-state relations and to progress in building a new type of international relations.

3. Please interpret the following passage by using the techniques illustrated above. Please pay attention to the underlined sentences as they require special treatment during interpreting.

2015 New Year Address by Chinese President Xi Jinping

① Comrades and friends, ladies and gentlemen:

② Time flies, Year 2014 is coming to an end and 2015 is approaching. At this turn of the year, I now extend my best wishes to people of all ethnic groups in China, to our compatriots from Hong Kong and Macau Special Administrative Regions, to compatriots in Taiwan and overseas Chinese, as well as to friends in other countries and regions in the world.

③ 2014 is unforgettable. In the past year, we pushed forward reforms with strong commitment, conquered many hardships and introduced a series of important reform measures, many of which are closely associated with the interests of the general public. We worked to adapt to the new normal of economic growth and actively pushed forward economic and social development, resulting in further improvement in people's lives. On December 12, the first phase of the central route of Water Diversion Project from South to North was officially completed. More than 400 thousand residents along the route were relocated. We pay our sincere tributes to them for their sacrifice, and wish them a happy life in their new homes. In the past year, we endeavored to improve our work style and strengthen party and government discipline, with efforts focusing on fighting against formalism, bureaucracy, hedonism and extravagance. The situation has greatly improved. We stepped up our efforts in our crackdown on corruption, and severely punished corrupt officials with zero tolerance. This demonstrates that we are strongly committed to fighting against corruption and other evil forces. In the past year, we enhanced our cooperation and exchanges with countries in the world. We hosted the informal leadership meeting of the Asia-Pacific Economic Cooperation Organization in Beijing. Chinese leaders visited many countries and received many foreign leaders. Such exchanges of visits have helped the rest of the world understand China better.

④ Officials at various levels have also spared no efforts performing their duty. Of course, those achievements would not have been possible without the support of the people. I would like to salute our great people.

⑤ In the past year, through legislation we established the Commemorative Day to mark the victory of Chinese People's War of Resistance against Japanese Aggression, the Commemorative Day of Martyrs, and the National Memorial Day to commemorate victims in the Nanjing Massacre. Solemn ceremonies were held on these days. Despite the change of times, we would always remember the sacrifice and contribution of those who gave their lives for the Chinese nation and for peace.

⑥ In the past year, we also recorded sad moments. We remember the more than 150 Chinese compatriots still missing after the loss of the Malaysian Airline flight MH370. We will continue our efforts to locate their whereabouts. In the past year, China suffered from a number of natural disasters and tragic work safety accidents, in which some compatriots lost their lives. The Ludian earthquake in Yunnan Province claimed more than 600 lives. Our hearts are with them and we wish their families all the best.

⑦ The New Year bell is about to ring. We will continue our efforts to act upon people's expectations and turn their aspirations into reality. We will continue to deepen the reform in an all-round way. This is an unstoppable train. Only those who brave hardships would prevail. We will push forward the rule of law in an all-round way, safeguard the rights of people in line with law, maintain social justice and promote national development. For an eventual accomplishment of building a moderately prosperous society in an all-round way in due time, both deepening the reforms and strengthening the rule of law should function as the two wings of a bird, or as wheels on both sides of a vehicle.

⑧ People's lives in our country are enjoying constant improvement, but we will always remember those still living in hardships. We will work with passion to improve their well-being, with efforts focusing on poverty-alleviation and guaranteeing basic living conditions. We will provide assistance to all those in need of help, including poverty-stricken farmers and urban residents with difficulties, so that their basic living conditions are guaranteed and they feel the warmth of care being in this society.

⑨ We will continue to comprehensively push forward strict party discipline, never hesitate in improving our work style. We will always resort to the anti-corruption drive as a sharp weapon, and consolidate mechanism-building as a cage to contain powers. In this socialist country led by the Communist Party of China, every corrupt official must be dealt with once evidence is found. There's absolutely no tolerance for corruption and graft.

⑩ We're engaged in a lofty mission. Only perseverance will lead to victory, while giving up halfway will end up with failure to do whatever. Our blueprint is magnificent, but our struggle will certainly be arduous. All party members and people of all ethnic groups in the country must be united as one, draw on collective wisdom and useful ideas to grasp opportunities, jointly face challenges with united strength, conquer problems with quick action, be bold to carry on innovation, making China a better country year by year and constantly improving people's lives.

⑪ Chinese people are not only concerned with the prospect of their own country, but also that of the whole world. We helped African people fight against the Ebola epidemic, and assisted people in the Maldivian capital suffering from severe water shortages. Many of those moves showed that Chinese people share weal and woe with people in the world. The world is not a tranquil place. We call for peace and we sincerely hope that people of all countries can work together to ensure that all people be free from the torture of hunger and cold, and all families from the threat of wars, all the children must flourish under the sun of peace.

⑫ Thank you!

6.4 社会主题词汇汇总(Vocabulary Build-up)

arena	活动场所
auditorium	观众席
watershed	转折点
transform	使改观
massive	大规模的
cease	停止
tribute	颂词，称赞
reconciliation	和解

(续表)

subsequent	随后的
contentious	有争议的
moral	道德的
context	背景，环境
destiny	命运
indispensable	必不可少的
assert	声明
oppression	压迫，镇压
genuine	真正的
passionate	热切的
macro	巨大的
auspices	资助
mute	减音，减弱
rectify	纠正
external	外部的
mandate	命令，指令
referendum	公民投票
radical	极端的
foreseeable	可预见的
symbolic	象征的
profound	深度的
intervention	介入
humanitarian	人道主义的
disarmament	裁军

6.5　扩展练习(Enhancement Practice)

Retelling.

Directions: Listen to the following passages once and then reproduce them in the same language at the end of each segment.

A. English Passage

When our men and women in uniform answer the call to serve, their families serve right along with them. Across this country, military spouses have been raising their families all alone during those long deployments. And let's not forget about our military kids, moving from base to base—and school to school—every few years, and stepping up to help out at home when mom or dad is away. Our military families sacrifice so much on our behalf, and Barack and I believe that we should serve them as well as they serve this country. That's why Dr. Jill Biden and I started Joining Forces—an effort to rally all Americans to honor and support our veterans and military families. Just go to joining forces. Government to find out how you can show your gratitude for their service. Because that's what this season is all about. For my family and millions of Americans, it's a time to celebrate the birth of Christ. To reflect on His life and learn from his example. Every year, we commit to love one another. To give of ourselves. To be our brother's keeper. To be our sister's keeper. But those ideas are not just part of our faith. They're part of all faiths. And they unite us as Americans. In this country, we take care of each other. And in this season of giving, it's inspiring to see so many people all across America taking the time to help those most in need. That's part of what makes us such a compassionate nation. And this year, I know many of you are extending that kindness to the families who are still picking up the pieces from Hurricane Sandy and extending your prayers to the people of Newtown, Connecticut.

B. Chinese Passage

　　无论你是否喜欢，过去20年，互联网对人类社会产生了巨大的影响，每个人都相信互联网为世界做出了伟大的贡献。而许多传统企业讨厌互联网，因为互联网毁掉了他们的生意。但是为什么互联网公司会担忧？我们觉得这里面一定有问题。我们必须找到一个解决方案，让我们的公司能够像奔驰、西门子一样，活得长久而健康。如果一个行业不能存活超过3年，如果不是所有的公司能够快乐地生存超过3年，则这个行业永远无法成为主流，这个行业永远不可能深深根植于经济——所以，我们要做什么才能找到解决方案？世界正在快速改变，我们今天的科技发展非常迅速，大部分人不知道IT是什么，互联网是什么。IT科技和数字科技，这不仅仅是不同的技术，还是人们思考方式的不同，人们对待这个世界方式的不同。我们不知道世界30年后会变成什么样，我们不知道数据在30年后会长成什么样——但是我们相信，整个世界在30年后会大大改变。如果第一次和第二次技术革命释放了人的体力，那么这次技术革命则释放了人的脑力，脑力在革新。未来的世界，我们将不再由石油驱动，而是由数据驱动；未来的世界，生意将是C2B而不是B2C，用户改变企业，而不是企业向用户出售——因为我们将产生大量的数据。制造商必须个性化，否则他们将非常困难。未来的世界，制造商的机器不仅会生产产品，还会说话和思考。机器不会再由石油和电力驱动，机器由数据来支撑。未来的世界，企业将不再会关注于规模，企业不再会关注于标准化和权力，他们会关注于灵活性、敏捷性、个性化和用户友好。而且我坚信，在未来的世界，我们会有很多女性领袖——因为在未来，人们将不会只关注肌肉力量，而会更加重视智慧，重视关怀和责任。我认为，互联网必须找到那个缺失的部分。这个缺失的部分就是鼠标和水泥携手合作，找到一个方法让互联网经济和实体经济结合。只有当鼠标和水泥结合时，互联网公司才能活下来，才能开心地活30年。

6.6 口译点滴(Information Link)

■ 习近平主席在多个场合对"一带一路"倡议的阐述(六)

习近平主席在日内瓦出席"共商共筑人类命运共同体"高级别会议,并发表主旨演讲

我提出"一带一路"倡议,就是要实现共赢共享发展。中国打造伙伴关系的决心不会改变。中国坚持独立自主的和平外交政策,在和平共处五项原则基础上同所有国家发展友好合作。中国率先把建立伙伴关系确定为国家间交往的指导原则,同90多个国家和区域组织建立了不同形式的伙伴关系。中国将进一步联结遍布全球的"朋友圈"。

——2017年1月18日

The Belt and Road Initiative I put forward aims to achieve win-win and shared development. China remains unchanged in its commitment to foster partnerships. China pursues an independent foreign policy of peace, and is ready to enhance friendship and cooperation with all other countries on the basis of the Five Principles of Peaceful Coexistence. China is the first country to make partnership-building a principle guiding state-to-state relations. It has formed partnerships of various forms with over 90 countries and regional organizations, and will build a circle of friends across the world.

——January 18th,2017

第7单元　口译笔记 II (Note-Taking in Interpreting II)

口译主题：家庭

单元学习目的(Unit Goals) 💡

➢ 掌握本课程所讲授的口译笔记系统的设计技巧。
➢ 学习家庭专题所涉及的常用词语和表达。

导入(Lead -in)

1. 口译笔记系统的设计的注意事项有哪些？
2. 口译笔记的基本格式是怎样的？
3. 口译笔记常用的符号有哪些？

7.1　技能讲解(Skill Introduction)

■ 7.1.1　口译笔记系统的设计的注意事项(Tips for Taking Notes)

口译笔记系统必须相对稳定，能确保译员顺利地解读笔记内容。使用的符号不能引起歧义或导致意义不明确，避免滥用符号。译员可以形成自己习惯的记录方式，可以使用自己经常使用的符号，避免频繁更换符号来指代某种意义。笔记应简洁明了，克服完整听写的冲动，争取用最少的符号来表达尽量完整的意义。但是一般不提倡采用速记的方式记录口译内容。

(1) 为了方便记录，可以使用母语，尽量用最少的汉字笔画来表示完整的意义。不必把整个词汇都写下来(不熟悉或理解有困难的除外)，只需记录核心字即可，如"政"表示"政治"。但是因为汉字笔画比较烦琐，所以可以按照自己的习惯简化笔画，无关对错，只要自己能认得就行。

(2) 如果目的语熟练，或是汉字笔画太烦琐，也可以使用目的语来记录，这样做在**翻**译时就会更加容易一些。

(3) 用哪国文字记录并不重要，只要是自己能正确解读，多种文字混用或是用第三国文字也未尝不可。

(4) 可以使用缩略语。最常用的缩略语是国家、机构名称，如USA、UN等，或各行业领域约定俗成的表达方式，如GDP。此外，也可采用来自拉丁语的缩略，如eg.，etc. 等。英语单词在缩写时可以按照拼写法取前几个字母，如"Eng"表示"English"，"acc"表示"account"或"accountant"，也可以抽取字母组成，"acpt"表示"accept"，"agt"表示"agent"，"amt"表示"amount"。有时一个单词可以简写到一个字母，如"m"表示"military"，"J"表示"judge"或"justice"。

(5) 可以利用线条来指代重复出现的信息。如果下文中提及的某个信息在上文中已经出现过，那么无须重复记录，只要把出现在上文中的记录圈起来，再画一条线拉下来，用箭头表明其应该在下文中出现的位置即可。此方法尤其适用于重复次数多且书写费时的信息。当然，如果译员觉得重写一次更方便，那么也可以选择重写。

(6) 可以使用符号。口译笔记中常用的符号包括标点符号、数学符号、图像符号等。如"□"表示"国家"，"□/□"表示国家之间；"＞"表示"优于"或"期待"；"＞＜"表示"冲突"；"√"表示"肯定，赞成"；"≠"表示"不等于，不意味着"；"？"表示"疑问，问题"；"→"表示"发送"或"导致"；"〇"表示"空洞"或"无效"；"∟"表示"将来"。

(7) 可以使用简笔画。如果条件允许，译员也可以尝试用简笔画来记录重要信息。

■ 7.1.2　口译笔记的基本格式(Typical Style of Note-Taking)

大体说来，没有必须遵守的口译笔记格式，口译笔记具有鲜明的个人风格。多数人惯用的格式如下。

(1) 先在左边画一条竖线，左侧页边距约为1~2厘米，用于记录承上启下或表达逻辑关系的连词，如"因为、所以、但是"等。或者当译员没有听清某个细节时可在其对应的左侧空格里做出问号标记，以便于在发言人结束发言、译员开始翻译前与发言人进行确认。

(2) 字体大而稀疏，便于译员在有限的时间内辨认出所记录的内容，不要怕浪费纸张。

(3) 如果段落很长，可以分成若干意群，为了清晰起见，可以在各个意群之间画上横线，以便分析整理。

(4) 按意群分行记录，既不要一个字一行，也不要把两个句子写在一行里。否则，一个完整的意群会被分得七零八落，不便于稍后的解读。

(5) 若是意群太长，需要另起一行时，注意在另起的一行开头缩进一定距离。

(6) 每个段落记录完成后，要标上"#"，使得开头和结尾一目了然，避免在稍后的**翻**译过程中出现遗漏或有重复翻译的错误。

■ 7.1.3 口译笔记常用的符号(Frequently-Used Notations)

(1) 地名简写

地名简写，如K=Korea，SD= Sweden，SW=Switzerland，等等。有时还可以借助"|—"来表示东、西、南、北、中等方位。Western Europe(西欧)表示为"|EU"。

(2) 缩略词

缩略词，如IMP为important，ASAP为as soon as possible。

缩略词的写法一般为四种方式。

a. 拿掉所有元音

| MKT | market |
| MGR | manager |

b. 保留前几个字母

| INFO | information |
| INS | insurance |

c. 保留开头和结尾的发音字母

| WK | week |
| RM | room |

d. 根据发音

| R | are |
| THO | though |

(3) 字母、图像

o 表示"人"，即people/person，因为"o"看上去像个人头，它通常被写在一个词或符号的右上角。

P 表示政治，即politics，political。希腊字母P读/pai/，近似politics，political。

G 表示效率，即efficient，effective。G为效率符号。

Q 表示"通货膨胀"，即inflation。因为这个符号酷似一个上升的气球。

B 表示商业，即business。

C× 表示冲突，矛盾，即conflict，confrontation。C×中的"×"表示反对。

W 表示工作，职业，即work，employ 等。它是work的第一个字母，所以WZ就可以用来表示worker。

O 表示"国家""民族""领土"等，即country，state，nation等。

⊙，圆圈表示一个圆桌，中间一点表示一盆花，这个符号就可以表示"会议""开会"等，即meeting, conference, negotiation, seminar, discussion, symposium。

∞，这个符号看上去像条鱼，所以表示"捕鱼业"等和fishery有关的词汇。

⊖，圆圈代表地球，横线表示赤道，所以这个符号就可以表示"国际的""世界的""全球的"等，即international，worldwide，global，universal等。

(4) 数学符号

+ 表示"多"，即many，lots of，a great deal of，a good many of 等。

++(+2) 表示"多"的比较级，即more。

+3 表示"多"的最高级，即most。

一 表示"少"，即little，few，lack，in short of/ be in shortage of 等。

× 表示"错误""失误"和"坏"的概念，即wrong/incorrect，something bad，notorious，negative 等。

> 表示"多于"概念，即bigger/larger/greater/more than/better than 等。

　表示"高"概念，即superior to，surpass 等。

< 表示"少于"概念，即less/smaller 等。

　表示"低"概念，即inferior to 等。

= 表示"同等"概念，即means，that is to say，in other words，the same as，be equal to 等。

　表示"对手"概念，即a match，rival，competitor，counterpart 等。

() 表示"在……之间"，即among，within 等。

≠ 表示"不同"概念，即be different from 等。

　表示"无敌"概念，即matchless，peerless 等。

~表示"大约"概念，即about/around，or so，approximately 等。

(5) 标点等

: 表示各种各样"说"的动词，即say，speak，talk，marks，announce，declare等。

? 表示"问题"，即question，issue，例如台湾问题可表示为"tw?"。

. (dot) 这个"."点的位置不同表示的概念也不一样。

".d"表示yesterday，".y"表示last year，".2m"表示two month ago，"y"表示this year，"y2."表示 two years later，"next week"表示为"wk."。

∧ 表示"转折"，即but，yet，however 等。

√ 表示"好的"状态，即right/good，famous/well-known 等。

　表示"同意"状态，即stand up for，support，agree with sb, certain / affirmative 等。

☆ 表示"重要的"状态，即important，exemplary(模范的) best，outstanding，brilliant 等。

& 表示"和"，"与"，即and，together with，along with，accompany，along with，further more 等。

// 表示"结束"，即end，stop，halt，bring sth to a standstill/stop 等。

7.2　主题口译(Topic Interpreting)

■ 7.2.1　单句口译(Sentence Practice)

Please interpret the following sentences by using the techniques illustrated above. You may interpret to your partner first and then he/she comments on your performance.

(1) It's generally accepted that the experiences of the child in his first years largely determine his character and later personality.

(2) In a society, both parents and teachers are responsible for the opportunities provided for the development of the child, so that upbringing and education are interdependent.

(3) Early upbringing in the home is naturally affected by the cultural pattern of the community and by the parents' capabilities and their aims and depends not only on upbringing and education but also on the innate abilities of the child.

(4) Every parent watches eagerly the child's acquisition of each skill——the first spoken words, the first independent steps, or the beginning of reading and writing.

(5) learning together is a fruitful source of relationship between children and parents because by playing together, parents learn more about their children and children learn more from their parents.

(6) 至于如何培养成长中的孩子的道德规范问题，重要的是家长在教育中要言行一致。

(7) 调查结果表明：男人与女人的意见有着实质性的差异。

(8) 在焦急地等待高考成绩的那些日日夜夜，我的心中充满了迷惑，不知道未来带给我的会是什么：惊奇、兴奋，还是失望、悲伤。

(9) 他的母亲被推进了手术室，他在外面一支接一支地吸着烟，来回走动。

(10) 在现实生活中，保持心态平衡十分必要。生活中心态失衡，既无法很好地工作，身心也不能得到全面的发展。

■ 7.2.2　对话口译(Dialogue Practice)

1. Vocabulary Work: Study the following words and phrases and translate them into the target language.

sustain	junior
be on track	share...with...
foremost	competent
Quality Time	personally

2. Read the following dialogue and interpret it into the target language .

A：您因为《夜现场》这一精彩的节目而名声大振，受到许多人的喜爱。

B：Thank you. But in my opinion, I am not only a writer, but also a father.

A：的确如此，您是一位成功的作家，同时也是一位好父亲。

B：Thank you.

A：今天想和观众们分享些什么呢？

B：Since those first glory days of Night Live, I've had my successes and I've had my failures, and I have to tell you, the successes have been more fun. But what has sustained me through all of it were the people closest to me: my parents, my wife, and my kids.

A：我听说您有一个女儿，是吗？

B：Yes, my daughter is a junior. And she's on track to graduate with honors.

A：太棒了！

B：Thank you. Parenting is the hardest job you'll ever love.

A：最难的工作？

B：Yes, the hardest job. First and foremost, being a good parent means spending lots of time with your children.

A：但是，有些家长太忙……

B：I personally hate the phrase, "Quality Time".

A：为什么呢？

B：Kids don't want Quality Time, they want Quality Time, big, lazy, non-productive Quality Time.

A：哦，的确如此。

B：On the other hand it's important for every parent to maintain balance in his or her life.

A：您的意思是……？

B：Don't be a slave to your child. No one respects a slave—unless he's played by Morgan Freeman.

7.2.3 篇章口译[Passage Practice (E to C)]

1. Vocabulary Work: Study the following words and phrases and translate them into the target language.

value	unresolved
highlight	addiction
mental health	social concerns
anchor	devotion

2. Please interpret the following paragraph by using the techniques illustrated above. Please pay attention to the underlined sentences as they require special treatment during interpreting.

I often get asked why I decided to spend time highlighting the mental health of children.

I imagine my answer might be similar to many of yours. // I know that I was lucky. My parents and teachers provided me with a wonderful and secure childhood where I always knew I was loved, valued and listened to.// But of course many children are not so lucky. Since beginning my work in areas like addiction, for example, I have seen time and time again that the roots of poor mental health in adulthood are almost always present in unresolved childhood challenges.// I am sure you will agree that all children deserve time, attention and love from the adults in their lives. These basic qualities are so much more valuable than the always changing material and social concerns that can seem so important to young people.// As today's theme reminds us, many children – even those from stable, happy homes – are finding that their heads are just too full. It is our duty, as parents and as teachers, to give all children the space to build their emotional strength and provide a strong foundation for their future.// Of course, not all children have the anchor of a strong family. Many will arrive through your school gates feeling a real lack of love and devotion in their lives. This often leaves them feeling insecure and without confidence and trust in the world around them. That is why your work is so important.// Parents, teachers and other school staff need the tools to help these young people early in their lives. And the earlier, the better. It is proven that early action prevents problems later in life.// Imagine if everyone was able to help just one child who needs to be listened to, needs to be respected, and needs to be loved – we could make such a huge difference for an entire generation.

3. Please interpret the following passage by using the techniques illustrated above. Please pay attention to the underlined sentences as they require special treatment during interpreting.

A Speech Delivered in Mother's Day[1] by Barack Hussein Obama[2]

① Hi, everybody.

② In our house, everybody knows that President is only the third-most important job in the family.

③ So this weekend, I'm going to take a little extra time to say thank you to Michelle for the remarkable way she does the most important joB：being a mom.

④ And I'm going to give extra thanks to my mother-in-law for the role model she's always been to Michelle and the countless selfless ways in which she's helped Michelle and me raise Malia and Sasha.

⑤ I am incredibly lucky to have these wonderful women help me raise, love, and look after our girls.

⑥ I hope you'll also take a moment to say thank you to the women in your life who love you in that special way mothers do. [3]

⑦ Biological moms, adoptive moms, and foster moms; single moms, grandmoms and godmothers; aunts and mentors – whomever you think of when you think of Mother's Day.

⑧ Or take a moment, like I will, to remember the moms who raised us, whose big hearts sustained us, and whom we miss every day, no matter how old we get.

⑨ Giving flowers is always a good idea.

⑩ But I hope that on this Mother's Day, we'll recommit ourselves to doing more than that: Through deeds that match our words.

⑪ Let's give mothers the respect they deserve, give all women the equality they deserve, and give all parents the support they need in their most important roles.

⑫ That includes paid maternity and paternity leave, sick leave, accommodations for workers who are pregnant, good health care, affordable child care, flexibility at work, equal pay, and a decent minimum wage.

⑬ We ask our mothers to do more than their fair share of just about everything.

⑭ Making sure they're treated fairly is the least we can do.

⑮ The idea of setting aside a Sunday in May for our mothers became an official holiday with a Congressional resolution a little more than 100 years ago.

⑯ They did it on May 8 – the same day we'll celebrate Mother's Day this year.

⑰ If Congress can make a holiday, surely they can back it up with the things that give it meaning.(4)

⑱ After all, that's what my mother taught me. I couldn't just say I was going to do the right thing, or say I agreed with it on principle. I had to actually do it.

⑲ So this Mother's Day, say thank you. Say, "I love you." And let's make sure we show that gratitude and appreciation through acts of respect throughout the year.

⑳ No one deserves that more than our moms.

㉑ Happy Mother's Day, and have a great weekend.

Notes on the text

(1) Mother's Day

母亲节(Mother's Day)，是一个感谢母亲的节日，目前所知最早的母亲节起源于古希腊。在这一天，古希腊人向希腊众神之母赫拉致敬。其后17世纪中叶，节日流传到英国。在这一天里，出门在外的年轻人会返家，送给母亲一些小礼物。美国的母亲节由安娜·贾维斯(Anna Jarvis，1864年—1948年)发起，她终身未婚，一直陪伴在母亲身边。安娜·贾维斯的母亲心地善良，极富同情心，她提出应设立一个纪念日来纪念默默无闻做出奉献的母亲们，可是这个愿望尚未实现，她就逝世了。她的女儿安娜·贾维斯于1907年开始举办活动，申请让母亲节成为一个法定节日。节日于1908年5月10日在美国的西弗吉尼亚和宾夕法尼亚州正式开始。1913年，美国国会确定将每年5月的第二个星期日作为法定的母亲节，并规定这一天家家户户都要悬挂国旗，表达对母亲的尊敬。而安娜·贾维斯的母亲生前最爱的康乃馨也就成了美国母亲节的象征。

(2) Barack Hussein Obama

贝拉克·侯赛因·奥巴马(Barack Hussein Obama)，1961年8月4日出生，美国民主党籍政治家，第44任美国总统，为美国历史上第一位非洲裔总统。1991年，奥巴马以优等生荣誉从哈佛法学院毕业。2007年2月10日，宣布参加2008年美国总统选举。2008年11月4日正式当选为美国总统。2009年10月9日，获得诺贝尔委员会颁发的诺贝尔和平奖。2012年11月6日，第57届美国总统大选中，奥巴马击败共和党候选人罗姆尼，成功连任。2017年1月10日，奥巴马在芝加哥发表告别演讲。2017年1月20日，结束了8年的美国总统生涯，由特朗普担任第45任美国总统。

(3) I hope you'll also take a moment to say thank you to the women in your life who love you in that special way mothers do.

我希望你们也能抽一点时间，向你们生命中给予你母亲般特别的爱的女性，说声谢谢。

(4) If Congress can make a holiday, surely they can back it up with the things that give it meaning.

国会既然能够设立这个节日，他们一定就能用行动赋予这个节日意义。

▌7.2.4　篇章口译[Passage Practice (C to E)]

1. Vocabulary Work: Study the following words and phrases and translate them into the target language.

非凡的成就	嫉妒
诋毁	认可
心存感激	天赋
组合拳	沮丧

2. Please interpret the following paragraph by using the techniques illustrated above. Please pay attention to the underlined sentences as they require special treatment during interpreting.

有太多人把幸福当作人生的终极目标，但如果你只是等待幸福来敲门，幸福可能永远都不会到来！// 你总是期待得到更多，总是期待着你变"幸福"的那一刻。然而，如果你陷入这种思维陷阱，那你永远也达不到这个目的。幸福不该是生活的目标，它应该是生活本身！// 幸福唯一该存在的时刻，就是每时每刻的现在！它是一种心态，而不是一连串的成就，或者物质财富的积累。你必须要接受的是：生活中总会有挑战，事情不会总朝着你期望的方向发展。// 事情的发展不如你所愿时不要沮丧，你要对拥有这次体验心存感激。不要幻想着明天会更美好、更幸福、更富有，要尽可能精彩地过好今天。// 幸福是我此刻就能做出的有意识的决定。思考未来、胸怀大志是幸福美满生活的基础，关键在于不要让对未来的思考掩盖当下的快乐和对现在生活中人和事的感激！// 没有通往幸福的路：幸福本身就是一条路！不要再等着幸福登门了，你需要做的仅仅是决定幸福地活着！这不是什么伟大的目的目标，只是生命的旅程和道路。

3. Please interpret the following passage by using the techniques illustrated above. Please pay attention to the underlined sentences as they require special treatment during interpreting.

如何应对欺负你的人

① 如果你想不走寻常路，做出些非凡的成就，那你就要明白总有那么一些人会对你的成就心生嫉妒与怨恨。 无论你工作有多努力，或者你做出了多大的牺牲才获得了现在的成就，那些"恨你的人"总能找到理由来批评你，甚至诋毁你。 对你心生不满的人看不惯你对自我的肯定，也见不得你得到别人的认可。他们无法忍受你的快乐、满足和成功。<u>这些嫉恨你的人不愿意去做你所做过的事，不愿意同你一样做出牺牲，也不愿意花时间心血去工作，他们只是嫉妒你的成功，却永远懒得去花时间和力气去完成自己的目标。</u>⁽¹⁾

② 诚然，有时候即使我们付出了时间和努力，也未必能成功。谁也不能保证生活会是一帆风顺的，有时，它也会跟你打个擦边球。 我喜欢蒂娜·菲在金球奖领奖时说过的话，她把奖杯高高举起，说道，"感谢那些讨厌我的人！"蒂娜就是富有天赋、工作努力而且获得成功的好例子，同时，她也收到了无数负面抨击，但她从未让这些流言蜚语影响到自己。

③ <u>你只要记住：这些嫉恨你的人，他们讨厌你的唯一理由就是他们想得到你所得到的，却不愿意付出你所付出的。</u>⁽²⁾讨厌你的人总觉得你只不过是运气好而已，或者你走了后门，但事实是，你是通过自己的不懈努力才做出了成绩的，这些努力才是你的"好运"所在。 对付嫉恨你的人的最好办法就是下面这套"组合拳"。

④ 第一，别让他们影响到你。尽情地为自己取得的成功而感到高兴和自豪吧，和那些欣赏你、赞美你、支持你的人在一起，不要怀疑，这些是你应得的。讨厌你的人都是善妒易怒的人，别去管他们说了什么，无论他们说什么，都不重要。

⑤ 第二，那些人越是欺负你、骚扰你，你就越要积极地去获得成功。对付那些贬损你的招数，你的回应就是更加努力工作，取得更大的成就。

⑥ <u>你对待敌意的方式会激励你取得更大的成就，到时，嫉恨者的恶言恶语就会转变成熊熊烈火帮助你创造出更大的辉煌。</u>⁽³⁾这些欺负你的人再也伤不了你，反而会鞭策你更上一层楼。

Notes on the text

(1) <u>这些嫉恨你的人不愿意去做你所做过的事，不愿意同你一样做出牺牲，也不愿意花时间心血去工作，他们只是嫉妒你的成功，却永远懒得去花时间和力气去完成自己的目标。</u>

These hateful individuals are unwilling to do the work that you've done; they rarely make the same kinds of sacrifices or put in the long, hard hours. They resent your success but are too lazy or spoiled to invest real time or energy in the pursuit of their own goals.

(2) 你只要记住：这些嫉恨你的人，他们讨厌你的唯一理由就是他们想得到你所得到的，却不愿意付出你所付出的。

The thing you need to know about these haters is that the only reason they behave this way is that you have something they want but they aren't willing to work for it.

(3) 你对待敌意的方式会激励你取得更大的成就，到时，嫉恨者的恶言恶语就会转变成熊熊烈火帮助你创造出更大的辉煌。

When your reaction to their hostility has inspired you to achieve further success, you've transformed the haters' negativity into fuel for your creative fires.

7.3 参考译文(Reference Version)

7.3.1 单句口译(Sentence Practice)

Please interpret the following sentences by using the techniques illustrated above. You may interpret to your partner first and then he/she comments on your performance.

(1) 人们一般认为孩子最初几年的经历对其性格以及以后个性的培养影响很大。

(2) 在社会里，家长与教师都要对孩子今后的发展负责，因而父母的抚养和学校的教育相辅相成，缺一不可。

(3) 早期的家庭抚养自然受社会文化模式、父母自身能力和他们培养孩子目标的影响，同时不仅受到孩子抚养和教育的制约，还受孩子先天能力的制约。

(4) 每一个父母都会怀着急切的心情去观察孩子掌握的各种技能，如会说的第一句话、会走的第一步或者会读写的第一个字。

(5) 共同学习是父母与孩子关系绵延的成功的源泉，因为通过共同玩耍，父母更了解孩子，孩子也能向父母学到更多的东西。

(6) As regards the development of moral standards in the growing child, consistency is very important in parental teaching.

(7) The findings show a substantial difference between the opinions of men and women.

(8) On those days and nights when I was waiting for the results of the Entrance Examination, my heart was filled with uncertainty, I wondered what the future held for me, of surprise and excitement or disappointment and sorrow.

(9) His mother was sent into the operation room. He walked to and fro outside, smoking one cigarette after another.

(10) A well-balanced life is necessary to live in today's world. Without a well-balanced life a person can neither function properly nor develop into a well-rounded individual.

7.3.2　对话口译(Dialogue Practice)

1. Vocabulary Work: Study the following words and phrases and translate them into the target language.

支持	大三学生
在按计划进行	与……分享
最重要的	有能力的
宝贵的时间	就本人而言

2. Read the following dialogue and interpret it into the target language.

A：You got famous for that wonderful Night Live, and you are so popular among the audience.

B：谢谢。不过，我觉得我不仅是一名作家，还是一位父亲。

A：Exactly. You are a successful writer and a good father.

B：谢谢。

A：Today, what do you want to share with the audience?

B：在《夜现场》一开始的那些光荣岁月里，我成功过也失败过，并且我要告诉你们的是，相比之下，还是成功有更多的乐趣。而一直支持我走到现在的是我的亲人们：我的父母、妻子和孩子。

A：I heard that you have a daughter, don't you?

B：是的，我的女儿是大三的学生，并且她将满载荣誉如期毕业。

A：That's great!

B：谢谢。为人父母既是最难的工作，也是你会永远热爱的工作。

A：The hardest job?

B：是的。首先，做名好家长，就意味着要花时间和你的孩子在一起。

A：But, some parents are too busy to ...

B：我个人不喜欢"宝贵的时间"这个词。

A：Why?

B：孩子们不想要宝贵时间，他们想要的是大量充足的、无拘无束的、无所事事的与父母在一起的时间。

A：Oh, yes.

B：另一方面，对每位家长来说都很重要的是，保持其生活的平衡。

A：What do you mean ?

B：不要成为孩子的奴隶。没有人会尊重一个奴隶——除非这个奴隶由好莱坞黑人明星摩根·弗里曼扮演。

7.3.3 篇章口译[Passage Practice (E to C)]

1. Vocabulary Work: Study the following words and phrases and translate them into the target language.

重视	未解决的
强调	上瘾
心理健康	社会关注
精神支柱	关照

2. Please interpret the following paragraph by using the techniques illustrated above. Please pay attention to the underlined sentences as they require special treatment during interpreting.

别人经常问我为什么我一直这么关注儿童心理健康的发展，我的答案可能和大家心里面想的差不多。//我很幸运，小时候，父母和老师的关爱让我度过了非常难忘的童年，那时候我能感觉到有人疼爱自己、欣赏自己、倾听自己。//但是世界上有很多的孩子并不像我这么幸运，比如说，自从我开始接触一些吸毒上瘾的人之后，我经常发现这些成年人之所以会出现严重的心理问题，其根源都是小时候曾经遭遇过巨大的创伤。//我相信大家都认为孩子应当得到大人的关怀、陪伴和理解，比起现代社会里年轻人层出不穷的物质需求和社会考量，这些才是他们最需要的东西。//就像今天活动的主题所不断提醒我们的一样，许多孩子，包括那些来自于幸福而稳定的家庭里的，都被太多的东西占据了自己的身心。作为家长和老师，我们有责任为孩子们打造一片他们能够用来建筑自己情感力量的天地，有责任来为他们未来的发展打下坚实的基础。//当然，并不是所有的孩子都有一个坚强的家庭来作为他们成长的后盾，许多每天穿梭于学校和家庭之间的孩子们总是深深地感觉到自己的生活里缺少父母的关爱。也正因如此，他们的心里总是充满了不安全感，对周围的世界没有信心和信任。我们工作的重要性也就是在这些孩子的身上所体现的。//家长、老师和其他所有的学校工作人员都需要用适当的方式尽早地帮助这些孩子，越早越好。很多的案例都已证明，如果我们能尽早采取措施，那么很多的问题后来就不会发生。//想像一下，如果每个人都能帮助一个需要倾听、需要尊重、需要疼爱的孩子，那么我们就能够改变整整一代人。

3. Please interpret the following passage by using the techniques illustrated above. Please pay attention to the underlined sentences as they require special treatment during interpreting.

奥巴马总统母亲节致辞

① 大家好。

② 在我们家，大家都知道总统是我在家里第三重要的工作。

③ 所以这个周末，我要额外地花一点时间，向米歇尔说声谢谢，谢谢她在母亲这个最重要的岗位上所做的杰出贡献。

④ 我还要特别感谢我的岳母，她一直以来都为米歇尔树立了一个好母亲的榜样，感谢她在帮助我和米歇尔抚养玛利亚和莎夏上做的无数无私的付出。

⑤ 我是如此幸运，有这两位女性帮助我抚养、爱护和照料我的女儿们。

⑥ 我希望你们也能抽一点时间，向你们生命中给予你母亲般特别的爱的女性，说声谢谢。

⑦ 无论生母、义母、养母，单亲妈妈，祖母，教母，以及姑姑阿姨和老师——只要是你母亲节这一天想起的人，都对她们说声谢谢。

⑧ 或者抽点时间，像我一样，牢记养育我们的妈妈，是她用宽广的胸怀给我们以支持，是她让我们日日牵挂，无论我们长多大。

⑨ 送花总是个好主意。

⑩ 但我希望在这个母亲节，我们能激励自己做得更多——用行动践行我们的承诺。

⑪ 让母亲得到应有的尊重，让所有女性受到公平的对待，让所有父母得到他们在承担这最重要的职务时所需的帮助。

⑫ 包括给所有怀孕的工人提供带薪产假、陪产假、病假以及住宿，为她们提供良好的卫生保健、儿童保健、工作上的自由、同工同酬并设定合理的最低工资标准。

⑬ 我们在所有的事情上，都让我们的母亲做了超出她们应做的事。

⑭ 我们至少要确保她们受到公正对待。

⑮ 把5月的一个星期日设为母亲节的想法，通过国会确立为法定节日，这一天已经过去100多年了。

⑯ 他们设置的日期是5月8日——跟今年的母亲节是同一天。

⑰ 国会既然能够设立这个节日，他们一定就能用行动赋予这个节日意义。

⑱ 毕竟，这是我母亲教我的。我不能只是嘴上说我要做一件正确的事，或者说我原则上同意它，我得把它做出来。

⑲ 因此在这个母亲节，请说出"谢谢您"，"我爱您"，并且保证在这一年里，我们都能通过满怀敬意的行动来表达我们的感激之情。

⑳ 我们的母亲当之无愧。

㉑ 祝大家母亲节快乐，周末愉快。

7.3.4 篇章口译[Passage Practice (C to E)]

1. Vocabulary Work: Study the following words and phrases and translate them into the target language.

something beyond the ordinary	be jealous
condemn	recognition
feel grateful	talent
one-two punch	feel disappointed

2. Please interpret the following paragraph by using the techniques illustrated above. Please pay attention to the underlined sentences as they require special treatment during interpreting.

Too many people think of happiness as the ultimate goal of life. But, if you're waiting for happiness to arrive then it's likely that it never will!// You're always wanting something more, always looking forward to a time when you'll be "happy". And, if you fall into this trap, you'll never reach that goal. Happiness should not be your life's goal, it should be your life! // The only time to be happy is right now! It's state of mind, not a set of accomplishments or the accumulation of material things. You must accept that life will always have challenges and things will not always go your way.// Instead of feeling disappointed when things don't work out the way you'd hoped, feel grateful for the experience. Instead of dreaming of a brighter, happier, richer tomorrow, make today as wonderful as you can.// Happiness is a conscious decision and that I can make it right now. Thinking of the future and having aspirations is essential to leading a happy and fulfilled life. The trick is not to let thoughts of the future overshadow your enjoyment of the present and the appreciation of the things and people you have in your life right now!// There is no way to happiness: happiness is the way! Stop waiting for happiness to arrive and simply decide to be happy! It's not some great goal or destination, it's a journey and a way of life.

3. Please interpret the following passage by using the techniques illustrated above. Please pay attention to the underlined sentences as they require special treatment during interpreting.

How to cope with the "Haters"

① If you're someone who aspires to something beyond the ordinary, you must have figured out by now that there will always be those who are jealous or resentful of your success. It doesn't matter that you've worked long and hard to get where you are, nor that you've made great sacrifices in achieving your goals. The "haters" will always find a reason to criticize and even condemn you. They're spiteful people who begrudge you the pride you have in yourself and the recognition you're receiving from others. They can't stand it that you're happy, fulfilled and achieving your goals. These hateful individuals are unwilling to do the work that you've done; they rarely make the same kinds of sacrifices or put in the long, hard hours. They resent your success but are too lazy or spoiled to invest real time or energy in the pursuit of their own goals.

② It's true that we aren't always going to succeed in our ventures, even if we put in the time and effort. Results are never guaranteed and life has a way of throwing curve balls at us. I loved it when Tina Fey went up to collect her Golden Globe and held it high, saying, "This is for all the haters!" She's a good example of a talented, hard-working and successful person who's received an inordinate amount of negative press. Ms. Fey may be besieged by haters but she refuses to let them get to her.

③ The thing you need to know about these haters is that the only reason they behave this way is that you have something they want but they aren't willing to work for it. The haters are convinced that you've been lucky or that you've had some unfair advantage but the truth is that your success is born of your untiring efforts, and it's these efforts that have brought about your "luck". The best way to deal with haters is what I call the "one-two punch".

④ First, don't let them phase you. Be happy about your success and proud of your accomplishments. Let in the approval and the recognition from affirming, supportive people and never doubt that you deserve all this. The haters are angry, jealous people. What they think or say is ultimately meaningless.

⑤ Next, the more the haters harass you, the more you should be motivated to succeed. They want to undermine you but your response should be to work that much harder in order to increase your level of success.

⑥ When your reaction to their hostility has inspired you to achieve further success, you've transformed the haters' negativity into fuel for your creative fires. Not only can they not hurt you but they've inadvertently spurred you on to even greater heights.

7.4　家庭主题词汇汇总(Vocabulary Build-up)

present address	目前住址
home phone	住宅电话
postal code	邮政编码
native place	籍贯
autonomous region	自治区
nationality	国籍
marital status	婚姻状况
dual citizenship	双重国籍
family status	家庭状况
married	已婚
single/unmarried	未婚
divorced	离婚
short-sighted	近视
far-sighted	远视
separated	分居

(续表)

ID card	身份证
lane	胡同
house number	门牌
key school	重点中学
nightdress	睡衣
bedding	床上用品
bed frame/bed base	床架
sprung base	弹簧床
mattress	床垫
coffee table	咖啡台
escalator	滚梯
rocking chair	摇椅
wardrobe	衣柜
meter box	水表
lamp shade	灯罩
socket	插座
traffic light	交通灯
trash bin	垃圾箱

7.5 扩展练习(Enhancement Practice)

Retelling.

Directions: Listen to the following passages once and then reproduce them in the same language at the end of each segment.

A. English Passage

I never really knew my own father. I was raised by a single mom and two wonderful grandparents who made incredible sacrifices for me. And there are single parents all across the country who do a heroic job raising terrific kids. But I still wish I had a dad who was not only around, but involved; another role model to teach me what my mom did her best to instill – values like hard work and integrity; responsibility and delayed gratification – all the things that give a child the foundation to envision a brighter future for themselves.

That's why I try every day to be for Michelle and my girls what my father was not for my mother and me. And I've met plenty of other people – dads and uncles and men without a family connection –who are trying to break the cycle and give more of our young people a strong male role model.

Being a good parent – whether you're gay or straight; a foster parent or a grandparent – isn't easy. It demands your constant attention, frequent sacrifice, and a healthy dose of patience. And nobody's perfect. To this day, I'm still figuring out how to be a better husband to my wife and father to my kids.

And I want to do what I can as President to encourage marriage and strong families. We should reform our child support laws to get more men working and engaged with their children. And my Administration will continue to work with the faith and other community organizations, as well as businesses, on a campaign to encourage strong parenting and fatherhood.

Because if there's one thing I've learned along the way, it's that all our personal successes shine a little less brightly if we fail at family. That's what matters most. When I look back on my life, I won't be thinking about any particular legislation I passed or policy I promoted. I'll be thinking about Michelle, and the journey we've been on together. I'll be thinking about Sasha's dance recitals and Malia's tennis matches – about the conversations we've had and the quiet moments we've shared. I'll be thinking about whether I did right by them, and whether they knew, every day, just how much they were loved.

That's what I think being a father is all about. And if we can do our best to be a source of comfort and encouragement to our kids; if we can show them unconditional love and help them grow into the people they were meant to be; then we will have succeeded.

B. Chinese Passage

今天，我开始新的生活。

今天，我爬出满是失败创伤的老茧。

今天，我重新来到这个世上，我出生在葡萄园中，园内的葡萄任人享用。

今天，我要从最高最密的藤上摘下智慧的果实，这葡萄藤是好几代前的智者种下的。

今天，我要品尝葡萄的美味，还要吞下每一个成功的种子，让新生命在我心里萌芽。

我选择的道路充满机遇，也有辛酸与绝望。失败的同伴数不胜数，叠在一起，比金字塔还高。

然而，我不会像他们一样失败，因为我手中持有航海图，可以领我越过汹涌的大海，抵达梦中的彼岸。

失败不再是我奋斗的代价。它和痛苦都将从我的生命中消失。失败和我，就像水火一样，互不相容。我不再像过去一样接受它们。我要在智慧的指引下，走出失败的阴影，步入富足、健康、快乐的乐园，这些都超出了我以往的梦想。

我要是能长生不老，就可以学到一切，但我不能永生，所以，在有限的人生里，我必须学会忍耐的艺术，因为大自然的行为一向是从容不迫的。造物主创造树中之王橄榄树需要一百年的时间，而洋葱经过短短的九个星期就会枯老。我不留恋从前那种洋葱式的生活，我要成为万树之王——橄榄树，成为现实生活中最伟大的推销员。

7.6 口译点滴(Information Link)

■ 习近平主席在多个场合对"一带一路"倡议的阐述(七)

中国国家主席习近平在"一带一路"国际合作高峰论坛开幕式上发表题为《携手推进"一带一路"建设》的主旨演讲

习近平提出，我们要将"一带一路"建成和平之路、繁荣之路、开放之路、创新之路、文明之路。"一带一路"是一项造福各国人民的世纪工程。和平合作、开放包容、互学互鉴、互利共赢。古丝绸之路，和时兴，战时衰。"一带一路"建设离不开和平安宁的环境。我们要构建以合作共赢为核心的新型国际关系，打造对话不对抗、结伴不结盟的伙伴关系。"一带一路"建设不是另起炉灶、推倒重来，而是实现战略对接、优势互补。不论来自亚洲、欧洲，还是非洲、美洲，都是"一带一路"建设国际合作的伙伴。

——2017年5月14日

Xi Jinping said Sunday the Belt and Road should be built into a road for peace, a road of prosperity, a road of opening-up, a road of innovation and a road connecting different civilizations. The Belt and Road Initiative is "a project of the century" that will benefit people across the world. The ancient silk routes embody the spirit of "peace and cooperation, openness and inclusiveness, mutual learning and mutual benefit". "The ancient silk routes thrived in times of peace, but lost vigor in times of war. The pursuit of the Belt and Road Initiative requires a peaceful and stable environment." "We should foster a new type of international relations featuring win-win cooperation; and we should forge partnerships of dialogue with no confrontation and of friendship rather than alliance." Xi Jinping said that the pursuit of the Belt and Road Initiative is not meant to reinvent the wheel. "Rather, it aims to complement the development strategies of countries involved by leveraging their comparative strengths." All countries, from either Asia, Europe, Africa or the Americas, can be international cooperation partners of the Belt and Road Initiative."

——May 14th, 2017

第二篇　提高篇

第8单元　转换法 I (Conversion I)

口译主题：国际热点

单元学习目的(Unit Goals)

➤ 掌握本课程所讲授的词语转换技巧。

➤ 学习国际热点专题所涉及的常用词语和表达。

导入(Lead -in)

1. 口译中常用的转换技巧有哪些？

2. 以下三句话的译文分别运用了什么转换方法？

In his article the author is critical of man's negligence toward his environment.

【译】作者在文章中，对人类疏忽自身环境做了批评。

In some of the European countries, the people are given the biggest social benefits such as medical insurance.

【译】在有些欧洲国家里，人民享受最广泛的社会福利，如医疗保险等。

All the students should develop morally, intellectually and physically.

【译】学生们都应该德、智、体全面发展。

8.1　技能讲解(Skill Introduction)

转换语言是决定翻译速度和质量的关键部分。英汉两种语言，有很多部分存在一一对应，如数字、专业术语、专有名词、固定表达等。但是英汉两种语言本身在词汇、句式、语篇等方面却有很大差异，需要借助一些语言转化技巧加以规范。常用的转换技巧包括：增译法(Amplification)、减译法(Deletion)、简化法(Simplification)转换法(Conversion Reconstruction)、反译法(Negation)、拆句法(Segmentation)及合并法(Combination)等。

8.1.1 增译法(Amplification)

增译法就是在翻译时根据意义上、修辞上、句法上的需要增加原文中虽无其词但有其义的一些词。目的是使译文忠实表达原文的信息与风格,并使译文合乎表达习惯。要注意的是,增译绝不是无中生有,不是随意增加原文没有的意义。

8.1.2 减译法(Deletion)

减译,指从全文出发根据逻辑、句法、修辞的需要在译文中删减一些不必要的语言单位的全译方法。减译不是删掉原文的某些内容,而是为了避免内容重复、文字累赘,使译文更加简练,更符合目的语的习惯,形式上看似省去了若干语言单位,实际未减意。减译的原则:减形不减意。如"We assure you of our prompt attention to this matter",可译为"我们保证立即处理此事"。

8.1.3 简化法(Simplification)

翻译时不按原语逐词逐句译,而直接使用目标语中常用的简称说法,达到省时更省力的目的。使用缩略语也属于简化法。如"我们应根据《联合国气候变化框架公约》及其《京都议定书》的要求,积极落实 '巴厘路线图' 谈判",可译为"We should act in keeping with the provisions of the UNFCCC and its Protocol and advance negotiations under the Bali Roadmap in real earnest"(UNFCCC,即 The United Nations Framework Convention on Climate Change,Protocol即Kyoto protocol,京都议定书)。

8.1.4 转换法(Conversion Reconstruction)

汉语和英语分别属于不同的语系,在词汇和句法方面有很多不同之处。要想把汉语句子译成一个完整的英文句子,源语言在译入语中有时要做适当调整,未必还直译成对应的词性或句子结构。为使翻译更加符合目的语的表达习惯,如果机械地按照原词翻译,则可能会使译文听起来别扭,有时即使在语法上通顺,听众听起来也会不舒服。转换法就是指在翻译过程中为了使译文符合目标语的表述方式、方法和习惯而对原句中的词类、句型和语态等进行转换。

(1) 词性的转换(The Conversion of Part of Speech)

所谓词性转换就是指在翻译过程中一种语言中所用的词汇在译成另一种语言时不能采用完全对等的表达方式,而是转换成其他别的词类。常用的词性转换包括把名词转换为代词、形容词、动词;把动词转换成名词、以名词为中心的短语、形容词、副词、介词短语。此外,动词还可转换为独立主格,把形容词转换成名词、副词和短语,把介词转换成动词，把名词转换成副词等。我们以下面几句话为例。

"对于我们这样一个发展中国家，更应该<u>注意</u>培养一批这样的参与者，让他们充分<u>认识理解</u>金融衍生产品的重要作用。"可译为："In a developing country like China, more <u>emphasis</u> should be put on the education of market participants so that they may gain an adequate <u>understanding</u> of the importance of financial derivatives."该译文中画线部分的动词被译为对等名词。

"我们要通过加强我们之间的经济、文化、科学、技术交流和人员往来<u>加深了解</u>。"可译为："We seek a <u>deep-rooted</u> understanding through the multiplication of our economic, cultural, scientific, technical and human ties."该译文中画线部分动词被译为对等形容词。

"I'm all <u>for</u> you opinion."可译为："我完全<u>赞成</u>你的意见。"该译文中画线部分介词被译为对等动词。

"学生们都应该<u>德、智、体</u>全面发展。"可译为："All the students should develop <u>morally, intellectually and physically</u>."该译文中画线部分名词被译为对等副动词。

"一些金属容易加工，而另一些金属却不容易。"可译为："Some metals are easy to machine; others are not."汉英两种语言有一个重大差别，那就是英语尽量避免重复，如果一句话里或相连几句话里需要重复某个词语，则用代词来代替，或以其他手段来避免重复。所以英译汉时要少用代词，多用实词。汉语不怕重复，连续使用某个词语很常见。汉语也使用代词，但不如英语用得多。

(2) 句子成分的转换(The Conversion of Sentence Constituent)

所谓句子成分转译的译法，是在翻译过程中把句子的某一成分译成另一成分。在多数情况下，词类转译必然导致句子成分的转换，如当英语的动词转译为汉语的名词或副词时，该动词的谓语成分也就相应地转译为汉语的主语、宾语或状语等。成分转换的目的是使译文通顺，符合目的语习惯。常用的转换包括主语转译为谓语、主语转译为宾语、主语转译为状语、主语转译为定语；谓语的动词转译为名词并在句子中充当主语成分；宾语转译为主语、谓语；状语转译为主语、定语等。具体如下面两句话。

"In recent years increasing attention had been paid to the economic benefit in the production of our factory."可译为："近年来，我厂越来越注重生产中的经济效益。"该译文中的主语是含动词意义的名词，翻译时被转译为谓语。

"High-tech products of various types also can be manufactured in our country."可译为："我国也能制造各种类型的高科技产品。"原文状语在译文中转化为主语。

■ 8.1.5 反译法(Negation)

在译语中采取与源语相反的表达方式，也就是人们常说的正话反说或者反话正说。比如"She is anything but a smart student"，是正话反说，可以译为她算不上是个聪明的学生。

8.1.6　拆句法、合并法(Segmentation and Combination)

(1) 拆句法：把一个长而复杂的句子拆译成几个简单、简短的句子。常用于英译汉，在原句的关系代词、关系副词、主谓连接处，并列或转折连接处，后续成分与主体的连接处切断，或按意群切断，译成汉语分句。如 "Our relationship with China is guided by the recognition that we live in an inter-connected world. " 可译为 "我们生活在一个相互联系的世界上，我们与中国的关系正是以这样一种认识为指导。"

(2) 合并法：把几个短句合并成一个长句，多数时用于汉译英。如 "中华民族是热爱和平的民族。中华民族的复兴对世界不是威胁，而是机遇和贡献。" 可译为 "The Chinese nation is a peace-loving nation whose rejuvenation is not threat to the world, but an opportunity and contribution to the world. "

8.2　主题口译(Topic Interpreting)

8.2.1　单句口译(Sentence Practice)

Please interpret the following sentences by using the techniques illustrated above. You may interpret to your partner first and then he/she comments on your performance.

(1) The United Nations calls on all of us to observe a day of global ceasefire and non-violence, and to honour a cessation of hostilities for the duration of the Day.

(2) It will be a major boost to Iran's economy and it coincided with the United Nations report that said Iran is doing its part to restrict its controversial nuclear program, though critics have said Iran will be a nuclear power in 15 years.

(3) The 2030 Agenda for Sustainable Development is the world's inspiring new manifesto for transforming our world and building a better future for all. But as we undertake this crucial journey of implementation, a broad barrier stands in our path: corruption.

(4) With a new U.S. president coming Friday, changes in foreign policies and aid will likely follow.

(5) One person asked: "How do we know Esteemed Electors isn't a Russian operation to influence our election?"

(6) 我们欢迎《联合国气候变化框架公约》第21次缔约方大会通过的《巴黎协定》。

(7) 加强同东盟国家友好合作，推动澜湄合作走深走实，坚持通过对话谈判解决南海问题的正确方向，使南海真正成为和平、友好、合作之海。

(8) 一切形式和表现的恐怖主义，无论在何地由何人所为，也无论出于何种动机，都是对国际和平与安全的威胁、对人权的严重侵犯以及反人类的罪行。

(9) 从长远看，只有调整国家产业结构或加快污染产业转型升级，减少污染物排放源，才能缓解污染问题。

(10) 马来西亚航空MH370航班神秘消失近3年之后，其搜寻行动正式结束。

8.2.2 段落口译(Paragraph Practice)

1. Vocabulary Work: Study the following words and phrases and translate them into the target language.

网络安全	speak for
六方会谈	expediency
双重标准	gun violence
无核化	gang violence

2. Please interpret the following paragraphs by using the techniques illustrated above.

(1) 在网络安全问题上，中方的立场是明确和一贯的。我们反对一切形式的网络攻击，反对在此问题上采取双重标准。网络空间需要合作和国际规则。希望各方切实本着互尊互信的精神，积极开展对话与合作，妥善处理网络安全问题，共同维护网络空间的和平与安全。

(2) 中方认为，尽管六方会谈经历了一些曲折，但仍是维护半岛和平稳定、实现半岛无核化的有效机制，也是有关各方接触对话、改善关系的重要平台。希望有关各方共同努力，多做有利于推动局势进一步缓和的事情，尽快回到对话协商轨道，为尽早重启六方会谈创造条件。中方将继续就此与包括韩国在内的有关各方保持密切沟通和协调。

(3) So ISIL speaks for no religion. Their victims are overwhelmingly Muslim, and no faith teaches people to massacre innocents. No just God would stand for what they did yesterday, and for what they do every single day. ISIL has no ideology of any value to human beings. Their ideology is bankrupt. They may claim out of expediency that they are at war with the United States or the West, but the fact is they terrorize their neighbors and offer them nothing but an endless slavery to their empty vision, and the collapse of any definition of civilized behavior.

(4) Gun violence is an issue in Chicago, Illinois, America's third largest city. The Brennan Center for Justice blames the increase on fewer police officers working in some cities, as well as poverty and increased gang violence. Gary Slutkin is founder of a group called Cure Violence. Slutkin said the workers often knew when a young person was planning a violent act just by living nearby. His group has trained people to work in their communities to persuade people to choose non-violent ways of dealing with conflicts. Often the "issue" with another young person was not that big a deal — maybe someone spoke to his girlfriend or owes him money. His workers, Slutkin said, could persuade young people that their problem with another person was not worth a violent response.

8.2.3 篇章口译[Passage Practice (E to C)]

1. Please interpret the following passage by using the techniques illustrated above. Please pay attention to the underlined sentences as they require special treatment during interpreting.

David Cameron's Resignation Speech

① Good morning everyone, the country has just taken part in a giant democratic exercise, perhaps the biggest in our history. Over 33 million people from England, Scotland, Wales, Northern Ireland and Gibraltar have all <u>had their say.</u>[1]

② We should be proud of the fact that in these islands we trust the people for these big decisions.

③ We not only have a parliamentary democracy, but on questions about the arrangements for how we are governed, there are times when it is right to ask the people themselves, and that is what we have done.

④ The British people have voted to leave the European Union and their will must be respected.

⑤ I want to thank everyone who took part in the campaign on my side of the argument, including all those who put aside party differences to speak in what they believed was the national interest. And let me congratulate all those who took part in the Leave campaign for the spirited and passionate case that they made.

⑥ The will of the British people is an instruction that must be delivered. It was not a decision that was taken lightly, not least because so many things were said by so many different organizations about the significance of this decision.

⑦ So there can be no doubt about the result.

⑧ Across the world people have been watching the choice that Britain has made. I would reassure those markets and investors that Britain's economy is fundamentally strong. And I would also reassure Britons living in European countries and European citizens living here that there will be no immediate changes in your circumstances. There will be no initial change in the way our people can travel, in the way our goods can move or the way our services can be sold.

⑨ We must now prepare for a negotiation with the European Union. This will need to involve the full engagement of the Scottish, Welsh and Northern Ireland governments, to ensure that the interests of all parts of our United Kingdom are protected and advanced.

⑩ But above all, this will require strong, determined and committed leadership. I'm very proud and very honored to have been Prime Minister of this country for six years.

⑪ <u>I believe we've made great steps, with more people in work than ever before in our history, with reforms to welfare and education, increasing people's life chances, building a bigger</u>

and stronger society, keeping our promises to the poorest people in the world, and enabling those who love each other to get married whatever their sexuality.⁽²⁾ But above all, restoring Britain's economic strength, and I'm grateful to everyone who has helped to make that happen.

⑫ I have also always believed that we have to confront big decisions, not duck them.

⑬ That is why we delivered the first coalition government in 70 years to bring our economy back from the brink. It's why we delivered a fair, legal and decisive referendum in Scotland. And it's why I made the pledge to renegotiate Britain's position in the European Union and to hold the referendum on our membership and have carried those things out.

⑭ I fought this campaign in the only way I know how, which is to say directly and passionately what I think and feel — head, heart and soul. I held nothing back. I was absolutely clear about my belief that Britain is stronger, safer and better off inside the European Union, and I made clear the referendum was about this and this alone — not the future of any single politician, including myself.

⑮ But the British people have made a very clear decision to take a different path, and as such I think the country requires fresh leadership to take it in this direction.

⑯ I will do everything I can as Prime Minister to steady the ship over the coming weeks and months, but I do not think it would be right for me to try to be the captain that steers our country to its next destination.

⑰ This is not a decision I've taken lightly, but I do believe it's in the national interest to have a period of stability and then the new leadership required.⁽³⁾ There is no need for a precise timetable today, but in my view we should aim to have a new prime minister in place by the start of the Conservative Party conference in October.

⑱ Delivering stability will be important and I will continue in post as Prime Minister with my Cabinet for the next three months.⁽⁴⁾The Cabinet will meet on Monday. The Governor of the Bank of England is making a statement about the steps that the Bank and the Treasury are taking to reassure financial markets.⁽⁵⁾

⑲ We will also continue taking forward the important legislation that we set before Parliament in the Queen's Speech. And I have spoken to Her Majesty the Queen this morning to advise her of the steps that I am taking.

⑳ A negotiation with the European Union will need to begin under a new Prime Minister, and I think it's right that this new Prime Minister takes the decision about when to trigger Article 50 ⁽⁶⁾and start the formal and legal process of leaving the EU.

㉑ I will attend the European Council next week to explain the decision the British people have taken and my own decision. The British people have made a choice. That not only needs to be respected — but those on the losing side of the argument, myself included, should help to make it work.

㉒ Britain is a special country. We have so many great advantages — a parliamentary democracy where we resolve great issues about our future through peaceful debate; a great trading nation with our science and arts; our engineering and our creativity, respected the world over.(7)

㉓ And while we are not perfect, I do believe we can be a model for the multi-racial, multi-faith democracy, where people can come and make a contribution and rise to the very highest that their talent allows.

㉔ Although leaving Europe was not the path I recommended, I am the first to praise our incredible strengths. I have said before that Britain can survive outside the European Union, and indeed that we could find a way.

㉕ Now the decision has been made to leave, we need to find the best way, and I will do everything I can to help.

㉖ I love this country, and I feel honored to have served it. And I will do everything I can in future to help this great country succeed.

㉗ Thank you very much.

Notes on the text

(1) had their say

表达个人的意见，发表意见

(2) I believe we've made great steps, with more people in work than ever before in our history, with reforms to welfare and education, increasing people's life chances, building a bigger and stronger society, keeping our promises to the poorest people in the world, and enabling those who love each other to get married whatever their sexuality.

我相信我们做出了巨大的进步：就业人数从未如此之多；我们对福利和教育进行改革，改善人民生活质量、建设更大更强的社会；保持对全世界最贫困人民做出的承诺；不论性别因素，让相爱的人们合法结婚。

注意介词和分词结构的译法。

(3) I do believe it's in the national interest to have a period of stability and then the new leadership required.

但从国家利益出发，我认为我们需要一段稳定期，之后便需要更换新的领导人。

注意介词短语"in the national interest"和分词"required"翻译。

(4) Delivering stability will be important and I will continue in post as Prime Minister with my Cabinet for the next three months.

保持稳定是非常重要的，在接下来的三个月里，我将继续作为首相和我的内阁一起为大家服务。

介词短语"be in post"意为继续工作，应译为动词。

(5) The Governor of the Bank of England is making a statement about the steps that the Bank and the Treasury are taking to reassure financial markets.

英格兰银行行长将发表声明，阐释央行与财政部关于确保金融市场稳定采取的下一步措施。

注意这句话中出现了两个现在进行时，表示的是将要采取的行动。

(6) Article 50

该演说中指《里斯本条约》(*The Treaty of Lisbon*)第50条。

(7) We have so many great advantages —a parliamentary democracy where we resolve great issues about our future through peaceful debate; a great trading nation with our science and arts; our engineering and our creativity, respected the world over.

我们拥有很多杰出的优点：我们实行议会民主制，通过和平辩论的方式解决关乎未来的重要事项；我们是强大的贸易国家，科学和艺术、工程和创造力深受世界推崇。

注意如何将名词短语译为句子。

2. Please interpret the following passage by using the techniques illustrated above. Please pay attention to the underlined sentences as they require special treatment during interpreting.

Remarks by the President at the September 11th Observance at the Pentagon Memorial (Excerpts)

① Secretary Hagel, General Dempsey, members of our Armed Forces and most of all, the survivors who bear the wounds of that day and the families of those we lost, it is an honor to be with you here again to remember the tragedy of twelve Septembers ago—to honor the greatness of all who responded and to stand with those who still grieve and to provide them some measure of comfort once more. Together we pause and we pray and we give humble thanks—as families and as a nation—for the strength and the grace that from the depths of our despair has brought us up again, has revived us again, has given us strength to keep on.

② We pray for the memory of all those taken from us—nearly 3 000 innocent souls. Our hearts still ache for the futures snatched away, the lives that might have been—the parents who would have known the joy of being grandparents, (1) the fathers and mothers who would have known the pride of a child's graduation, the sons and daughters who would have grown, maybe married and been blessed with children of their own. Those beautiful boys and girls just beginning to find their way who today would have been teenagers and young men and women looking ahead, imagining the mark they'd make on the world.

③ They left this Earth. They slipped from our grasp.(2) But it was written, "What the heart has once owned and had, it shall never lose." What your families lost in the temporal, in the here and now, is now eternal. The pride that you carry in your hearts, the love that will never die, your loved ones' everlasting place in America's heart.

④ We pray for you, their families, who have known the awful depths of loss. And in the

的重大问题。无论是叙利亚还是中东地区，都不能再承受一场新的战争之乱。安理会在处理叙利亚问题时，必须铭记《宪章》的宗旨和原则，<u>本着对叙利亚人民负责、对世界负责、对历史负责的态度，</u>[2] 确保所做的任何决定都经得起历史的检验。

② 数周前，<u>围绕叙利亚问题曾战云密布，</u>[3]许多国家忧心忡忡。中国一贯反对在国际关系中使用武力。我们始终认为，军事手段不但解决不了叙利亚问题，反而会带来更大动荡与灾难。<u>令人欣慰的是，安理会刚刚一致通过了第2118号决议，将叙利亚局势从一触即发的战争边缘拉回到和平轨道，为推动叙利亚问题政治解决提供了新的机遇。</u>[4] 这是一年多来，安理会首次就叙利亚问题一致采取的重大行动。这份决议符合政治解决叙利亚问题的大方向，体现了安理会的作用，也维护了安理会的团结。中方对此表示欢迎。

③ 中国在二战期间曾深受侵华日军使用化学武器之害。<u>我们坚决反对任何国家、任何组织和个人使用化武，</u>[5] 无论谁使用化武，都应受到一致谴责。

④ 中国欢迎叙利亚政府日前加入《禁止化学武器公约》。安理会第2118号决议制定了销毁叙利亚化武的总体目标，明确了下步工作的路线图。中方愿派专家参与有关工作，并为此提供资助。我们希望有关各方保持密切合作，履行各自责任，全面、准确执行禁化武组织决定和安理会决议，最终实现叙利亚化武问题的妥善解决。

⑤ 叙利亚人道主义局势日趋严峻，中方对此深表关注。中国政府已经向叙利亚境内外平民提供了1100多万美元的人道主义援助。中国正在落实对约旦提供的1500万元人民币紧急人道主义物资援助，并将向世界粮食计划署和世界卫生组织提供2400多万元人民币紧急人道现汇援助，分别用于救助叙利亚境内的流离失所者和黎巴嫩境内的叙利亚难民。我们将继续向叙利亚及其邻国提供力所能及的人道主义帮助。

⑥ 政治解决是叙利亚问题的唯一出路，应同销毁叙利亚化武进程并行推进。安理会第2118号决议明确要求落实日内瓦会议公报，呼吁召开第二次日内瓦国际会议。<u>叙利亚有关各方应以国家和人民的利益为重，尽快停火止暴，通过对话结束危机，重建家园，</u>[6]中方希望国际社会凝聚共识，推动第二次日内瓦国际会议尽快召开。中方将继续支持潘基文秘书长和普拉希米联合特别代表的斡旋努力。

⑦ 叙利亚问题十分错综复杂，无论是销毁化武，还是政治解决进程，都难以一帆风顺，今后很可能会遇到这样或那样的问题。我们希望各方保持耐心和定力，坚持和平处理争端的方针，坚持政治解决的方向。中国作为安理会常任理事国，愿同各方一道，为叙利亚问题的全面、妥善、长期解决继续做出不懈努力。

Notes on the text

(1) <u>逾700万叙利亚平民流离失所，生命和财产均蒙受惨重损失。</u>

... over seven million Syrians became homeless and there was tremendous loss of life and property.

注意动词转译为名词。

(2) <u>本着对叙利亚人民负责、对世界负责、对历史负责的态度……</u>

...act with a sense of responsibility to the Syrian people, the world and history...

(3) 围绕叙利亚问题曾战云密布

... dark clouds of war overshadowed the Syrian issue...

注意状语转译为宾语。

(4) 令人欣慰的是，安理会刚刚一致通过了第2118号决议，将叙利亚局势从一触即发的战争边缘拉回到和平轨道，为推动叙利亚问题政治解决提供了新的机遇。

We are heartened to see that the Security Council has just unanimously adopted Resolution 2118, bringing the Syrian situation back to the track of peace from the verge of war and presenting a new opportunity for seeking a political settlement of the Syrian issue.

注意两个并列谓语"将……拉回"和"为推动……"被转译为分词引导的状语。

(5) 我们坚决反对任何国家、任何组织和个人使用化武。

We are firmly opposed to the use of chemical weapons by any country, any group or any individual.

注意将动词转译为名词。

(6) 利亚有关各方应以国家和人民的利益为重，尽快停火止暴，通过对话结束危机，重建家园。

Relevant parties in Syria should keep in mind the interests of Syria and its people, realize a ceasefire and cession of violence as soon as possible, put an end to the crisis through dialogue and rebuild the homes for Syrians.

注意动词到名词的转译。

8.3　参考译文(Reference Version)

■ 8.3.1　单句口译(Sentence Practice)

Please interpret the following sentences by using the techniques illustrated above. You may interpret to your partner first and then he/she comments on your performance.

(1) 联合国呼吁所有人纪念全球停火和无暴力日，并在国际日期间停止敌对行动。

(2) 此举将会促进伊朗经济的发展，同时也符合联合国在报告中指出在限制伊朗的核项目上这个国家要负上自己的责任，但批评人士称这个国家会在未来15年内成为核强国。

(3) 国际社会以《2030年可持续发展议程》发出了鼓舞人心的新宣言，要让世界改观，要为所有人建设更美好的未来。然而，就在我们踏上落实《议程》这一重要征程之际，一道巨大的障碍挡住了去路，那就是腐败。

(4) 周五美国候任总统将宣誓就职，其外交和援助政策可能会做相应的调整。

(5) 有人反问，"难道'尊敬的选举人'不是俄罗斯为了干涉美国大选而搞的鬼？"

(6) We welcomed the adoption of the Paris Agreement at the 21st Session of the Conference of the Parties to the United Nations Framework Convention on Climate Change (UNFCCC).

(7) We will intensify friendly cooperation with ASEAN countries, promote solid and in-depth Lancang-Mekong Cooperation, keep to the right approach of settling the South China Sea issue through dialogue and negotiation, and turn the relevant waters into a sea of peace, friendship and cooperation.

(8) Terrorism in all its forms and manifestations committed by whomever, wherever, and for whatever purposes, is a threat to international peace and security, a grave violation of human rights and a crime against humanity.

(9) In the long run, the pollution problem can only be eased by adjusting the country's industrial structure, or accelerating the upgrading of polluting industries, so as to cut down the emission sources of pollutants.

(10) The search for Malaysia Airlines Flight 370 has officially ended, nearly three years after the plane mysteriously disappeared.

8.3.2　段落口译[Paragraph Practice]

1. Vocabulary Work: Study the following words and phrases and translate them into the target language.

cyber security	代表
the Six-Party Talks	从自身利益考虑、私利
double standard	枪支暴力
denuclearization	帮派暴力

2. Please interpret the following paragraphs by using the techniques illustrated above.

(1) China's position on cyber security is consistent and clear. China is opposed to all forms of cyber attacks and a double standard on this issue. What we need in the cyber space is cooperation and international regulations. We hope that all parties could conduct dialogue and cooperation actively in the spirit of mutual respect and trust and handle the issue of cyber security properly so as to jointly uphold peace and security of the cyber space.

(2) China believes that despite some setbacks, the Six-Party Talks remains an effective mechanism for peace, stability and denuclearization of the Korean Peninsula as well as a major platform for contact, dialogue and improvement of relations among relevant parties. We hope that all parties could make joint efforts to further ease the tensions, return to the track of dialogue and consultation and create conditions for an early resumption of the Six-Party Talks. China will maintain close communication and coordination with all relevant parties including the ROK.

(3) 因此，ISIL不代表任何宗教。他们的受害人绝大多数是穆斯林。没有任何信仰教人屠杀无辜。没有任何正直的天主支持他们昨天的行径和他们每一天的作为。ISIL没有任何具有人类价值的意识形态。他们的意识形态是邪恶的。他们可以出于自身需要而声称是在与西方交战，但事实是，他们让邻里处于恐怖之中，除了使人沦为他们空妄之想的永无尽头的奴隶和毁灭任何意义上的文明举止之外，丝毫不能给人带来任何好处。

(4) 枪支暴力是成为美国第三大城市伊利诺伊州芝加哥市的一项棘手问题。布伦南司法中心将该现象归咎于一些城市在职警员人数的减少以及贫困和帮派暴力的增加。加里·斯卢克金是"治愈暴力"团体的创始人。斯卢克金说，当周围的年轻人商议暴力行为时，职员们容易得到消息。该组织已经培训人们在自己的社区工作，说服人们以非暴力手段处理冲突。年轻人之间的"矛盾"通常不是什么大问题，也许有人出言调戏自己的女朋友或是欠钱不还。斯卢克金说，他的职员就能够劝导年轻人，这等鸡毛蒜皮的小事不值得诉诸暴力。

8.3.3 篇章口译[Passage Practice (E to C)]

1. Please interpret the following passage by using the techniques illustrated above. Please pay attention to the underlined sentences as they require special treatment during interpreting.

戴维·卡梅伦辞职演说

① 各位早上好，这个国家刚刚进行了一场大型的民主活动，这也许是我们历史上最大的一次。超过3300万来自英格兰、苏格兰、威尔士、北爱尔兰和直布罗陀的人民表达了他们的声音。

② 我们应该为这个事实感到骄傲。在这片国土上，我们相信人民是重大的决策者。

③ 我们不仅拥有议会民主制度，而且在如何管理这个国家的问题上，我们也会适时征求人民的意愿。对此我们已经做到了。

④ 英国人民投票选择离开欧盟，他们的意愿必须得到尊重。

⑤ 我要感谢在这场活动里和我持相同意见的每个人，这其中包括摈弃政党偏见来表达他们对国家利益信念的所有人。同时，我也祝贺所有进行脱欧活动的人们，他们进行了活跃和充满热情的活动。

⑥ 英国人民的意愿是必须执行的指令。这不是一个轻易做出的决定，并不仅仅是因为众多不同组织对这一决定的重要性阐述了众多观点。

⑦ 因此对这个结果不应持有疑问。

⑧ 全世界的人民都已经看到了英国做出的决定。我想对市场及投资者重申的是，英国的经济基础非常强劲。另外我也向居住在欧洲国家的英国公民以及在英国居住的欧洲公民保证，你们的现状不会立刻发生改变。我们的人民在出行方式上目前不会有任何改变。物品运送、服务提供都将照常进行。

⑨ 我们现在必须做出准备，与欧盟进行协商。协商需要苏格兰、威尔士以及北爱尔兰政府的共同参与，以确保联合王国各方面的利益都受到保护和推进。

⑩ 但要做到以上全部，我们需要强劲、坚定且负责任的领导者。我非常骄傲和荣幸能在过去的六年里担任这个国家的首相。

⑪ 我相信我们做出了巨大的进步：就业人数从未如此之多；我们对福利和教育进行改革，改善人民生活质量，建设更大更强的社会；保持对全世界最贫困人民做出的承诺；

不论性别因素，让相爱的人们合法结婚。所有这一切都将让英国继续保持其经济实力。我对帮助实现这一切的所有人表示感谢。

⑫ 我始终相信，对重大决策，我们应该面对，而不是回避。

⑬ 这就是为什么我们成立了70年来首个联合政府，带领经济脱离濒危边缘。这就是为什么我们在苏格兰进行了公正、合法、有决定意义的公投。这也是为什么我做出承诺，与欧盟重新商议英国的地位，开启英国与欧盟关系的公投，并实现它们。

⑭ 我以自己知道的唯一方法进行着这个过程，那就是直接、用心地表达我内心的想法和感受。我没有任何保留，我的立场很明确，英国在欧盟内将会更加强大、安全和繁荣。我也强调了这次公投跟任何政客的前途，包括我自己，没有任何关系。

⑮ 但是英国民众已经做出了明确且不同的选择，因此我认为英国需要新的领导人来带领我们的国家向前。

⑯ 我将以首相的身份尽我所能在未来几个星期、几个月中稳定局面。但我认为并不应该由我作为领导人带领我们的国家向新的目的地前进。

⑰ 这是我经过慎重考虑做出的决定。但从国家利益出发，我认为我们需要一段稳定期，之后便需要更换新的领导人。我们不需要今天就制定一个详细的时间进度表，但是我认为，在10月保守党大会开始之前，我们需要一个新的首相继任。

⑱ 保持稳定是非常重要的，在接下来的三个月里，我将继续作为首相和我的内阁一起为大家服务。内阁将在周一举行会谈。英格兰银行行长将发表声明，阐释央行与财政部关于确保金融市场稳定采取的下一步措施。

⑲ 我们也会继续推进在女王议会讲话中制定的重要立法议程。我今天早晨也跟女王陛下通话并告知我即将采取的行动。

⑳ 与欧盟的协商需要由新的首相开启，我认为应该由新任首相去决定何时启动《里斯本条约》第50条，开启脱离欧盟的正式法律程序。

㉑ 我将在下周举行的欧洲理事会会议上阐释英国人民的选择和我个人的决定。英国人民已经做出决定，这不仅需要被尊重；同时，失败的一方，包括我本人在内，还应该努力去协助实现这一决定。

㉒ 英国是一个特别的国家。我们拥有很多杰出的优点：我们实行议会民主制，通过和平辩论的方式解决关乎未来的重要事项；我们是强大的贸易国家，科学和艺术、工程和创造力深受世界推崇。

㉓ 虽然我们并不完美，但我相信我们能为多种族、多信仰的民主系统树立典范。人们可以来到英国，作出贡献，并凭借才华能力达到自己的顶峰。

㉔ 尽管离开欧洲并不是我推崇的道路，但我是第一个赞扬我们卓越力量的人。以前我说过，脱离欧盟英国也能继续下去，我们肯定会找到一条出路。

㉕ 现在决定已经做出，英国脱离欧盟。我们需要找到最正确的方向，而我也将尽我所能去帮助实现它。

㉖ 我热爱这个国家，能够为之效力我感到十分自豪。未来我也将尽我所能去帮助这个伟大国家取得成功。

㉗ 谢谢！

2. Please interpret the following passage by using the techniques illustrated above. Please pay attention to the underlined sentences as they require special treatment during interpreting.

总统在五角大楼9·11纪念仪式上的讲话(节选)

① 国防部长哈格尔、登普西将军、我国武装部队成员，最重要的是，饱含那一日伤痛的幸存者以及遇难者家属，我有幸与你们一起再一次回顾12年前的那场悲剧，纪念全体有关人员的伟大精神，他们纷纷参加抢救工作，支持那些至今仍然悲不自胜的人们，再一次给他们一些慰藉。我们一起静默片刻，我们一起祈祷。我们作为一个个家庭，作为一个国家，一起谦卑地感谢我们获得的力量和恩典，使我们再一次从深度绝望中得到拯救，使我们再一次重整旗鼓，给予我们继续蹈厉奋发的力量。

② 我们为从我们身边被夺走的生命祈祷——近3 000名无辜的亡灵。我们的心依然悲痛，因为他们的未来被无情地掠去，原来应该享有的生活被扼杀——作为祖父母，本应享受子孙绕膝之乐；作为父母，本应看到儿女毕业感到自豪；作为儿女，本应长大成人，也可能结婚并生儿育女；那些奔向花样年华的漂亮的男孩和女孩，本应成长为今天的翩翩少年或青春少女；那些年轻的男男女女，本应憧憬着未来，想象着他们将给这个世界留下什么样的印记。

③ 他们离开了这个世界。他们从我们的手中被夺走。但有人曾这样写道："心中珍惜和挚爱的东西永远不会丢失。"你们的家庭暂时失去的，此时此刻已永世长存。你们心中承载的骄傲、永不消逝的爱、你们所爱的人永远活在美国的心中。

④ 我们为你们祈祷，为他们的家人祈祷，你们深深体会到失去亲人的无限伤悲。在我们共同静默的时刻，通过你们讲述的故事，我感慨万分，你们在日常生活中表现了坚强意志，精神抖擞，兴微继绝；你们继续人生之路，重施仁爱，再展欢颜。

⑤ 你们的生活是对亡者最好的祭奠，胜于砖墙水泥建成的纪念碑。当你像他那样露出微笑，像她那样意气风发，或者为改善这个世界建立以亡者命名的奖学金和服务项目时，他们留下的精神就通过你们得到发扬光大。当你像他们一样成为消防队的一员，穿上军装或者投身于为他人的崇高事业时，就向他们证明了这一切。你们以坚韧不拔的毅力教导我们所有的人：没有我们不能承受的困难，没有我们无法战胜的灾难。

⑥ 我们为所有在战争岁月中挺身而出的人员祈祷——坚持在危险岗位上服务的外交人员，正如去年的这一天我们在班加西看到的，往往默默无闻却以各种方式保护我们的专业情报人员，以及保卫我们所爱的祖国的男女将士。

⑦ 今天，我们不仅缅怀那些在9月的那一天失去的生命。我们还向自那时以来作出了最大奉献的6 700多名爱国者——军人或平民——表达诚挚的敬意。通过他们缔结的友谊、他们阻止的袭击、他们挽救的无辜生命，以及他们在阿富汗正在最后完成使命并在明年年底结束这场战争的战友们，我们看到他们留下的财富。

⑧ 这是我们一起共同走过的征途。这些是需要继续愈合的创伤。这些表明了对上帝的信仰和我们彼此之间的信任，由此引领我们前进，让我们重振雄风，使我们每一次来到这些令人激越悲壮的地方——在这栋大楼旁，在宾夕法尼亚州的田野，在双子塔曾高高耸

立的土地上——我们都会再一次听见信义的召唤。在这里，在这个庄严的时刻，我们获得新生。在这里，我们重申必须指引我们前进的价值和美德。

⑨ 让我们积聚力量抗击凶顽的威胁，尽管这些威胁可能与12年前不同。只要有人妄图袭击我国人民，我们就要保持警惕，保卫家园。

⑩ 让我们运用智慧获得领悟，尽管有时需要使用武力，但单凭武力无法建立我们追求的世界。因此我们再次承诺发展合作伙伴关系，积极取得进展，相互尊重，加深信任，让更多的人在获得尊严、繁荣和自由的条件下生活。

⑪ 让我们信守体现美国本质的价值观，我们决不能失去信念；坚持使我们成为世界灯塔的欣欣向荣的自由；维持使我们日益强盛的丰富的多样性；秉持我们在全国服务与纪念日强调的团结精神和共同承诺。

⑫ 最重要的是，让我们以今天在场的幸存者和家属们为榜样勇敢奋进，无论夜晚多么黑暗，无论白天多么艰难。"你是叫我们多经历重大急难的，必使我们复活，从地的深处救上来。求你使我越发昌大，又转来安慰我。"

⑬ 愿上帝赐福于我们对遇难者的怀念。愿他抚慰你们和你们的家人。上帝保佑美利坚合众国。

8.3.4　篇章口译[Passage Practice(C to E)]

1. Please interpret the following passage by using the techniques illustrated above. Please pay attention to the underlined sentences as they require special treatment during interpreting.

Chinese President Xi Jinping's Speech at the Opening of the UN Climate Change Conference in Paris(Excerpts)

① Thanks to joint efforts of all parties since the United Nations Framework Convention on Climate Change entered into force over 20 years ago, global actions on climate change have made progress although there are still numerous difficulties and challenges. This Paris Conference is hence convened to strengthen implementation of the UNFCCC and bring about a comprehensive, balanced, ambitious and binding agreement on climate change. The conference is also expected to come up with equitable, reasonable and effective global solutions to climate change and explore pathways and governance models for mankind to achieve sustainable development.

② A successful international agreement should not just address immediate challenges but more importantly, it should also present a vision for the future. The Paris agreement should focus on strengthening post-2020 global actions on climate change and boost global efforts to pursue sustainable development.

③ The Paris agreement should help meet the goals of the UNFCCC and chart the course for green development. The agreement should follow the principles and rules set out in the UNFCCC and contribute to its full and effective implementation. The agreement should put effective control on the increase of atmospheric concentration of greenhouse gases and set up incentive mechanisms to encourage countries to purse green, circular and low-carbon development featuring both economic growth and an effective response to climate change.

④ The Paris agreement should help increase input of resources to ensure actions on climate change. To obtain financial and technical support for capacity building is essential for developing countries to address climate change. Developed countries should honor their commitment of mobilizing US$100 billion each year before 2020 and provide stronger financial support to developing countries afterwards. It is also important that climate-friendly technologies should be transferred to developing countries to help them build green economy.

⑤ The Paris agreement should accommodate the national conditions of various countries and lay emphasis on practical results. It is imperative to respect differences among countries, especially developing countries, in domestic policies, capacity building and economic structure. A one-size-fits-all approach must be avoided. Addressing climate change should not deny the legitimate needs of developing countries to reduce poverty and improve their people's living standards. Special needs of the developing countries must be well attended to.

⑥ The Paris Conference is not the finishing line but a new starting point. As an important part of global governance, the global efforts on climate change can be taken as a mirror for us to reflect on what models to have for future global governance and how to build a community of shared future for mankind. Much valuable inspiration may thus be drawn.

⑦ China has been actively engaged in the global campaign on climate change. China is both sincere and determined to contribute its share to the success of the Paris Conference.

⑧ In the past few decades, China has seen rapid economic growth and significant improvement in people's lives. However, this has taken a toll on the environment and resources. Having learned the lesson, China is vigorously making ecological endeavors to promote green, circular and low-carbon growth. We have integrated our climate change efforts into China's medium- and long-term program of economic and social development. We attach equal importance to mitigation and adaption, and try to make progress on all fronts by resorting to legal and administrative means, technologies and market forces. China's installed capacity of renewable energy accounts for 24% of the world's total, with the newly installed capacity accounting for 42% of the global total. China tops the world in terms of energy conservation and utilization of new and renewable energies.

⑨ "All things live in harmony and grow with nourishments." Chinese culture values harmony between man and nature and respects nature. Going forward, ecological endeavors will feature prominently in China's 13th Five-Year Plan. China will work hard to implement the vision of innovative, coordinated, green, open and inclusive development. China will, on the basis of technological and institutional innovation, adopt new policy measures to improve industrial mix, build low-carbon energy system, develop green building and low-carbon transportation, and build a nation-wide carbon emission trading market so as to foster a new pattern of modernization featuring harmony between man and nature. In its Intended Nationally Determined Contributions, China pledges to peak CO_2 emissions by around 2030 and strive to achieve it as soon as possible, and by 2030, reduce CO_2 per unit of GDP by 60%~65% over the 2005 level, raise the share of non-fossil fuels in primary energy consumption to about 20% and increase forest stock by around 4.5 billion cubic meters over 2005. This requires strenuous efforts, but we have confidence and resolve to fulfill our commitments.

⑩ China upholds the values of friendship, justice and shared interests, and takes an active part in international cooperation on climate change. Over the years, the Chinese government has earnestly fulfilled its policy commitments of South-South cooperation regarding climate change to support developing countries, especially the least developed countries, landlocked developing countries and small island developing states, in confronting the challenge of climate change. In a show of greater support, China announced in September the establishment of an RMB 20 billion South-South Climate Cooperation Fund. Next year, China will launch cooperation projects to set up 10 pilot low-carbon industrial parks and start 100 mitigation and adaptation programs in other developing countries and provide them with 1 000 training opportunities on climate change. China will continue to promote international cooperation in such areas as clean energy, disaster prevention and mitigation, ecological protection, climate-smart agriculture, and low-carbon and smart cities. China will also help other developing countries to increase their financing capacity.

2. Please interpret the following passage by using the techniques illustrated above. Please pay attention to the underlined sentences as they require special treatment during interpreting.

Statement by Wang Yi, Foreign Minister of China, at UN Security Council Meeting On the Issue of Chemical Weapons in Syria(Excerpts)

① The issue of Syria is now the top concern of the international community. In the past two years and more, over seven million Syrians became homeless and there was tremendous loss of life and property. In this august hall, the Security Council has discussed major issues involving war or peace on many occasions. Neither Syria nor the Middle East region can afford another war. In dealing with the Syrian issue, the Security Council must bear in mind the purposes and principles of the UN Charter, act with a sense of responsibility to the Syrian people, the world and history, and ensure that any decision it takes can stand the test of history.

② Several weeks ago, dark clouds of war overshadowed the Syrian issue and many countries were deeply worried. China opposes the use of force in international relations. We believe that military means cannot solve the Syrian issue. Rather it will bring greater turmoil and disaster. We are heartened to see that the Security Council has just unanimously adopted Resolution 2118, bringing the Syrian situation back to the track of peace from the verge of war and presenting a new opportunity for seeking a political settlement of the Syrian issue. This is the first time that the Security Council takes a joint major action on the Syrian issue in the past over one year. This resolution is in keeping with the general direction of a political settlement of the Syrian issue, reflects the role of the Security Council and upholds the solidarity of the Security Council. The Chinese side welcomes the adoption of the resolution.

③ China suffered deeply from the use of chemical weapons by Japanese invaders during the Second World War. We are firmly opposed to the use of chemical weapons by any country, any group or any individual. whoever uses chemical weapons should be condemned by all.

④ China welcomes the fact that the Syrian government joined the Chemical Weapons Convention (CWC) not long ago. Resolution 2118 has set out the overall objective of the destruction of chemical weapons in Syria and the roadmap for the follow-up work. The Chinese side is ready to send experts to participate in relevant work and provide financial support in this regard. We hope that the relevant parties will stay in close cooperation, fulfill their respective responsibilities and implement the OPCW decision and Security Council resolution in a comprehensive and accurate manner so as to eventually achieve a proper settlement of the issue of chemical weapons in Syria.

⑤ The humanitarian situation in Syria is getting grimmer. China is deeply concerned. The Chinese government has provided over 11million US dollars of humanitarian assistance to Syrian civilians in and outside of Syria. China is now providing 15 million RMB Yuan worth of emergency humanitarian aid to Jordan and will provide over 24 million RMB Yuan in cash remittance for emergency humanitarian aid to the World Food Program and the World Health Organization, which will be used to help the displaced people inside Syria and Syrian refugees in Lebanon. We will continue providing humanitarian help to Syria and its neighbors to the best of our capability.

⑥ Political settlement is the only way out for Syria. This process should go side by side with the process of destruction of chemical weapons in Syria. Resolution 2118 clearly asks for the implementation of the Geneva Communiqué and calls for the convocation of the Geneva II Conference. Relevant parties in Syria should keep in mind the interests of Syria and its people, realize a ceasefire and cession of violence as soon as possible, put an end to the crisis through dialogue and rebuild the homes for Syrians. China hopes that the international community will build consensus and promote the early convening of the Geneva II Conference. China will continue with its support for the mediation efforts of Secretary-General Ban Ki-moon and Joint Special Representative Alkhdar Brahimi.

⑦ The Syrian issue is highly complex. Neither the destruction of chemical weapons nor the process of political settlement will be a plain sailing. Going forward, there will probably be this problem or that. We hope that all parties will keep their patience and composure, uphold the principle of peaceful settlement of disputes and stick to the direction of political settlement. As a permanent member of the Security Council, China stands ready to work with all the parties and make unremitting efforts for comprehensive, proper and long-term settlement of the Syrian issue.

8.4 外事接待主题词汇汇总(Vocabulary Build-up)

National Association of Securities Deal Automated Quotations (NASDAQ)	纳斯达克
North-South dialogue	南北对话
refugee camp	难民营
in-fighting	内耗
annual State Budget	年度国家预算
age structure	年龄结构
attend a conference without voting rights	列席会议
zero-sum game	零和博弈
Brexit	英国脱欧
Departure from Asia for Europe	脱亚入欧
Grexit	希腊脱欧
frontier region, border region	边界地区
boundary negotiation	边界谈判
never to attach any conditions	不附带任何条件
non-aligned countries	不结盟国家
generally-accepted principles of international relations	公认的国际关系原则
joint action	共同行动
normalization of relations	关系正常化
international waters	国际水域、公海
maritime resources	海洋资源
exchange of needed goods	互通有无
mutual understanding and mutual accommodation	互谅互让
right of residence	居留权
territorial sea	领海
territorial air	领空
territorial waters	领水
territorial jurisdiction	领土管辖权
complete prohibition and thorough destruction of nuclear weapons	全面禁止和彻底销毁核武器
sacred and inviolable	神圣不可侵犯
ecocide	生态灭绝
sole legal government	唯一合法政府
colonialism and neo-colonialism	新老殖民主义
extradition	引渡
Zionism	犹太复国主义
political offender	政治犯

racial segregation, apartheid	种族隔离
to take concerted steps	采取协调行动
Pacific Rim	环太平洋地区
armed conflict	武装冲突
bloody conflict	流血冲突

8.5　扩展练习(Enhancement Practice)

Making comments on a given topics.

Directions: Please read paragraph (1) and (2) carefully and then express your views on the given topics.

(1)

In recent years, with competition in the job market getting more and more intense, college graduates are lowering their salary expectations in order to gain employment opportunities. Statistics show that one third of graduates are willing to accept a salary of about 1,000 yuan RMB per month if they cannot find better jobs while two-thirds are not. Do you think college graduates should take low-paying jobs when satisfactory jobs are not available? Why or why not?

(2)

Every September 22 is a "Car Free Day" in many countries around the world. Chengdu, capital of southeast China's Sichuan Province, pioneerd China's first "Car Free Day" on October 14, 2000. So far, over 100 Chinese cities have responded positively to the "Car Free Day" idea. Residents of these cities are urged to take public transport, ride bikes or walk instead of using their cars. Do you think this "Car Free Day" campaign is meaningful?

8.6　延伸口译(Extended Interpreting)

习近平主席在乌兹别克斯坦媒体发表的署名文章

"Grass-covered land is lush green and snow-clad mountains are translucent and silvery," to quote a poem written by a Chinese envoy in Ming Dynasty after his mission to Central Asia over 600 years ago. The magnificent landscape of Uzbekistan is familiar to and admired by the Chinese people since ancient times. I first visited your beautiful country in September 2013 and was deeply impressed by its distinct natural scenery, time-honored history and cultural heritage, and the hard-working and talented people.

"绿野草铺茵，空山雪积银。"这是600多年前明代中国官员出使中亚后写下的诗句。乌兹别克斯坦的壮美景色自古为中国人所熟知和向往。2013年9月，我第一次访问美丽的乌兹别克斯坦，这里独具特色的自然风光、积淀千年的历史文化、勤劳智慧的人民给我留下深刻印象。

The people of our two countries are diligent, courageous and honest. They cherish friendship and share similar views on personal dedication to the welfare of the nation and the world. Over 2 000 years ago, the ancient Silk Road connected China and Uzbekistan and has since witnessed the growth of two-way trade, mutual learning and people-to-people friendship. Zhang Qian in Western Han Dynasty, Xuan Zang in Tang Dynasty and Chen Cheng in Ming Dynasty traveled to Uzbekistan as an envoy or for a stopover. Renowned historical and cultural figures in Uzbekistan such as Alisher Navoi, Mirza Ulugbek and Muhammad Al Khwarizmi are known in China for their works and thoughts. Central Asia is the meeting place of Chinese and Western cultures, and Uzbekistan has played an important role as a bridge of communication. Over the centuries, China and Uzbekistan have maintained close contacts and fostered a fine tradition of friendly exchanges, thus laying a solid foundation for the good-neighborly relations we enjoy today.

中乌两国人民勤劳勇敢、诚实守诺、重情重义，对家国天下有着相似的理解。2000多年前，古老的丝绸之路将中乌两国和两国人民连接在一起，拉开了双方互通有无、互学互鉴的友谊大幕。中国西汉张骞、大唐玄奘、明代陈诚曾经出使或途经乌兹别克斯坦，纳沃伊、兀鲁伯、花拉子米等乌兹别克斯坦历史文化名人的作品和思想在中国流传。中西文化在中亚彼此交融，乌兹别克斯坦从中发挥了重要桥梁作用。千百年来，中国同乌兹别克斯坦保持密切联系，形成相互交好的优良传统，为今天中乌睦邻友好关系打下了坚实基础。

Uzbekistan is a major country in Central Asia. China views its relations with Uzbekistan from a strategic and long-term perspective. China was among the first countries to establish diplomatic relations with Uzbekistan shortly after its independence. Over the past 24 years, bilateral relations have stood the test of time and changes in the international landscape and kept a momentum of sound and steady growth. Our two sides have rendered each other firm support on issues concerning our respective core interests and achieved fruitful results in cooperation in various fields.

乌兹别克斯坦是中亚大国，中国始终从战略高度和长远角度看待中乌关系。在乌兹别克斯坦独立之初，中国率先同乌兹别克斯坦建立外交关系。24年来，中乌关系经受住时间和国际风云变幻的考验，保持健康稳定的发展势头。双方在涉及彼此核心利益问题上相互坚定支持，各领域合作取得丰硕成果。

Since 2013, President Karimov and I have stayed in close touch by way of meetings, phone calls and correspondence, and have developed good working relations and deep personal friendship. Our two sides have signed such important documents as the Treaty on Friendly

Cooperation and the Development Plan for the Strategic Partnership (2014—2018), thus cementing the political and legal foundation of bilateral relations. We are jointly building the Belt and Road, synergizing our national strategies, seeking innovative drivers for cooperation, and enhancing international coordination and security cooperation. With bilateral cooperation growing in both breadth and depth, China-Uzbekistan relations have entered a golden era of rapid development.

2013年以来,我同卡里莫夫总统以会晤、通话、互致信函等多种方式保持密切交往,建立起良好的工作关系和深厚的个人友谊。双方签署了《中乌友好合作条约》《中乌2014—2018年战略伙伴关系发展规划》等重要文件,双边关系的政治和法律基础更加牢固。双方共建"一带一路",加紧国家战略对接,创新合作驱动,加强国际协作和安全合作。中乌合作领域越来越宽,合作质量越来越高,双边关系已经进入快速发展的黄金时期。

Jointly building the Belt and Road is a highlight and priority in our bilateral cooperation. In policy communication, our two countries have signed the cooperation document on jointly building the Belt and Road and are working on an outline of cooperation plan. China appreciates that Uzbekistan was one of the first countries to express interest in the Asian Infrastructure Investment Bank and has joined it as a founding member.

当前,共建"一带一路"是中乌合作的亮点和主线。在政策沟通方面,中乌签署了共建"一带一路"合作文件,正在研究编制中乌合作规划纲要。中方赞赏乌方率先成为亚洲基础设施投资银行创始成员国。

We need to enhance political mutual trust and mutual support. The ancient Chinese philosopher Confucius said, "In his dealings with friends, one should be trustworthy in what he says." Political mutual trust is an important basis for the sound growth of China-Uzbekistan relations. We will continue to extend each other firm support on issues concerning each other's core interests such as sovereignty, security and development. China firmly supports Uzbekistan in its independent choice of a development path that suits its national conditions, understands and respects the measures taken by the Uzbek government for national stability and economic and social development, and opposes interference by external forces in Uzbekistan's internal affairs.

我们要增强政治互信,加大相互支持。中国古代思想家孔子说:"与朋友交,言而有信。"政治互信是中乌关系健康发展的重要保障。双方将继续在涉及彼此国家主权、安全、发展等核心利益问题上相互坚定支持。中方坚定支持乌兹别克斯坦根据本国国情自主选择的发展道路,理解和尊重乌兹别克斯坦政府为保持国内稳定、促进经济社会发展所采取的措施,反对外部势力干涉乌兹别克斯坦内政。

We need to work together to ensure the success of the major initiative of the Belt and Road and explore broader space for cooperation based on mutual benefit. While strengthening cooperation in the energy and resources sector, we also need to explore other areas of cooperation, facilitate bilateral trade and make it better-structured. We should seek converging interests, deepen production capacity cooperation in light of local conditions and translate our economic complementarity into more tangible outcomes of cooperation.

我们要做好共建"一带一路"这篇大文章，在互利共赢基础上开辟更广阔的合作空间。在加强能源资源合作的同时，拓展非资源领域合作，努力构建结构优化、条件便利的中乌经贸新格局。寻找利益契合点，因地制宜深化产能合作，将经济互补优势转化为更多实实在在的合作成果。

We need to increase understanding between our peoples and deepen cultural, education, tourism, archaeological and sub-national cooperation to foster a greater sense of pride and confidence in China and Uzbekistan, both ancient civilizations along the Silk Road. We should leverage the two Confucius Institutes in Uzbekistan as bridges between our youth and nurture China-Uzbekistan friendship among future generations. We need to support cultural events such as the Chinese "Happy Spring Festival" and the Uzbek "Oriental Charm" staged in each other's country and bring well-received performances and fine artistic works to more people.

我们要精心打造中乌民心相通工程，通过深化文化、教育、旅游、考古、地方合作提升中乌作为丝绸之路古国的自豪感和自信心。发挥两所孔子学院的纽带作用，加强青年学生交流，培养更多的中乌友好事业接班人。支持中国"欢乐春节"和乌兹别克斯坦"东方韵律"访演活动，鼓励品牌节目和优秀文艺作品深入民间。

As the rotating chair of the SCO this year, Uzbekistan has done a lot to secure tangible outcomes of cooperation in various fields. China stands ready to work with Uzbekistan and other member states and take the Tashkent summit as a new starting point to further enhance cooperation across the board so that the SCO will bring more benefits to this region and its people.

乌兹别克斯坦作为上海合作组织轮值主席国，为推动组织各领域合作取得实际成果作出了积极贡献。中方愿同乌方及其他成员国一道努力，以塔什干峰会为新起点，全面提高合作水平，使上海合作组织更好地造福地区和各国人民。

A Uzbek proverb goes, "A tree gets attention only when it bears fruits." China-Uzbekistan cooperation across the board has yielded fruitful results, and has benefited and won the support of our two peoples. I believe that in realizing our respective national development and rejuvenation, our two countries will join hands and write a glorious new chapter of China-Uzbekistan friendship.

乌兹别克斯坦谚语说："只有结满果实的大树才会引人注意。"中乌全方位合作已经结出累累硕果，造福两国人民，也得到两国人民拥护和支持。我相信，在实现各自国家发展振兴的征途上，中乌两国一定能够携手同行，谱写中乌友好新华章。

第9单元　转换法 Ⅱ(Conversion Ⅱ)

口译主题：外交

单元学习目的(Unit Goals) 💡

➤ 掌握本课程所讲授的词语转换技巧。
➤ 学习外交专题所涉及的常用词语和表达。

导入(Lead -in)

1. 什么是"意合""形合"？
2. 英汉两种语言在语态的使用上各有什么特点？
3. China is a country with vast territory, a big population and a long history.
【译】中国疆域辽阔，人口众多，历史悠久。
这句话翻译后在句子结构方面发生了什么变化？

9.1　技能讲解(Skill Introduction)

9.1.1　句子转换(The Conversion of Sentences)

(1) 顺句驱动(Syntactic linearity)

按照听到的与原语的相同的语序把整个句子切成意群单位或信息单位，再使用连接词把这些单位自然连接起来，译出整体的意思。如"China doesn't pose a threat to world energy security because it has depended maily on domestic resources to power its economic and social development."可按照原语语序译为"中国没有威胁世界能源安全，因为中国主要依靠国内资源来促进经济和社会发展。"

(2) 适当调整(Appropriate adjustment)

不按源语顺序，稍微调整语序或表达方式。

(3) 倒置法(Reversion)

在汉语中，定语修饰语和状语修饰语往往位于被修饰语之前；在英语中，许多修饰语常常位于被修饰语之后，因此翻译时往往要把原文的语序颠倒过来。倒置法通常用于英译汉，即对英语长句按照汉语的习惯表达法进行前后调换，按意群或进行全部倒置，原则是使汉语译句符合现代汉语论理叙事的一般逻辑顺序。有时倒置法也用于汉译英。

如"改革开放以来，中国发生了巨大的变化。"可将句子全部倒置，译为"Great changes have taken place in China since the introduction of the reform and opening policy."而"I believe strongly that it is in the interest of my countrymen that Britain should remain an active and energetic member of the European Community."这句话可进行部分倒置，译为"我坚信，英国依然应该是欧共体中的一个积极的和充满活力的成员，这是符合我国人民利益的。"

(4) 包孕法(Reversion)

这种方法多用于英译汉。所谓包孕是指在把英语长句译成汉语时，把英语后置成分按照汉语的正常语序放在中心词之前，使修饰成分在汉语句中形成前置包孕。但修饰成分不宜过长，否则会形成拖沓，或造成汉语句子成分在连接上的纠葛。如"You are the representative of a country and of a continent to which China feels particularly close."可译为"您是一位来自于使中国倍感亲切的国家和大洲的代表。"

(5) 插入法(Embedment)

插入法指把难以处理的句子成分用破折号、括号或前后逗号插入译句中。这种方法主要用于笔译中。其偶尔也用于口译中，即用同位语、插入语或定语从句来处理一些解释性成分。比如"如果说宣布收回香港就会像夫人说的带来灾难性的影响，那么我们要勇敢地面对这个灾难，做出决策。"译为"If the announcement of the recovery of Hong Kong would bring about，as Madam put it，'disastrous effects'，we will face that disaster squarely and make a new policy decision."

(6) 重组法(Reorganization)

重组法指在进行英译汉时，为了使译文流畅和更符合汉语叙事论理的习惯，在理清长句的结构、弄懂原意的基础上，彻底摆脱原文语序和句子形式，对句子进行重新组合。

9.1.2　语态的转换(The Conversion of Voice)

汉语和英语中都有主动语态和被动语态之分，但对于两种语态的运用却不尽相同，英语里运用被动语态的频率明显高于汉语。英语的某些文体为了使叙述公正、口气客观正式，常用被动句以迎合其表达的需要，尤其是新闻文体、公文文体及法律文体。

(1) 汉语常使用无主语句子，翻译时可采用被动语态补充主语。比如"要制造飞机，就必须仔细考虑空气阻力问题。"可译为"Air resistance must be given careful consideration when the aircraft is to be manufactured."

(2) 英语里常常运用被动结构把动作的承受者作为句子里的主语，来突出它的地位，强调它的重要性。因此，翻译时汉语的主动句往往变换为英语的被动句。

(3) 英语中，常常为了上下文的连贯，使句子之间的连接紧密自然而运用被动结构。翻译这类英文句子时则需根据汉语习惯变被动为主动。如 "He appeared on the stage and was warmly applauded by the audience." 可译为 "他出现在台上，观众给予热烈掌声。"

(4) 汉语中有一些习惯用语，有的用 "人们" "有人" "大家" 等作主语；有的是无主句或独立结构，如 "已经证明" "据悉" "应该说" "必须指出" 等。这些习惯用语，从语态上来说是主动语态，但翻译时都转化为被动语态，在表达方式上，则可充分利用it做形式主语的句型。常见翻译有："必须指出" 可译为 "It must be pointed out that..."；"必须承认" 可译为 "It must be admitted that..."；"可见" 可译为 "It will be seen that..."；"无可否认" 可译为 "It cannot be denied that..."；"已经证明" 可译为 "It has been proved/demonstrated that..."；"可以肯定" 可译为 "It may be confirmed that..."。

9.1.3 汉语的 "意合" 与英语的 "形合" 之间的转换(The Conversion Between Parataxis & Hypotaxis)

英汉在连贯方式上的 "形合" 和 "意合"：汉语句子之间的连接及语篇内的连贯往往隐含在上下文中，呈 "隐形" 状态；但这并不妨碍汉语读者对其阅读和理解，因为汉语是借助语篇的语境意义来弥补其在逻辑和连贯方面的不足。而英语注重句法结构，它的逻辑关系是通过外在的形式来体现的，因此其逻辑和连贯关系表现出 "形合" 的特征。在翻译中要学会借助英语表达中词法和句法的结构来将汉语表达中隐形的逻辑和连贯关系显性化。比如 "文化特色和个性是历史文化名城的独特和珍贵的标志，历史文化名城间的文化交流与合作将极大地促进城市文化可持续发展与繁荣。" 可译为 "Cultural exchanges among historical and culturally-significant cities, whose respective features and individuality are their unique and invaluable symbols, will greatly contribute to the sustainable development and prosperity of their cultures."

9.2 主题口译(Topic Interpreting)

9.2.1 单句口译(Sentence Practice)

Please interpret the following sentences by using the techniques illustrated above. You may interpret to your partner first and then he/she comments on your performance.

(1) The Ministers reiterated their strong commitment to the United Nations as a universal multilateral organization entrusted with the mandate of helping the world community maintain international peace and security, advance common development and promote and protect human

rights.

(2) The Ministers noted that preventing arms race in outer space is in the interests of maintaining international peace and security and for the promotion and strengthening of international cooperation in the exploration and the use of outer space for peaceful purposes, highlighting the prevention of placement of weapons of any kind in outer space as one of its main elements.

(3) Support the establishment of a China-CEEC (Central and Eastern European Countries) think tanks exchange and cooperation center.

(4) China and Australia have a lot to offer each other economically and our development strategies complement each other in many ways.

(5) We should deepen result-oriented cooperation and be close partners of mutual benefit.

(6) 朋友越走越近，邻居越走越亲。

(7) 亚洲各国就像一盏盏明灯，只有串联起来，才能让亚洲的夜空灯火辉煌。

(8) 中国发展对世界各国是重要机遇。中国正在加快推进新型工业化、信息化、城镇化、农业现代化，新的经济增长点将不断涌现。

(9) 中国积极帮助其他发展中国家建设基础设施，加强能力建设和贸易发展，加大对环境保护领域的援助投入，帮助受援国实现经济社会发展。

(10) 当前，中国人民正在为实现中华民族伟大复兴的中国梦而不懈奋斗。中国梦就是要实现国家富强、民族振兴、人民幸福。

■ 9.2.2　段落口译(Paragraph Practice)

1. Vocabulary Work: Study the following words and phrases and translate them into the target language.

超级大国	harmonious coexistence
独立自主的和平外交政策	forge ahead
人均国内生产总值	reform and opening-up
以……自居	peace and stability

2. Please interpret the following paragraphs by using the techniques illustrated above.

(1) 第一，中国不是什么"超级大国"，而是一个发展中国家。虽然我们是世界最大的发展中国家，经济总量居世界前列，但是人均国内生产总值还排在世界80位以后，谈不上有超级大国的基础，更不要说我们根本没有做所谓超级大国的想法。第二，在同邻国相处当中，中国从来没有以"老大哥"自居。中国奉行的是独立自主的和平外交政策，秉持亲诚惠容的周边外交理念，主张国家不论大小一律平等。如果我们之间都有诚挚的愿望，就能成为好兄弟、好朋友，不存在谁是大哥的问题。

(2) 自1991年以来，中国外交延续了一个好的传统，那就是中国的外长在每年新年之际的第一次出访就访问非洲国家。这体现了中国对非洲的重视，对中非传统友谊的珍视。这次也不例外，王毅外长传承了中国外交的这个好传统。这也是中国新一届政府执政以来，中国外长首次访问撒哈拉以南非洲，双方都非常期待此次访问。

(3) In closing, I would like to call upon the international community to forge ahead and work in unison to uphold peace and stability, embrace harmonious coexistence, and boost the impetus for openness and innovation. By doing so, I am confident we will be able to overcome whatever difficulty or obstacle that stand in our way, and bring about a better future for the world that we all call home.

(4) It must be pointed out that China is still a developing country and still has a long way to go before achieving modernization. While peace is the basic condition for China's development, reform and opening-up along with our people's desire for a happy life constitute the strongest impetus propelling development. The space of development in China's rural and urban areas and various regions is enormous, and the country's domestic demand will simply generate great potential of growth. Development at medium-to-high speed for another ten to twenty years will bring even bigger changes to China and create more development opportunities for the world.

▍9.2.3 篇章口译[Passage Practice (E to C)]

1. Please interpret the following passage by using the techniques illustrated above. Please pay attention to the underlined sentences as they require special treatment during interpreting.

Starting a New Phase in Sino-US Relations
Max Baucus, US Ambassador to China

① I often say this, and I mean it from the heart: serving as the United States Ambassador to China is the best job I've ever had. It has been the greatest pleasure to work with Chinese and Americans to advance the world's most important bilateral relationship.

② But, as they say, all good things must come to an end. The United States just had an election and, with our country's transition to a new administration, the time has come to bid you farewell as the United States Ambassador. When you say "goodbye" in Chinese it means "see you again", and that's how I like to think of this farewell – I'll be seeing you again!

③ Before my wife Mel and I depart from Beijing for a new chapter in our lives, I would like to share some parting thoughts with you as we start a new phase in our countries' relationship, at a time fraught with global challenges – from economic uncertainty to climate change to terrorism.[1]

④ Over my 35 years in the United States Senate and especially my time as the United States Ambassador, I've witnessed first-hand China's remarkable transformation and re-emergence on the global stage.

⑤ Since Deng Xiaoping launched China's opening up and reform three decades ago, China has lifted hundreds of millions out of poverty, becoming the world's second-largest economy. <u>Our economies, in turn, have grown increasingly interconnected, with more than $650 billion in annual bilateral trade.</u>(2)

⑥ I've seen China's rise play out in impressive ways. China joined the United States to help lead the world toward an ambitious agreement on climate change in Paris. <u>It played a positive role in the global response to Ebola, working closely with the United States and other partners.</u>(3)

China served as the host of the Six Party Talks on the denuclearization of the Korean Peninsula and can play an equally important role in seeing those talks resumed.

⑦ These examples make clear the benefits to China and the world that come from China's engagement and responsible leadership. <u>US policy, decades old and upheld by successive administrations from both parties, has been to welcome the rise of a stable, peaceful and prosperous China.</u>(4) <u>We welcome China as a global leader that assumes its responsibilities within the transparent, rules-based system underpinning the peace and prosperity that the Asia-Pacific region has enjoyed for many decades.</u>(5)

⑧ I worked hard as a U.S. Senator to get China into the World Trade Organization because I knew it would be good for China, good for the United States, and good for the entire world. And it was! Looking ahead, we hope China will work closely with the new US administration to continue this process of opening up to the world.

⑨ We live in a time of interconnectedness, unlike any other in history. Our countries' relationship, in fact, is a testament to and a direct benefactor of these trends.

⑩ And a key part of keeping this going in the right direction will be fostering an encouraging environment for American and foreign companies to invest and do business here – just as Chinese companies can expect to do in the United States.

⑪ Strengthening innovation, one of China's top priorities, is another critical factor. That's why we encourage China to continue to open up, which will help enable talent – like that of Jack Ma, Tu Youyou, or Wang Jianlin – to flourish across the globe. Similarly, we hope that China will welcome the constructive role of non-government organizations that help societies drive innovation, contribute to social stability and bring us together to protect the environment.

⑫ Another key element will be ensuring that China's peaceful rise is bolstered by regional engagement and creative diplomacy that manages disputes in ways that benefit all, in line with President Xi and President Obama's efforts during their numerous meetings that I've had the privilege to join.

⑬ <u>At the end of the day, I can't stress enough the importance for us all to ask honest, constructive, good-faith questions, and to really listen to each other's point of view.</u>(6) As my mentor and former United States Senator from Montana Mike Mansfield once said, "Remember, the other person isn't always wrong, and you're not always right." This is the path to honest dialogue.

⑭ While this is a time of transition, and some question the path ahead, I think both of our countries agree on the importance of making this relationship work. That has been true since President Nixon first came to China and met with Chairman Mao in what is called "the week that changed the world." Their work was carried on by President Carter and Deng Xiaoping, who normalized relations between our two countries in 1979.[7] Our leaders have changed, and we've had our ups and downs, but we've never given up our shared goal to create a better future for our kids and grandchildren.

⑮ I've seen this commitment first-hand, time and time again. When I first came to China, I promised President Xi that I would visit all of China's provinces – a goal I achieved last October. What I learned along the way is that it doesn't matter if you're American or Chinese, we all basically want the same things in life – a good job, a good education for our children, and a clean, safe environment to live in. That's a big part of the American dream. And it's part of what I've come to learn—the Chinese dream.

⑯ With patience, persistence and the positive attitude I've seen in students, everyday people, business people, or government officials throughout this country – from Qufu to Kunming, from Shanghai to Urumqi – I know there is nothing we can't accomplish when we work together. And when we succeed – whether that's working on those many issues on which we agree, or being frank and wisely in managing our differences – the world stands to benefit.

Notes on the text

(1) Before my wife Mel and I depart from Beijing for a new chapter in our lives, I would like to share some parting thoughts with you as we start a new phase in our countries' relationship, at a time fraught with global challenges – from economic uncertainty to climate change to terrorism.

在我妻子梅尔与我离开北京开启我们新的生活篇章之前，当我们在充满全球挑战的时刻(从经济不确定到气候变化，再到恐怖主义)开启我们国家关系新的篇章之时，我想分享一些临别的想法。

这段话中出现了若干个状语，翻译时注意状语的语序。

(2) Our economies, in turn, have grown increasingly interconnected, with more than $650 billion in annual bilateral trade.

我们的经济日益相互关联，每年双边贸易额超过6500亿美元。

注意原文状语部分翻译时被转换为并列句。

(3) It played a positive role in the global response to Ebola, working closely with the United States and other partners.

中国在全球应对埃博拉方面发挥了积极作用，与美国及其他伙伴密切合作。

注意原文复杂句被转译为并列句。

(4) US policy, decades old and upheld by successive administrations from both parties, has been to welcome the rise of a stable, peaceful and prosperous China.

历经几十年且一直得到两党历届政府支持的美国的对华政策，一直是欢迎一个稳定、和平与繁荣的中国的崛起。

注意从"中心词+修饰语"到"修饰语+中心词"的转换。

(5) We welcome China as a global leader that assumes its responsibilities within the transparent, rules-based system underpinning the peace and prosperity that the Asia-Pacific region has enjoyed for many decades.

我们欢迎中国在透明的、以规则为基础的制度中作为一个承担自己责任的全球领导者，这个制度巩固了亚太地区几十年来所享有的和平与繁荣。

注意将英文复杂句转译为并列句。

(6) At the end of the day, I can't stress enough the importance for us all to ask honest, constructive, good-faith questions, and to really listen to each other's point of view.

最后，就我们大家诚实、建设性和真诚地提问以及真正倾听对方观点的重要性来说，我再怎么强调都不为过。

(7) Their work was carried on by President Carter and Deng Xiaoping, who normalized relations between our two countries in 1979.

在卡特总统与邓小平的推动下，中美于1979年实现了两国建交。

注意被动语态到主动语态的转译。

2. Please interpret the following passage by using the techniques illustrated above. Please pay attention to the underlined sentences as they require special treatment during interpreting.

Stop Meddling in the South China Sea

Liu Xiaoming(Chinese Ambassador to the UK)

① The issue of the South China Sea is being ramped up by those in the US and the UK who accuse China of causing tension in the region. They proclaim the principle of free navigation and overflight,[1] but in reality their prejudice and partiality will only increase tension.

② Their suggestion that China's "hard line" position about the sea increases friction is not based on fact. We were the first to discover and name its islands and reefs and the first to govern them. Despite this, more than 40 are now illegally occupied by other countries. Our talks with neighbours to resolve our differences shows how committed we are to regional peace and stability. China's construction on its own islands and reefs is a matter for us. These actions are not targeted at any other country. Apart from minimum defence facilities, the building works are primarily civilian in purpose.[2]

③ The claim that there is a threat to the freedom of navigation and overflight in the sea is false.[3] Is there a single case in which this freedom has been affected? More than 100 000 vessels pass through the sea unimpeded every year. Is the freedom of navigation that every country is entitled to really the issue? Or is it the "freedom" of certain countries to flex military muscle and moor warships on other nations' doorsteps and fly military jets over others countries' territorial airspace? If it is the latter, such "freedom" should be condemned as a flagrantly hostile act and stopped.

④ Some appear eager to label China as "not abiding by international law" and "undermining the rule-based international system" because it rejects the arbitration imposed on it under the UN Convention on the Law of the Sea. <u>China made a clear declaration in accordance with this law in 2006 to exclude compulsory arbitration on sovereign disputes and maritime delimitation.</u>[4] More than 30 other countries, including the UK, have made similar declarations.

⑤ Some countries outside the South China Sea claim to be taking no side in sovereignty disputes, but they are actually doing all they can to get involved. <u>The military vessels and planes they sent to the region and the accusations they throw at China</u>[5] only encourage certain countries in the region to behave even more recklessly, increasing the tension.

⑥ China and the UK have co-hosted events marking the 400th anniversary of William Shakespeare's death. Some of his characters are good at stirring up enmity. But they can fool only their victims in the play, never the audience. Likewise, the world will see clearly who is making trouble in the South China Sea. These nations should desist from meddling and muddling. Such actions pose a threat to regional stability and world peace.

Notes on the text

(1) <u>The issue of the South China Sea is being ramped up by those in the US and the UK who accuse China of causing tension in the region. They proclaim the principle of free navigation and overflight.</u>

最近，南海问题又被炒得沸沸扬扬。美国、英国都有人在南海问题上高调发声，指责中国造成了南海局势的紧张，鼓吹所谓"捍卫航行和飞越自由"。

(2) <u>China's construction on its own islands and reefs is a matter for us. These actions are not targeted at any other country. Apart from minimum defence facilities, the building works are primarily civilian in purpose.</u>

中国在南海的岛礁建设，完全是中国主权范围内的事，不针对任何国家，除满足必要的军事防卫需求外，更多的是为各类民事需求服务。

注意英语形合到汉语意合的转换。

(3) <u>The claim that there is a threat to the freedom of navigation and overflight in the sea is false.</u>

这些人鼓吹的所谓"捍卫航行和飞越自由"实际上是伪命题。

译文将主语变为人，使批驳的针对性更强，文风更加有力。

(4) <u>China made a clear declaration in accordance with this law in 2006 to exclude compulsory arbitration on sovereign disputes and maritime delimitation.</u>

中国不参与、不接受仲裁，是由于中国早在2006年就根据《联合国海洋法公约》相关规定作出了排除性声明，将主权争议和海洋划界等问题排除在强制性争端解决机制之外。

(5) <u>The military vessels and planes they sent to the region and the accusations they throw at China...</u>

他们一方面出动飞机军舰，另一方面对中国妄加指责。

注意根据汉语语言习惯转换主语。

9.2.4 篇章口译[Passage Practice (C to E)]

1. Please interpret the following passage by using the techniques illustrated above. Please pay attention to the underlined sentences as they require special treatment during interpreting.

李克强在联合国一般性辩论上的重要讲话(节选)

① <u>去年联合国发展峰会通过《2030年可持续发展议程》，为全球发展描绘了新愿景。</u>(1)中国国家主席习近平在峰会上围绕"<u>谋共同永续发展，做合作共赢伙伴</u>"(2)，阐述了中国的原则立场，表明了中国的积极态度。

② 今年是落实可持续发展议程的开局之年。前不久召开的二十国集团领导人杭州峰会，就推动世界经济增长达成杭州共识，<u>为构建创新、活力、联动、包容的世界经济描绘了愿景。</u>(3)峰会共同承诺积极落实2030年可持续发展议程，并制定了落实2030年可持续发展议程行动计划，<u>为全球可持续发展事业注入新的动力。</u>(4)中国政府还率先批准并发布了《中国落实2030年可持续发展议程国别方案》。联大一般性辩论以"可持续发展目标：共同努力改造我们的世界"为主题，很有现实意义。

③ 可持续发展首先是要发展，基础也在于发展。离开了发展，也就谈不上可持续。当今世界的很多问题，都是由于发展不足引起的。无论是贫困、难民危机，还是战乱冲突、恐怖主义等，都能从发展落后上找到根源，也都需要通过发展寻求根本解决之道。唯有发展，才能保障人民的基本权利。唯有发展，才能消除全球性挑战的根源。唯有发展，才能推动人类文明进步。

④ 发展必须是可持续的。可持续有着丰富内涵，哪个方面做不到，都将使发展陷入停滞与困顿。如果发展不平衡、不平等，南北差距、贫富差距拉大，则不可持续。如果发展方式粗放，高消耗、高污染、高排放，超过资源环境承受能力，也不可持续。如果经济社会发展不协调，一条腿长一条腿短，同样不可持续。<u>只有深刻认识和把握可持续的内涵，全面推进减贫、南北合作和南南合作、应对气候变化等各项事业，促进公平共享和绿色发展，发展才能立得稳、走得远。</u>(5)

⑤ 可持续发展必须包容联动。当前，可持续发展面临严峻挑战。地区冲突和热点问题此起彼伏，传统和非传统安全威胁相互交织，可持续发展环境堪忧。世界经济复苏乏力，经济全球化阻力加大，可持续发展动力不足。重大疫情、自然灾害频发等问题日益突出，能源资源安全、粮食安全、金融安全问题交织，可持续发展任务艰巨。越是在艰难时刻，越要提振信心。人类总是有智慧找到办法、有能力突破困境的，关键是要相互合作、同舟共济。国际社会应以命运共同体、利益攸关者的新视角，采取一致行动，共同应对全

球性挑战。

⑥ 推动可持续发展，要近期和远期结合，[6]以务实的行动应对当前的挑战，积极变革和改造我们的世界。

⑦ 我们必须维护《联合国宪章》的宗旨和原则。没有和平稳定的环境，就没有可持续发展，已经取得的发展成果也会丧失。世界能保持70多年的和平，是来之不易的，这说明以联合国为核心的现行国际体系和以《联合国宪章》为基础的国际关系准则行之有效，必须坚决予以维护。这不仅符合各国人民的共同利益，也是实现可持续发展目标最重要的保障。各国要把《联合国宪章》的宗旨和原则真正落到实处，支持联合国及其安理会在国际事务中发挥主导作用，支持不断改革完善全球治理机制，以适应国际政治、经济格局出现的新变化。要树立共同、综合、合作、可持续的新安全观，建设"对话而不对抗、结伴而不结盟"的全球伙伴关系。

Notes on the text

(1) 去年联合国发展峰会通过《2030年可持续发展议程》，为全球发展描绘了新愿景。

The UN Sustainable Development Summit held last year adopted the 2030 Agenda for Sustainable Development, opening a new vision for global development.

注意根据英语"形合"特点将汉语并列句转换为英语的复杂句。

(2) 谋共同永续发展，做合作共赢伙伴

Towards Win-win Partnership for Sustainable Development

(3) 为构建创新、活力、联动、包容的世界经济描绘了愿景。

A blueprint was drawn for building an innovative, invigorated, interconnected and inclusive world economy.

为使句式富于变化，译文将主语进行调整，将原文主动语态变为被动语态。

(4) 峰会共同承诺积极落实2030年可持续发展议程，并制定了落实2030年可持续发展议程行动计划，为全球可持续发展事业注入新的动力。

Participants at the Summit pledged to actively implement the 2030 Agenda for Sustainable Development and formulated an action plan toward that end, which injected new vigor to global sustainable development.

"新动力"即"行动计划"，通过定语从句使句子结构清晰，指向更加明确。

(5) 只有深刻认识和把握可持续的内涵，全面推进减贫、南北合作和南南合作，应对气候变化等各项事业，促进公平共享和绿色发展，发展才能立得稳、走得远。

Only when we keep a profound understanding of the implication of sustainability, make all-round progress in poverty reduction, North-South and South-South cooperation, climate change and other fields, and work to promote equal sharing and green development can we ensure that development is truly solid and sustainable.

汉语句子结构较松散，前后主语不一致。译文将主语统一为we，以此为轴将多个动词统一在一起。

(6) 推动可持续发展，要近期和远期结合……

To advance sustainable development, we must keep both short-term and long-term interests in mind...

注意"意合"到"形合"的转换。

2. Please interpret the following passage by using the techniques illustrated above. Please pay attention to the underlined sentences as they require special treatment during interpreting.

继往开来，努力构建中美新型大国关系——纪念中美建交35周年

外交部部长 王毅

① 35年前的今天，中美两国正式建立了外交关系。<u>发生在1979年的这一历史事件堪称20世纪下半叶国际关系史上最具战略意义的事件。</u>(1)它不仅翻开了中美两国关系新的一页，而且对国际形势的演变产生了深远影响。

（一）

② 35年来，在中美几代领导人和两国人民的共同努力下，<u>中美关系走过了风风雨雨，取得了历史性的发展。</u>(2)

③ 1979年，两国双边贸易额仅24.5亿美元；2013年，已突破5000亿美元。双向投资也从建交初期的微乎其微发展到目前超过1000亿美元。今天，中美两国已互为第二大贸易伙伴，中国是美国第一大进口来源地、第三大出口市场。

④ 1979年，两国官方交往屈指可数。而过去5年中，中美元首进行了14次会晤。两国还建立了战略与经济对话、人文交流高层磋商等90多个对话与合作机制，以及41对友好省州和201对友好城市关系。

⑤ 1979年，中美人员往来仅几千人次。2013年，两国人员往来已近400万人次。两国每天有上万人穿梭于太平洋两岸，<u>通过互联网、手机互动的民众更难以计数。</u>(3)

⑥ 1979年，中美在国际和地区问题上的合作也远未像今天这样广泛和密切。<u>目前，无论在应对国际金融危机、气候变化、能源安全、粮食安全等全球性挑战上，还是在推动解决朝核、伊朗核、叙利亚等地区热点问题方面，中美都保持着密切的沟通与协调，发挥着重要作用。</u>(4)

⑦ 35年弹指一挥间。中美两国已从当初的相对隔绝状态变成了你中有我、我中有你的利益共同体，中美关系的战略意义与全球影响愈来愈凸显。35年的历史证明，一个良好的中美关系不仅符合两国人民的根本利益，也有利于促进亚太地区乃至世界的和平、稳定与发展。

（二）

⑧ 35年的中美关系给了我们很多启示，其中几点值得特别铭记。

⑨ 把握正确方向是发展中美关系的关键所在。中美关系走向始终牵动世界。中美和则两利，斗则俱伤。合作是双方的唯一正确选择。只要坚持从两国人民的根本利益出发，坚持中美三个联合公报指出的方向，坚持两国元首达成的一系列重要共识，"咬定青山不放松"，就能确保中美关系始终沿着健康稳定的轨道持续向前发展。

⑩ 积极寻求共同利益是推进中美关系发展的动力源泉。作为世界上最大的发展中国家和最大的发达国家，中美拥有广泛的共同利益，肩负重要的共同责任。任何情况下，双方都不能忘了这一基本事实。只要双方聚焦共同利益，不断做大合作蛋糕，中美关系就能永葆青春、永续发展。

⑪ 相互尊重是管控好两国分歧的正确方法。中美政治制度、发展水平、历史文化传统不同，存在这样那样的矛盾与分歧是正常的。只要尊重彼此的核心利益和重大关切，通过对话协商积累互信，聚同化异，就能避免两国关系受到不必要的干扰。

⑫ 人民之间的友谊永远是中美关系发展的重要基础。中美关系的发展离不开两国人民的广泛参与和大力支持。双方要努力拓宽渠道，鼓励各界双向交流，厚植民间友好情谊，这样才能使中美关系始终保持生机与活力。(5)

Notes on the text

(1) 发生在1979年的这一历史事件堪称20世纪下半叶国际关系史上最具战略意义的事件。

It is fair to say that this historic event in 1979 exerted the greatest strategic impact on the international relations in the latter half of the 20th century.

注意译文的句子结构，用it做主语。

(2) 中美关系走过了风风雨雨，取得了历史性的发展。

China-US relations have achieved historic growth despite ups and downs.

注意汉语并列句的翻译。

(3) 通过互联网、手机互动的民众更难以计数。

It is hard to keep a record of many more Chinese and Americans who interact with each other through the Internet and mobile phones.

原句主语过长，译文采用it做形式主语，避免头重脚轻，使句子协调。

(4) 目前，无论在应对国际金融危机、气候变化、能源安全、粮食安全等全球性挑战上，还是在推动解决朝核、伊朗核、叙利亚等地区热点问题方面，中美都保持着密切的沟通与协调，发挥着重要作用。

The two countries now maintain close consultation and dialogue on global challenges such as the international financial crisis, climate change, energy security and food security as well as hot-spot issues such as the Korean nuclear issue, the Iranian nuclear issue and Syria, and the two countries have played an important role in addressing these challenges and issues.

(5) 双方要努力拓宽渠道，鼓励各界双向交流，厚植民间友好情谊，这样才能使中美关系始终保持生机与活力。

The two sides need to deepen people-to-people friendship by expanding the channels of communication and encouraging two-way exchanges among the people from all walks of life. This will inject everlasting vitality into China-US relations.

注意汉语零散的并列句的翻译。

9.3 参考译文(Reference Version)

9.3.1 单句口译(Sentence Practice)

Please interpret the following sentences by using the techniques illustrated above. You may interpret to your partner first and then he/she comments on your performance.

(1) 外长们重申坚定支持联合国作为最普遍的多边组织，协助国际社会维护国际和平与安全、促进共同发展、促进和保护人权。

(2) 外长们注意到阻止外空军备竞赛，尤其是防止在外空部署任何武器，将有利于维护国际和平与安全，也有利于促进和加强和平开发和利用外空的国际合作。

(3) 支持组建中国—中东欧国家智库交流与合作中心。

(4) 中澳经济互补性强，发展战略契合度高。

(5) 双方应深化务实合作，做互利共赢的紧密搭档。

(6) Friends and neighbors become closer when they visit each other more often.

(7) Asian countries are just like a cluster of bright lanterns. Only when we link them together, can we light up the night sky of Asia.

(8) China's development offers an important opportunity to the world. China is speeding up a new type of industrialization, IT application, urbanization and agricultural modernization, which will create many new growth areas.

(9) China has actively helped other developing countries in infrastructure construction, and assisted their efforts in strengthening capacity building and trade development. China has also increased the amount of foreign assistance in environmental protection, helping the recipient countries realize economic and social development.

(10) We Chinese are striving to achieve the Chinese dream, which is the great rejuvenation of the Chinese nation. The Chinese dream is about enhancing the strength and prosperity of the nation and the well-being of the Chinese people.

9.3.2 段落口译[Paragraph Practice]

1. Vocabulary Work: Study the following words and phrases and translate them into the target language.

superpower	和谐相处、和谐共存
an independent foreign policy of peace	奋勇前进、继续前行
per capita GDP	改革开放
posed itself as	和平稳定

2. Please interpret the following paragraphs by using the techniques illustrated above.

(1) First, China is not "superpower", but a developing country. Though being the biggest First, China is not "superpower", but a developing country. Though being the biggest developing country with one of the largest economies in the world, China still ranks behind some 80 countries in terms of per capita GDP. We don't have the basis to be a superpower, still less do we intend to be one. Second, in developing relations with its neighbors, China has never posed itself as a "big brother". China follows an independent foreign policy of peace, a neighborhood policy featuring amity, sincerity, mutual benefit and inclusiveness, and believes that all countries, big or small, are equals. We could all be good brothers and good friends when we share such sincere wish. There is no such thing as one being the "big brother".

(2) China's diplomacy has kept up a fine tradition since 1991, that is, Chinese foreign ministers would choose African countries as the destinations of their first overseas visits at the beginning of every new year. It embodies the importance attached by China to Africa and China-Africa traditional friendship. This time is no exception. Foreign Minister Wang Yi carries forward the tradition of China's diplomacy. This will also be the first time for the Chinese Foreign Minister to visit the Sub-Saharan Africa under the new leadership. Both sides are looking forward to the visit.

(3) 我相信，只要国际社会携起手来，坚守和平稳定的底线，秉持和谐相处的理念，激活开放创新的动力，就没有克服不了的艰难险阻，我们赖以生存的这个世界就会迎来一个更加美好的未来！

(4) 要看到，中国还是一个发展中国家，实现现代化还有很长的路要走。和平是中国发展的基础条件，改革开放和人民对幸福美好生活的追求是发展的最大动力。中国城乡和区域发展空间广阔，国内需求潜力巨大。以中高速再发展一、二十年，中国的面貌就会持续改善，也会给世界带来更多发展机遇。

9.3.3 篇章口译[Passage Practice (E to C)]

1. Please interpret the following passage by using the techniques illustrated above. Please pay attention to the underlined sentences as they require special treatment during interpreting.

开启美中关系的新篇章

美国驻华大使马克斯·博卡斯

① 我常这么说，也真心这么认为：担任美国驻中国大使是我所拥有过的最好的工作。与美中两国人民一起推动世界上最重要的双边关系是莫大的荣幸。

② 但是，正如人们所说的，所有的好事都有结束的时候。美国刚刚举行过选举，随着我们国家向一个新政府过渡，现在是我作为美国大使与你们告别的时候了。当你用中文

说"goodbye"时，它的意思是"再见"，对我的这次道别来说，我就是这么想的——我会再次见到你！

③ 在我妻子梅尔与我离开北京开启我们新的生活篇章之前，当我们在充满全球挑战的时刻(从经济不确定到气候变化，再到恐怖主义)开启我们国家关系新的篇章之时，我想分享一些临别的想法。

④ 在我35年的美国国会参议员生涯中，特别是我作为美国大使的日子里，我亲眼见证了中国显著的转型及在全球舞台上的重现。

⑤ 自邓小平30多年前在中国开启改革开放以来，中国已使数以亿计的人摆脱了贫困，成为世界第二大经济体。我们的经济日益相互关联，每年双边贸易额超过6500亿美元。

⑥ 我看到中国的崛起以令人印象深刻的方式展开。中国与美国一起，帮助领导世界在巴黎达成一项富有雄心的气候协议。中国在全球应对埃博拉方面发挥了积极作用，与美国及其他伙伴密切合作。中国曾担任朝鲜半岛核问题六方会谈的东道方，并能在这些会谈的恢复过程中发挥同样重要的作用。

⑦ 这些例子清楚地表明中国的参与和负责任领导对中国及世界的好处。历经几十年且一直得到两党历届政府支持的美国的对华政策，一直是欢迎一个稳定、和平与繁荣的中国的崛起。我们欢迎中国在透明的、以规则为基础的制度中作为一个承担自己责任的全球领导者，这个制度巩固了亚太地区几十年来所享有的和平与繁荣。

⑧ 我曾作为一名美国会参议员作了很大的努力，帮助中国加入世界贸易组织，因为我知道这对中国有利，对美国有利，对整个世界都有利。它确实是！展望未来，我们希望中国与美国新政府密切合作，继续这个向世界开放的进程。

⑨ 我们生活在一个史无前例的相互联系的时代。中美两国关系事实上是这些趋势的证明和直接受益者。

⑩ 继续让此朝正确方向行进的一个关键是为美国和外国公司在这里投资和做生意创造一个令人鼓舞的环境——就像中国公司期望在美国那样。

⑪ 作为中国首要任务之一的加强创新是另一个关键因素。这就是为什么我们鼓励中国继续努力保持开放，这样的开放将有助于让像马云、屠呦呦或王健林这样的人才在全球蓬勃发展。同样，我们希望中国欢迎非政府组织的建设性作用，它们帮助社会推动创新、促进社会稳定，并让我们走到一起来保护环境。

⑫ 另一个关键因素将是确保中国的和平崛起是以区域参与及创造性外交为支撑的，即以有利于大家的方式管控争端，这符合习近平主席与奥巴马总统在我有幸参加的许多会见中所做的努力。

⑬ 最后，就我们大家诚实、建设性和真诚地提问以及真正倾听对方观点的重要性来说，我再怎么强调都不为过。正如我的导师、来自蒙大拿州的美国前参议员迈克·曼斯菲尔德曾经说过的，"记住，别人并不总是错的，你也不总是对的。"这正是通往诚实对话的道路。

⑭ 虽然这是一个过渡时期，有些人对前方的路有疑问，但我认为，我们两国都认同让这种关系成功的重要性。自从尼克松总统第一次来到中国，并在"改变世界的那一周"

会晤毛主席以来，这一直是如此。在卡特总统与邓小平的推动下，中美于1979年实现了两国建交。我们经历了领导人的更迭，经历了我们间的起起伏伏，但我们从没有放弃为自己的子孙创造更美好未来的共同目标。

⑮ 我一次又一次亲眼看到这样的决心。当我第一次来中国时，我向习主席许诺，我将访问中国大陆所有的省份——去年10月我实现了这个目标。我一路上学到的是，无论美国人还是中国人，我们基本上都想在生活中得到同样的东西——一份好的工作，我们孩子的良好教育，一个干净、安全的生活环境。这是美国梦的一大部分。它也是我了解到的中国梦的一部分。

⑯ 从曲阜到昆明、从上海到乌鲁木齐，从学生、老百姓、商人或政府官员的身上，我在这个国家看到了耐心、坚持和积极的态度，我知道当我们一起努力时，没有什么是我们完成不了的。当我们成功时——无论是就我们看法一致的许多问题进行努力，还是开诚布公并明智地管控我们的分歧——世界都受益。

2. Please interpret the following passage by using the techniques illustrated above. Please pay attention to the underlined sentences as they require special treatment during interpreting.

停止插手南海事务
刘晓明(中国驻英大使)

① 最近，南海问题又被炒得沸沸扬扬。美国、英国都有人在南海问题上高调发声，指责中国造成了南海局势的紧张，鼓吹所谓 "捍卫航行和飞越自由"。但实际上，他们这些充满偏见和偏袒的言论恰恰加剧了南海地区的紧张形势。

② 首先，这些人指责中国的所谓"强硬行动"造成了南海局势的紧张。这种看法罔顾事实。中国人最早发现了南海诸岛，最早为其命名，最早实施行政管辖。然而，迄今为止南海有40多个岛礁被个别国家非法侵占。对此，中国始终坚持通过双边谈判协商解决争议，致力于共同维护南海地区的长期和平稳定。中国在南海的岛礁建设，完全是中国主权范围内的事，不针对任何国家，除满足必要的军事防卫需求外，更多的是为各类民事需求服务。

③ 第二，这些人鼓吹的所谓"捍卫航行和飞越自由"实际上是伪命题。请问南海航行和飞越自由受影响了吗？事实上，每年世界各国十万多艘船只在南海地区畅通无阻，从未发生问题。我不清楚这些人所称的"航行和飞越自由"到底是什么？是各国依据国际法享有的航行自由？还是个别国家耀武扬威，可以为所欲为地将军舰开到别人家门口，将军机飞越别国领空的自由？如果是后者，我想这样的自由实质上是一种公然的挑衅和敌对行为，应当受到谴责和禁止。

④ 第三，这些人说中国必须接受菲律宾单方面提起的南海仲裁，否则就要给中国扣上"不遵守国际法"和"破坏基于规则的国际体系"的大帽子。这完全是颠倒黑白。中国不参与、不接受仲裁，是由于中国早在2006年就根据《联合国海洋法公约》相关规定作出

了排除性声明，将主权争议和海洋划界等问题排除在强制性争端解决机制之外。要特别指出的是，包括英国在内的30多个国家都做出了类似声明。

⑤ 一些域外国家声称对南海主权争议不选边站队，但同时又竭力介入南海问题。他们一方面出动飞机军舰，另一方面对中国妄加指责。这只能助长区域内少数国家的肆意妄为，使局势进一步紧张。

⑥ 今年是莎士比亚逝世400周年。中英两国将举办一系列纪念活动。莎翁笔下的一些角色惯于搬弄是非、无事生非，尽管剧中人难免受骗上当，但读者和观众总能洞若观火，明辨是非。今天，谁在南海问题上搅浑水，世人也看得一清二楚。我奉劝那些域外国家，不要再搅浑水，他们的行为已对地区稳定与世界和平构成了直接威胁。

9.3.4 篇章口译[Passage Practice (C to E)]

1. Please interpret the following passage by using the techniques illustrated above. Please pay attention to the underlined sentences as they require special treatment during interpreting.

The Speech delivered by Li Keqiang at the UN General Debate (Excerpts)

① The UN Sustainable Development Summit held last year adopted the 2030 Agenda for Sustainable Development, opening a new vision for global development. At the summit, Chinese President Xi Jinping gave a speech entitled "Towards Win-win Partnership for Sustainable Development" to expound on China's principles and position as well as its readiness to advance the agenda for sustainable development.

② This year is the first in the Agenda's implementation. The G20 Summit held not long ago in Hangzhou of China reached the Hangzhou consensus on world economic growth. A blueprint was drawn for building an innovative, invigorated, interconnected and inclusive world economy. Participants at the Summit pledged to actively implement the 2030 Agenda for Sustainable Development and formulated an action plan toward that end, which injected new vigor to global sustainable development. The Chinese government was also among the first to adopt and release the country's National Plan on Implementation of the 2030 Agenda for Sustainable Development. As for the General Assembly, it has decided that for this year's session, the general debate will focus on the theme "The Sustainable Development Goals: a universal push to transform our world". These, in my view, are all highly relevant.

③ Sustainable development is first and foremost about development. Development underpins every human achievement. Without development, nothing can be sustainable. The lack of development is often at the root of many problems facing the world. Be it poverty or the refugee crisis, war, conflicts or terrorism, they all could be attributed to insufficient development and none can be addressed properly without development. Only development can guarantee people's fundamental rights. Only development can root out the cause for global challenges. And only development can advance human civilization and progress.

④ Development must be sustainable. It must be sustainable in all dimensions, otherwise development will be stalled and strained. Development won't be sustainable if it is unbalanced, unequal and widens the gap between the North and the South and the rich and the poor. Development won't be sustainable if it is achieved in an extensive manner, driven by high consumption, high pollution and high emissions and depletes resources and strains the environment. Development won't be sustainable if economic growth and social progress are not well coordinated. Only when we keep a profound understanding of the implication of sustainability, make all-round progress in poverty reduction, North-South and South-South cooperation, climate change and other fields, and work to promote equal sharing and green development can we ensure that development is truly solid and sustainable.

⑤ Sustainable development must be inclusive and interconnected. Currently, the sustainable development endeavor is faced with grave challenges: regional conflicts and hot spots are incessant, traditional and non-traditional security threats intertwine, and the environment for sustainable development gives no reason for optimism. World economic recovery remains lukewarm, economic globalization faces strong headwind, and the momentum for sustainable development is weak. Frequent occurrence of major infectious diseases and natural disasters is increasingly prominent, the issues of energy and resource security, food security and financial security are interwoven, and sustainable development remains an uphill journey. Difficult moments call for stronger confidence. I believe mankind has the wisdom and capability to find a way out of difficulty. For that to happen, there must be cooperation and a spirit of working together to tide over difficulties. It is time that the international community take on a new perspective. It should see itself as a community of shared future in which all are stakeholders, and should make concerted efforts to jointly tackle global challenges.

⑥ To advance sustainable development, we must keep both short-term and long-term interests in mind, tackle challenges with concrete efforts and work actively to transform and change our world.

⑦ We must uphold the purposes and principles of the UN Charter. Without peace and stability, there will be no sustainable development; even the fruits of development already reaped risk being lost. The hard-won peace that has prevailed over the past 70 years or more testifies to the effectiveness of the existing international system with the UN at its core and of the norms of international relations established on the basis of the UN Charter. This international system and these norms governing international relations must be upheld resolutely, for they not only serve the common interests of people of all countries, but also provide the most essential guarantee for the attainment of the sustainable development goals. Countries need to honor the purposes and principles of the UN Charter in letter and in spirit, and should support the leading role of the

UN and its Security Council in global affairs. Countries need to be supportive of steady reform and improvement of global governance mechanisms, so as to adapt to the changing international political and economic landscape. A new concept of common, comprehensive, cooperative and sustainable security should be nurtured and a global partnership should be established that features "dialogue instead of confrontation, and partnership instead of alliance".

2. Please interpret the following passage by using the techniques illustrated above. Please pay attention to the underlined sentences as they require special treatment during interpreting.

Build on Past Progress to Develop a New Model of Major-country Relations Between China and the United States—In Commemoration of the 35th Anniversary of the Establishment of China-US Diplomatic Relations
Chinese Foreign Minister Wang Yi

① Thirty-five years ago today, China and the United States entered into official diplomatic relations. It is fair to say that this historic event in 1979 exerted the greatest strategic impact on the international relations in the latter half of the 20th century. It not only opened a new page in the history of China-US relations, but also had a far-reaching impact on the evolving international environment.

I

② Thanks to joint efforts of successive leaders and the people of both countries, China-US relations in the past 35 years have achieved historic growth despite ups and downs.

③ In 1979, the annual trade between the two countries was just 2.45 billion dollars, while in 2013, it surged to over half a trillion dollars. Two-way investment which was insignificant in the early days of our relations has now exceeded 100 billion dollars. Today, China and the United States are each other's second largest trading partner. China is the largest source of import and third largest export market of the United States.

④ In 1979, the official exchanges between the two countries were limited. Whereas in the past 5 years, our presidents have met 14 times. There are over 90 mechanisms for dialogue and cooperation between the two countries, including the Strategic and Economic Dialogues and the High-level Consultation on People-to-people Exchange. Moreover, there are 41 pairs of sister province/state and 201 pairs of sister city relationships between China and the United States.

⑤ In 1979, only several thousand Chinese and Americans visited the other country. In 2013, the number was close to four million. Every day, over ten thousand Chinese and Americans fly across the Pacific Ocean for mutual visits, and it is hard to keep a record of many more Chinese and Americans who interact with each other through the Internet and mobile phones.

⑥ In 1979, cooperation between China and the United States was nothing like what we have today in terms of scope and intensity. The two countries now maintain close consultation and dialogue on global challenges such as the international financial crisis, climate change, energy security and food security as well as hot-spot issues such as the Korean nuclear issue, the Iranian nuclear issue and Syria, and the two countries have played an important role in addressing these challenges and issues.

⑦ In just 35 years, China and the United States have moved away from a state of no contact and become a community of intertwined interests. The strategic dimension and global influence of China-US relations have become increasingly prominent. The growth of China-US relations in the past 35 years shows that sound relations between China and the United States not only meet the fundamental interest of the two peoples; they also contribute to peace, stability and development of the Asia-Pacific and the world.

II

⑧ The growth of China-US relations over the past 35 years is a source of inspiration for us. In particular, we should bear in mind the following principles guiding the growth of the relations:

⑨ Adhering to the right direction holds the key to growing China-US relations. Where China-US relations are headed has an impact on the whole world. A good relationship benefits the two sides, while confrontation does harm to both countries. Cooperation is thus the best choice for us. We should act in the fundamental interests of our two peoples, adhere to the direction set by the three China-US joint communiqués and the important common understanding on numerous issues reached by our presidents, and stay on the right track. By doing so, we can ensure the sound and steady growth of China-US relations.

⑩ Identifying common interests provides the driving force for growing China-US relations. Respectively being the world's largest developing and developed countries, China and the United States share broad common interests and shoulder important common responsibilities. Both countries must not lose sight of this crucial fact under any circumstances. As long as the two countries focus on our common interests and expand cooperation, China-US relations will have a bright future.

⑪ Mutual respect offers the right approach to managing our differences. Given differences in political system, level of development, history and cultural tradition, it is only natural for the two countries to have disagreement and differences. By respecting each other's core interests and major concerns, building trust through dialogue and consultation, and seeking common ground while narrowing differences, we can keep the bilateral relations from being adversely affected by differences.

⑫ The friendship between our peoples underpins the growth of China-US relations. Extensive involvement by and strong support of our peoples are vital to the growth of bilateral relations. The two sides need to deepen people-to-people friendship by expanding the channels of communication and encouraging two-way exchanges among the people from all walks of life.

This will inject everlasting vitality into China-US relations.

9.4　外事接待主题词汇汇总(Vocabulary Build-up)

Ministry of Foreign Affairs	外交部
Protocol Department	礼宾司
Information Department	新闻司
diplomatic mission	外交代表机构、外交使团
consulate-general	总领事馆
embassy	大使馆
consulate	领事馆
office of the charged' affaires	代办处
commercial counsellor's office	商务处、商务参赞处
liaison office	联络处
diplomat	外交家，外交官
diplomatic rank	外交官衔
diplomatic representative	外交代表
members of the administrative and technical staff	行政技术人员
ambassador	大使
ambassador extraordinary and plenipotentiary	特命全权大使
minister-counsellor	公使衔参赞
counsellor	参赞
charged' affaires ad interim	临时代办
first secretary	一等秘书
second secretary	二等秘书
third secretary	三等秘书
attache	随员
commercial secretary	商务参赞
cultural secretary	文化参赞
dean of the diplomatic corps	外交使团团长
special envoy	特使
memorandum	备忘录
persona non-grat	不受欢迎的人
communique	公报
announcement	公告，通告
letter of credence, credentials	国书
mutual recognition	互相承认
establishment of diplomatic relations	建立外交关系
during one's absence	离任期间

(续表)

diplomatic immunities	外交豁免
diplomatic channels	外交途径
diplomatic courier	外交信使
letter of appointment	委任书
letter of recall	召回公文
note	照会
normalization	正常化
to express regret	表示遗憾
to sever diplomatic relations	断绝外交关系
to resume diplomatic relations	恢复外交关系
to proceed to take up one's post	赴任
to return to one's post	返任
to exchange ambassadors	互派大使
to present one's credentials	递交国书
to establish diplomatic relations at ambassadorial level	建立大使级外交关系
to establish consular relations	建立领事关系
to upgrade diplomatic relations	外交关系升格
to make representations to	向……交涉
to lodge a protest with	向……提出抗议
to request the consent of...	征求……的同意
to suspend diplomatic relations	中断外交关系
state visit	国事访问
private visit	私人访问
obituary	讣告
questions of common interest, question of common concern	共同关心的问题
state banquet	国宴
message of greeting, message of congratulation	贺电

9.5 扩展练习(Enhancement Practice)

Making comments on the given topics.

Directions: Please read paragraph (1) and (2) carefully and then express your views on the given topics.

(1)

In many big cities, firecrackers and fireworks have been banned for a number of years because of safety and environmental concerns. Recently, however, some people have suggested that the government should lift the ban during the Spring Festival, because, in their opinion, firecrackers and fireworks are an integral part of the traditional Chinese New Year celebration and, without them, the Spring Festival lacks a true festival atmosphere. Some cities have thus lifted the ban but many others have not. Suppose you were the mayor of a big city, where people's views on this issue could not be reconciled. What do you think the government should do? Please give reasons to support your ideas.

(2)

Nowadays more and more city residents like to keep pet and dogs at home. However, some people think pet breeding should be forbidden or at least discouraged in urban areas. What is your opinion? Why?

9.6　延伸口译(Extended Interpreting)

习近平主席在蒙古国国家大呼拉尔的演讲

尊敬的额勒贝格道尔吉总统及夫人，尊敬的恩赫包勒德主席，尊敬的阿勒坦呼亚格总理，各位议员，各位部长，各位嘉宾，女士们，先生们，朋友们：

Your Excellency President Elbegdorj and Mrs. Elbegdorj, Your Excellency Chairman Enkhbold, Your Excellency Prime Minister Altankhuyag, Distinguished Members of the State Great Khural, Ministers, Distinguished Guests, Ladies and Gentlemen, Dear Friends,

大家好！今天，有机会来到蒙古国国家大呼拉尔，同各位朋友们见面，我感到十分高兴。首先，我谨代表中国政府和中国人民，并以我个人的名义，向在座各位，并通过你们向全体蒙古国人民，致以诚挚的问候和良好的祝愿！

Good Morning! It is a great pleasure to meet you here at the State Great Khural of Mongolia. At the outset, please allow me to extend, on behalf of the Chinese government and people and in my own name, sincere greetings and best wishes to all of you and, through you, to the entire people of Mongolia!

2008年，我担任国家副主席时首次出访就选择了蒙古国。踏上这块美丽的土地，我深深感到这里是物华天宝的好地方。贵国著名文学家那楚克道尔吉在他的诗作《我的故乡》中曾写到："肯特、杭爱、萨彦岭的巍峨群山，是点缀北国的层峦叠嶂；漠南、沙尔克、诺敏的无边戈壁，是横亘南疆的沙漠瀚海。这就是我生长的地方，美丽的蒙古大地！"

Mongolia was the first country I visited as Vice President of China in 2008. As soon as I set foot on the beautiful land of Mongolia, I was deeply impressed by its naturally endowed abundance. Natsagdorj, a well-known Mongolian writer, depicted a poetic and beautiful scene of Mongolia in his poem My Native Land: High stately mountains of Khentei, Khangai and Soyon;

Forests and thick-wooded ridges-the beauty of the North; The Great Gobi desert-the spaces of Menen, Sharga and Nomin; And the oceans of sand deserts that dominate the South; This, this is my native land, The lovely country-my Mongolia.

时隔6年，我再次来到蒙古国，看到这里是一片欣欣向荣的景象，充满生机活力，感到由衷的高兴，我对勤劳勇敢的蒙古国人民取得的发展成就，表示衷心的祝贺！

Six years later, I am here again. What I see is a thriving country dynamic and full of vitality. With heartfelt joy, I wish to extend our sincere congratulation to you, the brave and hardworking people of Mongolia, on your achievements.

昨天，我同额勒贝格道尔吉总统举行了会谈，刚才又分别会见了恩赫包勒德主席、阿勒坦呼亚格总理。我同蒙古国领导人就中蒙关系和共同关心的问题深入交换意见，达成广泛共识。双方一致决定，将中蒙关系提升为全面战略伙伴关系并发表联合宣言，还签署了涉及政治、经贸、人文等各个领域的20多项合作文件。我对这次访问的成果感到满意，对中蒙关系更加充满信心。

Yesterday, I had talks with President Elbegdorj. Before I came here, I met with both Chairman Enkhbold and Prime Minister Altankhuyag. Mongolian leaders and I have had an in-depth exchange of views on our bilateral ties as well as issues of shared interest. We have reached broad consensus. The two sides have agreed to elevate China-Mongolia relations to a comprehensive strategic partnership and issue a joint statement. We have signed more than 20 cooperation documents covering political, economic, trade and cultural fields. I am happy with the outcomes of my visit. And I have greater confidence in the relations between China and Mongolia.

女士们、先生们、朋友们！

Ladies and Gentlemen,

Dear Friends,

"路遥知马力，日久见人心。"65年前，中蒙正式建立外交关系。蒙古国是最早承认新中国的国家之一。我们不会忘记贵国对新中国给予的支持。我愿再次重申：无论国际和地区形势如何变化，中国都将始终按照中蒙友好合作关系条约精神，尊重蒙古国独立、主权、领土完整，尊重蒙古国人民自主选择的发展道路。这是我们将长期坚持的一项基本政策。

Just as distance tests a horse's strength, time will reveal a person's sincerity. China and Mongolia officially established diplomatic relations 65 years ago. Mongolia was one of the first countries to recognize New China and we will always remember the support you have rendered us. Let me reiterate that no matter how the international and regional situation may evolve, China will always follow the spirit enshrined in the the friendship and cooperation treaty between China and Mongolia, respect Mongolia's independence, sovereignty and territorial integrity and the Mongolian people's independent choice of development path. This is a basic and long-term policy that we will uphold.

我们高兴地看到，进入第二个甲子的中蒙关系正朝着更高水平不断发展。特别是过去20年间，中蒙高层交往频繁，政治互信不断加深。两国经贸务实合作快速发展，中国连续多年保持贵国最大贸易伙伴国和最大投资来源国地位。2013年，中蒙人员往来130多万人次，其中蒙古国公民赴华超过100万人次。应该说，中蒙全面战略伙伴关系的建立恰逢其时、水到渠成，标志着中蒙关系进入历史最好的发展时期。

Sixty years are a cycle according to the Chinese zodiac. We are pleased to see that China-Mongolia ties, now in their second cycle, are moving further ahead. The past two decades, in particular, have witnessed frequent exchange of high-level visits and increased political mutual trust. Practical business ties have grown fast. China has, for many years in a row, remained Mongolia's largest trading partner and source of investment. In the year 2013 alone, more than 1.3 million visits were made between China and Mongolia, with more than 1 million from Mongolia to China. No doubt, the establishment of China-Mongolia comprehensive strategic partnership, a natural development at a most opportune time, has ushered the bilateral ties into the best development period in history.

中蒙是山水相连的友好邻邦，同为本地区重要国家。今年是中蒙建交65周年、中蒙友好合作关系条约修订20周年和中蒙友好交流年，双方应该以建立全面战略伙伴关系为契机，推动中蒙关系不断迈上更高台阶。

China and Mongolia are friendly neighbours sharing common mountains and rivers and both are important countries in the region. This year marks the 65th anniversary of China-Mongolia diplomatic ties, 20th anniversary of the amendment to the friendship and cooperation treaty between the two countries, and the year of China-Mongolia friendship and exchanges. The two sides should take the advantage of the establishment of our comprehensive strategic partnership and work together to bring China-Mongolia ties to an even higher level.

第一，中蒙要做守望相助的好邻居。不论国际风云如何变幻，双方都要牢牢把握两国关系大方向，站在战略伙伴的角度多为对方着想，在涉及彼此主权、安全、领土完整等重大核心利益和重大关切问题上相互予以坚定支持。

First, China and Mongolia should be good neighbors that support each other. Whatever changes may take place in the international landscape, our two countries should always keep in mind the overall interests of the bilateral relations. We should think more for each other from the perspective of strategic partners and firmly support each other on issues involving our respective core interests or major concerns, such as sovereignty, security and territorial integrity.

两国要保持高层交往势头，两国领导人可以通过各种渠道保持经常性会晤，加强战略沟通、深化政治互信。我邀请额勒贝格道尔吉总统今年11月赴华出席亚太经合组织领导人非正式会议期间举行的互联互通伙伴对话会，中方欢迎恩赫包勒德主席今年赴华进行正式访问。双方已经决定建立中蒙立法机关定期交流机制和中蒙外交部门战略对话机制，双方将在防务安全磋商框架内，继续加强两国国防合作。

Our two countries should maintain the momentum of exchanging high-level visits. It is beneficial for leaders of the two countries to keep regular contacts through various channels so as to enhance strategic communication and political mutual trust. I would like to invite President Elbegdorj to a dialogue meeting on connectivity to be held during the APEC Economic Leaders' Meeting in China in the coming November. China looks forward to Chairman Enkhbold's official visit to China this year. Our two countries have agreed to put in place a regular exchange mechanism between our legislatures and a strategic dialogue program between the two foreign ministries, and enhance our cooperation in national defense within the framework of defense security consultation.

中方支持蒙方加入亚太经合组织，支持蒙方积极参与东亚合作，支持蒙方以适当方式参与东亚峰会和中日韩合作，支持蒙方提出的东北亚安全乌兰巴托对话倡议，愿在联合国、亚欧会议、亚信会议、上海合作组织等框架内同蒙方加强合作。

China supports Mongolia in joining the APEC and actively participating in East Asia cooperation. We support Mongolia in engaging in the East Asia Summit and China-Japan-ROK cooperation in an appropriate manner and Mongolia's initiative of Ulaanbaatar Dialogue on Northeast Asian Security. We are ready for closer cooperation with Mongolia in the United Nations, Asia-Europe Meeting, Conference on Interactions and Confidence-Building Measures in Asia, and the Shanghai Cooperation Organization.

中方愿同蒙方加强在丝绸之路经济带倡议下合作，对蒙方提出的草原之路倡议持积极和开放态度。双方可以在亚洲基础设施投资银行等新的平台上加强合作，共同发展，共同受益。

China is also ready to increase cooperation with Mongolia in matters covered by the Silk Road Economic Belt project. China is positive and open to Mongolia's initiative for passage to grassland. Our two countries may step up cooperation for common development and mutual benefit through new platforms such as the Asian Infrastructure Investment Bank.

第二，中蒙要做互利共赢的好伙伴。"近水楼台先得月"，中蒙地理相邻、经济互补，中方的市场、资金、技术、通道和蒙方的资源富集优势互补性很强，有许多合作机遇。去年，中国商品进出口总额达到4.16万亿美元。未来5年，中国预计将进口超过10万亿美元商品，对外投资规模预计超过5000亿美元。去年，中国公民出境旅游近1亿人次，估计到2020年这一数字将超过每年1.5亿人次。中国持续发展将为包括蒙古国在内的合作伙伴带来巨大的市场和机遇。

Second, China and Mongolia should become good partners in win-win cooperation. Just as we say in China "one gets a better view of the rising moon at a waterfront pavilion or a favorable position", the geographical proximity and economic complementarity between our two countries — China's market, capital, technology and transportation corridors and Mongolia's rich natural endowment, promise great opportunities for closer cooperation between us. Last year, China's imports and exports totaled US$4.16 trillion. For the coming five years, China will import over US$10 trillion of goods and make outbound investment worth over US$500 billion.

Last year, about 100 million Chinese tourists travelled abroad, and the number is estimated to top 150 million annually by 2020. Sustained development in China will offer Mongolia and other cooperation partners a big market and enormous opportunities.

我这次访问期间，蒙方长期关心的过境运输、出海口等问题都得到了妥善解决。双方成立了矿能和互联互通合作委员会，签署了《中蒙经贸合作中期发展纲要》，确定了到2020年双边贸易额达到100亿美元的目标。双方就加强口岸、铁路合作等进行了深入探讨，达成了共识。双方决定将双边本币互换规模扩大至150亿元人民币，双方同意研究在中国二连浩特—蒙古国扎门乌德等地建立跨境经济合作区。双方还将在矿产品深加工、新能源、电力、农牧业、环保等领域开展全方位合作。这些新的合作必将增进两国人民福祉，给两国人民带来实实在在的利益。

During my current visit, the issues of transit transport and sea access that Mongolia had long sought to solve have been properly resolved. Our two countries have established a cooperation committee on minerals, energy and connectivity, and signed an Outline for Midterm Development of China-Mongolia Economic Cooperation, whose goal is to increase the two-way trade to US$10 billion by 2020. We have had an in-depth discussion and reached consensus on port and railway cooperation. We have decided to expand bilateral currency swap to RMB15 billion and agreed to study the possibility of establishing a cross-border economic cooperation zone spanning China's Erenhot and Mongolia's Zamyn-Uud. We will conduct full cooperation in the deep-processing of minerals and development of new energy, electricity, agriculture and animal husbandry, environmental protection and other areas. These new cooperation programs will surely deliver real benefits to our two peoples and enhance their well-being.

第三，中蒙要做常来常往的好朋友。路熟了走起来容易，人熟了聊起来容易。昨天，我同额勒贝格道尔吉总统会谈时，双方商定将进一步活跃人员往来，相互给予更加便利的签证政策，继续加强青年、媒体等领域机制性交流，营造更加有利的社会氛围，大力宣传中蒙友好。

Third, China and Mongolia should be good friends who will visit each other frequently. Travel is easy on familiar roads, and conversation is easy between friends. In my talks with President Elbegdorj yesterday, we agreed to encourage more people-to-people exchanges through greater visa facilitations, and increase exchanges between the youth, media and other sectors of the two countries so as to create a more favorable social environment and foster a culture of China-Mongolia friendship.

中方欢迎更多蒙方公民赴华留学、旅游、经商、就医。今后5年内，中方将向蒙方提供1000个培训名额，增加提供1000个中国政府全额奖学金名额，为蒙军培训500名留学生，邀请500名蒙方青年访华，邀请250名蒙方记者访华，并向蒙方免费提供25部中国优秀影视剧译作。相信这将对增进两国人民的相互了解和友好感情发挥重要促进作用。

China welcomes more Mongolian citizens to China for purposes of study, travel, business or medical treatment. In the coming five years, China will offer training opportunities for 1 000

Mongolians, provide an extra 1 000 full government scholarships to Mongolia, and train 500 Mongolian officers and soldiers. We will invite 500 Mongolian youth and 250 Mongolian journalists to China and offer free of charge 25 popular Chinese movies and TV plays that have been translated into Mongolian language. I believe all these will help boost the mutual understanding and friendship between our peoples.

当前，中国人民正在致力于实现"两个一百年"奋斗目标，努力到2020年全面建成小康社会，到21世纪中叶建成富强民主文明和谐的社会主义现代化国家。我们形象地把这个目标概括为实现中华民族伟大复兴的中国梦。同时，蒙古国人民也正致力于国家改革和经济社会发展，可以说蒙古国人民心中也有一个蒙古梦。

At present, the Chinese people are working towards the "two centennial goals", which is to complete the building of a moderately prosperous society in all respects by 2020 and build China into a modern socialist country that is prosperous, democratic, culturally advanced and harmonious by the middle of the century. These two goals together make up the Chinese dream of the great renewal of the Chinese nation. At the same time, the people of Mongolia are also committing themselves to advancing reform and achieving economic and social development. In other words, there is also a Mongolian dream in the hearts of the Mongolian people.

中国进行改革开放和现代化建设，将辐射和带动包括蒙古国在内的周边国家，中蒙双方发展战略完全可以进行有效对接，促进共同发展，实现共同繁荣。

China's ongoing reform, opening-up and modernization process will provide catalyst and impetus for the growth of Mongolia and other neighboring countries. This makes it possible for us to effectively align our respective development strategies for the benefit of common development and prosperity.

同时，我们也十分清楚，实现"两个一百年"奋斗目标，对中国这样一个拥有13亿多人口、发展还不平衡的国家来说并非易事，可以说任重而道远，需要继续长期艰苦奋斗。实现"两个一百年"奋斗目标，必须有一个良好周边环境。家门口太平，我们才能安心、踏实办好自己的事情。

On the other hand, we are soberly aware that it is not easy to realize the "two centennial goals" in China, a country with a population of over 1.3 billion and uneven development. It is going to be a long and arduous process that requires a long-term commitment. In the meantime, to realize these two goals, we need a sound neighboring environment. Without a peaceful neighborhood, we will not be able to keep our mind on our goals and manage our own affairs well.

随着中国不断发展起来，世界上有一些人对中国走向产生疑虑，担心中国发展强大后构成威胁。这要么是一种误解，要么就是一种曲解。

As China grows, some people in the world have begun to doubt how China would go about. They are worried that a stronger China might become a threat to them. This is either a misunderstanding or a misinterpretation of China's intention.

中国多次公开声明，中国将坚定不移地走和平发展道路，同时也将推动各国共同坚持和平发展。中国将积极承担更多国际责任，同世界各国一道维护人类良知和国际公理，在世界和地区事务中主持公道、伸张正义。中国将继续以最大诚意和耐心，坚持通过对话协商以和平方式解决分歧和争端。

China has publicly stated on numerous occasions that it will stick to the path of peaceful development and encourage all countries to pursue peaceful development. China will take up more international responsibilities, work with other countries to uphold human conscience and international justice, and stand for justice in regional and international affairs. China will continue to handle differences and disputes peacefully through dialogues and consultations with utmost sincerity and patience.

中国也多次公开声明，中国尊重各国人民自主选择发展道路的权利，绝不把自己的意志强加于人，也绝不允许任何人把他们的意志强加于中国人民。我们主张以和平方式解决国际争端，反对各种形式的霸权主义和强权政治，永远不称霸，永远不搞扩张。

China has also publicly stated on numerous occasions that it respects the right of people of all countries to independently choose their path of development, and that it will never impose its will on others, nor will it allow others to impose their will on the Chinese people. China stands for peaceful solutions to international disputes, opposes hegemonism and power politics in all forms, and will never seek hegemony or expansion.

中华民族历来是爱好和平的民族，中华文化崇尚和谐。在5000多年的文明发展中，中华民族一直追求和传承着和平、和睦、和谐的坚定理念。以和为贵，与人为善，己所不欲、勿施于人等观念和传统在中国代代相传，深深植根于中国人的精神中，深深体现在中国人的行为上。自古以来，中华民族就积极开展对外交往通商，而不是对外侵略扩张；执着于保家卫国的爱国主义，而不是开疆拓土的殖民主义。中国近代史，是一部充满灾难的悲惨屈辱史，是一部中华民族抵抗外来侵略、实现民族独立的伟大斗争史。历经苦难的中国人民珍惜和平，绝不会将自己曾经遭受过的悲惨经历强加给其他民族。中国人民愿意同世界各国人民和睦相处、和谐发展，共谋和平、共护和平、共享和平。

The Chinese nation is a peace-loving nation, and the Chinese culture values harmony. For over 5 000 years of its civilization, the Chinese nation has unswervingly advocated and promoted the ideas of peace, amity and harmony. For generations, the Chinese people have strongly believed in the traditional ideas that peace is the most precious, that one should be friendly to others and that one should not do onto others what he does not want others do unto him. All these ideas have taken deep root in the heart of the Chinese people and shaped their character and behavior. Since ancient times, the Chinese nation has actively engaged itself in exchanges and trade with foreign countries, instead of external aggression or expansion. We have committed ourselves to the patriotic cause of defending our homeland, instead of colonialist pursuit of territorial expansion. The modern history of China is a humiliating and tragic record of miserable sufferings, and at the same time, it also captures the epic struggle of the Chinese people to resist foreign aggression and realize national independence. Emerging from untold suffering, the

Chinese people cherish the value of peace, and will never want to see other nations go through the same pains it endured in the past. The Chinese people want, more than anything else, to live in peace and harmony with the people of other countries, and work with them to promote, defend and share peace together.

中国改革开放30多年的历史已经证明，和平发展是中国基于自身国情、社会制度、文化传统作出的战略抉择，顺应时代潮流，符合中国根本利益，符合周边国家利益，符合世界各国利益，我们没有理由去改变它。

The experience of China's reform and opening-up over the past 30 years and more has proved that peaceful development is a strategic choice that suits China's own national conditions, social system and cultural traditions. It conforms to the trend of the times, and serves the fundamental interests of China. It also meets the interests of China's neighboring countries and those of all countries in the world. So there is no reason whatsoever to change this policy.

中国始终把包括蒙古国在内的周边邻国视作促进共同发展的合作伙伴、维护和平稳定的真诚朋友，同绝大多数邻国建立了不同形式的伙伴关系。我们将继续坚持与邻为善、以邻为伴的方针，坚持睦邻、安邻、富邻的政策，在同邻国相处时秉持亲、诚、惠、容的理念。

China has always regarded Mongolia and other neighboring countries as partners for pursuing common development and sincere friends for maintaining peace and stability. We have established partnerships with most of our neighbors in one form or another. We will continue the policy of enhancing good-neighborliness and partnership with neighbors, remain committed to living in harmony and security with neighbors for common prosperity, and uphold the principles of amity, sincerity, mutual benefit and inclusiveness in our relations with neighbors.

"众人拾柴火焰高。"中国愿意为包括蒙古国在内的周边国家提供共同发展的机遇和空间，欢迎大家搭乘中国发展的列车，搭快车也好，搭便车也好，我们都欢迎，正所谓"独行快，众行远"。我多次讲，中国开展对发展中国家的合作，将坚持正确义利观，不搞我赢你输、我多你少，在一些具体项目上将照顾对方利益。中国人讲求言必信、行必果。中国说到的话、承诺的事，一定会做到，一定会兑现。

"Many hands make light work." China wishes to provide Mongolia and other neighboring countries with both opportunities and space for common development. All countries are welcome to get on board the express train of China's development. As a saying goes, "If you want to go fast, go alone; if you want to go far, go together." I have said many times that in our cooperation with other developing countries, China will set store by upholding moral principles while pursuing its interests. China will not subscribe to the zero-sum approach. When it comes to specific projects, China will give more consideration to the interests of our cooperation partners. We Chinese people attach great importance to taking action to keep promises. We will do whatever it takes to honor our commitment.

女士们、先生们、朋友们！

Ladies and Gentlemen,

Dear Friends,

蒙古国有"邻里心灵相通，命运与共"的谚语。中国人讲"好邻居金不换。"中国是世界上邻国最多的国家，我们把这当作宝贵财富。

As a Mongolian saying goes, "Neighbors are connected at heart and share a common destiny." In the same vein, we often say in China, "Good neighbors are more precious than gold." China has more neighbors than any other country in the world. And this we take as a precious gift.

当今世界，亚洲是经济发展最具活力的地区，同时也是热点敏感问题较多的地区，亚洲国家如何正确处理同邻国关系，实现邻国和睦相处、共同发展，妥善解决彼此争议和矛盾，是一个重大课题。我认为，要破解这一课题，关键在于要顺应时代潮流和民心所向，坚持相互尊重、求同存异、面向未来、合作共赢的原则，更多地用东方智慧来解决问题、化解矛盾、促进和谐。

Although, in the world today, Asia is the most dynamic region for economic development, it is also a region with more hot spots and sensitive issues than other regions. How to properly manage relations with neighbors, live in harmony with each other for common development, and properly handle disputes and differences remains a major issue for Asian countries. I believe that to find a solution, it is essential to follow the trend of the times and the will of the people. We should uphold the principle of mutual respect, seek common ground while reserving differences, adopt a forward-looking approach and seek win-win cooperation. Above all, we should rely more on our oriental wisdom to solve problems, diffuse tension and advance harmony.

60年前，中国、印度、缅甸共同倡导和平共处五项原则，成为指导国与国关系的基本准则，是亚洲国家为促进国际关系发展作出的重要贡献。在推进区域合作进程中，亚洲国家交流互鉴，坚持相互尊重、协商一致、照顾各方舒适度的亚洲方式，这是符合本地区特点的处理相互关系的传统。这个传统体现着亚洲的邻国相处之道，在今天应该继续发扬光大，为亚洲国家以及整个地区和平、发展、合作激发出源源不断的内生动力。坚持和实践这一传统，要做到以下几点。

The Five Principles of Peaceful Coexistence, jointly initiated by China, India and Myanmar sixty years ago, have become basic norms governing state-to-state relations and thus represent an important contribution that Asian countries have made to the development of international relations. While moving forward with regional cooperation, Asian countries have embraced the Asian approach that features learning from each other through exchanges, mutual respect, consensus-building, and accommodating each other's comfort level. This approach to state-to-state relations fits in well with the specific conditions in Asia. Embodying the Asian tradition of handling relations with neighbors, this approach should be carried forward in order to unleash the endless inherent strength for peace, development and cooperation in Asian countries and the region as a whole. To uphold and practice this approach, we need to do the following:

——互尊互信。历史上，许多亚洲国家饱受外来欺凌之苦，深感国家独立自主之可贵。尊重独立、主权、领土完整，尊重各国自主选择社会制度和发展道路，互不干涉内政，照顾彼此重大关切，这是亚洲各国友好相处的重要基础。亚洲多样性突出，具有开放包容的传统，各国应该在平等基础上，促进不同文明交流对话，加深相互理解和彼此认同，为亚洲稳定和繁荣构筑坚实依托。

Respect and trust each other. Many Asian countries had the agonizing experience of being bullied and humiliated by foreign powers, and know full well the value of national independence. Mutual respect for each other's independence, sovereignty and territorial integrity, mutual respect for each other's independent choice of social system and development path, mutual non-interference in each other's internal affairs, mutual accommodation of each other's major concerns are an important foundation on which Asian countries have lived with each other in amity. A region of great diversity, Asia has a tradition of openness and inclusiveness. Countries in this region should increase inter-civilization exchanges and dialogue on an equal footing for better mutual understanding and trust and lay a solid foundation for stability and prosperity in Asia.

——聚同化异。在亚洲各国交往史上，友好合作是主流，但也不乏一些遗留问题。邻国之间磕磕碰碰在所难免，关键是如何对待和处理。只有以对话和合作凝聚共识、化解分歧，才是地区长治久安最有效的保障。我们应该着眼大局、友好协商，共同参与国际和地区治理，为促进国际政治经济秩序朝着更加公正合理的方向发展发挥积极作用。

Seek common ground while resolving differences. Although friendship and cooperation have been the mainstream in the history of relations among Asian countries, there are still numerous issues left over from history yet to be resolved. Differences and frictions are hardly avoidable among neighboring countries. What is important is how to handle and manage them properly. The most effective way to ensure long-term peace and stability in the region is to build consensus and resolve differences through dialogue and cooperation. We, Asian countries, should bear in mind the overall interests of the world, engage in friendly consultations, jointly participate in regional and international governance and contribute to the building of a more fair and equitable international political and economic order.

——合作共赢。发展经济、改善民生是亚洲各国面临的首要任务，加强互利合作是促进亚洲和睦相处的重要粘合剂。亚洲各国应该秉持联合自强、守望相助的亚洲意识，互帮互助，优势互补，扩大利益交融，合力推进自由贸易区和互联互通建设，深化区域经济一体化，实现共同发展，做大共同利益的蛋糕，增进亚洲各国人民福祉。

Pursue win-win cooperation. It is a task of primary importance for Asian countries to grow economy and improve their people's well-being. Efforts to enhance mutually beneficial cooperation among them provide a strong adhesive for Asian countries to live in harmony with one another. Asian countries should, in the Asian spirit of strength through unity and mutual assistance, help each other and complement each other's strengths to expand converging interests.

We should work in concert to make progress in building free trade areas, promote greater connectivity and deepen regional economic integration for the benefit of common development. Together, we should make a bigger pie of common interests and bring more benefits to all the people in Asia.

女士们、先生们、朋友们！

Ladies and Gentlemen,

Dear Friends,

我这次访问蒙古国，深深感到中蒙友好已经植根于两国人民心中，这是中蒙关系发展最大的信心和动力源泉。我相信，在两国人民支持下，中蒙关系的明天一定会更加美好。

This trip has made me feel even more strongly that China-Mongolia friendship has already taken deep root in the hearts of our peoples. This is the biggest source of confidence and strength for the continued growth of our bilateral relations. I am confident that with the support of the people in both countries, China-Mongolia relationship will usher in an even brighter future.

今年是中国和蒙古国的马年。马是力量和进取的象征，深受中蒙两国人民喜爱。我衷心祝愿蒙古国国家建设龙马精神、万马奔腾，衷心祝愿中蒙全面战略伙伴关系快马加鞭、马到功成。让我们携手努力，让中蒙世代友好的种子广泛播撒在两国人民心中。

This year marks the Year of Horse in both China and Mongolia. Horse symbolizes strength and progress, and it is therefore very popular among people in both countries. It is my sincere wish that Mongolia will make great strides forward in its national development just like ten thousand horses galloping ahead with full vitality. I also sincerely hope that China-Mongolia comprehensive strategic partnership will advance at fast speed and achieve resounding success. Let us work hand in hand to sow the seed of lasting friendship in the hearts of our two peoples.

巴耶里拉！谢谢！

Bayarlalaa! Thank you!

第10单元　数字口译 I (Figures in Interpreting I)

口译主题：经济

单元学习目的(Unit Goals) 💡

➢ 数字的类型。
➢ 不同类型数字的读法和表达。
➢ 学习经济专题所涉及的常用词语和表达。

导入 (Lead -in)

1. 请用英语读出数字：一万，87 654 321，100 000 000
2. 如何翻译这句话：这是您第几次访问中国？
3. 数字口译有哪些类型？

10.1　技能讲解(Skill Introduction)

数字有几种特殊的表达方式，如序数词、分数、小数、百分数等，此外与数字相关的短语如几年、时间、倍数等的读法和表达也是数字口译的难点。

■ 10.1.1　数字的读法(Numeration)

英语和汉语对于四位数以上的数字的表达，有不同的段位概念和分段方法。英语数字以每三位数为一段位，而汉语则以每四位数为一段位。

1. 英语数字分段方法	汉语数字分段方法
第一段位 one，ten，hundred	第一段位 个 十 百 千
第二段位 thousand，ten thousand，hundred thousand	第二段位 万 十万 百万 千万
第三段位 million，ten million，hundred million	第三段位 亿 十亿 百亿 千亿
第四段位 billion，ten billion，hundred billion	第四段位 兆
第五段位 trillion	

2. 3~5位数的读法

304读作：three hundred (and) four

762读作：seven hundred (and) sixty-two

4 241读作：four thousand two hundred (and) forty one

● 在英式英语中，一个数的最后两位(十位和个位)用"and"，但美式英语中则不用。如：1 021，读作：one thousand twenty-one.

● 不定冠词"a"只在数的开头才和hundred，thousand等连用。

如：506，读作：five hundred (and) six；

3 251，读作：three thousand, two hundred (and) fifty one。

● 读整数1000是a thousand，在and前我们也可读a thousand，但是在一个有百位数的数目前就得说one thousand。

如：1 091，读作：a thousand, (and) ninety-one；

1 238，读作：one thousand, two hundred (and) thirty-eight。

● hundred，thousand和million的单数可以和"a"或"one"连用，但不能单独使用。在非正式文体中"a"比较常用；当表达比较准确信息的时候用"one"。

如： John wants to live for a hundred years.

The task took exactly one hundred days.

3. 多位数的读法

以一组13位数字为单位的阿拉伯数字1234567891234为例，用英语和汉语表达时，前者按下标分段记号(,)为单位朗读，后者按上标分段记号(')为单位朗读。

英语朗读法(以下面逗号为分割点)：

1,234,567,891,234

one trillion

two hundred and thirty-four billion

five hundred and sixty-seven million

eight hundred and ninety-one thousand

two hundred and thirty-four

汉语朗读法(以上面逗号为分割点)：

1' 2345' 6789' 1234

一兆/万亿

二千三百四十五亿

六千七百八十九万

一千二百三十四

■ 10.1.2 序数词的读法 (Ordinal numeral)

1st，读作：(the)first.

2nd，读作：(the)second。

3nd，读作：(the)third。

4th，读作：(the)fourth。

20th，读作：(the)twentieth。

21st，读作：(the)twenty-first。

22nd，读作：(the)twenty-second。

23rd，读作：(the)twenty-third。

如：She was (the) third in the exam.

China's economy is ranked the 6th in the world and its foreign trade is ranked the 4th.

It is a great pleasure to join you in Vientiane as we mark the 25th anniversary of China-ASEAN dialogue relations.

■ 10.1.3 分数的读法(Fraction)

通常将分子读为基数，将分母读为序数。

1/2 = a (or one) half

1/3 = a (or one) third

1/4 = a quarter or one fourth

1/5 = a (or one) fifth

2/3 = two thirds

7/9 = seven ninths

7 3/4 = seven and three quarters

● 比较复杂的分数可用over表示。

如： 10/41 = ten over (or by) forty-one

147/587 = one hundred and forty-seven over five hundred and eighty-seven

● 其他实际使用例子，如：

3/4 hour = three quarters of an hour (三刻钟)

8/10 mile = eight tenths of a mile (十分之八英里)

Harry Potter and Platform 9 3/4 = Harry Potter and Platform nine and three quarters (哈利·波特与9 3/4月台)

■ 10.1.4 小数的读法 (Decimal)

1. 不满 "1" 的小数的读法

小数点读作 "point"，小数点左边的零读作 "naught "(英) 或 "zero"(美)，也可不读。小数点右边的小数部分按个位基数词依次读出。在小数点后遇到零时，多读作字母

"O"的音，具体如下。

0.5：naught/zero point five；point five。

0.136：naught/zero point one three six；point one three six。

0.006%：naught/zero point O O six percent。

2. 整数带小数的读法

小数点左边的整数部分按整数读法或按个位基数词依次读出。小数点右边的小数部分按个位基数词依次读出。在小数点后遇到零时，可读作"naught/zero"，也可以读作字母"O"的音，具体如下。

4.09：four point naught/zero nine；four point O nine。

6.002：six point naught naught/zero zero two；six point O O two。

15.31%：fifteen point three one percent。

44.44……：forty-four point four recurring。

3. 万位和亿位以上整数带小数的读法

汉语里有万位和亿位以上整数带小数的写法或读法。英语里没有相应的表示"万"或"亿"的单词。译成英语时，先将万理解为十个千，将亿理解为一百个百万，然后将小数点左边的整数部分和小数点右边的小数部分做相应的变化，例如：

3.5万：35,000，thirty-five thousand。

753.24万：7,532,400，seven million, five hundred and thirty-two thousand, four hundred。

12.05亿：1,205,000,000，one point two O five billion；one billion, two hundred and five million。

10.1.5　百分比的读法 (Percentage)

42%，读作forty-two percent。

22.3%，读作twenty-two point three percent。

10‰，读作two per mill (per mill，每千，permillage *n*. 千分率[比])。

10.1.6　时间的读法 (Time)

1. 年份

关于四位数年份的读法有下列几种情形。

(1) 一般情况下，将表示年份的4个数字按前后分为两组，每一组的数字都按基数词来读。如：

1961年读作 nineteen sixty-one；

1795年读作 seventeen ninety-five。

(2) 如果前两个数字为非"零"数字，后两位数分别为"零"，则先读出前两位数，然后将后面的两个"零"读为hundred。如：

1900年读作 nineteen hundred；

1800年读作 eighteen hundred。

(3) 第三个数字为"零"(其他数字不是"零")的年份的读法应当将该"零"读为"O"。如：1505年，读作 fifteen O five。

(4) 关于千年的一些读法。

2000年，读作 two thousand。

2006年，读作 two thousand and six(或twenty O six)。

1005年，读作 one thousand and five(或ten O five)。

另外，还有一些非四位数的年份，它们有两种读法：一种是按照基数词的方法来读，另一种是一个一个数字来读。如：

431BC，读作 four three one BC(或four hundred and thirty-one BC)。

2.日期

(1) 日期的写法可以采用基数词和序数词两种形式。如：

May 1，可以写成 May 1st。

March 20，可以写成 March 20th。

(2)日期的表达英式和美式有所不同，在日期的写法上，英式先写日子，美式先写月份。如：

(英)2000年5月8日，为8th May 2000。

(美)2000年5月8日，为May 8, 2000。

(3) 日期的读法只能用序数词的形式。如：

January 21(January 21st)，读作January(the)twenty-first。

July 22(July 22th)，读作July(the)twenty-second。

(4) 在读法上，英国人有两种表达方式，如：

April the fifth，nineteen ninety-nine。

The fifth of April，nineteen ninety-nine。

美国人则一般这样表示：April fifth，nineteen ninety-nine(省略"the")。

10.1.7 温度 (Temperature)

表示温度有华氏(Fahrenheit)和摄氏(Centigrade)两种。英美均使用华氏作为温度的计量单位。摄氏用法现已日渐普及，如：

35℃，为thirty-five degrees Centigrade(或Celsius)；

50℉，为fifty degrees Fahrenheit；

0C，为naught degrees Centigrade；

−2C，为two degrees below zero。

10.2 主题口译(Topic Interpreting)

■ 10.2.1 单句口译(Sentence Practice)

Please interpret the following sentences by using the techniques illustrated above. You may interpret to your partner first and then he/she comments on your performance.

(1) The global population of older persons is expected to rise from just over 900 million in 2015 to 1.4 billion by 2030 and 2.1 billion by 2050.

(2) Our people-to-people exchanges are also growing. Each week 90 or so flights crisscross between us, making possible more than 1.3 million visits between us last year.

(3) Currently, China-Canada trade only accounts for 1.4% of China's total foreign trade and 8.1% of that of Canada.

(4) In 2015, trade volume between the two sides reached 472.2 billion dollars and China was the biggest trade partner of the ASEAN for the 7th consecutive year.

(5) The accumulative volume of mutual investment between the two sides exceeded 160 billion dollars and the number of annual personnel exchanges exceeded 23 million.

(6) 25年来，双方贸易额从80亿美元增长到4722亿美元，增长近60倍。

(7) 人文交流日益频繁，双向留学生达18万，年度人员往来超过2300万人次，中国成为东盟第一大游客来源国。

(8) 中方欢迎将2017年确定为"中国—东盟旅游合作年"，愿与东盟探讨制定旅游合作计划，确立2020年双方人员往来达到3000万人次的目标。

(9) 随着中美旅游年活动的开展，两国互访旅游人数有望达到500万人次，创历史新高。

(10) 民生不断改善，居民收入与经济增长基本保持同步，城镇新增就业每年超过1300万人。

■ 10.2.2 段落口译(Paragraph Practice)

1. Vocabulary Work: Study the following words and phrases and translate them into the target language.

two-way trade	in a row
volume	accumulative
register	gross domestic product
folds	overheating
fixed asset	cool down

2. Please interpret the following paragraphs by using the techniques illustrated above.

(1) Over the past 25 years, the two-way trade volume has gone from $8 billion to $472.2

billion, an increase of almost 60 folds. China has been ASEAN's biggest trading partner for seven years running and ASEAN has been China's third largest trading partner for five years in a row. Two-way investment has registered fast and balanced growth with a total amount of $160 billion in accumulative terms. Chinese companies have set up 26 projects in eight ASEAN countries. These projects, being overseas economic and trade cooperation zones in nature, have attracted over 300 Chinese companies, achieving a total investment of $1.77 billion and an output of $9.02 billion.

(2) China's State Information Center predicts China's gross domestic product will grow by 9.3 percent for all of this year, with a total of 13.4 trillion yuan or US$1.6 trillion. The center says China's overall economy runs from overheating to normal status. It predicts the increase of fixed asset investment this year will be slower than last year. It says trade surplus will decrease from last year's 25.4 billion US dollars to this year's US$4.4 billion. In another development report, the World Bank says China's policy which measures to cool down the economy are starting to show some success. It predicts China's GDP to grow by 9.25 percent this year.

(3) 1950年至2016年，中国在自身长期发展水平和人民生活水平不高的情况下，累计对外提供援款4000多亿元人民币，实施各类援外项目5000多个，其中成套项目近3000个，举办11 000多期培训班，为发展中国家在华培训各类人员26万多名。改革开放以来，中国累计吸引外资超过1.7万亿美元，累计对外直接投资超过1.2万亿美元，为世界经济发展做出了巨大贡献。国际金融危机爆发以来，中国经济增长对世界经济增长的贡献率年均在30%以上。这些数字，在世界上都是名列前茅的。

(4) 中国将积极营造宽松有序的投资环境，放宽外商投资准入，建设高标准自由贸易试验区，加强产权保护，促进公平竞争，让中国市场更加透明、更加规范。预计未来5年，中国将进口8万亿美元的商品、吸收6000亿美元的外来投资，对外投资总额将达到7500亿美元，出境旅游将达到7亿人次。这将为世界各国提供更广阔市场、更充足资本、更丰富产品、更宝贵合作契机。

■ 10.2.3 篇章口译[Passage Practice (E to C)]

1. Please interpret the following passage by using the techniques illustrated above. Please pay attention to the underlined sentences as they require special treatment during interpreting.

Mobilizing Agricultural Science and Technology for Ending Poverty in Africa and Beyond
World Bank Africa Region Vice President Makhtar Diop

Mr. Chairman, Distinguished Guests, Ladies and Gentlemen, thank you for the honor of your invitation.

① This is my second visit to China since being appointed Vice President for Africa at the World Bank. I look forward to nurturing the China-World Bank partnership particularly on today's vital topic: mobilizing agricultural science and technology for ending poverty, in Africa and beyond.

② We meet at a critical time in the global economy. Even as industrialized countries are suffering from anemic growth rates, Sub-Saharan Africa's 49 countries are booming with growth rates of five percent and more. Demand for food is rising globally, and food prices are more volatile. Adding to this complex mix, we know that climate change will impact Africa's agricultural potential, particularly in dry land areas that are home to a majority of poor people.

③ As you may be aware, under the leadership of our new President, Jim Yong Kim, the World Bank has set new goals for ending poverty and achieving shared prosperity in our lifetime. Reducing the percentage of people living on less than $1.25 a day to three percent by 2030 and increasing the incomes of the bottom 40 percent of the population in every developing country will require a thriving agricultural sector that provides jobs, food and income security, as well as greater, more open market access and trade, including within Africa.[1]

④ I am here to talk about Africa and its unrealized – but achievable – potential in the farm sector. China feeds nearly 20 percent of the human family. Africa can and must benefit from the wealth of China's experiences in sustainable food production and rural transformation. Nowhere is the need for an agricultural transformation greater than in Africa's dryland areas. In the Sahel sub-region, over 10 million people are facing chronic food insecurity. In the Horn of Africa, over 8.32 million people are facing a stressed or crisis phase of food insecurity.[2] We are taking a strategic, regional approach to tackling these challenges focusing on reducing vulnerability and increasing resilience, and promoting greater economic opportunity and integration.

⑤ The World Bank is committed to making a positive difference in Africa's farm economy. Given the importance of the agricultural sector, the World Bank's Action Plan commits us to providing $8—$10 billion annually. A significant portion of this, up to one-third, is being directed to the specific needs of Africa's farm sector.[3]

⑥ We have scaled-up the World Bank's agricultural program in Africa quantitatively and qualitatively. Notably, we are:

-Expanding our lending program, from US$0.4 billion in 2008 to US$1.2 billion a year. In addition to budget support and traditional investment projects, these investments will support public-private partnerships and larger, sub-regional operations that generate economies of scale and transformational impact.[4]

-Working to boost Africa's irrigated area, from 20 percent currently to 40 percent by 2030. This goal will require US$40 billion, with the Bank potentially financing one-quarter of the investment needed. [5]

-Moving from modest and fragmented pilot efforts to bold, systematic projects in land administration. It is time for a big push to scale-up best practices, and we aim to deliver at least two new land administration projects per year, US$150 million each, leading to at least US$1.5 billion over 10 years. A target worth striving for would be to reduce time required for registering property from 65 days to 30.[6]

⑦ Working to increase market access, remove trade barriers, and improve competitiveness to double food trade in ten years. We want to be ambitious, improve trade, transport, infrastructure and food safety systems with a 10-year target of cutting by half the costs of bringing produce to market.

Notes on the text

(1) Reducing the percentage of people living on less than $1.25 a day to three percent by 2030 and increasing the incomes of the bottom 40 percent of the population in every developing country will require a thriving agricultural sector that provides jobs, food and income security, as well as greater, more open market access and trade, including within Africa.

要想在2030年以前把每个发展中国家每天生活消费在1.25美元以下的人口比例降至3%、使收入最低的40%的人口收入增加，这需要一个生机勃勃的农业部门来提供就业、粮食和收入保障，还需要更多、更开放的市场准入和贸易——包括非洲内部的市场准入和贸易。

(2) Nowhere is the need for an agricultural transformation greater than in Africa's dryland areas. In the Sahel sub-region, over 10 million people are facing chronic food insecurity. In the Horn of Africa, over 8.32 million people are facing a stressed or crisis phase of food insecurity.

非洲干旱地区面临的农业变革需求比世界其他任何地区都更为迫切。在萨赫勒(Sahel)地区，有1000多万人长期缺乏粮食保障。在非洲之角，超过832万人面临粮食紧张和粮食危机。

(3) Given the importance of the agricultural sector, the World Bank's Action Plan commits us to providing $8—$10 billion annually. A significant portion of this, up to one-third, is being directed to the specific needs of Africa's farm sector.

由于农业部门的重要性和世界行动的行动计划承诺，我们将每年为农业提供80亿~100亿美元的资金。其中很大一部分(近1/3)是用于满足非洲农业部门的具体需要。

(4) Expanding our lending program, from US$0.4 billion in 2008 to US$1.2 billion a year. In addition to budget support and traditional investment projects, these investments will support public-private partnerships and larger, sub-regional operations that generate economies of scale and transformational impact.

我们正在扩大贷款项目，从2008年的4亿美元增长到每年12亿美元。除了用于预算支持和传统的投资项目外，这些资金还将支持公私伙伴关系和更大规模的次区域业务，以产生规模效应和深刻影响。

(5) <u>Working to boost Africa's irrigated area, from 20 percent currently to 40 percent by 2030. This goal will require US$40 billion, with the Bank potentially financing one-quarter of the investment needed.</u>

我们正在努力扩大非洲的灌溉区域,要从现在的20%增长到2030年的40%。实现这一目标需要400亿美元,世界银行可能会提供1/4的投资。

(6) <u>Moving from modest and fragmented pilot efforts to bold, systematic projects in land administration. It is time for a big push to scale-up best practices, and we aim to deliver at least two new land administration projects per year, US$150 million each, leading to at least US$1.5 billion over 10 years. A target worth striving for would be to reduce time required for registering property from 65 days to 30.</u>

从小规模、零散的土地管理试点项目转变为大胆、系统性的项目。现在是大规模推广土地管理最佳实践的时候了,我们的目标是每年至少推出两个新的土地管理项目,每个1.5亿美元,10年时间里共投资至少15亿美元。一个值得努力推动的目标是将登记土地资产所需的时间从65天降为30天。

2. Please interpret the following passage by using the techniques illustrated above. Please pay attention to the underlined sentences as they require special treatment during interpreting.

REPORT ON THE WORK OF THE GOVERNMENT (Excerpts)

Delivered at the Second Session of the Twelfth National People's Congress on March 5, 2014

Li Keqiang, Premier of the State Council

Fellow Deputies,

① On behalf of the State Council, I now present to you the report on the work of the government for your deliberation, and I welcome comments on my report from the members of the National Committee of the Chinese People's Political Consultative Conference (CPPCC).

Review of Work in 2013

② Last year was the first year for this government to perform its functions in accordance with the law, and it had arduous tasks. We faced a complex environment: the world economic recovery was difficult. In China, downward pressure on the economy increased, natural disasters occurred frequently, and there was an array of interrelated problems. However, the people of all of China's ethnic groups, under the leadership of the Central Committee of the Communist Party of China (CPC) with Comrade Xi Jinping as General Secretary, confidently met all challenges, strove to overcome difficulties, fully attained the main targets for economic and social development for the year, and made impressive achievements in reform and opening up and in the socialist modernization drive.

③ -<u>The economy was stable and improved. The gross domestic product (GDP) reached</u>

56.9 trillion yuan, an increase of 7.7% over the previous year. The rise in the consumer price index (CPI) was kept at 2.6%. The registered urban unemployment rate was kept at 4.1% and 13.1 million urban jobs were created, an all-time high. Total imports and exports exceeded US$4 trillion, reaching a new high.[1]

④ -Personal income continued to rise, and economic performance continued to improve. The per capita disposable income of urban residents rose by 7% in real terms, and the per capita net income of rural residents rose by 9.3% in real terms. The number of rural people living in poverty was reduced by 16.5 million and the urban-rural income gap continued to narrow. The profits of industrial enterprises with annual revenue of 20 million yuan or more from their main business operations rose by 12.2%. Government revenue increased by 10.1%.[2]

⑤ -Progress was achieved in adjusting the economic structure. Grain output exceeded 600 million metric tons, increasing for the tenth consecutive year. The value-added of the service sector accounted for 46.1% of GDP, surpassing secondary industry for the first time. The proportion of the gross regional product of the central and western regions to China's GDP continued to rise, and development in different regions became better balanced. China's total electricity consumption increased by 7.5%, and the volume of freight transport rose by 9.9%. Main real physical indexes matched economic growth.[3]

⑥ Last year, we adhered to the general work guideline of making progress while maintaining stability. We worked to maintain stable growth, make structural adjustments and carry out reform in a holistic way. We ensured that the government's macro policies are stable, micro policies are flexible and social policies meet people's basic needs. We improved the ways of exercising macro-control and adopted measures with both short-term and long-term benefits in mind. We strove to break new ground, improve quality, and make progress while ensuring stability. All our work got off to a good start.

⑦ First, we deepened reform and opening up, invigorated the market, and stimulated internal impetus to growth. In the face of complex international and domestic developments and difficult choices in macro-control, we endeavored to resolve deep-seated problems and difficulties, took reform and opening up as the fundamental way to advance development, and gave full rein to both the invisible hand of the market and the visible hand of the government to promote steady economic growth. Taking government reform as our starting point, we made accelerating the transformation of government functions, streamlining administration and delegating more power to lower-level governments the top priority of this government. Reform of State Council bodies was carried out in an orderly manner. We abolished or delegated to lower-level governments 416 items previously subject to State Council review and approval in batches, revised the list of investment projects requiring government review and approval, and carried forward reform of the business registration system. Local governments actively transformed their functions and reformed their departments, and greatly reduced the matters requiring their review and approval. The pilot project to replace business tax with value-added tax (VAT) was expanded, and 348 administrative fees were either canceled or exempted, thus reducing the burden on businesses by more than 150 billion yuan.[4]

⑧ Second, we improved our thinking on and ways of conducting macro-control and ensured that the economy performed within a proper range. In the face of economic fluctuations, we maintained confidence, and stressed the need to maintain steady growth and ensure that employment does not fall below the prescribed minimum level and that inflation does not rise above the projected level. As the economic performance remained within the proper range, we concentrated our efforts on improving the growth model and making structural adjustments by unswervingly following the underlying principles of our macro-control policy. This enhanced public confidence in the market and kept expectations stable.

⑨ Third, we focused on adjusting the economic structure and raising the quality and returns of development. To address structural problems that hinder development, we strove to take well-targeted steps and used both the market and differential policies to maintain steady growth while upgrading the economic structure. And we also promoted industrial transformation in the course of carrying out innovation-driven development, thereby raising the quality and returns of development, promoting industrial upgrading and creating conditions for sustaining long-term development. The foundation of agriculture was consolidated and strengthened. We carried out integrated and comprehensive pilot reforms to modernize agriculture and supported the development of diversified and large-scale farming. Reinforcement of 15 000 small reservoirs was completed. More than 63 million additional rural people gained access to safe drinking water. Ecological conservation and development were strengthened, and China's forest coverage increased to 21.6% of the total land area.[6]

⑩ Adjustment of the industrial structure was accelerated. We encouraged the development of the service sector, and supported the development of strategic emerging industries. The 4G mobile communications system was put into commercial operation. We worked actively to resolve the serious problem of excess production capacity in some industries. We tried hard to conserve energy, reduce emissions and prevent and control pollution. Energy intensity was cut by 3.7%, and emissions of sulfur dioxide and chemical oxygen demand decreased by 3.5% and 2.9%, respectively.[7]

⑪ Infrastructure was strengthened. The first phase of the eastern route of the South-to-North Water Diversion Project was put into operation ahead of plan, and the main part of the first phase of the central route was completed as planned. Underground pipe networks and other urban infrastructure were improved. Oil, natural gas and electric power networks were expanded, and electricity generated from non-fossil energy amounted to 22.3% of the total electricity output. Civil aviation, water transport, information and postal service networks were improved. The total length of expressways and railways in service both exceeded 100 000 kilometers, with the length of high-speed railways in service reaching 11 000 kilometers, ranking first in the world.[8]

⑫ Fourth, we ensured and improved people's wellbeing and upheld social fairness and justice. At a time when government expenditures exceeded government revenue by a large amount, we took improving people's wellbeing as the starting point and goal of our work, gave high priority to improving the relevant systems, ensured that people's basic living needs are met, and promoted the development of social programs. We ensured that the people have access to basic daily necessities. We implemented the program for promoting employment of university graduates, thus enabling the vast majority of new college graduates to find jobs. We improved employment services and vocational skills training for rural migrant workers, and provided employment assistance to urban residents having difficulties in finding jobs. We improved the systems of social aid and old-age insurance. Subsistence allowances for urban and rural residents were raised by 13.1% and 17.7% respectively, and basic pension benefits for enterprise retirees were increased by 10%. Construction of 6.66 million government-subsidized housing units was started, and 5.44 million such housing units were basically completed. Thanks to these efforts, over ten million people with housing difficulties moved into new homes.[9]

⑬ We promoted education development and reform. We launched the project to alleviate poverty through education and continued to implement the plan to improve poorly built and low performing rural schools providing compulsory education. The project to improve nutrition of rural students covered 32 million students, and living allowances were issued to rural teachers in contiguous poor areas. The number of students from poor rural areas who were enrolled by key colleges and universities increased by 8.5% over the previous year.[10]

Notes on the text

(1) The economy was stable and improved. The gross domestic product (GDP) reached 56.9 trillion yuan, an increase of 7.7% over the previous year. The rise in the consumer price index (CPI) was kept at 2.6%. The registered urban unemployment rate was kept at 4.1% and 13.1 million urban jobs were created, an all-time high. Total imports and exports exceeded US$4 trillion, reaching a new high.

经济运行稳中向好。国内生产总值达到56.9万亿元，比上年增长7.7%。居民消费价格涨幅控制在2.6%。城镇登记失业率4.1%。城镇新增就业1310万人，创历史新高。进出口总额突破4万亿美元，再上新台阶。

(2) Personal income continued to rise, and economic performance continued to improve. The per capita disposable income of urban residents rose by 7% in real terms, and the per capita net income of rural residents rose by 9.3% in real terms. The number of rural people living in poverty was reduced by 16.5 million and the urban-rural income gap continued to narrow. The profits of industrial enterprises with annual revenue of 20 million yuan or more from their main business operations rose by 12.2%. Government revenue increased by 10.1%.

居民收入和经济效益持续提高。城镇居民人均可支配收入实际增长7%，农村居民人均纯收入实际增长9.3%，农村贫困人口减少1650万人，城乡居民收入差距继续缩小。年收入2 000万元以上工业企业利润增长12.2%。财政收入增长10.1%。

(3) Grain output exceeded 600 million metric tons, increasing for the tenth consecutive year. The value-added of the service sector accounted for 46.1% of GDP, surpassing secondary industry for the first time. The proportion of the gross regional product of the central and western regions to China's GDP continued to rise, and development in different regions became better balanced. China's total electricity consumption increased by 7.5%, and the volume of freight transport rose by 9.9%. Main real physical indexes matched economic growth.

粮食产量超过1.2万亿斤，实现"十连增"。服务业增加值比重达到46.1%，首次超过第二产业。中西部地区生产总值比重继续提高，区域发展协调性增强。全社会用电量增长7.5%，货运量增长9.9%，主要实物量指标与经济增长相互匹配。

(4) Local governments actively transformed their functions and reformed their departments, and greatly reduced the matters requiring their review and approval. The pilot project to replace business tax with value-added tax (VAT) was expanded, and 348 administrative fees were either canceled or exempted, thus reducing the burden on businesses by more than 150 billion yuan.

各地积极推进政府职能转变和机构改革，大幅减少行政审批事项。扩大"营改增"试点，取消和免征行政事业性收费348项，减轻企业负担1500多亿元。

(5) The number of newly registered businesses increased by 27.6% nationwide. Private investment increased to 63% of the country's total investment. Interest rate controls on loans were completely lifted.

全国新注册企业增长27.6%，民间投资比重上升到63%。全面放开贷款利率管制，在全国进行中小企业股份转让系统试点。

(6) Reinforcement of 15 000 small reservoirs was completed. More than 63 million additional rural people gained access to safe drinking water. Ecological conservation and development were strengthened, and China's forest coverage increased to 21.6% of the total land area.

全面完成1.5万座小型水库除险加固，新解决农村6300多万人饮水安全问题。加强生态保护与建设，全国森林覆盖率上升到21.6%。

(7) The 4G mobile communications system was put into commercial operation. We worked actively to resolve the serious problem of excess production capacity in some industries. We tried hard to conserve energy, reduce emissions and prevent and control pollution. Energy intensity was cut by 3.7%, and emissions of sulfur dioxide and chemical oxygen demand decreased by 3.5% and 2.9%, respectively.

第四代移动通信正式商用。积极化解部分行业产能严重过剩矛盾。推进节能减排和污染防治，能源消耗强度下降3.7%，二氧化硫、化学需氧量排放量分别下降3.5%、2.9%。

(8) Oil, natural gas and electric power networks were expanded, and electricity generated from non-fossil energy amounted to 22.3% of the total electricity output. Civil aviation, water transport, information and postal service networks were improved. The total length of expressways and railways in service both exceeded 100 000 kilometers, with the length of high-speed railways in service reaching 11 000 kilometers, ranking first in the world.

拓展油气、电力输配网络，非化石能源发电量比重达到22.3%。加强民航、水运、信息、邮政网络建设，铁路、高速公路运营里程均超过10万公里，其中高速铁路运营里程达到1.1万公里，居世界首位。

(9) We improved the systems of social aid and old-age insurance. Subsistence allowances for urban and rural residents were raised by 13.1% and 17.7% respectively, and basic pension benefits for enterprise retirees were increased by 10%. Construction of 6.66 million government-subsidized housing units was started, and 5.44 million such housing units were basically completed. Thanks to these efforts, over ten million people with housing difficulties moved into new homes.

推进养老保险、社会救助制度建设，城乡低保标准分别提高13.1%和17.7%，企业退休人员基本养老金水平提高10%。新开工保障性安居工程666万套，基本建成544万套，上千万住房困难群众乔迁新居。

(10) The project to improve nutrition of rural students covered 32 million students, and living allowances were issued to rural teachers in contiguous poor areas. The number of students from poor rural areas who were enrolled by key colleges and universities increased by 8.5% over the previous year.

启动教育扶贫工程，实施农村义务教育薄弱学校改造计划，学生营养改善计划惠及3200万孩子。对集中连片特困地区乡村教师发放生活补助，贫困地区农村学生上重点高校人数比上年增长8.5%。

■ 10.2.4 篇章口译[Passage Practice (C to E)]

1. Please interpret the following passage by using the techniques illustrated above. Please pay attention to the underlined sentences as they require special treatment during interpreting.

2015年工作回顾 (节选)
国务院总理 李克强

① 过去一年，我国发展面临多重困难和严峻挑战。在以习近平同志为总书记的党中央坚强领导下，全国各族人民以坚定的信心和非凡的勇气，攻坚克难，开拓进取，经济社会发展稳中有进、稳中有好，完成了全年主要目标任务，改革开放和社会主义现代化建设取得新的重大成就。

② 经济运行保持在合理区间。<u>国内生产总值达到67.7万亿元，增长6.9%，在世界主要经济体中位居前列。粮食产量实现"十二连增"，居民消费价格涨幅保持较低水平。特别是就业形势总体稳定，城镇新增就业1312万人，超过全年预期目标，成为经济运行的一大亮点。</u>⁽¹⁾

③ <u>结构调整取得积极进展。服务业在国内生产总值中的比重上升到50.5%，首次占据"半壁江山"。消费对经济增长的贡献率达到66.4%。高技术产业和装备制造业增速快于一般工业。单位国内生产总值能耗下降5.6%。</u>⁽²⁾

④ 发展新动能加快成长。创新驱动发展战略持续推进，互联网与各行业加速融合，新兴产业快速增长。<u>大众创业、万众创新蓬勃发展，全年新登记注册企业增长21.6%，平均每天新增1.2万户。</u>⁽³⁾新动能对稳就业、促升级发挥了突出作用，正在推动经济社会发生深刻变革。

⑤ 人民生活进一步改善。<u>全国居民人均可支配收入实际增长7.4%，快于经济增速。去年末居民储蓄存款余额增长8.5%，新增4万多亿元。同时，解决了6434万农村人口的饮水安全问题。扶贫攻坚力度加大，农村贫困人口减少1442万人。</u>⁽⁴⁾

⑥ 科技领域一批创新成果达到国际先进水平，第三代核电技术取得重大进展，国产C919大型客机总装下线，屠呦呦获得诺贝尔生理学或医学奖。对我国发展取得的成就，全国各族人民倍感振奋和自豪！回顾过去一年，成绩来之不易。

⑦ 这些成绩，是在极为复杂严峻的国际环境中取得的。<u>去年世界经济增速为6年来最低，国际贸易增速更低，大宗商品价格深度下跌，国际金融市场震荡加剧，对我国经济造成直接冲击和影响。</u>⁽⁵⁾这些成绩，是在国内深层次矛盾凸显、经济下行压力加大的情况下取得的。面对"三期叠加"的局面，经济工作遇到不少两难甚至多难问题，需要远近结合，趋利避害，有效应对。<u>这些成绩，是在我国经济总量超过60万亿元的高基数上取得的。现在国内生产总值每增长1个百分点的增量，相当于5年前1.5个百分点、10年前2.5个百分点的增量。经济规模越大，增长难度随之增加。</u>⁽⁶⁾在困难和压力面前，全国各族人民付出了极大辛劳，一步一步走了过来。这再次表明，任何艰难险阻都挡不住中国发展前行的步伐！

Notes on the text

(1) <u>国内生产总值达到67.7万亿元，增长6.9%，在世界主要经济体中位居前列。粮食产量实现"十二连增"，居民消费价格涨幅保持较低水平。特别是就业形势总体稳定，城镇新增就业1312万人，超过全年预期目标，成为经济运行的一大亮点。</u>

GDP reached 67.7 trillion yuan, representing an increase of 6.9% over the previous year-a growth rate faster than that of most other major economies. Food crop production increased for the 12th year in a row. Consumer prices grew slowly. Of particular note, the employment situation overall remained stable, with 13.12 million new urban jobs created over the course of the year, surpassing the year's target and becoming an economic highlight.

(2) <u>结构调整取得积极进展。服务业在国内生产总值中的比重上升到50.5%，首次占据"半壁江山"。消费对经济增长的贡献率达到66.4%。高技术产业和装备制造业增速快于</u>

一般工业。单位国内生产总值能耗下降5.6%。

Encouraging progress was made in structural adjustment. The service sector as a proportion of GDP rose to 50.5%, accounting for more than half for the first time. The contribution of consumption toward economic growth reached 66.4%. High-tech industries and equipment manufacturing grew faster than other industries. Energy consumption per unit of GDP fell by 5.6%.

(3) 大众创业、万众创新蓬勃发展，全年新登记注册企业增长21.6%，平均每天新增1.2万户。

Business startups and innovations by the general public flourished, with the number of newly registered businesses rising by 21.6% in 2015, or an average of 12,000 new businesses per day.

(4) 人民生活进一步改善。全国居民人均可支配收入实际增长7.4%，快于经济增速。去年末居民储蓄存款余额增长8.5%，新增4万多亿元。同时，解决了6434万农村人口的饮水安全问题。扶贫攻坚力度加大，农村贫困人口减少1442万人。

Living standards improved. Personal per capita disposable income increased by 7.4% in real terms, overtaking the growth rate of the economy. By the end of last year, personal savings deposits had risen by 8.5%, an increase of more than four trillion yuan. In rural areas, another 64.34 million people gained access to safe drinking water and greater alleviation efforts reduced the number of people living in poverty by 14.42 million.

(5) 去年世界经济增速为6年来最低，国际贸易增速更低，大宗商品价格深度下跌，国际金融市场震荡加剧，对我国经济造成直接冲击和影响。

In 2015, world economic growth fell to its lowest rate in six years, growth in international trade slowed, commodity prices plummeted, and there was growing volatility in the global financial market. All this had a direct impact on China's economy.

(6) 这些成绩，是在我国经济总量超过60万亿元的高基数上取得的。现在国内生产总值每增长1个百分点的增量，相当于5年前1.5个百分点、10年前2.5个百分点的增量。经济规模越大，增长难度随之增加。

Finally, they were made at a time when China's economic output had exceeded 60 trillion yuan. Every percentage point of GDP growth today is equivalent to 1.5 percentage points of growth five years ago or 2.5 percentage points of growth ten years ago. The larger the economy grows, the greater the difficulty of achieving growth.

2. Please interpret the following passage by using the techniques illustrated above. Please pay attention to the underlined sentences as they require special treatment during interpreting.

中国的大门对尼日利亚更加开放
周平剑

① 此次中国进出口银行应尼方请求拟向拉伊铁路项目提供的优惠性质贷款12.75亿

美元，是习近平主席2015年12月在中非合作论坛峰会上宣布的600亿美元资金支持的一部分。[1]中方在王外长访尼后不久批准该笔贷款意味深长，表明中国将对尼日利亚进一步开放，推动两国互利合作迈上新台阶。未来5年，中国将进口8万亿美元的商品、吸收6000亿美元的外来投资，对外投资总额将达到7500亿美元，出境旅游将达到7亿人次。这将为包括尼日利亚在内世界各国提供更大市场和更多资本、产品和合作契机。开着门，世界能够进入中国，中国也才能走向世界。中国对世界始终打开大门。[2]

② 事实上，正如中国将向尼日利亚和其他国家更加开放，尼日利亚也在致力于改善营商环境，利用全球机会推进经济多元化。今年1月20日世界经济论坛年会期间，尼日利亚正式提交接受世界贸易组织《贸易便利化协定》议定书，成为第107个接受协定的世贸组织成员。作为非洲第一大经济体，尼日利亚此举被广泛解读为对经济全球化的促进。[3]"经济全球化曾经被人们视为阿里巴巴的山洞，现在又被不少人看作潘多拉的盒子。"习主席在世界经济论坛2017年年会开幕式主旨演讲中指出，国际社会围绕经济全球化问题展开了广泛讨论。"我想说的是，困扰世界的很多问题，并不是经济全球化造成的，"习主席强调，"经济全球化确实带来了新问题，但我们不能就此把经济全球化一棍子打死，而是要适应和引导好经济全球化，消解经济全球化的负面影响，让它更好地惠及每个国家、每个民族。"

③ 中国自1978年开始实行改革开放。自那以来，中国累计吸引外资超过1.7万亿美元，累计对外直接投资超过1.2万亿美元，为世界经济发展作出了巨大贡献。国际金融危机爆发以来，中国经济增长对世界经济增长的贡献率年均在30%以上。2016年，中国经济增长6.7%，对世界经济贡献率达33.2%。从这些数字可以看出，中国的发展是世界的机遇，中国是经济全球化的受益者，更是贡献者。中国改革开放持续推进，为开放型世界经济发展提供了重要动力。[4]

④ 中国对经济全球化也曾经有过疑虑，但我们最终还是认定，融入世界经济是历史大方向，中国经济要发展，只能拥抱世界市场。中国在2001年成为世界贸易组织的一员，这是正确的战略抉择。今年5月14至15日，中国将在北京主办"一带一路"国际合作高峰论坛，共商合作大计，共建合作平台，共享合作成果，为解决当前世界和区域经济面临的问题寻找方案，为实现联动式发展注入新能量，让"一带一路"倡议更好地造福各国人民。

⑤ 中国2014年在北京成功主办亚太经合组织领导人非正式会议、2016年在杭州成功主办二十国集团领导人峰会。"一带一路"国际合作高峰论坛同这两次会议的理念一脉相承，都强调开放包容、合作共赢，都强调互联互通、联动发展，都强调创新发展，挖掘动能，为各国民众福祉贡献力量。经济全球化进程应更有活力、更加包容、更可持续。正如习主席在2016年亚太经合组织领导人非正式会议上所言，"我们要主动作为、适度管理，让经济全球化的正面效应更多地释放出来，实现经济全球化进程再平衡；我们要顺应大势、结合国情，正确选择融入经济全球化的路径和节奏；我们要讲求效率、注重公平，让不同国家、不同阶层、不同人群共享经济全球化的好处。"

Notes on the text

(1) 此次中国进出口银行应尼方请求拟向拉伊铁路项目提供的优惠性质贷款，是习近平主席2015年12月在中非合作论坛峰会上宣布的600亿美元资金支持的一部分。

What China Exim Bank has agreed this time is to provide $1.275 billion concessionary loan to support the Lagos-Ibadan rail line project as requested by the Nigeria side. The loan is part of the $60 billion funding support Chinese President Xi Jinping announced at the FOCAC Johannesburg Summit in December 2015.

(2) 未来5年，中国将进口8万亿美元的商品、吸收6000亿美元的外来投资，对外投资总额将达到7500亿美元，出境旅游将达到7亿人次。这将为包括尼日利亚在内世界各国提供更大市场和更多资本、产品和合作契机。开着门，世界能够进入中国，中国也才能走向世界。中国对世界始终打开大门。

In the coming five years, China is expected to import $8 trillion of goods, attract $600 billion of foreign investment, make $750 billion of outbound investment, and Chinese tourists will make 700 million overseas visits. All these will create a bigger market, more capital, more products and more business opportunities for other countries including Nigeria. An open door allows both other countries to access the Chinese market and China itself to integrate with the world. China will keep its door wide open and not close it.

(3) 今年1月20日世界经济论坛年会期间，尼日利亚正式提交接受世界贸易组织《贸易便利化协定》议定书，成为第107个接受协定的世贸组织成员。作为非洲第一大经济体，尼日利亚此举被广泛解读为对经济全球化的促进。

On January 20 this year, Nigeria submitted the instrument of acceptance of World Trade Organization's Protocol on Trade Facilitation Agreement (TFA) on the sideline of World Economic Forum in Davos, Switzerland. With this, Nigeria became the 107th WTO member state to ratify the agreement. Giving its position as the largest economy in Africa, the recent step Nigeria took is widely interpreted as a timely big boost to economic globalization.

(4) 中国自1978年开始实行改革开放。自那以来，中国累计吸引外资超过1.7万亿美元，累计对外直接投资超过1.2万亿美元，为世界经济发展作出了巨大贡献。国际金融危机爆发以来，中国经济增长对世界经济增长的贡献率年均在30%以上。2016年，中国经济增长6.7%，对世界经济贡献率达33.2%。从这些数字可以看出，中国的发展是世界的机遇，中国是经济全球化的受益者，更是贡献者。中国改革开放持续推进，为开放型世界经济发展提供了重要动力。

China initiated its reform and opening-up policy in late 1978. Since then, China has attracted over $1.7 trillion of foreign direct investment (FDI) and made over $1.2 trillion of outbound direct investment (ODI), making huge contribution to global economic development. In the years following the outbreak of international financial crisis around 2008, China contributed to over 30% of global growth every year on average. In 2016, China's economy expanded at an annual rate of 6.7% and contributed 33.2% of global growth. The figures speak for themselves. China's development is an opportunity for the world; China has not only benefited from economic globalization but also contributed to it. China's continuous progress in reform and opening-up has lent much momentum to an open world economy.

10.3 参考译文(Reference Version)

10.3.1 单句口译(Sentence Practice)

Please interpret the following sentences by using the techniques illustrated above. You may interpret to your partner first and then he/she comments on your performance.

(1) 全球老年人人口预计将从2015年的刚刚过9亿增加到2030年的14亿和2050年的21亿。

(2) 两国人文交流日益频繁，目前每周约有90个航班穿梭于中加之间，去年人员往来超过130万人次。

(3) 目前，中加贸易规模仅占中国外贸总额的1.4%、加拿大外贸总额的8.1%。

(4) 2015年，双方贸易额达4722亿美元，中国已连续7年成为东盟最大贸易伙伴。

(5) 双方相互投资累计超过1600亿美元，年度人员往来超过2300万人次。

(6) Over the past 25 years, the two-way trade volume has gone from $8 billion to $472.2 billion, an increase of almost 60 folds.

(7) Our cultural and people-to-people exchanges have increased day by day, with 180,000 students studying in each other's countries, and over 23 million mutual visits being made every year.

(8) China applauds making 2017 the China-ASEAN Year of Tourism Cooperation. We could discuss a plan for tourism cooperation and set a target to achieve 30 million mutual visits by 2020.

(9) As programs of the China-U.S. Year of Tourism continue to unfold, the two countries are on the way to having a new record of five million two-way visits by the end of the year.

(10) People's livelihood kept improving, personal income growth was basically in sync with economic growth, and over 13 million new urban jobs were being created on an annual basis.

10.3.2 段落口译(Paragraph Practice)

1. Vocabulary Work: Study the following words and phrases and translate them into the target language.

双方贸易、双向贸易	连续
量、额	累计
注册	国内生产总值
倍数	过热
固定资产	降温

2. Please interpret the following paragraphs by using the techniques illustrated above.

(1) 25年来，双方贸易额从80亿美元增长到4722亿美元，增长近60倍。中国连续7年成为东盟最大贸易伙伴，东盟连续5年成为中国第三大贸易伙伴。双方相互投资快速均衡发展，累计双向投资超过1600亿美元。中国企业在东盟8个国家设立了26个具有境外经贸合作区性质的项目，引入超过300家中资企业入区，已累计投资17.7亿美元，实现产值90.2亿美元。

(2) 国家信息中心预计，今年全年中国的国内生产总值将增长9.3%，总计13.4万亿元(1.6万亿美元)。该中心称中国的经济整体上将从过热转向正常，并预测说今年的固定资产投资的增长将低于去年，中国的贸易顺差将从去年的253亿美元下降到今年的44亿美元。在另一项发展报告中，世界银行认为中国给经济发展降温的政策开始显出成效，它预测中国今年的国内生产总值增长率为9.25%。

(3) Between 1950 and 2016, despite its modest level of development and living standard, China provided more than 400 billion yuan of foreign assistance, undertook over 5 000 foreign assistance projects, including nearly 3 000 complete projects, and held over 11 000 training workshops in China for over 260 000 personnel from other developing countries. Since it launched reform and opening-up, China has attracted over 1.7 trillion US dollars of foreign investment and made over 1.2 trillion US dollars of direct outbound investment, making huge contribution to global economic development. In the years following the outbreak of the international financial crisis, China contributed to over 30% of global growth every year on average. All these figures are among the highest in the world.

(4) China will foster an enabling and orderly environment for investment. We will expand market access for foreign investors, build high-standard pilot free trade zones, strengthen protection of property rights, and level the playing field to make China's market more transparent and better regulated. In the coming five years, China is expected to import eight trillion US dollars of goods, attract 600 billion US dollars of foreign investment and make 750 billion US dollars of outbound investment. Chinese tourists will make 700 million overseas visits. All this will create a bigger market, more capital, more products and more business opportunities for other countries.

10.3.3 篇章口译[Passage Practice (E to C)]

1. Please interpret the following passage by using the techniques illustrated above. Please pay attention to the underlined sentences as they require special treatment during interpreting.

利用农业科技来终结非洲及其他地区的贫困
世界银行非洲地区副行长马克塔·迪奥普

主席先生，尊敬的来宾，女士们，先生们：

感谢你们对我的邀请。

① 这是我担任世界银行非洲地区副行长以来第二次访问中国。我期待着进一步发展中国与世行的伙伴关系——特别是在今天这个至关重要的议题上：利用农业科技来终结非洲及其他地区的贫困。

② 当前全球经济正处于一个严峻时刻。尽管工业化国家经济增长乏力，但撒哈拉以南非洲的49个国家却在繁荣增长，增长率达到5%或更高。全球食品需求增长，而食品价格的波动加剧。此外，我们也知道，气候变化将影响非洲的农业生产潜力，特别是在大多数贫困人口所生活的干旱地区。这使我们面临的形势更加复杂。

③ 你们可能已经知道，在我们的新行长金塘的领导下，世界银行已经确定了在我们这一代结束贫困、实现共同繁荣的新目标。要想在2030年以前把每个发展中国家每天生活消费在1.25美元以下的人口比例降至3%、使收入最低的40%的人口收入增加，这需要一个生机勃勃的农业部门来提供就业、粮食和收入保障，还需要更多、更开放的市场准入和贸易——包括非洲内部的市场准入和贸易。

④ 今天我要谈的就是非洲以及它在农业领域尚未发挥——但可以发挥——的潜力。中国养活了人类大家庭里20%的人口。中国在可持续的粮食生产和农村转型方面有着丰富的经验，非洲可以也必须学习这些经验，以便从中受益。非洲干旱地区面临的农业变革需求比世界其他任何地区都更为迫切。在萨赫勒(Sahel)地区，有1000多万人长期缺乏粮食保障。在非洲之角，超过832万人面临粮食紧张和粮食危机。我们正在采取一个战略性、地区性的方式来解决这些挑战，把重点放在降低脆弱性和提高韧性上，同时努力扩大经济机会和经济融合。

⑤ 世界银行致力于对非洲的农业经济作出积极贡献。由于农业部门的重要性和世界行动的行动计划承诺，我们将每年为农业提供 80亿~100亿美元资金。其中很大一部分(近1/3)是用于满足非洲农业部门的具体需要。

⑥ 我们已经从数量上和质量上加强了世界银行在非洲的农业项目。特别值得一提的是：

——我们正在扩大贷款项目，从2008年的4亿美元增长到每年12亿美元。除了用于预算支持和传统的投资项目外，这些资金还将支持公私伙伴关系和更大规模的次区域业务，以产生规模效应和深刻影响。

——我们正在努力扩大非洲的灌溉区域，要从现在的20%增长到2030年的40%。实现这一目标需要400亿美元，世界银行可能会提供1/4的投资。

——从小规模、零散的土地管理试点项目转变为大胆、系统性的项目。现在是大规模推广土地管理最佳实践的时候了，我们的目标是每年至少推出两个新的土地管理项目，每个1.5亿美元，10年时间里共投资至少15亿美元。一个值得努力推动的目标是将登记土地资产所需的时间从65天降为30天。

⑦ 我们正在推动扩大市场准入，消除贸易壁垒，改善竞争力，从而使食品贸易在10年内翻一番。我们要充满雄心，改善贸易、交通、基础设施和食品安全体系，在10年内把农产品销售到市场上的成本降低一半。

2. Please interpret the following passage by using the techniques illustrated above. Please pay attention to the underlined sentences as they require special treatment during interpreting.

政府工作报告 (节选)
——2014年3月5日在第十二届全国人民代表大会第二次会议上
国务院总理 李克强

各位代表：

① 现在，我代表国务院，向大会作政府工作报告，请予审议，并请全国政协各位委员提出意见。

2013年工作回顾

② 过去一年是本届政府依法履职的第一年，任务艰巨而繁重。面对世界经济复苏艰难、国内经济下行压力加大、自然灾害频发、多重矛盾交织的复杂形势，全国各族人民在以习近平同志为总书记的党中央领导下，从容应对挑战，奋力攻坚克难，圆满实现全年经济社会发展主要预期目标，改革开放和社会主义现代化建设取得了令人瞩目的重大成就。

③ ——经济运行稳中向好。国内生产总值达到56.9万亿元，比上年增长7.7%。居民消费价格涨幅控制在2.6%。城镇登记失业率4.1%。城镇新增就业1310万人，创历史新高。进出口总额突破4万亿美元，再上新台阶。

④ ——居民收入和经济效益持续提高。城镇居民人均可支配收入实际增长7%，农村居民人均纯收入实际增长9.3%，农村贫困人口减少1650万人，城乡居民收入差距继续缩小。年收入2000万元以上工业企业利润增长12.2%。财政收入增长10.1%。

⑤ ——结构调整取得积极成效。粮食产量超过1.2万亿斤，实现"十连增"。服务业增加值比重达到46.1%，首次超过第二产业。中西部地区生产总值比重继续提高，区域发展协调性增强。全社会用电量增长7.5%，货运量增长9.9%，主要实物量指标与经济增长相互匹配。

⑥ 过去一年，困难比预料的多，结果比预想的好。经济社会发展既有量的扩大，又有质的提升，为今后奠定了基础。这将鼓舞我们砥砺前行，不断创造新的辉煌。一年来，我们坚持稳中求进工作总基调，统筹稳增长、调结构、促改革，坚持宏观政策要稳、微观政策要活、社会政策要托底，创新宏观调控思路和方式，采取一系列既利当前、更惠长远的举措，稳中有为，稳中提质，稳中有进，各项工作实现了良好开局。

⑦ 一是着力深化改革开放，激发市场活力和内生动力。在国内外环境错综复杂、宏观调控抉择两难的情况下，我们深处着力，把改革开放作为发展的根本之策，放开市场这只"看不见的手"，用好政府这只"看得见的手"，促进经济稳定增长。我们从政府自身改起，把加快转变职能、简政放权作为本届政府开门第一件大事。国务院机构改革有序实施，分批取消和下放了416项行政审批等事项，修订政府核准的投资项目目录，推动工商登记制度改革。各地积极推进政府职能转变和机构改革，大幅减少行政审批事项。扩大"营改增"试点，取消和免征行政事业性收费348项，减轻企业负担1500多亿元。

⑧ 二是创新宏观调控思路和方式，确保经济运行处于合理区间。面对跌宕起伏的经济形势，我们保持定力，明确守住稳增长、保就业的下限和防通胀的上限，只要经济在合

理区间运行，就集中精力抓住转方式调结构不放松，保持宏观政策基本取向不动摇，以增强市场信心、稳定社会预期。

⑨ 三是注重调整经济结构，提高发展质量和效益。针对阻碍发展的结构性问题，我们注重精准发力，运用市场手段和差别化政策，在优化结构中稳增长，在创新驱动中促转型，推动提质增效升级，为长远发展铺路搭桥。巩固和加强农业基础。推进现代农业综合配套改革试点，支持发展多种形式适度规模经营。全面完成1.5万座小型水库除险加固，新解决农村6300多万人饮水安全问题。加强生态保护与建设，全国森林覆盖率上升到21.6%。

⑩ 加快产业结构调整。鼓励发展服务业，支持战略性新兴产业发展，第四代移动通信正式商用。积极化解部分行业产能严重过剩矛盾。推进节能减排和污染防治，能源消耗强度下降3.7%，二氧化硫、化学需氧量排放量分别下降3.5%、2.9%。

⑪ 加强基础设施建设。南水北调东线一期工程提前通水，中线一期主体工程如期完工。推进地下管网等城市基础设施建设。拓展油气、电力输配网络，非化石能源发电量比重达到22.3%。加强民航、水运、信息、邮政网络建设，铁路、高速公路运营里程均超过10万公里，其中高速铁路运营里程达到1.1万公里，居世界首位。

⑫ 四是切实保障和改善民生，促进社会公平正义。在财政收支矛盾较大的情况下，我们竭诚尽力，始终把改善民生作为工作的出发点和落脚点，注重制度建设，兜住民生底线，推动社会事业发展。保障群众基本生活。实施大学生就业促进计划，应届高校毕业生绝大部分实现就业。加强农村转移劳动力就业服务和职业培训，对城镇就业困难人员进行就业援助。推进养老保险、社会救助制度建设，城乡低保标准分别提高13.1%和17.7%，企业退休人员基本养老金水平提高10%。新开工保障性安居工程666万套，基本建成544万套，上千万住房困难群众乔迁新居。

⑬ 推进教育发展和改革。启动教育扶贫工程，实施农村义务教育薄弱学校改造计划，学生营养改善计划惠及3200万孩子。对集中连片特困地区乡村教师发放生活补助，贫困地区农村学生上重点高校人数比上年增长8.5%。

10.3.4 篇章口译[Passage Practice (C to E)]

1. Please interpret the following passage by using the techniques illustrated above. Please pay attention to the underlined sentences as they require special treatment during interpreting.

Review of the Work We Did in 2015 (Excerpts)
Li Keqiang Premier of the State Council

① In the past year, China has encountered many difficulties and challenges in its development.

However, under the leadership of the Central Committee of the Communist Party of China

(CPC) headed by General Secretary Xi Jinping, and with confidence and courage, all the people of China have worked to overcome obstacles and have pressed ahead with a pioneering spirit. As a result, progress has been achieved and stability ensured in economic and social development, the main tasks and targets for the year have been fulfilled, and major achievements have been made in reform, opening up, and socialist modernization.

② The economy operated within an appropriate range. GDP reached 67.7 trillion yuan,representing an increase of 6.9% over the previous year-a growth rate faster than that of most other major economies. Food crop production increased for the 12th year in a row. Consumer prices grew slowly. Of particular note, the employment situation overall remained stable, with 13.12 million new urban jobs created over the course of the year, surpassing the year's target and becoming an economic highlight.

③ Encouraging progress was made in structural adjustment. The service sector as a proportion of GDP rose to 50.5%, accounting for more than half for the first time. The contribution of consumption toward economic growth reached 66.4%. High-tech industries and equipment manufacturing grew faster than other industries. Energy consumption per unit of GDP fell by 5.6%.

④ New driving forces for development grew rapidly. Further progress was made in implementing the strategy of innovation-driven development, the penetration of the Internet into all industries picked up pace, and emerging industries grew rapidly. Business startups and innovations by the general public flourished, with the number of newly registered businesses rising by 21.6% in 2015, or an average of 12 000 new businesses per day. New driving forces played a major role in keeping employment stable and pushing ahead industry upgrading, and are now driving profound economic and social change in China.

⑤ Living standards improved. Personal per capita disposable income increased by 7.4% in real terms, overtaking the growth rate of the economy. By the end of last year, personal savings deposits had risen by 8.5%, an increase of more than four trillion yuan. In rural areas, another 64.34 million people gained access to safe drinking water and greater alleviation efforts reduced the number of people living in poverty by 14.42 million.

⑥ A number of world-class innovations were made in science and technology. Major headway was made in the development of 3G nuclear power technology, China's self-developed C919 large jetliner rolled off the assembly line, and Tu Youyou was awarded the Nobel Prize for Physiology or Medicine. These achievements in China's development, a source of pride and motivation for our people, did not come easily.

⑦ They were made in the context of an extremely complicated and challenging international environment. In 2015, world economic growth fell to its lowest rate in six years, growth in international trade slowed, commodity prices plummeted, and there was growing volatility in the global financial market. All this had a direct impact on China's economy. They were made at the same time as deep-seated domestic problems were becoming prominent and downward pressure on the economy was mounting. While dealing with the slowdown in economic growth, making difficult structural adjustments, and absorbing the effects of previous economic stimulus policies, China was also confronted with many difficult problems and choices in the running of the economy, and this called for effective responses based on the need both to combine long-term and short-term considerations and to seek benefit and avoid harm. Finally, they were made at a time when China's economic output had exceeded 60 trillion yuan. Every percentage point of GDP growth today is equivalent to 1.5 percentage points of growth five years ago or 2.5 percentage points of growth ten years ago. The larger the economy grows, the greater the difficulty of achieving growth. In the face of these difficulties and pressures, all our people have truly exerted themselves and progressed step by step to get us where we are today. This once again demonstrates that no difficulty or hardship will ever stop China from moving forward.

2. Please interpret the following passage by using the techniques illustrated above. Please pay attention to the underlined sentences as they require special treatment during interpreting.

China Opens Door Wider to Nigeria
Zhou Pingjian

① What China Exim Bank has agreed this time is to provide $1.275 billion concessionary loan to support the Lagos-Ibadan rail line project as requested by the Nigeria side. The loan is part of the $60 billion funding support Chinese President Xi Jinping announced at the FOCAC Johannesburg Summit in December 2015.The approval of the loan shortly after Foreign Minister Wang's visit to Nigeria speaks volumes. China is set to open its door even wider to Nigeria and elevate the mutually beneficial bilateral cooperation to a new height. In the coming five years, China is expected to import $8 trillion of goods, attract $600 billion of foreign investment, make $750 billion of outbound investment, and Chinese tourists will make 700 million overseas visits. All these will create a bigger market, more capital, more products and more business opportunities for other countries including Nigeria. An open door allows both other countries to access the Chinese market and China itself to integrate with the world. China will keep its door wide open and not close it.

② As a matter of fact, just as China stands ready to open its door wider to Nigeria and other countries, Nigeria is making real efforts to improve ease of doing business towards diversifying its economy and taking advantage of global opportunities. On January 20 this year,　Nigeria submitted the instrument of acceptance of World Trade Organization's Protocol on Trade Facilitation Agreement (TFA) on the sideline of World Economic Forum in Davos,

Switzerland. With this, Nigeria became the 107th WTO member state to ratify the agreement. Giving its position as the largest economy in Africa, the recent step Nigeria took is widely interpreted as a timely big boost to economic globalization. "Economic globalization was once viewed as the treasure cave found by Ali Baba in The Arabian Nights, but it has now become the Pandora's box in the eyes of many," observed President Xi Jinping in his keynote speech at the opening ceremony of the 2017 World Economic Summit in Davos on January 17, "The international community finds itself in a heated debate on economic globalization." "The point I want to make is that many of the problems troubling the world are not caused by economic globalization," he stressed, "It is true that economic globalization has created new problems, but this is no justification to write economic globalization off completely. Rather, we should adapt to and guide economic globalization, cushion its negative impact, and deliver its benefits to all countries and all nations."

③ China initiated its reform and opening-up policy in late 1978. Since then, China has attracted over $1.7 trillion of foreign direct investment (FDI) and made over $1.2 trillion of outbound direct investment (ODI), making huge contribution to global economic development. In the years following the outbreak of international financial crisis around 2008, China contributed to over 30% of global growth every year on average. In 2016, China's economy expanded at an annual rate of 6.7% and contributed 33.2% of global growth. The figures speak for themselves. China's development is an opportunity for the world; China has not only benefited from economic globalization but also contributed to it. China's continuous progress in reform and opening-up has lent much momentum to an open world economy.

④ There was a time when China also had doubts about economic globalization and was not sure whether it should join the World Trade Organization (WTO) or not. But at the end of the day we concluded that integration into the global economy is a historical trend. To grow its economy, China had no choice but to embrace the global market. Therefore, China became a member of WTO in 2001. It has proved to be a right strategic choice. From 14 to 15 May 2017, China will host in Beijing the Belt and Road Forum for International Cooperation (BRF), which aims to discuss ways to boost cooperation, build cooperation platforms and share cooperation outcomes. The Forum will also explore ways to address problems facing global and regional economy, create fresh energy for pursuing interconnected development and make the Belt and Road Initiative put forward by President Xi Jinping over three years ago deliver greater benefits to the people of all countries.

⑤ China successfully hosted the APEC Economic Leaders' Meeting in Beijing in 2014 and the G20 Summit in Hangzhou in 2016. These two events and the BRF follow the same idea, namely, the emphasis on openness, inclusiveness and win-win cooperation, on connectivity and interconnected development and on innovative development to tap potential driving forces and contribute to the well-being of people around the world. The process of economic globalization should be more invigorated, more inclusive and more sustainable, however. As President Xi Jinping pointed out at the APEC Economic Leaders' Meeting in late 2016, "We should act pro-actively and manage economic globalization as appropriate so as to release its positive impact and rebalance the process of economic globalization. We should follow the general trend, proceed form our respective national conditions and embark on the right pathway of integrating into economic globalization with the right pace. We should strike a balance between efficiency and equity to ensure that different countries, different social strata and different groups of people all share in the benefits of economic globalization."

10.4 经济主题词汇汇总(Vocabulary Build-up)

socialist economy	社会主义经济
capitalist economy	资本主义经济
protectionism	保护主义
autarchy	闭关自守
private/ public sector	私营/公共部门
economic channels	经济渠道
economic balance	经济平衡
economic fluctuation	经济波动
economic depression	经济衰退
economic stability	经济稳定
economic policy	经济政策
understanding	约定
holding company	控股公司
rate of growth	增长
economic trend	经济趋势
economic situation	经济形势
infrastructure	基本建设
purchasing power, buying power	购买力
scarcity	短缺
stagnation	停滞，萧条，不景气
fixed assets	固定资产
real estate	不动产，房地产
circulating capital, working capital	流动资本
available capital	可用资产
capital goods	资本货物

(续表)

reserve	准备金，储备金
allocation of funds	资金分配
contribution of funds	资金捐献
working capital fund	周转基金
self-financing	自筹经费，经费自给
bank	银行
current account	经常账户 (美作：checking account)
current-account holder	支票账户 (美作：checking-account holder)
cheque	支票 (美作：check)
transfer	转让，转账，过户
exchange rate	汇率，兑换率
ready money business, no credit given	现金交易，概不赊欠
foreign exchange	外汇
floating exchange rate	浮动汇率
free exchange rates	自由汇兑市场
foreign exchange certificate	外汇兑换券
securities business	证券市场
stock exchange	股票市场
stock exchange corporation	证券交易所
GNP (Gross National Product)	国民生产总值
per capita GNP	人均国民生产总值
international balance of payments	国际收支
circulation system	流通制度
sideline production	副业
primary industry	第一产业
secondary industry	第二产业
tertiary industry	第三产业
means of production	生产资料
private ownership	私有制
ownership by the entire/whole people	全民所有制
socialist collective ownership	社会主义集体所有制
to practice strict economy and combat waste	厉行节约，反对浪费
foreign-funded enterprise	外资企业
joint venture	合资企业
cooperative enterprise	合作企业
wholly foreign owned/funded enterprise	独资企业

10.5 扩展练习(Enhancement Practice)

Making comments on the given topics.
Directions: Please read paragraph (1) and (2) carefully and then express your views on the given topics.

(1) How should public money be allocated?

Some people argue that the government should provide funds for arts, while some other people suggest that the money should be used for public health and education. Discuss both views and give your reasons.

(2) Who should be responsible for scientific research, governments or private companies?

It is universally acknowledged that scientific research plays a vital role in a nation's long-term development and planning. So, when it comes to which side, whether the state or some private enterprises, should implement and dominate scientific research projects, opinions tend to be various. To what extent do you agree or disagree? Give your reasons.

10.6 延伸口译(Extended Interpreting)

习近平主席在阿拉伯国家联盟总部的演讲

China follows the path of peaceful development, an independent foreign policy of peace and a win-win strategy of opening-up. One of our priorities is to take an active part in global governance, pursue mutually beneficial cooperation, assume international responsibilities and obligations, expand convergence of interests with other countries and forge a community of shared future for mankind.

中国坚持走和平发展道路，奉行独立自主的和平外交政策，实行互利共赢的对外开放战略，着力点之一就是积极主动参与全球治理，构建互利合作格局，承担国际责任义务，扩大同各国利益汇合，打造人类命运共同体。

We need to make good use of the coming five years as the crucial period to jointly build the Belt and Road and set out the guiding principles of peace, innovation, guidance, governance and integration. We should be builders of peace, promoters of development, boosters of industrialization, supporters of stability and partners of people-to-people exchanges in the Middle East.

我们要抓住未来5年的关键时期共建"一带一路"，确立和平、创新、引领、治理、交融的行动理念，做中东和平的建设者、中东发展的推动者、中东工业化的助推者、中东稳定的支持者、中东民心交融的合作伙伴。

China is ready to work with Arab states to jointly build the Belt and Road and expand common ground in our respective effort to achieve national renewal.

中方愿同阿拉伯国家开展共建"一带一路"行动，推动中阿两大民族复兴形成更多交汇。

First, we need to hold high the banner of peace and dialogue and take steps to promote stability. The Belt and Road Initiative calls for exchanges between nations and civilizations for mutual understanding, rather than mutual resentment. It is important to remove, rather than erect, walls between each other, take dialogue as the golden rule and be good neighbors with each other.

第一，高举和平对话旗帜，开展促进稳定行动。"一带一路"建设，倡导不同民族、不同文化要"交而通"，而不是"交而恶"，彼此要多拆墙、少筑墙，把对话当作"黄金法则"用起来，大家一起做有来有往的邻居。

The ancient Chinese philosopher Mencius said, "Ensuring the right conduct and uphold justice should be the way to follow across the land." With regard to China's policy measures toward the Middle East, China decides its position on issues on the basis of their own merits and the fundamental interests of the people in the Middle East. Instead of looking for a proxy in the Middle East, we promote peace talks; instead of seeking any sphere of influence, we call on all parties to join the circle of friends for the Belt and Road Initiative; instead of attempting to fill the "vacuum", we build a cooperative partnership network for win-win outcomes.

中国古代圣贤孟子说："立天下之正位，行天下之大道。"中国对中东的政策举措坚持从事情本身的是非曲直出发，坚持从中东人民根本利益出发。我们在中东不找代理人，而是劝和促谈；不搞势力范围，而是推动大家一起加入"一带一路"朋友圈；不谋求填补"真空"，而是编织互利共赢的合作伙伴网络。

The Chinese people believe in the philosophy of change and adaptation. The Arabs also say "continuing in the same state is impossible". We respect the Arab states' aspiration for reform, and support Arab states in their efforts to independently explore the path of development. To properly handle the relations between reform, development and stability is of vital importance. This is like camel racing, a popular sport in the Arab world. If the camel runs too fast at the beginning, it may be exhausted toward the end of the race. Yet if it starts too slow, it may lag behind in the end. Only the rider who keeps a good balance between speed and stamina can claim the final victory.

中国人有穷变通久的哲学，阿拉伯人也说"没有不变的常态"。我们尊重阿拉伯国家的变革诉求，支持阿拉伯国家自主探索发展道路。处理好改革发展稳定关系十分重要。这就好比阿拉伯喜闻乐见的赛骆驼，前半程跑得太快，后半程就可能体力透支；前半程跑得太慢，后半程又可能跟不上。骑手只有平衡好速度和耐力，才能够坚持到最后。

The spread of terrorist and extremist ideas poses a serious challenge to peace and development. Countries need to have consensus about the fight against terrorist and extremist forces. Terrorism knows no borders. There is no distinction between good and bad terrorism. And there should be no double standards in fighting terrorism. For the same reason, terrorism shall not be linked with any specific ethnic group or religion, as it will only create ethnic and religious tensions. No policy can be effective on its own, and a comprehensive strategy that addresses both symptoms and root causes must be applied in the fight against terrorism.

恐怖主义和极端思潮泛滥，是对和平与发展的严峻考验。打击恐怖主义和极端势力，需要凝聚共识。恐怖主义不分国界，也没有好坏之分，反恐不能搞双重标准。同样，也不能把恐怖主义同特定民族宗教挂钩，那样只会制造民族宗教隔阂。没有哪一项政策能够单独完全奏效，反恐必须坚持综合施策、标本兼治。

To this end, China will set up a China-Arab research center on reform and development. We will hold a roundtable on inter-civilization dialogue and eradicating extremism within the framework of the China-Arab States Cooperation Forum and organize exchange of visits by 100 renowned religious leaders. We will enhance cooperation on cyber security, block the online transmission of audio and video materials instigating violence and terrorism, and jointly participate in the formulation of an international counter-terrorism convention in the cyberspace. We will provide US$300 million of assistance to support such projects as law enforcement cooperation and police training to help regional countries enhance their capacity in maintaining law and order.

为此，中方将建立中阿改革发展研究中心；在中阿合作论坛框架内召开文明对话与去极端化圆桌会议，组织100名宗教界知名人士互访；加强中阿网络安全合作，切断暴力恐怖音视频网络传播渠道，共同参与制定网络空间国际反恐公约；提供3亿美元援助用于执法合作、警察培训等项目，帮助地区国家加强维护稳定能力建设。

Second, we need to advance structural adjustment and adopt new ways of cooperation. Given the ever more fierce global competition in development, we need to upgrade our cooperation. We need to advance the "oil and gas plus" cooperation model and further tap the potential of cooperation. China is ready to strengthen cooperation with Arab states across the entire industrial chain from upstream to midstream to downstream, renew long-term oil purchase agreement, and enter into strategic energy cooperation with Arab states that features mutual benefit, reliability and enduring friendship. It is important to set up new mechanism for trade and investment and expand space for cooperation.

第二，推进结构调整，开展创新合作行动。日趋激烈的国际发展竞争，需要我们提高合作档次。要推进"油气+"合作新模式，挖掘合作新潜力。中方愿同阿方加强上中下游全产业链合作，续签长期购油协议，构建互惠互利、安全可靠、长期友好的中阿能源战略合作关系。要创新贸易和投资机制，拓展合作新空间。

As China is already on the fast track of outbound investment and Arab states boast strong sovereign wealth funds, we may sign more currency swap and mutual investment agreements, expand RMB settlement business, accelerate investment facilitation and steer the investment fund and private capital of our two sides toward major projects under the Belt and Road Initiative. It is important to step up high-tech cooperation and foster new driving force for our cooperation. On the basis of the existing technology transfer and training centers, the two sides may speed up the introduction of new and high technologies such as high-speed rail, nuclear power, aerospace, new energy and genetic engineering so as to add more value to the pragmatic cooperation between China and Arab states.

中国对外投资已经进入快车道，阿拉伯国家主权基金实力雄厚，我们可以更多签署本币互换、相互投资协议，扩大人民币结算业务规模，加快投资便利化进程，引导双方投资基金和社会资金参与"一带一路"重点项目。双方要加强高新领域合作、培育合作新动力，可以依托已经成立的技术转移、培训中心等，加快高铁、核能、航天、新能源、基因工程等高新技术落地进程，提高中阿务实合作含金量。

For this purpose, China will implement the action plan for new ways of cooperation, explore a model of package cooperation involving oil, loan and project, and extend the traditional oil and gas cooperation chain to the development of new and renewable energy. China will take part in the development of industrial parks in the Middle East with priority given to the Suez Economic and Trade Cooperation Zone. By means of personnel training and joint planning and building of factories, we will integrate the whole process from processing and manufacturing to transportation and export. We will launch China-Arab states scientific and technological partnership program and jointly build 10 laboratories on modern agriculture, ICT and health. We will hold China-Arab States BeiDou Cooperation Forum.

为此，中方将实施创新合作行动，愿同阿方探索"石油、贷款、工程"一揽子合作模式，延伸传统油气合作链条，合作开发新能源、可再生能源。中方将参与中东工业园区建设，重点推进苏伊士经贸合作区建设，通过人员培训、共同规划、合作建厂等方式，实现加工制造、运输出口一体化。我们将启动中阿科技伙伴计划，在现代农业、信息通信、人口健康等领域共建10个联合实验室。我们还要举办中阿北斗合作论坛。

Third, we need to advance industrialization in the Middle East and carry out production capacity cooperation. Production capacity cooperation is consistent with the overall trend of economic diversification in the Middle East. It can help Middle East countries embark on a new path of efficient, people-oriented and green industrialization.

第三，促进中东工业化，开展产能对接行动。产能合作契合中东国家经济多元化大趋势，可以引领中东国家走出一条经济、民本、绿色的工业化新路。

Chinese equipment is of high quality yet inexpensive price. Combined with technology transfer, personnel training and strong financing support, they can help countries in the Middle East develop urgently needed industries such as iron and steel, non-ferrous metals, construction materials, glass, car manufacturing and power plant with relative low cost to fill the gap in their industrial structure and foster new comparative advantages. China's competitive production capacity and the human resources in the Middle East, when combined, will deliver more and better job opportunities for the region.

中国装备性价比高，加上技术转让、人才培训、强有力融资支持，可以帮助中东国家花较少的钱建立起钢铁、有色金属、建材、玻璃、汽车制造、电厂等急需产业，填补产业空白，培育新的比较优势。中方优势产能和中东人力资源相结合，可以创造更多、更好的就业机会。

This morning, I attended the inauguration ceremony of the second phase of the China-Egypt Suez Economic and Trade Cooperation Zone. The project will bring to Egypt over 100 companies in such sectors as textile, garment, oil equipment, motorcycle and solar energy, and create over 10,000 job opportunities for Egypt.

今天上午，我出席了中埃苏伊士经贸合作区二期揭牌仪式，这一项目将引进纺织服装、石油装备、摩托、太阳能等100多家企业，可以为埃及创造1万多个就业机会。

In order to promote the industrialization process of the Middle East, China will work with Arab states to launch an action plan for production capacity cooperation. Under this initiative, China will set up a US$15 billion special loan for industrialization in the Middle East to be used on production capacity cooperation and infrastructure projects in regional countries, and provide countries in the Middle East with US$10 billion of commercial loans to support production capacity cooperation. China will also provide US$10 billion of concessional loans with even more favorable terms for regional countries. Meanwhile, China will launch a US$20 billion joint investment fund with the UAE and Qatar to primarily invest in traditional energy, infrastructure development and high-end manufacturing industries in the Middle East.

为促进中东工业化进程，中国将联合阿拉伯国家，共同实施产能对接行动，包括设立150亿美元的中东工业化专项贷款，用于同地区国家开展的产能合作、基础设施建设项目，同时向中东国家提供100亿美元商业性贷款，支持开展产能合作；提供100亿美元优惠性质贷款，并提高优惠贷款优惠度；同阿联酋、卡塔尔设立共计200亿美元共同投资基金，主要投资中东传统能源、基础设施建设、高端制造业等。

Fourth, we need to strengthen cultural exchanges and mutual learning and take actions to enhance friendship. Like the diverse species in Mother Nature, cultural diversity gives life to our planet. The Middle East is the meeting place of ancient human civilizations and home to diverse and splendid civilizations and cultures. China will continue to unswervingly support Middle East and Arab states in preserving their ethnic and cultural traditions, and oppose all forms of discrimination and prejudice against specific ethnic group and religion.

第四，倡导文明交流互鉴，开展增进友好行动。文明具有多样性，就如同自然界物种的多样性一样，一同构成我们这个星球的生命本源。中东是人类古老文明的交汇之地，有着色彩斑斓的文明和文化多样性。中国将继续毫不动摇支持中东、阿拉伯国家维护民族文化传统，反对一切针对特定民族宗教的歧视和偏见。

The Chinese and Arab civilizations each have their own systems and distinctive features, yet they both embody the common ideals and aspirations of mankind for development and progress, and they both champion such values as moderation, peace, forgiveness, tolerance and self-restraint. We should promote dialogue among civilizations in a spirit of inclusiveness and mutual learning and explore together values in our respective cultural tradition that remain relevant today as positive guidance for good relations.

中华文明与阿拉伯文明各成体系、各具特色，但都包含有人类发展进步所积淀的共同理念和共同追求，都重视中道平和、忠恕宽容、自我约束等价值观念。我们应该开展文明对话，倡导包容互鉴，一起挖掘民族文化传统中积极处世之道同当今时代的共鸣点。

The regions covered by the Belt and Road Initiative are vibrant in people-to-people exchanges. The close ties between our peoples must be nurtured through constant efforts. Yesterday, I met with ten old Arab friends who received the Award for Outstanding Contribution to China-Arab Friendship. It is the hard work of generations of friendly people from both sides that has enabled the seedlings of China-Arab friendship to grow into luxuriant and evergreen trees.

"一带一路"延伸之处，是人文交流聚集活跃之地。民心交融要绵绵用力，久久为功。昨天，我会见了获得"中阿友好杰出贡献奖"的10位阿拉伯老朋友。正是有一代接一代的友好人士辛勤耕耘，中阿友好的大树才能枝繁叶茂、四季常青。

第11单元　数字口译Ⅱ(Figures in Interpreting Ⅱ)

口译主题：外贸

单元学习目的(Unit Goals) 🔆

➤ 数字的记录。
➤ 数字变化趋势的表达。
➤ 学习外贸专题所涉及的常用词语和表达。

导入(Lead -in)

1. 你将听到一些带有数字的句子，请把它们记录下来：全年入境旅游人数43 904万人次，国际旅游外汇收入1 284亿美元，增长27.9%。
2. 请列举你所知道的有关数字变化趋势的用语。
3. 数字记录的技巧有哪些？

11.1　技能讲解(Skill Introduction)

■ 11.1.1　数字的记录方法(Recording Numbers)

迅速、准确地记录听到的数字是做好数字口译的第一步。

当听到英语"one hundred twenty-three million, four hundred and fifty-six thousand"时，我们可以用下面的方法记录。

(1) 123m456t

用英文字母"t""m""b"和"tr"分别表示"thousand""million""billion"和"trillion"等段位。

(2) 123, 456, 或 123, 456 / 或 123, 456—— 或 123, 456K

用逗号"，"、斜杠号"/"、横线"——"或用字母"k"表示"000"。

(3) 1亿2345万6千

我们可以将其转换成目的语记录。

如果听到汉语"1亿2千3百45万6千"时，我们可以用下面的方法记录：

- 1.23456亿，用小数点表示；
- 1亿2345万6千，用原语记录；
- 123m456t，用目的语记录。

11.1.2 数字趋势变化的表达 (The Expression of Number Fluctuation)

讲话人经常利用数字来说明事物的趋势变化，因此译员应该掌握一些趋势用语以丰富口译表达。

向上趋势	向下趋势	波动趋势
增加： increase，rise，grow，go up 增长到： expand to，increase to，go up to，be up to，rise to 增长了： go up by x%，increase by x% 爬升： climb，pick up 飙升： surge up，hike sth. up，jump up，shoot up，soar，skyrocket	下降： decrease，decline，drop，fall，go down，reduce 猛跌： slump，plunge，be slashed，tumble 稍降： be trimmed，dip	超过： surpass，exceed，be more than，be over 达到： reach，amount to，be up to，arrive at，hit 总计： total，add up to，amount to 占(百分比)： account for，occupy，make up，take 多达： be as much as，be as many as，be up to 大约： about，around，approximately，roughly，more or less 少于： less than，fewer than，under，below 多于： more than，over，above 差不多： nearly，almost 介于……之间： from A to B，between A and B，somewhere between A and B

1. 增/减百分比的口译

(1) 增/减了……%

具体短语为：increase/rise/grow... %；decrease/drop/fall/sink ... %；increase/rise/grow/go up by ... %；decrease/drop/fall/go down by ... %。

如：Between 1995 and 1996, Adidas' sales dropped 17 percent and profits sank by more than 38 percent as a result of competition with Converse.

与"匡威"鞋业竞争的结果，从1995年到1996年，阿迪达斯(鞋)的销售额下降了17%，利润下降了38%多。

Procter & Gamble just raised prices on its paper products by as much as 7.7%.

(美国) 普罗科特—甘布尔公司刚刚把他们的纸制品价格提高了7.7%。

In the fiscal year of 2001, ending on May 30, export slumped 11.3 percent in Japan, 8.7 percent in Thailand, 10percent in South Korea and 2.2 percent in Hong Kong. However, the Chinese mainland posted a respectable 8.3 percent rate in the first quarter.

在5月30日刚刚结束的2001财政年度，日本的出口猛跌了11.3%，泰国8.7%，韩国10%，香港2.2%。然而，中国大陆却公布了第一季度8.3%的可观增长。

(2) 与……相比，增/减了……%

具体短语为：increase/rise/grow /go up by ... % (as) compared with /as against / as opposed to / over ...，decrease/drop/fall/go down by ... % (as) compared with /as against / as opposed to /over ...。

如，同1999年相比，2000年工业排污减少了12.3%；家庭排污增加了3.1%。

Compared with 1999, the discharge of industrial wastewater dropped by 12.3 percent, while that of domestic sewage rose by 3.1 percent in 2000.

因受亚洲金融危机的冲击，1998年中国进出口总额比上年下降0.5%，其中进口总额下降1.4%，出口总额增长0.6%。

As a result of Asian financial crises, China's total volume of import and export in 1998 dropped by 0.5 percent over the previous year, of which the volume of import went down by 1.4 percent, and the value of export went up by 0.6 percent.

(3) 增/减率

具体短语为：be ... % increase/ rise /growth ... ；be ... % decrease/drop /decline ... ；an increase / a rise / a growth rate of ... %；a decrease / drop / decline of ... %；be ... % up /down ...；be up / down ... %。

如，去年收入总计人民币150亿元，比上年增长20%

The revenue of last year totaled RMB 15 b yuan, a 20% increase over the previous year.

(4) 增/减具体数字的英译也可用 "by" + 具体数字表示

如：我国水土流失面积每年以9987平方公里的速度在扩大。目前，水土流失面积已达357万平方公里，占总土地面积将近40%。

The area of soil erosion in China has been increasing by 9987 square km. annually to 3.57 million square km. at present, accounting for nearly 40 percent of the total land area.

由于低温多雨的影响，我国夏粮减产1502万吨。

China's output of summer grain declined by 15.02 million tons due to low temperature and rainy days during the growing period.

2. 倍数的表达

(1) 特殊倍数的表达

a. 翻两番

翻两番一般会用到quadruple。

如，到2020年实现国内生产总值比2000年翻两番，达到40 000亿美元左右。

By 2020, China's GDP will quadruple that of 2000 to approximately USD 4 trillion.

b. 3成

今年的粮食产量比去年增长3成.

The output of grain this year increased by 30% over the last year.

(2) 汉语倍数的表示方法

汉语增加倍数的说法很多，英译时，首先要仔细区分是包括基数在内的增加倍数还是净增倍数，然后决定用N times 还是(N+1)times 来表达。

如，The earth is 49 times the size of the moon.

地球的大小是月球的49倍(或地球比月球大48倍)。

Since mid-century, the global economy has nearly quintupled, While the population has doubled, demand for grain has nearly tripled, and the burning of fossil fuels has increased nearly fourfold.

自21世纪中叶以来，全球经济增长了将近四倍，人口翻了一番。结果，粮食的需求增加了近两倍，石油燃料增加了近三倍。

Within 30 years there will be twice as many urban people as countryside people in the world.

30年内，全世界的城市居民将是农村人口的两倍。

由于汉语很少用"减少了若干倍"的说法，而多用"减少了百分之几"或"减少了几成"的说法，因此，减少多用百分数和分数表示。

如：由于水灾，去年的收成减少了两成。

Owing to flood, the crop last year was declined by 20 percent.

该公司的员工裁减了近1/3，开支减少了1/4。

The personnel of the company have been reduced nearly by one-third and the expenses by one-fourth.

1997年，政府机构改革目标实现。国务院下设部门从40个减少到29个，人员减少了近一半。

In 1997，the targets of restructuring governmental institutions were met. Departments under the State Council were reduced from 40 to 29 and personnel were cut nearly by half.

11.2 主题口译(Topic Interpreting)

■ 11.2.1 单句口译(Sentence Practice)

Please interpret the following sentences by using the techniques illustrated above. You may interpret to your partner first and then he/she comments on your performance.

(1) GDP growth averaged 10 percent a year, and over 500 million people were lifted out of poverty.

(2) Last year, the two way trade volume exceeded US$400 billion, mutual investment hit US$100 billion, and the number of mutual visits made by our peoples reached 15 million.

(3) Since the beginning of the new century, Africa has on the whole maintained peace and stability. The African economy has entered a period of rapid growth, expanding by 4.8% in 2012 despite the global economic downturn. It is expected that Africa will extend its relatively fast growth into the next decade.

(4) In particular, we will provide stronger and more targeted support to those living in difficulty, so that the over 57 million poor rural population below the current poverty line will all be lifted out of poverty and poverty will be alleviated in all poor counties by 2020.

(5) We will double China's 2010 GDP and per capita income of urban and rural residents by 2020 and complete the building of a moderately prosperous society in all respects that benefits the over one billion Chinese people.

(6) 去年，中瑞贸易达到263亿美元，其中瑞士对华出口228亿美元，如果平均到每个瑞士人就是2800美元。

(7) 改革开放以来，中国有7亿多人口摆脱贫困，13亿多人民的生活质量和水平大幅度提升，用几十年时间完成了其他国家几百年走过的发展历程。

(8) 今年上半年，中国经济增长6.7%，产业升级和结构调整步伐加快，最终消费支出对国内生产总值的贡献率达到73.4%，第三产业增加值占到国内生产总值的54.1%，居民收入稳定增长，城镇新增就业717万人。

(9) 从总量看，"十一五"时期，我国工业增加值年均增长11.3%，2010年达到16万亿元，约占国内生产总值的40%。

(10) 截至目前，500多种工业产品中我国有220余种产量位居世界前列，制造业增加值占全球的19.8%，规模位居世界第一，是名副其实的全球制造业基地和世界工厂。

▌11.2.2　段落口译(Paragraph Practice)

1. Vocabulary Work: Study the following words and phrases and translate them into the target language.

sustain	urbanization
rural population	urban residents
unleashing	underscore
enormous	all-round
mutual visits	medical care

2. Please interpret the following paragraphs by using the techniques illustrated above.

(1) China's 2012 GDP, in comparable terms, more than doubled that of 2000, registering an increase of 3.2 times. To double the GDP of 2010 by 2020, China will need to sustain an annual growth rate of around 7 percent. Over the next five years, China will import some 10 trillion

dollars' worth of goods from the rest of the world, and its overseas investment will reach 500 billion dollars. By vigorously advancing urbanization in a steady manner, China will see hundreds of millions of its rural population turn into urban residents, unleashing increasing market demand along the way. All these underscore the enormous prospect of China's economic development and the growth opportunities it will bring to Switzerland and other countries.

(2) Today, thanks to the concerted efforts of both sides, China-Africa relations have entered a fast track of all-round development. We have set up the Forum on China-Africa Cooperation and established a new type of strategic partnership. Our cooperation in various fields has produced notable results. In 2012, China-Africa trade approached US$200 billion. There were over 1.5 million mutual visits between the two sides. China's cumulative direct investment in Africa topped US$15 billion. This year marks the 50th anniversary of Chinese medical teams in Africa. Over the last half century, 18 000 Chinese medical personnel have worked in Africa, providing medical care and treatment to 250 million local patients.

(3) 一是全球增长动能不足，难以支撑世界经济持续稳定增长。二是全球经济治理滞后，难以适应世界经济新变化和全球产业布局新调整。三是全球发展失衡，难以满足人们对美好生活的期待。全球最富有的1%人口拥有的财富量超过其余99%人口财富的总和，7亿多人口生活在极端贫困之中。

(4) 习主席还指出，中国的发展是世界的巨大机遇。他表示，从1950年至2016年，中国累计对外提供援款4000多亿元人民币，实施各类援外项目5000多个，其中成套项目近3000个。习主席还宣布，预计未来5年，中国将进口8万亿美元的商品，对外投资总额将达7500亿美元，出境旅游将达7亿人次。

▌11.2.3 篇章口译[Passage Practice (E to C)]

1. Please interpret the following paragraphs by using the techniques illustrated above. Please pay attention to the underlined sentences as they require special treatment during interpreting.

Economic Openness Serves Everyone Better
Li Keqiang

① This is a testing time. Almost a decade on, the world is still reeling from the fallout of the global financial crisis. China faces its fair share of challenges, but we choose to confront them head on. Above all, we remain convinced that economic openness serves everyone better, at home and abroad. The world is a community of shared destiny. It's far preferable for countries to trade goods and services and bond through investment partnerships than to trade barbs and build barriers. Should differences arise, it behooves us all to discuss them with respect and a keen sense of equality.

② China stands resolute with the World Trade Organization and multilateral free-trade agreements designed to be inclusive. Economic globalization has enabled the creation and sharing of wealth on an unprecedented scale. There are problems, too, more on the sharing side. These can be addressed, but only if countries work together to ensure that a rising tide really does lift all boats.

③ At home, the government is opting for a lighter, more balanced touch while engaging the market. To make doing business in China easier, the state is consolidating administrative reviews and focusing more on compliance oversight, risk preparedness, and providing services. We keep improving implementation of the VAT reform to make sure that tax costs drop across the board. We are opening new sectors of the economy to investment and widening access to many others. We are piloting a "negative list" model before a nationwide rollout, where investment access is assumed unless specifically restricted. More measures are in the pipeline to ensure all businesses registered in China are treated equally. Companies can enjoy additional incentives if they invest in less-developed western regions or in the northeastern industrial belt.

④ While the government is continuing to invest in infrastructure to boost domestic demand, more resources are going to improving rural roads, water supply, sewage systems, and information networks—areas that traditionally haven't been as visible. In parallel with such hardware improvements, we're continuing efforts to expand the safety net, not least for the more vulnerable members of society. Structural reforms are showing results. In 2016, China shed more than 65 million and 290 million tons of inefficient steel and coal-mining capacity, respectively. [(1)] We plan to raise those numbers to 140 million and 800 million tons within the next three to five years to restore healthier fundamentals to those industries.[(2)]Meanwhile, the government is working with business communities on various retraining programs. In 2016 alone, 700 000 workers once employed in downsized industries moved on to new jobs.[(3)]

⑤ At the same time, new growth drivers are emerging strong. Services, which have surpassed manufacturing as a share of the economy, keep consolidating their lead. Consumption now contributes more than 60 percent of the growth in China's gross domestic product. While creating new value, these drivers are also boosting the efficiency and competitiveness of traditional sectors, with high-tech and equipment manufacturing leading industrial expansion.[(4)] Entrepreneurship and innovation are taking root. Meanwhile, new business models are thriving, transforming many previously unimaginable services into daily conveniences. The mobile-internet-enabled sharing economy is only one obvious case. Besides ordering takeout or hailing cars, housekeeping, health consulting, and many more services are now just a swipe away.

⑥ The numbers bear out the case. The economy grew a healthy 6.7 percent last year. More important, despite industrial consolidation and ever more robots finding their way into factories, the job market is proving resilient.[(5)] The economy has added more than 13 million jobs every year since 2013. Unemployment stands at a multiyear low.[(6)]

In a world with a plethora of uncertainties, China offers an anchor of stability and growth with its consistent message of support for reform, openness, and free trade. The times may be difficult. But that's all the more reason not to lose sight of these principles, which have stood China—and the world—in good stead.

Notes on the text

(1) <u>In 2016, China shed more than 65 million and 290 million tons of inefficient steel and coal-mining capacity, respectively.</u>

2016年，中国压减落后过剩钢铁产能6500万吨以上、煤炭产能2.9亿吨以上。

(2) <u>We plan to raise those numbers to 140 million and 800 million tons within the next three to five years to restore healthier fundamentals to those industries.</u>

我们计划在三至五年内钢铁、煤炭产能分别压减1.4亿吨和8亿吨，使相关行业恢复更加健康的基本面。

(3) <u>In 2016 alone, 700 000 workers once employed in downsized industries moved on to new jobs.</u>

仅2016年，转岗安置人数就达到70万。

(4) <u>Consumption now contributes more than 60 percent of the growth in China's gross domestic product. While creating new value, these drivers are also boosting the efficiency and competitiveness of traditional sectors, with high-tech and equipment manufacturing leading industrial expansion.</u>

中国经济增长的新动能正在蓬勃兴起。服务业占经济总量的比重已超过制造业，领军地位更加巩固，消费对GDP增长的贡献率在六成以上。新动能不仅创造新价值，也提升了传统产业的效率和竞争力，推动高技术产业和装备制造业增长领跑整个工业。

(5) <u>The numbers bear out the case. The economy grew a healthy 6.7 percent last year. More important, despite industrial consolidation and ever more robots finding their way into factories, the job market is proving resilient.</u>

数字最能说明问题。去年中国经济实现了6.7%的健康增长。更重要的是，尽管产业进一步优化整合、工业机器人应用日益广泛，中国就业市场的弹性不降反增。

(6) <u>The economy has added more than 13 million jobs every year since 2013. Unemployment stands at a multiyear low.</u>

2013年以来，我们每年新增城镇就业1300多万人，失业率当前处于多年来最低水平。

2. Please interpret the following passage by using the techniques illustrated above. Please pay attention to the underlined sentences as they require special treatment during interpreting.

The Chinese Economy Is Still Full of Power

Liu Xiaoming, Chinese ambassador to the UK

① A glass is filled halfway with water. Pessimists would say it's half empty, while optimists would say it's half full. The same is true when it comes to the Chinese economy. Quite a few pessimists have been forecasting doom and gloom since the beginning of the year. However, they have failed to see the country's resilience and the new driving forces that have emerged.

② In fact, the recent moderation in China's growth is the anticipated result of reform measures and regulation. This is therefore the "new normal": we are seeing slower yet better quality growth helped along by proactive and deeper reforms. <u>Of course, China's growth rate could easily have exceeded 7 per cent if the energy- and- pollution-intensive industries had been given free rein, or if massive stimulus measures had been applied.</u>[(1)]China, however, chose not to opt for this kind of unsustainable growth-because it would come with a huge cost and would sacrifice the long-term development of China and the world. Instead, China has chosen to focus on the following five key areas: addressing excess capacity, downsizing property inventories, expanding effective supply, helping enterprises reduce cost and guarding against financial risks. This approach, like losing weight, won't be without its discomforts or pain. But just as perseverance will see one through a diet-to less fat, stronger muscles and a healthier body-so it is with the Chinese economy.

③ <u>Despite the moderation in growth, the fundamentals of the Chinese economy remain strong. While the stock and foreign exchange markets have their own patterns, the key is to look at the bigger picture. It is true that the 6.9 per cent growth in 2015 was the lowest for China in 25 years. But this was achieved by an economy that is 10 trillion dollars in size. The actual increment is equivalent to the yearly GDP of a medium-sized country and it is larger than the amount generated by double-digit growth years ago.</u>[(2)] <u>In other words, against the background of the sluggish world economy, China remains one of the fastest-growing major economies – and it contributes over one quarter of global growth. Consumption now accounts for two thirds of China's growth and the service sector now makes up more than half of GDP.</u>[(3)] China's solid material foundation, abundant human resources and vast market potential will continue to provide a sound basis and condition for sustained economic growth. The gap between the eastern and western regions, and between the urban and rural areas, indicates ample spaces and untapped potentials for further development. Moreover, the ongoing process of new industrialization, IT application, urbanization and agricultural modernization is generating strong driving forces for growth. China's fiscal deficit and government debt is also secure and much lower than that of the US, Europe and Japan, leaving enough room for further positive regulation.

④ Going forward, five new engines will drive forward China's economy. The first engine is the 13th Five-Year Plan. With its five key development concepts-innovation, balanced growth, a green economy, opening up and inclusive development — this Plan will map out the way for China to get over the "middle — income trap" and join the high-income economies. The second engine is supply-side reform. Rather than being a copy of Reaganomics or Thatcherism, China's supply-side reform is a response to the economic "new normal" in China. Its core mechanism is to replace ineffective and low-end supply with effective and high-end supply, which will increase competitiveness. The third engine is open development. China will continue to improve its domestic business environment in terms of legal, international and business-friendly practices. The fourth engine is China's active involvement in global economic governance and in providing public goods. The Asian Infrastructure Investment Bank, officially inaugurated last month, is just one example of this. The fifth engine is innovation-driven development. China will optimize the allocation of key resources in order to stimulate innovation, to create new demands and new supply, and to give rise to new businesses.

⑤ Since the financial crisis, China has made an outstanding contribution to global growth. It is widely recognized as the world's economic powerhouse and has fulfilled its responsibility as a key global player. Make no mistake: that engine is still full of power and will continue to bring opportunities and benefits to the world. "Although Zhou was an ancient state, it had a reform mission." This line from a 3000-year-old Chinese work, the Classic of Poetry, best portrays the country's commitment to reform. Today, reform and innovation remain the source of confidence and strength for China. There is every reason to look to a world-embracing China for steady progress and for a promising economic future.

Notes on the text

(1) Of course, China's growth rate could easily have exceeded 7 per cent if the energy- and-pollution-intensive industries had been given free rein, or if massive stimulus measures had been applied.

如果我们听任高能耗、高污染的产能继续扩张，或者采取大规模刺激手段，增长数字完全可能超过7%，甚至更高。

(2) Despite the moderation in growth, the fundamentals of the Chinese economy remain strong. While the stock and foreign exchange markets have their own patterns, the key is to look at the bigger picture. It is true that the 6.9 per cent growth in 2015 was the lowest for China in 25 years. But this was achieved by an economy that is 10 trillion dollars in size. The actual increment is equivalent to the yearly GDP of a medium-sized country and it is larger than the amount generated by double-digit growth years ago.

中国经济基本面仍然长期向好。股市和汇市的波动有其自身运行规律，观察中国经济关键要看基本面。2015年中国经济增速为6.9%，虽然增幅为25年来最小，但这是在10万亿美元高基数之上的增长，增量相当于一个中等国家全年的国内生产总值，比以前两位数的增量还要大。

(3) In other words, against the background of the sluggish world economy, China remains one of the fastest-growing major economies-and it contributes over one quarter of global growth. Consumption now accounts for two thirds of China's growth and the service sector now makes up more than half of GDP.

这也是在世界经济增长放缓大背景下的增长，在主要经济体中名列前茅，对世界经济增长贡献率超过1/4。消费对经济增长的贡献率已达2/3，服务业比重超过一半。

▌11.2.4　篇章口译[Passage Practice (C to E)]

1. Please interpret the following passage by using the techniques illustrated above. Please pay attention to the underlined sentences as they require special treatment during interpreting.

在中美工商界午餐会上的主旨演讲(节选)

中华人民共和国国务院副总理　汪洋

尊敬的普里茨克部长，弗罗曼大使，各位工商界朋友，女士们，先生们：

① 感谢美国中国总商会、美国州长协会的盛情邀请，使我有机会在商贸联委会期间与两国工商界朋友齐聚一堂。也感谢你们给我安排这样一个演讲的机会，让我能为中美经贸合作和中国投资环境做个广告。长期以来，在座各位为中美经贸关系发展做出过重要贡献，我谨代表中国政府，向大家致以崇高敬意！

② 中美商贸联委会是一个有着30多年历史的机制性安排，但每届联委会都有不同的背景和任务。本届联委会最大的背景，就是美国大选落下帷幕，特朗普先生当选总统。现在大家都关心美国新一届政府对华经贸政策取向以及中美经贸合作的前景。美国怎么做，我们拭目以待，预测是困难的，如同你们预测美国大选一样。面对今天的高朋满座，我最大的感慨是，虽然美国政府要换届了，但美国工商界与中国开展经贸合作的热情没有改变。如果以今天午餐会的盛况预测中美经贸合作的态势，前景一定看好！

③ <u>中国现在是美国最大的贸易伙伴。2008－2015年，尽管全球贸易处在寒冬期，但中美贸易逆势而上，年均增速超过7%。去年美国对华出口前四位的产品依次是飞机、大豆、汽车和集成电路。美国22%的棉花、26%的波音飞机、56%的大豆销往中国，美国对华货物和服务出口创造了近百万个就业岗位。</u>⁽¹⁾中国对美国也有大量出口，而且是顺差。不过要说明的是，中国从美国进口的不少是中国生产不了的高端产品，向美国出口的则大多是美国没有比较优势也不生产的产品。<u>中国企业对美投资迅猛发展，已遍及美国42个州，尤其是纽约、伊利诺伊、弗吉尼亚、马萨诸塞、加利福尼亚等州，为美国创造了近10万个就业机会。</u>⁽²⁾总体上看，中美经贸关系具有很强的互补性，市场选择已让两国形成了你中有我、我中有你、谁也离不开谁的利益格局。

④ 中美经贸关系越密切，分歧和摩擦也就越多。有时候你越在乎对方，可能就越容易吵架。如果不吵架了，那意味着对彼此失去了信心，离分手就不远了。其实工商界的朋友们对此可能体会更深，很多合作成果常常是吵出来的。积极面对分歧、有效化解分歧，正是中美经贸合作强劲的动力。现在双方已建立了众多管控分歧的机制。在经贸领域，不仅有商贸联委会、战略与经济对话等老机制，去年还建立了经济事务定期通话的新机制。我和普里茨克部长、弗罗曼大使、雅各布·卢财长都保持着热线联系，讨论的议题大到

两国重要经济领域的体制机制，小到双方具体产品的贸易。坦率地说，沟通不能解决全部问题，但增进了互信，管控了分歧，为更多的合作创造了条件。

⑤ 作为全球最大的两个经济体，中美经济增势良好，为两国工商界的合作创造了广泛的空间。<u>预计未来5年，中国进口总额将达到8万亿美元，利用外资总额达到6000亿美元，对外投资总额达到7500亿美元，出境旅游达到7亿人次，这必将为包括美国在内的各国企业带来巨大商机。</u>⁽³⁾为了自己，帮助别人，这是中国营商文化的重要内容。面对中国这样一个巨大的成长性市场，相信美国政府和企业也能够做出正确的选择。

⑥ 实际上，中美工商界已经做出了选择。<u>上个月美中贸委会发布的《2016年中国商业环境调查报告》显示，近3/4的受访美资企业看好中国经济的增长前景，90%的企业在中国实现盈利，近一半的企业表示要扩大在华投资。</u>⁽⁴⁾<u>今年前三季度，美国企业对华投资增长21.3%，中国企业对美非金融类直接投资增长1.8倍，这些数据可能比任何政治家、经济学家对中美经贸关系的解读更有说服力。</u>⁽⁵⁾一句话，中美经贸合作是市场行为，根本动力在民间、在工商界。如果中美经贸合作出现大问题，那不仅是对中美经济的破坏，更会增加全球经济复苏进程的不确定性。作为两个负责任的大国，合作是唯一正确的选择。

Notes on the text

(1) <u>中国现在是美国最大的贸易伙伴。2008—2015年，尽管全球贸易处在寒冬期，但中美贸易逆势而上，年均增速超过7%。去年美国对华出口前四位的产品依次是飞机、大豆、汽车和集成电路。美国22%的棉花、26%的波音飞机、56%的大豆销往中国，美国对华货物和服务出口创造了近百万个就业岗位。</u>

China is the largest trading partner of the US. Despite the lackluster growth in global trade from 2008 to 2015, China-US trade defied the downward trend and recorded an average annual growth of over 7%. Last year, the top four US exports to China were airplane, soybean, automobile and integrated circuit. China imported 22% of US cotton, 26% of Bowing airplanes and 56% of US soybean. Exports of goods and services to China generated nearly 1 million jobs in the US.

(2) <u>中国企业对美投资迅猛发展，已遍及美国42个州，尤其是纽约、伊利诺伊、弗吉尼亚、马萨诸塞、加利福尼亚等州，为美国创造了近10万个就业机会。</u>

The investment of Chinese companies in the US has rapidly increased, now reaching 42 American states, including New York, Illinois, Virginia, Massachusetts and California. Chinese investment has generated some 100 000 job opportunities for America. Generally speaking, China-US economic relationship is highly complementary.

(3) <u>预计未来5年，中国进口总额将达到8万亿美元，利用外资总额达到6000亿美元，对外投资总额达到7500亿美元，出境旅游达到7亿人次，这必将为包括美国在内的各国企业带来巨大商机。</u>

It is estimated that over the next five years, China will import US$8 trillion of goods, utilize US$600 billion of foreign investment, and make US$750 billion of outward investment.

Outbound Chinese tourists are also expected to reach 700 million. All these mean enormous business opportunities for companies around the globe, including American companies.

(4) 上个月美中贸委会发布的《2016年中国商业环境调查报告》显示，近3/4的受访美资企业看好中国经济的增长前景，90%的企业在中国实现盈利，近一半的企业表示要扩大在华投资。

The China Business Environment Survey published by the US-China Business Council last month shows that nearly three quarters of the American companies surveyed are optimistic about the growth prospect of the Chinese economy; 90% of the companies have made profits in China; and nearly half of the companies are ready to increase investment in China.

(5) 今年前三季度，美国企业对华投资增长21.3%，中国企业对美非金融类直接投资增长1.8倍，这些数据可能比任何政治家、经济学家对中美经贸关系的解读更有说服力。

In the first three quarters of this year, the investment of US companies in China was up by 21.3%, while the direct investment made by Chinese companies in the non-financial sectors of the US expanded by 1.8 folds. These figures may be more convincing than the interpretation of China-US economic relations by any politician or economist.

2. Please interpret the following passage by using the techniques illustrated above. Please pay attention to the underlined sentences as they require special treatment during interpreting.

美元走强致美跨国企业收入减少

① 英国《金融时报》一份分析报告显示，美元大幅升值可能导致今年部分美国大型跨国公司以美元计价的收入减少逾1000亿美元，这一数字将超过耐克(Nike)、麦当劳(McDonald's)以及高盛(Goldman Sachs)三家企业的收入总额。[1]

② 今年上半年，10家美国大型跨国公司——包括苹果(Apple)、通用汽车(General Motors)、IBM、亚马逊(Amazon)及通用电气(General Electric)等蓝筹公司——的收入共计减少310亿美元，而且人们现在越来越担心美联储(Fed)今年晚些时候的加息举措会进一步推高美元汇率。[2]

③ "大型跨国公司正受到美元走强的冲击，"摩根大通资产管理(JPMorgan Asset Management)市场策略师戴维莱博维茨(David Lebovitz)表示，"欧元与日元面临各自地区央行施加的下行压力，而且，考虑到新兴市场相对不利的处境，我们看到这些地区的货币正在贬值。"

④ 标普道琼斯指数公司(S&P Dow Jones Indices)数据显示，2014年，标普500指数(S&P 500)成份股公司约48%的收入来自海外。弱势美元在过去几年提振了美国跨国公司的业绩，这些公司的海外收入以美元计价的话增幅要大一些。

⑤ 但各地区日趋分化的货币政策已使贸易加权美元指数比上年同期升高了19%，美元相对欧元则升值了22%。这削弱了收入增长，尤其是互联网与科技企业的收入增长，这些

企业的海外收入比例比任何其他行业都高。⁽³⁾尽管在标普500指数成份股公司当中，有逾70%的公司的盈利强于预期，但只有42%的公司的收入强于预期，有41%的公司的收入逊于共识预期。⁽⁴⁾

⑥ 瑞银财富管理(UBS Wealth Management)股票策略师戴维•莱夫科维茨(David Lefkowitz)说："从收入增长看，整个扩张趋势并不强劲。"他表示，瑞银认为，今年美元升值将令标普500指数成份股公司10.7万亿美元的总收入减少3%~4%，相当于3000亿美元以上。⁽⁵⁾

⑦ 英国《金融时报》的分析显示，到目前为止，第二季度销售收入减少289亿美元，相当于8630亿美元报告收入的3.3%。而今年第一季度销售收入减少230亿美元，相当于第一季度收入的2.7%。⁽⁶⁾

⑧ 英国《金融时报》的分析报告涵盖了标普500指数成份股公司中逾100家已公布第一季度和第二季度财报的美国公司，但其局限之处在于，有数十家公司没有披露自己受到的汇率影响。

Notes on the text

(1) 英国《金融时报》一份分析报告显示，美元大幅升值可能导致今年部分美国大型跨国公司以美元计价的收入减少逾1000亿美元，这一数字将超过耐克(Nike)、麦当劳(McDonald's)以及高盛(Goldman Sachs)三家企业的收入总额。

The sharp rise in the US dollar may slice more than $100bn off dollar-denominated revenues at some of America's largest multinationals this year, a sum larger than the combined sales of Nike, McDonald's and Goldman Sachs, according to a Financial Times analysis.

(2) 今年上半年，10家美国大型跨国公司——包括苹果(Apple)、通用汽车(General Motors)、IBM、亚马逊(Amazon)及通用电气(General Electric)等蓝筹公司——的收入共计减少310亿美元，而且人们现在越来越担心美联储(Fed)今年晚些时候的加息举措会进一步推高美元汇率。

In the first half of the year, 10 of the largest US multinationals have had their sales reduced by a combined $31bn — including blue-chip companies like Apple, General Motors, IBM, Amazon and General Electric — and concerns have mounted that a move by the Federal Reserve to lift interest rates later this year will push the dollar higher.

(3) 但各地区日趋分化的货币政策已使贸易加权美元指数比上年同期升高了19%，美元相对欧元则升值了22%。这削弱了收入增长，尤其是互联网与科技企业的收入增长，这些企业的海外收入比例比任何其他行业都高。

But diverging monetary policies have pushed the trade-weighted dollar 19 per cent above year-ago levels, including a 22 per cent gain against the euro. That has depressed top-line growth, particularly for internet and technology groups, which earn more revenues outside the US than any other sector.

(4) 尽管在标普500指数成份股公司当中，有逾70%的公司的盈利强于预期，但只有

42%的公司的收入强于预期，有41%的公司的收入逊于共识预期。

Although more than 70 per cent of S&P 500 companies have beaten earnings expectations, just 42 per cent have eclipsed sales projections — 41 per cent have fallen short of consensus revenue forecasts.

(5) 瑞银认为，今年美元升值将令标普500指数成份股公司10.7万亿美元的总收入减少3%~4%，相当于3000亿美元以上。

UBS believed the dollar would shave 3 to 4 per cent from total S&P 500 revenues of $10.7tn this year, or upwards of $300bn.

(6) 英国《金融时报》的分析显示，到目前为止，第二季度销售收入减少289亿美元，相当于8630亿美元报告收入的3.3%。而今年第一季度销售收入减少230亿美元，相当于第一季度收入的2.7%。

The FT analysis showed a $28.9bn loss to sales in the second quarter so far, or 3.3 per cent of the $863bn in reported revenues. That compares with $23bn in the first three months of the year, or 2.7 per cent of first-quarter revenues.

11.3　参考译文(Reference Version)

11.3.1　单句口译(Sentence Practice)

Please interpret the following sentences by using the techniques illustrated above. You may interpret to your partner first and then he/she comments on your performance.

(1) GDP年均增长10%，5亿多人摆脱贫困。

(2) 去年双方贸易额突破4000亿美元，相互投资达到1000亿美元，人员交往1500万人次，建立了中国—东盟中心。

(3) 新世纪以来，非洲形势总体保持和平稳定，经济进入快速增长期。2012年，在全球经济形势低迷的情况下，非洲经济增长率达到4.8%。预计未来十年，非洲仍将保持较快增长。

(4) 特别是要加大对困难群众精准帮扶力度，在2020年前实现现行标准下5700多万农村贫困人口全部脱贫，贫困县全部摘帽。

(5) 2020年国内生产总值和城乡居民人均收入比2010年翻一番，全面建成惠及十几亿人口的小康社会。

(6) Last year, two-way trade reached 26.3 billion U.S. dollars, including 22.8 billion dollars of Swiss exports to China. That is to say, every Swiss man, woman and child exported 2,800 dollars to China.

(7) Thanks to this reform and opening-up endeavor, China has lifted over 700 million

people out of poverty and significantly made life better for its 1.3 billion-plus people. In pursuing development, we have accomplished just in a few decades what has taken other countries several hundred years to achieve.

(8) In the first half of this year, China's GDP grew by 6.7%, its industrial upgrading and structural adjustment picked up pace, the final consumption expenditure contributed 73.4% to GDP, and the added value of the tertiary industry took up 54.1% of GDP. Household income grew steadily, and 7.17 million urban jobs were created.

(9) In terms of overall output, China's industrial added value grew at an average rate of 11.3% per year during the Eleventh Five-Year Plan, reaching 16 trillion yuan in 2010, which accounted for 40% of the GDP.

(10) As of the present, of the 500-plus industrial products that China produces, the output of over 220 has climbed towards the top of the world rankings. The added value of China's manufacturing industry accounted for 19.8% of global industry value-added, higher than any other country.

■ 11.3.2　段落口译(Paragraph Practice)

1. Vocabulary Work: Study the following words and phrases and translate them into the target language.

维持	城镇化
农村人口、农民	城镇人口
释放	表明、强调
广阔、巨大	全面
往来、互访	医疗

2. Please interpret the following paragraphs by using the techniques illustrated above. Please pay attention to the underlined sentences as they require special treatment during interpreting.

(1) 2012年中国的GDP按可比价算是2000年的3.2倍，翻了一番还多；到2020年通过努力在2010年的基础上再翻一番，需年均增长7%左右。今后五年，中国将进口10万亿美元左右的商品，对外投资规模将达到5000亿美元。中国正在积极稳妥地推进城镇化，数亿农民转化为城镇人口会释放更大的市场需求。这些都表明，中国经济发展的前景十分广阔，也会给包括瑞士在内的各国发展带来更多机遇。

(2) 今天，在双方共同努力下，中非关系已经进入全面发展的快车道。双方成立了中非合作论坛，构建起新型战略伙伴关系，各领域合作取得显著成果。2012年，中非贸易额接近2000亿美元，中非人员往来超过150万人次。截至去年，中国对非洲的直接投资累计超过150亿美元。今年是中国向非洲派出医疗队50周年，50年来累计派出1.8万人次的医疗人员，诊治了2.5亿人次的非洲患者。

(3) Firstly, lack of robust driving forces makes it difficult to sustain the steady growth of the global economy. Secondly, inadequate global economic governance makes it difficult to adapt to new changes and readjustment of industrial layout in the global economy. Thirdly, uneven global development makes it difficult to meet people's expectations for better lives. The richest one percent of the world's population owns more wealth than the remaining 99 percent. Over 700 million people in the world are still living in extreme poverty.

(4) President Xi also pointed out that China's development is a great opportunity to the world. He said that between 1950 and 2016, China provided more than 400 billion yuan of foreign assistance, undertaken over 5 000 foreign assistance projects. He also announced that in the coming five years, China is expected to import $8 trillion of goods from other countries and make $750 billion of outbound investment. Chinese tourists will make 700 million overseas visits.

▌ 11.3.3　篇章口译[Passage Practice (E to C)]

1. Please interpret the following passage by using the techniques illustrated above. Please pay attention to the underlined sentences as they require special treatment during interpreting.

开放经济，造福世界
李克强

① 这是一个充满考验的时代。国际金融危机爆发近十年后，世界经济仍未能完全摆脱其负面影响，中国也面临不少挑战，但我们选择迎难而上。我们坚信，开放的经济符合各方利益，对中国如此，对世界亦然。世界各国是命运共同体，相互间开展贸易与投资合作，远比相互攻讦、高筑壁垒好。出现分歧，本着相互尊重、平等相待的精神商谈解决之道，最符合各方利益。

② 中国坚定支持世界贸易组织和一切旨在推动包容发展的自贸安排。经济全球化在前所未有的规模上推动了财富的创造和分享，但这一进程也存在问题，主要是在分享方面。只要各国齐心协力，确保所有人都能从全球化中受益，这些问题是完全可以解决的。

③ 在国内，中国政府在处理同市场关系时采取介入更少、更加平衡的方式。为改善中国的营商环境，我们推动简政放权、放管结合、优化服务等改革，着力防范各种风险隐患，并将不断完善营改增改革，确保各行业税负只减不增。我们将开放更多行业，并放宽更多行业准入。我们正在对基于负面清单管理模式的外资准入制度进行推广前的试点，未来还将出台更多措施，让所有在华注册的企业都能一视同仁享受政策。在西部欠发达地区或东北老工业基地投资的企业，还可享受更多优惠政策。

④ 政府将继续投资基础设施建设，增加国内需求。更多资源将投向乡村公路、供排水系统和信息网络建设等以往并不显眼的短板领域。在改善硬件的同时，努力加强民生保

障，特别是对弱势群体的保障力度。结构性改革正在收到成效。2016年，中国压减落后过剩钢铁产能6500万吨以上、煤炭产能2.9亿吨以上。我们计划在三至五年内钢铁、煤炭产能分别压减1.4亿吨和8亿吨，使相关行业恢复更加健康的基本面。与此同时，政府还联手企业，为转岗人员提供多种形式的再培训。仅2016年，转岗安置人数就达到70万。

⑤ 中国经济增长的新动能正在蓬勃兴起。服务业占经济总量的比重已超过制造业，领军地位更加巩固，消费对GDP增长的贡献率在六成以上。新动能不仅创造新价值，也提升了传统产业的效率和竞争力，推动高技术产业和装备制造业增长领跑整个工业。大众创业、万众创新向纵深发展。新的商业模式不断涌现，此前许多意想不到的服务正日益成为生活中随处可享的便利。一个典型的例子是建立在移动互联网基础上的共享经济。除了订餐、约车等基本服务，家政、健康咨询等很多新服务也都只需轻点手机就可获得。

⑥ 数字最能说明问题。去年中国经济实现了6.7%的健康增长。更重要的是，尽管产业进一步优化整合、工业机器人应用日益广泛，中国就业市场的弹性不降反增。2013年以来，我们每年新增城镇就业1300多万人，失业率当前处于多年来最低水平。在一个不确定性层出不穷的世界上，中国是稳定之锚、增长之源，并始终如一传递深化改革、扩大开放和推进自由贸易的积极信息。时局不易，但正因如此，我们更不应忽视这些中国和世界从中受益良多的原则。

2. Please interpret the following passage by using the techniques illustrated above. Please pay attention to the underlined sentences as they require special treatment during interpreting.

中国经济动力十足
中国驻英国大使　刘晓明

① 桌上放着半杯水，悲观者看是半空，乐观者看则是半满。对于中国经济，悲观者和乐观者持有完全不同的看法。今年初以来，出现不少悲观的论调，看空唱衰中国经济发展前景，这完全忽视了中国经济的韧性和新动力。

② 首先，中国经济增速适当放缓是改革调控的预期结果。中国经济进入新常态，速度放慢是为了提高质量，是主动深化改革的结果。如果我们听任高能耗、高污染的产能继续扩张，或者采取大规模刺激手段，增长数字完全可能超过7%，甚至更高。但是，中国没有选择这种不可持续的增长，因为这必将付出巨大代价，不利于中国和世界经济的长远发展。因此，中国将今年经济的重点放在了化解过剩产能、减少房地产库存、扩大有效供给、帮助企业降低成本和防范化解金融风险5个方面。这个过程犹如减肥，过程不会舒适，甚至会有痛苦，但只要坚持，去掉了赘肉，增加了肌肉，身体就会更加健康。

③ 第二，中国经济基本面仍然长期向好。股市和汇市的波动有其自身运行规律，观察中国经济关键要看基本面。2015年中国经济增速为6.9%，虽然增幅为25年来最小，但这是在10万亿美元高基数之上的增长，增量相当于一个中等国家全年的国内生产总值，比以前两位数的增量还要大。这也是在世界经济增长放缓大背景下的增长，在主要经济体中名

列前茅，对世界经济增长贡献率超过1/4。消费对经济增长的贡献率已达2/3，服务业比重超过一半。中国物质基础雄厚，人力资源丰富，市场空间广阔，持续增长的良好支撑基础和条件没有变。中国东西差距、城乡差距比较大，意味着发展空间和潜力还相当充分。此外，新型工业化、信息化、城镇化、农业现代化同步发展正创造强劲的增长动能。中国的财政赤字和政府债务余额均处于安全线内，远低于美、欧、日等主要经济体，为下一步积极调控留下了较大空间。

④ 第三，五大新动力将促进中国经济继续前行。一是"十三五"规划确立了创新、协调、绿色、开放、共享五大发展理念，将引领中国跨越"中等收入陷阱"，进入高收入国家行列。二是"供给侧结构性改革"，这并非里根和撒切尔时代"供应学派"的翻版，而是针对中国经济新常态提出的改革新理念，其核心是减少无效和低端供给，扩大有效和中高端供给，提升竞争力。三是开放发展，中国将完善法治化、国际化和便利化的营商环境。四是积极参与全球经济治理和公共产品供给。亚投行于今年1月16日正式开业就是一个例证。五是创新驱动发展，中国将通过优化要素配置，激发创新创业活力，释放新需求，创造新供给，推动新业态蓬勃发展。

⑤ 国际金融危机以来，中国对全球经济增长的贡献突出，是名副其实的动力源，体现了大国责任和担当。展望未来，中国这辆发动机仍然马力十足，将为世界各国带来更多合作机遇和红利。大约三千年前，中国文化典籍《诗经》写道："周虽旧邦，其命维新"。今天，改革和创新依然是我们信心和动力的源泉。我们有足够的理由相信，中国将在拥抱世界的过程中行稳致远，中国经济的发展前景依然精彩可期。

▌ 11.3.4 篇章口译[Passage Practice (C to E)]

1. Please interpret the following passage by using the techniques illustrated above. Please pay attention to the underlined sentences as they require special treatment during interpreting.

Keynote Speech at the China-US Business Luncheon (Excerpts)
H.E. Wang Yang, Vice Premier of the State Council of the People's Republic of China

The Honorable Secretary Pritzker,

Ambassador Froman,

Friends from the business community,

Ladies and Gentlemen,

① Thank you to the China General Chamber of Commerce – USA and the National Governors Association for the warm hospitality and the chance to meet friends from the business communities of both countries during this session of Joint Commission on Commerce and Trade (JCCT). I also want to thank you for giving me this speaking opportunity so that I can make some advertising for China-US trade and economic cooperation as well as China's investment environment. On behalf of the Chinese government, I would like to pay high tribute to you all for your years of important contribution to China-US economic relations.

② The JCCT is an over 30-years-old institutional arrangement, yet each session takes place with a different background and mission. The biggest background of this JCCT is the election of Mr. Trump as the new president. People are now all interested in the direction of the new US administration's trade policy on China and the future of China-US business cooperation. As for what actions the US will take, we will wait and see. The presidential election told us making prediction is difficult. However, today's large gathering gives me one strong impression, that is, although there will be a change of administration in the US, the passion of the US business community for cooperation with China remains unchanged. If today's luncheon gives us a clue about China-US business cooperation, it is that we have every reason to be optimistic about its future.

③ China is the largest trading partner of the US. Despite the lackluster growth in global trade from 2008 to 2015, China-US trade defied the downward trend and recorded an average annual growth of over 7%. Last year, the top four US exports to China were airplane, soybean, automobile and integrated circuit. China imported 22% of US cotton, 26% of Bowing airplanes and 56% of US soybean. Exports of goods and services to China generated nearly 1 million jobs in the US. The US is also a big market for Chinese exports and in China-US trade, China is on the surplus side. But I want to stress that many of China's imports from the US are high-end products which China cannot produce, and what we export to the US are mostly products which the US, with no comparative advantage, no longer produces. The investment of Chinese companies in the US has rapidly increased, now reaching 42 American states, including New York, Illinois, Virginia, Massachusetts and California. Chinese investment has generated some 100 000 job opportunities for America. Generally speaking, China-US economic relationship is highly complementary. The bond of the market has made us interconnected and indispensable to each other.

④ As our economic and trade ties grow closer, we also face growing differences and frictions. Sometimes, the more you care about the other side, the easier it is to get into quarrel. If there is no quarrel, it probably means a complete loss of faith in each other, and a breakup will not be far. In fact, since you are in the business world, you should know this better. Many cooperation deals were made after quarrels. As we face up to our differences and effectively resolve them, we find the strong driving force for China-US economic cooperation. Now we have a host of bilateral mechanisms for managing differences. In the economic and trade field, we not only have old mechanisms like the JCCT and the Strategic and Economic Dialogue (S&ED), but also the new arrangement of routine telephone communication on economic affairs initiated last year. I have maintained hotline communication with Secretary Pritzker, Ambassador Froman and Secretary Lew. The topics of our conversation ranged from big issues like institutions and mechanisms in important economic areas to small issues like trade of specific products. To be honest, communication can not solve all the problems, but it has enabled us to increase mutual trust and manage differences and created conditions for more cooperation.

⑤ China and the US, the two largest economies in the world, have both demonstrated strong momentum of growth, which has opened broad space for business cooperation. It is estimated that over the next five years, China will import US$8 trillion of goods, utilize US$600 billion of foreign investment, and make US$750 billion of outward investment. Outbound Chinese tourists are also expected to reach 700 million. All these mean enormous business opportunities for companies around the globe, including American companies. To help others is to help oneself. This is an important part of China's business culture. I am confident that, seeing a big emerging market like China, American government and companies will make the right choice.

⑥ As a matter of fact, the Chinese and American business communities have already made their choice. The China Business Environment Survey published by the US-China Business Council last month shows that nearly three quarters of the American companies surveyed are optimistic about the growth prospect of the Chinese economy; 90% of the companies have made profits in China; and nearly half of the companies are ready to increase investment in China. In the first three quarters of this year, the investment of US companies in China was up by 21.3%, while the direct investment made by Chinese companies in the non-financial sectors of the US expanded by 1.8 folds. These figures may be more convincing than the interpretation of China-US economic relations by any politician or economist. In one word, China-US business cooperation is market driven, and its ultimate driving force comes from the people, from the business community. If China-US business cooperation gets into serious trouble, it will not only damage the two economies but also add to the uncertainties of global economic recovery. As two responsible major countries, we can only choose to cooperate.

2. Please interpret the following passage by using the techniques illustrated above. Please pay attention to the underlined sentences as they require special treatment during interpreting.

The sharp rise in the US dollar may slice more revenues of at some of America's largest multinationals

① The sharp rise in the US dollar may slice more than $100bn off dollar-denominated revenues at some of America's largest multinationals this year, a sum larger than the combined sales of Nike, McDonald's and Goldman Sachs, according to a *Financial Times* analysis.

② In the first half of the year, 10 of the largest US multinationals have had their sales reduced by a combined $31bn — including blue-chip companies like Apple, General Motors, IBM, Amazon and General Electric — and concerns have mounted that a move by the Federal

Reserve to lift interest rates later this year will push the dollar higher.

③ "Large multinationals are taking a hit from the stronger US currency," David Lebovitz, market strategist with JPMorgan Asset Management, said. "You have downward pressure on the euro and yen coming from central banks in those regions and given a relatively unfavourable backdrop in emerging markets, we're seeing currency depreciation there."

④ Companies within the S&P 500 earned roughly 48 per cent of their revenues abroad in 2014, according to data from S&P Dow Jones Indices. A weak US dollar in years past had bolstered American multinationals, which benefited when they translated sales earned abroad back into the greenback.

⑤ But diverging monetary policies have pushed the trade-weighted dollar 19 per cent above year-ago levels, including a 22 per cent gain against the euro. That has depressed top-line growth, particularly for internet and technology groups, which earn more revenues outside the US than any other sector. Although more than 70 per cent of S&P 500 companies have beaten earnings expectations, just 42 per cent have eclipsed sales projections — 41 per cent have fallen short of consensus revenue forecasts.

⑥ "This whole expansion has not been strong in terms of revenue growth," said David Lefkowitz, an equity strategist at UBS Wealth Management. He said UBS believed the dollar would shave 3 to 4 per cent from total S&P 500 revenues of $10.7tn this year, or upwards of $300bn.

⑦ The FT analysis showed a $28.9bn loss to sales in the second quarter so far, or 3.3 per cent of the $863bn in reported revenues. That compares with $23bn in the first three months of the year, or 2.7 per cent of first-quarter revenues.

⑧ The report covered more than 100 of the US corporates in the S&P 500 that have reported both first and second-quarter earnings — and was limited by a lack of disclosure of foreign exchange effects from dozens of companies.

11.4 经济主题词汇汇总(Vocabulary Build-up)

WTO (World Trade Organization)	世界贸易组织
IMF (International Monetary Fund)	国际货币基金组织
CTG (Council for Trade in Goods)	货币贸易理事会
EFTA (European Free Trade Association)	欧洲自由贸易联盟
AFTA (ASEAN Free Trade Area)	东盟自由贸易区
JCCT (China-US Joint Commission on Commerce and Trade)	中美商贸联委会
NAFTA (North American Free Trade Area)	北美自由贸易区
UNCTAD (United Nations Conference on Trade and Development)	联合国贸易与发展会议

(续表)

GATT (General Agreement on Tariffs and Trade)	关贸总协定
world / international favorable balance of trade	贸易顺差
unfavorable balance of trade	贸易逆差
special preferences	优惠关税
tariff barrier	关税壁垒
trade partner	贸易伙伴
manufacturer	制造商，制造厂
middleman	中间商，经纪人
dealer	经销商
wholesaler	批发商
retailer, tradesman	零售商
merchant	商人，批发商，零售商
consumer	消费者，用户
client, customer	顾客，客户
buyer	买主，买方
carrier	承运人
inland trade, home trade, domestic trade	国内贸易
international trade	国际贸易
foreign trade, external trade	对外贸易，外贸
import, importation	进口
importer	进口商
export, exportation	出口
exporter	出口商
import license	进口许可证
export license	出口许可证
commercial transaction	买卖，交易

11.5　扩展练习(Enhancement Practice)

Making comments on a given topics.

Directions: Please read paragraph (1) and (2) carefully and then express your views on the given topics.

(1)

Countries on your planet vary in terms of their resource distribution, climatic conditions and topography, which, to a great extent, affect their population as well as food production. However, there is much discussion nowadays as to whether a country should take measures to prepare all the food for its citizens and import as little food as possible. Give reasons for your answer. Discuss both sides and give your own poinion.

(2)

With the rapid development of economy, the sales of consumer goods show a significant increase in many countries. Some countries encourage people to buy more and more products, while others believe it has negative effects on society

11.6　延伸口译(Extended Interpreting)

习近平主席：奏响中捷关系的时代强音

The Czech Republic is known for picturesque landscape, rich cultural heritage and talented people. I visited this country in the 1990s and was deeply impressed by the hard work and ingenuity of the Czech people, dynamic economic and social progress and the Bohemian culture nourished by the Vltava river.

捷克人杰地灵，山川秀美，人文历史底蕴深厚。20世纪90年代，我曾经到访捷克，勤劳智慧的捷克人民、蓬勃开展的捷克经济社会建设、伏尔塔瓦河孕育的波西米亚文明都给我留下了深刻的印象。

In recent years, China-Czech relations entered a period of fast growth. In a short span of two years, President Zeman and I met four times and reached broad common understanding on strengthening high-level exchanges, deepening strategic mutual trust and intensifying exchanges and cooperation across the board. At the end of 2015, the two governments signed an MOU on jointly promoting the "Belt and Road" initiative, which created even wider prospects for bilateral exchanges and cooperation in all fields.

近年来，中捷关系发展驶入快车道。两年内，我同泽曼总统四度会面，就加强两国高层交往、深化战略互信、提升各领域交流合作水平达成广泛共识。2015年年底，双方签署关于共同推进"一带一路"建设的政府间谅解备忘录，为两国各领域交流合作开辟了更加广阔的空间。

For many years in a row, China has been the Czech Republic's largest trading partner outside the European Union and the Czech Republic China's second largest trading partner in Central and Eastern Europe. In 2015, our bilateral trade topped 11 billion U.S. dollars. Our cooperation in nuclear power, finance, aviation, science and technology and agriculture scaled new heights both in level and scale. Many Chinese and Czech companies have investments and booming business operations in each other's countries.

中国连续多年是捷克在欧盟外第一大贸易伙伴，捷克是中国在中东欧地区第二大贸易伙伴。2015年，中捷双边贸易额达到110亿美元。中捷核电、金融、航空、科技、农业等领域合作日新月异，合作水平和规模不断提升。两国多家企业到对方国家投资兴业，业务发展迅速。

Our people-to-people and cultural exchanges are flourishing. The Czech Republic is an attractive destination to Chinese tourists, who made a record number of more than 300,000 visits here in 2015, making tourism a bright spot in China-Czech cooperation. Today, the Czech Republic hosts the first traditional Chinese medicine research center in Central and Eastern Europe. Cooperation on film and TV production is gaining momentum. The 2022 Winter Olympics to be held in China also offers a great opportunity for sports exchanges between our two countries.

中捷人文交流活力迸发。捷克已经成为中国游客憧憬和向往的旅游目的地。2015年，来捷克旅游的中国游客总数突破30万人次，创历史新高。旅游合作已经成为中捷交流合作的一张亮丽"名片"。中东欧首家中医中心在捷克落户。中捷影视合作方兴未艾。中国将举办2022年冬奥会，为双方加强体育交流提供了良好机遇。

This visit also marks my first trip to a Central and Eastern European country (CEEC) as China's president. With our deep-rooted friendship, political good-will and popular support as a strong basis, China and CEECs launched "16+1" cooperation, which has since made solid progress. Over the past four years, under the principles of mutual respect, mutual benefit, inclusiveness and openness, China and CEECs have built new cooperation mechanisms and platforms. Thanks to these efforts, China-CEECs cooperation is entering a maturing phase and delivering early harvests. Our cooperation on the "Belt and Road" initiative and efforts to strengthen synergy between China and the EU in their development strategies will create even greater impetus and potential for "16+1" cooperation.

这次访问也是我担任国家主席后第一次访问中东欧国家。中国同中东欧国家有着源远流长的深厚友谊。得益于双方的强烈政治意愿和良好的民意基础，中国—中东欧国家合作（"16+1合作"）应运而生，方兴未艾。4年来，中国同中东欧国家一道，本着相互尊重、互利共赢、包容开放的原则，建机制、搭平台、促合作，共同推动"16+1合作"逐渐步入成熟期和早期收获期。中国同中东欧国家开展共建"一带一路"合作以及中欧不断加强战略对接，为"16+1合作"汇聚了更为蓬勃的动力，开辟了更为广阔的空间。

The EU is China's comprehensive strategic partner. In March 2014, during my visit to the EU headquarters, the EU leaders and I agreed to develop partnerships for peace, growth, reform and civilization, pointing the strategic direction for China-EU relations. Last year, marking the 40th anniversary of diplomatic ties, the two sides decided to promote synergy between the "Belt and Road" initiative and the Investment Plan for Europe and set up the China-EU co-investment vehicle and the Connectivity Platform, broadening the new framework of China-EU practical cooperation. China-EU relations are at their best period in history and are presented with unprecedented historic opportunities of further growth.

欧盟是中国的全面战略伙伴。2014年3月，我访问欧盟总部期间，同欧方领导人一道决定打造中欧和平、增长、改革、文明四大伙伴关系，为新时期中欧关系指明了战略方向。2015年中欧建交40周年之际，双方决定推进"一带一路"倡议同欧洲投资计划等发展战略对接，组建中欧共同投资基金、互联互通平台等，进一步确立了中欧务实合作的新框架。中欧关系正处于历史发展最好时期，面临前所未有的历史机遇。

China and the EU are both deepening structural reforms to unleash greater social and economic vitality. People in China are now striving to complete the building of a moderately prosperous society in all respects, advance towards the "Two Centenary Goals" of development (i.e. to double 2010 GDP and per capita income and finish the building of a moderately prosperous society in all respects by the time the CPC celebrates its centenary in 2021 and to turn the PRC into a modern socialist country that is prosperous, strong, democratic, culturally advanced and harmonious by the time it celebrates its centenary in 2049) and realize the Chinese dream of national rejuvenation. The Outline of the 13th Five-Year Plan for Social and Economic Development, which was recently promulgated, calls for innovative, coordinated, green, open and inclusive development and sets forth the targets of maintaining stable growth, upgrading the growth model and economic structure, aiming at a medium-to-high growth speed for the comingfive years. The EU is working to keep the momentum of economic recovery and boost its economic competitiveness. Such a high complementarity in our development strategies and great potential of our cooperation hold out great promise for the future of China-EU relations. China will join hands with the EU for win-win cooperation, and together contribute to world economic development.

当前，中欧双方都在推进结构性改革，激发经济社会发展活力。中国人民正在为全面建成小康社会、实现"两个一百年"奋斗目标、实现中华民族伟大复兴的中国梦而不懈努力。不久前颁布实施的中国国民经济和社会发展第十三个五年规划纲要，贯彻创新、协调、绿色、开放、共享的发展理念，致力于稳增长、转方式、调结构，努力在未来5年保持经济中高速增长。欧盟正致力于保持经济复苏势头，大力提升欧盟经济发展竞争力。在此背景下，中欧双方发展战略契合度高、合作潜力巨大、前景广阔。中国愿同欧盟一道，发扬同舟共济、合作共赢的精神，共同为世界经济发展贡献力量。

China-CEECs cooperation and China-EU relations need to be underpinned by strong bilateral relationships. This is an opportune time for the development of China-Czech relations. I look forward to working with Czech leaders to further enhance bilateral relations and push for new progress in "16+1" cooperation and China-EU relations.

中国—中东欧国家合作和中欧关系的发展需要依靠双边关系的有力支撑。当前，中捷两国面临着双边关系发展的重要历史机遇。我期待通过这次访问，同捷克领导人一道，提高双边关系水平，推动"16+1合作"以及中欧关系不断向前发展。

We should enhance political mutual trust and establish a clear direction for the development of our ties. As people say in China, a tree can grow tall only when its roots are strong. China and the Czech Republic should consider upgrading the bilateral relationship in due time, adopt a strategic and long-term perspective, follow the principle of mutual respect and equality, and render firm support to each other on issues concerning our core interests and major concerns, to ensure long-term sound and stable development of bilateral ties and set the right direction for our relations.

加强政治互信，指明发展方向。"求木之长者，必固其根本。"中捷双方应该适时提高双边关系定位，坚持从战略高度和长远角度看待双边关系，本着互相尊重、平等相待的原则，坚定支持对方的核心利益和重大关切，确保中捷关系长期健康稳定发展，牢牢把握两国关系发展的大方向。

We should better align our development strategies to tap the potential of cooperation. The MOU of cooperation on the joint development of the "Belt and Road" between China and the Czech Republic offers fresh opportunity for the two countries to better align our development strategies and plans, and prepare the ground for identifying major cooperation projects for early harvest.

加强战略对接，释放合作潜力。中捷双方应该以签署共同推进"一带一路"建设政府间谅解备忘录为重要契机，加强各自发展战略和愿景的对接，进一步梳理和筹备重大合作项目，争取早期收获。

We should enhance economic cooperation for the benefit of our people. More than 30 years of reform and opening-up has sharpened China's competitive edge in terms of capital, technology and equipment, especially in railway and nuclear plant construction. Situated in the heartland of Europe, the Czech Republic enjoys advantageous location, strong industrial foundation and unique strengths in machining, automobile manufacturing and aero-industry. China hopes to cooperate with the Czech side to carry out industrial capacity cooperation in the manufacturing sector, and on that basis, expand practical cooperation in such areas as finance, telecommunications, smart industry, nano technology and environmental protection, to deliver greater fruits of this mutually beneficial cooperation to our two peoples.

加强经贸合作，惠及两国民众。经过30多年的改革开放，中国在资金、技术、装备方面已经形成较大优势，特别是在铁路、核电建设等领域优势明显。捷克位于欧洲心脏地带，地理位置优越，工业基础雄厚，在机械加工、汽车制造、航空等领域具有独特优势。中方愿同捷方一道，以制造业为基础推进产能合作，带动金融、通信、智能工业、纳米、环保等各领域务实合作，让两国民众分享更多互利合作成果。

We should encourage people-to-people and cultural exchanges. The Chinese and Czech peoples have long admired and appreciated each other's civilization and culture, and such exchanges have boomed in recent years. We should expand exchanges in culture, education, film and television, tourism and health sectors, encourage young people and students to interact more with each other to renew our traditional friendship.

加强人文交流，赋予时代内涵。中捷两国人民素来互相欣赏对方的文明、文化，近年来更是不断掀起交流高潮。我们要继续扩大文化、教育、影视、旅游、卫生等领域人文交流，鼓励青年和学生交往，让两国人民的传统友谊世代相传、历久弥新。

We should step up regional cooperation by bringing into play the role of multilateral platforms. The Czech Republic has actively supported and participated in China-CEECs cooperation, demonstrating its important role by spearheading health cooperation and cooperation at sub-national levels. We hope to work together with the Czech Republic and other CEECs to make the "16+1" a premier framework for regional cooperation.

加强区域合作，用好广阔平台。捷克一直积极支持和参与中国—中东欧国家合作，在卫生、地方合作等方面一直走在中东欧国家前列，在"16+1合作"中发挥了积极重要作用。我们愿同包括捷克在内的中东欧国家一道，为做大做强"16+1合作"共同努力。

We should strengthen China-EU cooperation for a better future. China and the EU should follow the trend of peace, development and win-win cooperation, further synergize development strategies, enhance communication and coordination in the international arena and work for new progress of the China-EU comprehensive strategic partnership.

加强中欧合作，共建美好未来。中欧双方应当顺应和平、发展、合作、共赢的时代潮流，不断深化各自发展战略对接，加强在国际舞台上的沟通和协调，携手努力，推动中欧全面战略伙伴关系不断迈上新台阶。

第12单元 跨文化技巧(Cross-Cultural Communication)

口译主题：文化娱乐

单元学习目的(Unit Goals) 💡

➢ 掌握本课程所讲授的跨文化口译技巧。

➢ 学习文化娱乐专题所涉及的常用词语和表达。

导入 (Lead -in)

1. 口译中的文化差异有哪些?

2. 如何翻译这句话：He who knows himself, knows others.

3. 口译中的文化障碍有哪些?

4. 译员应具备哪些跨文化交际意识?

12.1 技能讲解(Skill Introduction)

■ 12.1.1 口译中的文化差异(Cultural Differences in Interpreting)

(1) 价值观念的差异。英汉两种文化价值观念的差异主要表现在称谓语、隐私观念和谦虚的表达方式上。汉语里亲属称谓严密繁多，既要表明性别，又要区分大小；英语里亲属称谓将同一代归入同一称谓层，仅区分性别，表达人人平等的思想。汉语文化中，年龄、婚姻、工资等话题在聊天中可以随意询问，而在英语国家文化中属于隐私内容。在听到称赞话语后，中文的回应态度往往礼貌客气，谦虚含蓄，而英语回应则积极直白。

(2) 思维方式的差异。思维支配语言，语言是内在思维的外化表现。由特定思维模式所形成的不同思维文化差异主要由知识来源和思维方法上的差异造成。偏于形象类比的汉语思维方式是通过物体的形象表达思想，注重经验和实践，善于从整体认知的角度探究和认识事物。英语则强调局部优先，偏于逻辑、分析和验证，注重科学性和逻辑性，善于形式思维，注重具体的事物。

(3) 社会习俗的差异。英汉民族各自形成特有的生活习俗，包括礼仪、习惯、喜好、禁忌、数字、颜色以及文化意象等方面。在一种文化中形成的风俗习惯难以在另一种文化中找到对等的事物，口译时应把握这些差异。

(4) 历史背景的差异。不同语言在各自历史、经济、文化等发展过程中，积累了丰富的成语、谚语、俗语、俚语、歇后语、双关语、寓言、格言、神话、传说等惯用语和常用语，蕴藏着浓厚的民族特色和深远的社会历史渊源。在翻译时，这些习语无法保留原文的语义意义，这就要求译员精通历史背景知识，了解语用意义，才能在翻译时消除语言文化差异的障碍。

12.1.2　口译中的文化障碍(Cultural Barriers in Interpreting)

(1) 文化意象差异构成的文化障碍。文化意象是各民族或社团文化中逐渐形成的一种文化符号，以其多种多样的表现形式、深远的联想和丰富的寓意展示其历史和文化。如果在口译过程中对这些差异处理不当，就会出现误译。因此译员应该增加相应的解释来弥补差异。

(2) 思维认知差异构成的文化障碍。中英思维差异在对时间、地点、方位和度量衡的表述上均有体现。例如汉语计数是以十进位的，而在英语中数字是以千进位的。这些障碍需要译员花费大量时间进行自我调节，以适应不同思维。

(3) 价值观差异构成的文化障碍。价值观既是社会文化的组成部分，又是社会文化因素在人们心中长期渗透、积淀的结果，是人们关于什么是最好的行为的一套持久的信念或是依重要性程度而排列的一种信念体系。

(4) 历史文化典故。历史典故和寓言由于包含特有的人名和地名而成为翻译中的难题，因为如果译员采用直译方式，会让听者无法理解，而采用意译法则会失去源语的特色。

12.1.3　跨文化口译的原则(Principles of Cross-culture Interpreting)

(1) 译员应设身处地体味说话人的情感，将自己代入对方的心境，以引起共鸣。

(2) 译员要承认并尊重母语文化与异文化之间存在的差异，克服民族中心意识，抛弃有关性别、民族和文化等方面错误，甚至歧视性的态度和看法。

(3) 译员要关注跨文化交际中异文化使用者及其现实的交际场景，注意对方的言语和非言语表达，理解对方自然的情感反应。

(4) 译员要提高对异文化价值观和风俗习惯、思维模式等的敏感度，避免以自己的文化来解释、评价异文化中他人的言语行为和非言语行为。

(5) 译员要了解跨文化交际双方的交际目的和交际需求，站在对方的角度上观察分析问题。

12.1.4 培养跨文化意识(The Development of Cross-culture Awareness)

(1) 跨文化意识是指在跨文化交际中，译员自觉或不自觉地形成的一种认知标准和调节方法，主要指译员所特有的思维方式和判断能力，这将使译员不受或少受文化差异的负面影响，得体、准确地传达信息，主动弥补说话者表达的失误与缺陷，全面考虑交际的需要，帮助双方建立成功的跨文化交际。

(2) 译员应提高语言功底和口头表达能力。熟悉其语言的文化背景，理解语言的雅俗、诙谐、夸张、婉转等修辞上的特征。注意表达上的言之有序、词能达意、严于流畅，保证语言层面的正确性，注重语言使用的灵活性和多变性。

(3) 译员要熟练掌握源语和译入语的转换模式，了解原语和目的语的语言概念完全对应、部分对应及其完全不对应的情况下该如何翻译，提高语言表达的高效率。

(4) 译员必须掌握口译翻译的基本技巧和策略，包括断句、转换、重复、增补、省略、反说、归纳等。

12.1.5 口译中跨文化非语言交际(Non-verbal Cross-culture Interpreting)

(1) 非语言交际包括使用语言之外的一切传递信息的方式，其形式多种多样，如：姿态动作、目光接触、面部表情、身体距离、衣着打扮、空间利用、触碰行为、声音暗示，甚至没有表情和动作都可以构成非语言交际的有效方式。

(2) 非语言交际在许多方面受到文化影响，对待同一事物时，不同文化的群体有不同的感情和表情，体现不同的社会思想内涵。所以译员在工作时必须考虑到各国非语言交际的文化差异。

(3) 译员应积极培养的跨文化意识，提高跨文化交际能力，学习文化知识，树立正确态度，加强职业素养，善于协调交际双方的文化差异，保障口译质量。

12.2 主题口译(Topic Interpreting)

12.2.1 单句口译(Sentence Practice)

Please interpret the following sentences by using the techniques illustrated above. You may interpret to your partner first and then he/she comments on your performance.

(1) The increase in international business and in foreign investment has created a need for executives with knowledge of foreign languages and skills in cross-cultural communication.

(2) The language and culture differences of cross-cultural communication mainly exist in semantics, pragmatics and body language.

(3) The idea of one human family under the sun is a nice little proverb, but it has serious implications for implementation in a global village.

(4) Modern libraries are advanced media for cross-cultural communication, which can realize the free exchange between the cultures with different characteristics and make today s culture spread in the world wide.

(5) All cultures value beauty, and a beautiful baby or woman or man is recognized as such whether African, Asian or European.

(6) 丝绸之路不仅是一条贸易线路，它还曾在促进中国与亚洲、欧洲、非洲各国间的友好关系和经济文化交流等方面起着重要的作用。

(7) 所有文化都珍爱家庭惩罚犯罪，对犯罪的定义也几乎相似。

(8) 在与世界各国的文化交流中，中国不断丰富自己的文化，同时也为世界文化艺术的发展做出贡献。

(9) 出国留学有很多好处：你可以有跨文化交流的经验，对你所学的专业有新的认识，并结交新朋友。

(10) 我们对声音、感觉和情况的反应不同是因为个人经历、文化差异和情感联想不同。

12.2.2　段落口译(Paragraph Practice)

1. Vocabulary Work: Study the following words and phrases and translate them into the target language.

吸引力	health care system
难民危机	a highly desirable destination
大影响	high-net worth
马上到	candlelit dinner
使糊涂	get out of hand
志同道合	a black market

2. Please interpret the following paragraphs by using the techniques illustrated above.

(1) 农工党中央将在两会期间提出有关太极拳申请联合国教科文组织世界非物质文化遗产名录的提案，以进一步保护和推广这项传统体育运动。作为一项既可防身又能健体的内修型武学艺术，太极拳已经传播到150多个国家和地区，全球习练人数超3亿。与此形成对比的是，有关太极拳的研究少之又少，太极拳的推广也主要靠民间力量。据澎湃新闻报道，太极拳是在全世界认可度较高的中国文化符号，2006年已被列入中国首批国家非物质文化遗产名录，但我国在保护和传播太极拳方面还落后于瑜伽等国外体育项目。农工党中央在提案中指出："瑜伽在2016年被列为联合国教科文组织非物质文化遗产，此举有助于保护瑜伽文化。我国有关部门应该尽快推荐太极拳申报人类非物质文化遗产，周边国家如韩国、日本，对太极拳文化十分推崇，有抢先申报太极拳为人类非物质文化遗产代表作的倾向。"

(2) 中国自2008年开始向联合国教科文组织推荐太极拳申报人类非物质文化遗产。但是，由于教科文卫组织对非物质文化遗产的评估标准严苛，这项申请到目前为止还在等待阶段。太极拳项目专家严双军2014年接受新华社采访时曾表示："太极拳申遗面临的最大困难是太极拳理论和哲学的精准翻译问题。比如，太极拳中讲究的'天人合一'，连我们中国人自己都不太能明白，更何况外国专家呢。" 农工党中央建议，设立国家级太极拳文化研究中心，将太极拳文化引进高校和医疗科研机构，提高太极拳文化学术水平。农工党中央1930年8月在上海成立，目前有14.4万多名成员，包括医药卫生界的高级知识分子。

(3) The US and UK have traditionally attracted the highest number of wealthy migrants. But the allure of Australia has increased in recent years, especially for wealthy citizens of China and India. New World Wealth said migrating millionaires are drawn to the sunny Australian lifestyle, as well as the country's highly rated health care system, which is considered to be in better shape than those in the US and UK. It's considered a safe place to live and raise children, and it's geographically isolated from conflicts in the Middle East and the refugee crisis in Europe. Business considerations also play a role: Australia is a good base for doing business in emerging Asian countries such as China, South Korea, Singapore and India, the researchers said. The US is still considered a highly desirable destination, welcoming 10 000 foreign millionaires last year. New World Wealth expects demand to remain high. "We don't think the new leadership in the US will have a big impact. We expect another big net inflow of high-net worth individuals into the US in 2017," said Andrew Amoils, head of research at New World Wealth. Canada also saw of surge of 8 000 new millionaires coming to its shores. Rich Chinese citizens are moving to Vancouver while Europeans generally head to Toronto and Montreal.

(4) Love it or loathe it, another Valentine's Day is just around the corner. And while you may be choosing cards and planning candlelit dinners, other couples around the world are preparing quite differently. In Japan, for example, women don't receive gifts from men at all, they give them. A month later on March 14th, however, men can return the favor on what is known as White Day. In South Africa, women write down the name of the person they are besotted with and pin it to their sleeves; while in Germany, the pig is viewed as a symbol of lust and is often seen on cards and presents. They are often accompanied by other symbols of luck, such as four-leaf clovers. In Finland and Estonia, the 14th of February is actually Friend's Day — an occasion to celebrate non-romantic kinship. A French Valentine's Day tradition had to be banned by the government because it started to get out of hand. Single men and women used to gather in houses that faced each other, and shout across to be paired up. Men who weren't happy with their match could leave them for another, and the women who were left unmatched would gather together to burn pictures of the men afterwards. And if you want to avoid Valentine's Day altogether? You'll

be in good company in Saudi Arabia, where it's strictly banned. There is even a black market for red roses.

12.2.3 篇章口译[Passage Practice (E to C)]

1. Please interpret the following passage by using the techniques illustrated above. Please pay attention to the underlined sentences as they require special treatment during interpreting.

Music is Medicine (Excerpts)
Robert Gupta

① One day, Los Angeles Time columnist Steve Lopez was walking along the streets of downtown Los Angeles when he heard beautiful music. And the source was a man, an African-American man, charming, rugged, homeless, playing a violin that only had two strings. <u>And I'm telling a story that many of you know, because Steve's columns became the basis for a book, which was turned into a movie with Robert Downey Jr. acting as Steve Lopez, and Jamie Foxx as Nathaniel Anthony Ayers, the Juilliard-trained double bassist whose promising career was cut short by a tragic affliction with paranoid schizophrenia.</u>[1] Nathaniel dropped out of Juilliard, he suffered a complete breakdown, and 30 years later he was living homeless on the streets of Skid Row in downtown Los Angeles.

② I encourage all of you to read Steve's book or to watch the movie to understand not only the beautiful bond that formed between these two men, but how music helped shape that bond, and ultimately was instrumental — if you'll pardon the pun — in helping Nathaniel get off the streets. I met Mr. Ayers in 2008. Two years ago, at Walt Disney Concert Hall. He had just heard a performance of Beethoven's First and Fourth symphonies and came backstage and introduced himself. <u>He was speaking in a very jovial and gregarious way about Yo-Yo Ma and Hillary Clinton and how the Dodgers were never going to make the World Series, all because of the treacherous first violin passage work in the last movement of Beethoven's Fourth Symphony.</u>[2] And we got talking about music, and I got an email from Steve a few days later saying that Nathaniel was interested in a violin lesson with me.

③ Now, I should mention that Nathaniel refuses treatment because when he was treated it was with shock therapy and Thorazine and handcuffs, and that scar has stayed with him for his entire life. <u>But as a result now, he is prone to these schizophrenic episodes, the worst of which can manifest themselves as him exploding and then disappearing for days, wandering the streets of Skid Row, exposed to its horrors, with the torment of his own mind unleashed upon him.</u>[3] And Nathaniel was in such a state of agitation when we started our first lesson at Walt Disney Concert Hall—he had a kind of manic glint in his eyes, he was lost. And he was talking about invisible demons and smoke, how someone was poisoning him in his sleep. And I was afraid, not for myself, but I was afraid that I was going to lose him, that he was going to sink into one of his states, and that I would ruin his relationship with the violin if I started talking about scales, and arpeggios and other exciting forms of didactic violin pedagogy.

④ So, I just started playing. And I played the first movement of the Beethoven Violin Concerto. And as I played, I understood that there was a profound change occurring in Nathaniel's eyes. It was as if he was in the grip of some invisible pharmaceutical, a chemical reaction, for which my playing the music was its catalyst. And Nathaniel's manic rage was transformed into understanding, a quite curiosity and grace. And in a miracle, he lifted his own violin, and he started playing, by ear, certain snippets of violin concertos which he then asked me to complete — Mendelssohn, Tchaikovsky, Sibelius. And we started talking about music, from Bach too Beethoven and Brahms, Bruckner all the B's, from Bartak, all the way up to Esa-Pekka Salonen.[4] And I understood that he not only had an encyclopedic knowledge of music, but he related to this music at a personal level. He spoke about it with the kind of passion and understanding that I share with my colleagues in the Los Angeles Philharmonic. And through playing music and talking about music, this man had transformed from the paranoid, disturbed man that had just come from walking the streets of downtown Los Angeles to the charming, erudite brilliant, Juilliard-trained musician.[5]

⑤ Music is medicine. Music changes us. And for Nathaniel, music is sanity. Because music allow him to take his thoughts and delusions and shape them through his imagination and his creativity into reality. And that is an escape from his tormented state. And I understood that this was the very essence of art. This was the very reason why we made music that we take something that exists within all of us at our very fundamental core, our emotions, and through our artistic lens, through our creativity, we're able to shape those emotions into reality. And the reality of that expression reaches all of us and moves us, inspires and unites us. And for Nathaniel, music brought him back into a fold of friends. The redemptive power of music brought him back into a family of musicians that understood him, that recognized his talents and respected his. And I will always make music with Nathaniel, whether we're at Walt Disney Concert Hall or on Skid Row, because he reminds me why I became a musician.[6] Thank you.

Notes on the text

(1) And I'm telling a story that many of you know, because Steve's columns became the basis for a book, which was turned into a movie with Robert Downey Jr. acting as Steve Lopez, and Jamie Foxx as Nathaniel Anthony Ayers, the Juilliard-trained double bassist whose promising career was cut short by a tragic affliction with paranoid schizophrenia.

我现在要讲的这个故事你们很多人已经知道了，因为史蒂夫的专栏后来成了一本书的基础，然后又被拍成电影，其中罗伯特·唐尼扮演史蒂夫·洛佩兹，杰米·福克斯扮演了纳撒尼尔·安东尼·艾耶尔。史蒂夫原本是茱莉亚音乐学院培训的双重贝斯手，不料他的职业生涯却因为患上了偏执型精神分裂症而不幸中断。

(2) <u>He was speaking in a very jovial and gregarious way about Yo-Yo Ma and Hillary Clinton and how the Dodgers were never going to make the World Series, all because of the treacherous first violin passage work in the last movement of Beethoven's Fourth Symphony.</u>

他的说话方式让人很愉快，他提到了马友友和希拉里·克林顿；道奇队不可能进入世界联赛。而这都是最后一刻贝多芬第四交响乐中开始的那段变幻莫测的小提琴演奏的作用。

(3) <u>But as a result now, he is prone to these schizophrenic episodes, the worst of which can manifest themselves as him exploding and then disappearing for days, wandering the streets of Skid Row, exposed to its horrors, with the torment of his own mind unleashed upon him.</u>

结果呢，他的精神分裂症现在变得更容易发作，最糟糕的表现是他发作后会消失几天，在贫民区的大街上流浪，暴露着内心的恐惧，让心灵煎熬释放在身上。

(4) <u>And in a miracle, he lifted his own violin, and he started playing, by ear, certain snippets of violin concertos which he then asked me to complete — Mendelssohn, Tchaikovsky, Sibelius. And we started talking about music, from Bach too Beethoven and Brahms, Bruckner all the B's, from Bartak, all the way up to Esa-Pekka Salonen.</u>

神奇的是，他拿起了他的小提琴，他也跟着开始演奏小提琴协奏曲的某些片断，然后他又要我来完成，门德尔松，柴可夫斯基，西贝柳斯。于是我们开始谈论音乐：从巴赫到贝多芬、布拉姆斯、布鲁克纳，所有名字以B打头的人，从巴托克一直到艾沙·佩卡·萨洛宁。

注意口译中人名的译法。

(5) <u>And through playing music and talking about music, this man had transformed from the paranoid, disturbed man that had just come from walking the streets of downtown Los Angeles to the charming, erudite brilliant, Juilliard-trained musician.</u>

通过演奏音乐，谈论音乐，这个人从一个偏执、不安、刚才还在洛杉矶大街上晃悠的流浪汉变成了一个迷人、博学、优秀的受过茱莉亚音乐学院教育的音乐家。

(6) <u>The redemptive power of music brought him back into a family of musicians that understood him, that recognized his talents and respected his. And I will always make music with Nathaniel, whether we're at Walt Disney Concert Hall or on Skid Row, because he reminds me why I became a musician.</u>

音乐的挽救力将他带回到音乐的大家庭，在这里人们理解他、承认他的天赋、尊重他。而我会永远为他创造音乐，无论是在迪士尼的音乐厅，还是在贫民区的大街上，因为他提醒着我为什么我要做音乐家。

2. Please interpret the following passage by using the techniques illustrated above. Please pay attention to the underlined sentences as they require special treatment during interpreting.

Emma Watson's Speech at the UN Headquarters

① Today we are launching a campaign called "He For She." I am reaching out to you because I need your help. We want to end gender inequality — and to do that we need everyone to be involved.

② This is the first campaign of its kind at the UN: <u>we want to try and galvanize as many men and boys as possible to be advocates for gender equality.</u> And we don't just want to talk about it, but make sure it is tangible.

③ I was appointed six months ago and the more I have spoken about feminism the more I have realized that fighting for women's rights has too often become synonymous with man-hating. If there is one thing I know for certain, it is that this has to stop.

④ For the record, feminism by definition is: "The belief that men and women should have equal rights and opportunities. It is the theory of the political, economic and social equality of the sexes."

⑤ I started questioning gender-based assumptions when at eight I was confused at being called "bossy," because I wanted to direct the plays we would put on for our parents — but the boys were not.

⑥ When at 14 I started being sexualized by certain elements of the press. When at 15 my girlfriends started dropping out of their sports teams because they didn't want to appear "muscly." When at 18 my male friends were unable to express their feelings. I decided I was a feminist and this seemed uncomplicated to me. But my recent research has shown me that feminism has become an unpopular word.

⑦ <u>Apparently I am among the ranks of women whose expressions are seen as too strong, too aggressive, isolating, anti-men and, unattractive.</u>

⑧ Why is the word such an uncomfortable one?

⑨ I am from Britain and think it is right that as a woman I am paid the same as my male counterparts. I think it is right that I should be able to make decisions about my own body. I think it is right that women be involved on my behalf in the policies and decision-making of my country. I think it is right that socially I am afforded the same respect as men. But sadly I can say that there is no one country in the world where all women can expect to receive these rights. No country in the world can yet say they have achieved gender equality.

⑩ These rights I consider to be human rights but I am one of the lucky ones. My life is a sheer privilege because my parents didn't love me less because I was born a daughter. My school did not limit me because I was a girl. <u>My mentors didn't assume I would go less far because I might give birth to a child one day.</u> These influencers were the gender equality ambassadors that made who I am today. They may not know it, but they are the inadvertent feminists who are. And we need more of those. And if you still hate the word — it is not the word that is important but the idea and the ambition behind it. Because not all women have been afforded the same rights that I have. In fact, statistically, very few have been.

⑪ In 1997, Hilary Clinton made a famous speech in Beijing about women's rights. Sadly many of the things she wanted to change are still a reality today. But what stood out for me the most was that only 30 per cent of her audience were male. How can we affect change in the world when only half of it is invited or feel welcome to participate in the conversation?

⑫ Men — I would like to take this opportunity to extend your formal invitation. Gender equality is your issue too.

Notes on the text

(1) We want to try and galvanize as many men and boys as possible to be advocates for gender equality.

我们想要努力鼓励男性们成为性别平等的倡议者。

(2) Apparently I am among the ranks of women whose expressions are seen as too strong, too aggressive, isolating, anti-men and, unattractive.

显然，我跻身于强烈表达自身想法的女性之间了，被认为太嚣张了，被认为是孤立的，仇视男性，甚至没有吸引力。

(3) My mentors didn't assume I would go less far because I might give birth to a child one day.

我的导师没有因为我有一天可能会生孩子而认为我没有多大发展。

12.2.4 篇章口译[Passage Practice (C to E)]

1. Please interpret the following passage by using the techniques illustrated above. Please pay attention to the underlined sentences as they require special treatment during interpreting.

用班卓琴来改善中美关系
阿比盖尔·沃什伯恩

① 如果我本科刚毕业时你在佛蒙特州议会大楼里遇到我，那时我还正在参加活动议案通过者培训；如果你同时问我，你的人生理想是什么，我会告诉你我刚通过了汉语水平考试而且我准备去北京进修法律，我要自上而下地修订政策，并改革司法系统，以改善中美关系。我是有个计划，但我没想到它会和班卓琴扯上什么关系。

② 我真没想到它将在某个晚上对我造成如此巨大的影响，当时我正参加一个派对，我听见从房间角落的录音机传来的声音。那是多克·沃森弹唱的《林荫》，"树林荫荫啊，我的小爱人，树林荫荫啊，我的小亲亲，树林荫荫啊，我的小爱人，让我们一起回哈兰。"那声音真是太美了，多克的嗓音和荡漾的班卓琴声。在完全彻底沉迷于悠久厚重的中国历史与文化这么久以后，我听到了这地道的美国风格，同时也是地道的一流音乐，这对我实在是一种解脱。这时候，我知道自己肯定会带着班卓琴去中国。在出发去中国的法学院之前，我买了个班卓琴，把它扔进我的红色小皮卡里，然后我一路开到了阿巴拉契

亚。我在途中也学了一堆美风老歌。最后我来到了肯塔基的国际蓝草音乐联盟大会。一天晚上，我坐在走廊里，几个姑娘走过来问我："嘿，来个小合奏呗？"我说："成啊！"然后我拿起班卓琴，非常紧张地和她们合奏了四首歌。然后一个唱片公司的管理人员走了过来，邀请我去田纳西的纳什维尔录专辑。

③ 八年过去了，我没去中国当律师。事实上，我去了纳什维尔。几个月之后我就开始自己写歌。第一首是用英文写的，第二首是中文。"门外有个世界，心中有个声音，四方等你来啊，远行吧我的姑娘，去远行，去追逐你的梦……"距离肯塔基那改变命运的一夜的确已经过去八年了。这期间我参加过数以千计的表演。我和不计其数的出色音乐人合作过，他们来自世界的各个地方。我感受到了音乐的力量。我感受到了音乐能联通不同文化的力量。

④ 我是在东弗吉尼亚一个蓝草音乐节的舞台上意识到的。当我的视线越过草坪上那堆密密麻麻的躺椅时，我突然想起了一段中文歌。"太阳出来了喽喂，喜洋洋喽，嘟喽！"大家都睁大了眼睛，好像眼珠子要掉出来似的。他们像是在问："她发什么神经呢？"表演后他们来找我，带着他们的故事。他们跑过来告诉我："你知道吗，我婶婶的姐姐的保姆家的狗的小鸡去过中国，还收养了一个小女孩。"我要跟你说的是：大家都是有故事的人，真是太难以置信了。

⑤ 后来我去了中国，我站在一个大学的舞台上，我又突然唱起了中文歌，然后每个人都跟我一起唱，他们跟我一起大吼，对着我这个长头发拿着乐器的普通女孩。这个女孩唱着他们的音乐，这时候我意识到更重要的是音乐能够联通心灵。有一次我去四川，在地震灾后的临时小学里给孩子们唱歌。然后一个小女孩走过来说："王大姐，可以给你唱一下我妈妈教我的歌曲吗？"我坐下来，她坐在我膝盖上，她开始唱。我感到了她身体的温度，我看到了眼泪从她绯红的脸颊滚落下来，我也哭了起来，她眼中闪烁的光是我愿意相伴一生的东西。在那一刻，我们不是美国人，也不是中国人，我们只是简单的人，静静地坐在将我们心灵带到一起的光里。我真想和你们所有人一起去那片光里看一看。我知道中美关系不再需要一个律师了。谢谢。

Notes on the text

(1) 在完全彻底沉迷于悠久厚重的中国历史与文化这么久以后，我听到了这地道的美国风格，同时也是地道的一流音乐，这对我实在是一种解脱。这时候，我知道自己肯定会带着班卓琴去中国。

And after being totally and completely obsessed with the mammoth richness and history of Chinese culture, it was like this total relief to hear something so truly American and so truly awesome. I knew I had to take a banjo with me to China.

(2) 距离肯塔基那改变命运的一夜的确已经过去八年了。这期间我参加过数以千计的表演。我和不计其数的出色音乐人合作过，他们来自世界的各个地方。我感受到了音乐的力量。我感受到了音乐能联通不同文化的力量。

It's really been eight years since that fates night in Kentucky. And I've played thousands of shows. And I've collaborated with so many incredible, inspirational musicians around the world. And I see the power of music. I see the power of music to connect cultures.

(3) 后来我去了中国，我站在一个大学的舞台上，我又突然唱起了中文歌，然后每个人都跟我一起唱，他们跟我一起大吼，对着我这个长头发拿着乐器的普通女孩。这个女孩唱着他们的音乐，这时候我意识到更重要的是音乐能够联通心灵。

And then I go to China and I stand on a stage at a university and I burst out into a song in Chinese and everybody sings along and they roar with delight at this girl with the hair and the instrument, and she's singing their music. And I see, even more importantly, the power of music to connect hearts.

(4) 在那一刻，我们不是美国人，也不是中国人，我们只是简单的人，静静地坐在将我们心灵带到一起的光里。我真想和你们所有人一起去那片光里看一看。

And in that moment, we weren't our American selves, we weren't our Chinese selves, we were just mortals sitting together in that light that keeps us here. I want to dwell in that light with you and with everyone.

2. Please interpret the following passage by using the techniques illustrated above. Please pay attention to the underlined sentences as they require special treatment during interpreting.

斯蒂夫·乔布斯在斯坦福大学毕业典礼上的演讲

① 在十七岁那年，我真的上了大学。但是我很愚蠢地选择了一个几乎和斯坦福大学一样昂贵的学校，我的养父母是工人，他们几乎把所有的积蓄都花在了我的学费上。六个月后，我已经看不到其中的价值所在。我不知道我想做什么，也不知道大学能帮我找到怎样的答案，而我却几乎花光了养父母一生的积蓄。所以我决定退学，我觉得这是个正确的决定。不可否认，我当时确实非常害怕，但是现在回头看看，那的确是我这一生中最棒的决定。在我决定退学的那一刻，我终于可以不必去读那些毫无兴趣的课程了，可以去学那些看起来有点意思的课程。

② 但这并不怎么浪漫。由于没有宿舍可住，我只能睡在朋友房间的地板上；为了有钱填饱肚子，我去捡5美分的可乐瓶子来卖；在星期天的晚上，我要走七英里的路，穿过这个城市到印度教克利须那派教堂，只是为了能吃上饭——这个星期唯一一顿好点的饭。但我喜欢这样，我跟随好奇心和直觉所做的事，后来被证明基本都是极其珍贵的经验。我举几个例子：那时候，里德大学提供了全美国最好的书法教育。整个校园里的每一张海报、每一个抽屉上的标签，都是漂亮的手写体。由于已经退学，不用再去上那些常规的课程，于是我选择了一个书法班，想学学怎么写出一手漂亮字。在这个班上，我学习了各种衬线和无衬线字体，如何改变不同字体组合之间的字间距，以及如何做出漂亮的版式。那是一种科学永远无法捕捉的充满美感、历史感和艺术感的微妙，我发现这太有意思了。

③ 当时，我压根儿没想到这些知识会在我的生命中有什么实际运用价值；但是8年之后，当我们设计第一款苹果电脑的时候，这些东西全派上了用场。我把它们全部设计进了苹果电脑，这是第一台可以排出好看版式的电脑。如果当时我在大学里没有旁听这门课程的话，苹果电脑就不会提供各种字体和等间距字体。自从视窗系统抄袭了苹果电脑以后，所有的个人电脑都有了这些东西。

④ 如果我没有退学，我就不会去书法班旁听，而今天的个人电脑大概也就不会有出色的版式功能。

⑤ 当然，在我念大学那会儿，不可能有先见之明，把那些生命中的点点滴滴都串起来；但10年之后再回头看，生命的轨迹变得非常清楚。再强调一次，你不可能充满预见地将生命的点滴串联起来。只有在你回头看的时候，你才会发现这些点点滴滴之间的联系。所以，你要坚信，你现在所经历的，将在你未来的生命中串联起来。你不得不相信某些东西，你的直觉、命运、生活、因缘际会……正是这种信仰让我没有失去希望，它使我的人生变得与众不同。

Notes on the text

(1) 我跟随好奇心和直觉所做的事，后来被证明基本都是极其珍贵的经验。

And much of what I stumbled into by following my curiosity and intuition turned out to be priceless later on.

(2) 那是一种科学永远无法捕捉的充满美感、历史感和艺术感的微妙，我发现这太有意思了。

It was beautiful, historical, artistically subtle in a way that science can't capture, and I found it fascinating.

(3) 你不得不相信某些东西，你的直觉、命运、生活、因缘际会……正是这种信仰让我没有失去希望，它使我的人生变得与众不同。

You have to trust in something — your gut, destiny, life, karma, whatever — because believing that the dots will connect down the road will give you the confidence to follow your heart, even when it leads you off the well-worn path, and that will make all the difference.

12.3　参考译文(Reference Version)

12.3.1　单句口译(Sentence Practice)

Please interpret the following sentences by using the techniques illustrated above. You may interpret to your partner first and then he/she comments on your performance.

(1) 国际贸易和对外投资的增长需要懂得外语和了解跨文化交流技巧的高层次人才。

(2) 跨文化交际的语言文化差异主要在语义、语用和体态语的差异上。

(3) 天下一家是一句不错的小谚语，可它却有实现地球村的严肃愿景。

(4) 现代图书馆是跨文化交流的先进媒介，可以使不同特色的文化在极大超越以往的程度上得以交流，从而使文化传播有了空前的广度与深度。

(5) 各种文化都喜欢美，无论是非洲人、亚洲人还是欧洲人，都认同一个漂亮婴儿、美女或帅哥。

(6) More than just a trade route, the Silk Road once played a great role in promoting friendly relations and economic and cultural exchanges between China and Asia, European and African countries.

(7) All cultures cherish families and punish crime, and define crime in fairly similar ways.

(8) Through international cultural exchange, China enriches its own culture and contributes to the development of art and culture around the world.

(9) There are many benefits to studying abroad: you will acquire cross-cultural experience, gain new perspectives on your chosen field of study, and make many new friends.

(10) We all react to sounds, sensations, and situations differently because of our personal experiences, cultural differences, and emotional associations.

12.3.2 段落口译(Paragraph Practice)

1. Vocabulary Work: Study the following words and phrases and translate them into the target language.

allure	医疗保健系统
refugee crisis	非常理想的目的地
a big impact	高净值
around the corner	烛光晚餐
besot	失控
be in good company	黑市

2. Please interpret the following paragraphs by using the techniques illustrated above.

(1) The Chinese Peasants and Workers Democratic Party will propose the inclusion of tai chi on the UNESCO World Intangible Cultural Heritage List at the annual Two Sessions, in an effort to protect and promote the traditional sport. As an internal martial art practiced both for self-defense and health, tai chi has spread to more than 150 countries and regions, being adopted by over 300 million practitioners. Despite its popularity, research on tai chi is scarce, and its promotion relies primarily on non-governmental forces. Though tai chi is widely recognized as a symbol of Chinese culture, and was listed as an intangible cultural heritage by Chinese authorities in 2006, its protection and promotion still lag behind foreign athletic practices like yoga, Thepaper.cn reported. "Yoga was listed as a UNESCO intangible cultural heritage in

2016, a status that helps to protect the culture of yoga. Chinese authorities should recommend tai chi to UNESCO as soon as possible, as surrounding countries like Japan and South Korea are also keen on the martial art, and may claim it as their own before China makes the move," read an announcement from CPWDP.

(2) China has been campaigning for the inclusion of tai chi on the UNESCO list since 2008. However, due to UNESCO's strict criteria for intangible cultural heritage evaluation, the application is still pending as of press time. "The biggest problem with Tai Ch's inclusion on the UNESCO list is the lack of accurate translations of tai chi theories and philosophy. For instance, the tai chi theory that man is an integral part of nature is hard even for Chinese practitioners to understand, let alone foreign experts," Yan Shuangjun, a tai chi expert, told Xinhua News Agency in 2014. CPWDP is now calling for the establishment of a national tai chi center, as well as the introduction of martial arts to universities and medical research facilities. Authorities hope these changes can increase academic research on Tai Chi. Founded in Shanghai in August 1930, the CPWDP now has more than 144 000 members, including many leading intellectuals in the fields of medicine and healthcare.

(3) 传统上，美国和英国吸引的富有移民人数最多。不过近年来澳大利亚的吸引力一直在增强，特别是对中国和印度的富人。新世界财富公司表示，澳大利亚的医疗保健系统评价很高，超越了美国和英国，移民的富豪们也被充满阳光的澳洲生活方式所吸引。澳大利亚在地理上与中东的战乱和欧洲的难民危机隔绝，被认为是生活和育儿的安全地方。研究人员称，商业上的考虑也是其中一个因素：对于中国、韩国、新加坡和印度等新兴亚洲国家的人而言，澳大利亚是做生意的好基地。美国仍然被视为非常理想的移民目的地，去年吸引了一万富豪移民。新世界财富公司预计移民美国的需求将会继续保持在高位。新世界财富公司的研究部主管安德鲁·阿莫伊尔斯说："我们认为美国的新领导人对移民趋势不会产生太大影响。2017年我们预计还将有大批高净值个人移民美国。"加拿大也迎来了8000个富豪新移民。富裕的中国公民选择移居温哥华，而有钱的欧洲人则移居多伦多和蒙特利尔。

(4) 不管你喜不喜欢，又一个情人节马上就要到了。你也许在挑选卡片并策划烛光晚餐，而此时来自世界各地的其他情侣正在做着不同的准备。比如，在日本，女士根本不会收到男士的礼物，她们是送礼物的一方。不过，一个月之后，也就是3月14日，男士可以在"白色情人节"回礼。在南非，女士写下自己深爱的人的名字并将其缝在袖子上；而在德国，猪被视为欲望的象征，猪的形象经常会出现在卡片和礼物上。该图案通常和四叶草等其他幸运象征一起出现。在芬兰和爱沙尼亚，2月14日实际上是朋友节——人们在这一天庆祝非情侣的亲密关系。法国情人节的一项传统因为难以控制而被政府禁止。单身男女分别聚在面对面的房子里互相喊话配对。对伴侣不满意的男士可以另择佳人，而没有配对成功的女士会聚在一起烧掉男士的照片。如果你想完全逃避情人节，那么你可以在沙特阿拉伯找到志同道合的人，在那里情人节是严令禁止的。该国甚至存在红玫瑰的黑市交易。

12.3.3 篇章口译[Passage Practice (E to C)]

1. Please interpret the following passage by using the techniques illustrated above. Please pay attention to the underlined sentences as they require special treatment during interpreting.

音乐是良药 (节选)
罗伯特·古普塔

① 有一天，洛杉矶时报的专栏作家史蒂夫·洛佩兹走在洛杉矶大街上，听到一曲美妙的乐曲。音乐是从一个男人，一个非裔男人，一个颇有魅力、粗犷的流浪汉用一把只剩下两根弦的小提琴在演奏。我现在要讲的这个故事你们很多人已经知道了，因为史蒂夫的专栏后来成了一本书的基础，然后又被拍成电影，其中罗伯特·唐尼扮演史蒂夫·洛佩兹，杰米·福克斯扮演了纳撒尼尔·安东尼·艾耶尔，他原本是茱莉亚音乐学院培训的双重贝斯手，不料他的职业生涯却因为患上了偏执型精神分裂症而不幸中断。纳撒尼尔从茱莉亚音乐学院辍学，他完全崩溃了，三十年后的他流落在洛杉矶贫民区的大街上无家可归。

② 我鼓励大家都去看看史蒂夫的书，或者看看电影。不光是去理解这两个男人之间建立的美好纽带，也看看音乐是如何帮助建立这种纽带的，而那是最终改变纳撒尼尔流浪生活的最有用的工具。我和艾耶尔先生在2008年相见，那是两年前在迪士尼音乐厅。他才听了贝多芬第一、第四交响乐后，来到后台进行自我介绍。他的说话方式让人很愉快，他提到了马友友和希拉里·克林顿；道奇队不可能进入世界联赛。而这都是最后一刻贝多芬第四交响乐中开始的那段变幻莫测的小提琴演奏的作用。我们谈了一会儿音乐。几天后我收到了史蒂夫的邮件，告诉我纳撒尼尔有兴趣跟我学小提琴。

③ 现在我应该提一下的是纳撒尼尔拒绝治疗，因为当初他接受的是电击疗法，用的是镇静剂和手铐，那些伤疤从此留在了他的生活中。结果呢，他的精神分裂症现在变得更容易发作，最糟糕的表现是他发作后会消失几天，在贫民区的大街上流浪，暴露着内心的恐惧，让心灵煎熬释放在身上。纳撒尼尔当初就是处在这样的一种状态下，我们在迪士尼音乐厅开始上第一课的时候，他的目光中夹杂这狂躁，他是一个迷失了方向的人。他提到了无形的恶魔和烟雾，有人怎样在他睡觉时给他下毒。我感到害怕，不是为我自己的安全担心，而是害怕我会失去他，我害怕如果我开始讲音阶和琶音和其他形式的精彩的说教式的小提琴教学法，他又会沉浸在他的某一种状态中，而我会毁了他和小提琴建立起来的关系。

④ 于是，我开始拉琴。我演奏了贝多芬小提琴协奏曲的第一乐章。当我演奏的时候，我知道纳撒尼尔的眼睛里有一种奥妙的变化，好像抓住了什么隐形的药，像是经历了化学反应，而我的演奏就是催化剂，他的狂躁愤怒也转化成理解、好奇和优雅。神奇的是，他拿起了他的小提琴，他也跟着开始演奏小提琴协奏曲的某些片断，然后他又要我来完成，门德尔松，柴可夫斯基，西贝柳斯。于是我们开始谈论音乐：从巴赫到贝多芬、布

拉姆斯、布鲁克纳，所有名字以B打头的人，从巴托克一直到艾沙·佩卡·萨洛宁。我了解到他不但是一本音乐百科全书，而且他能将这些音乐跟他个人的感受联系起来。他讲到那些东西时充满了激情和对音乐深刻的理解，仿佛是我与我在洛杉矶交响乐团的同事们之间交流时一样。通过演奏音乐，谈论音乐，这个人从一个偏执、不安、刚才还在洛杉矶大街上晃悠的流浪汉变成了一个迷人、博学、优秀的受过茱莉亚音乐学院教育的音乐家。

⑤ 音乐是良药，音乐改变着我们。对纳撒尼尔来说，音乐帮助他开启心智，因为音乐可以帮他将他的思维、妄想转换成形，通过他的想象力和创造力变成现实。正是这个，帮助他从煎熬中解脱出来。而我知道这就是艺术的真髓。这就是我们创造音乐的原因，我们用我们每个人都拥有的一种内在、我们的最根本的核心、我们的感情，通过我们的艺术的镜头，通过我们的创造力，将我们的情感塑造成现实。而这种现实的表达传递给我们所有的人，感动我们、启迪我们、团结我们。而对纳撒尼尔来说，音乐把他带回到一群朋友中。音乐的挽救力将他带回到音乐的大家庭，在这里人们理解他、承认他的天赋、尊重他。而我会永远为他创造音乐，无论是在迪士尼的音乐厅，还是在贫民区的大街上，因为他提醒着我为什么我要做音乐家。谢谢。

2. Please interpret the following passage by using the techniques illustrated above. Please pay attention to the underlined sentences as they require special treatment during interpreting.

Emma Watson's Speech at the UN Headquarters

① 今天，我们要开展一次叫做"He For She"运动的活动。在得到你们的帮助和支持之前，我想先说说我的想法。我们想要结束性别歧视，为了实现这个目标，我们需要每个人的努力。

② 这是在联合国首次进行的类似的活动。我们想要努力鼓励男性们去改变性别歧视，不是停留在说说而已。我们想让它产生实际效果。

③ 6个月前，我被任命为联合国妇女署亲善大使。我对女权主义说得越多，越发现为妇女权利的斗争往往成为仇恨男人的代名词。这是必须应该停止的。

④ 女权主义，顾名思义，就是男性和女性应该享有同样的权利和机会。它是关于政治、经济和社会等方面性别平等的理论。我从很久之前就开始质疑基于性别歧视的假设。

⑤ 我8岁的时候，因为想要自己导演一次为父母表演的节目，结果被说是霸道，但是男生却不会被这么说，我对此感到很困惑。

⑥ 14岁的时候，我开始被媒体的特定元素性别化；15岁时，我的女性朋友们放弃了她们喜爱的球队，只因为她们不想看起来肌肉发达；18岁的时候，我决定成为一个女性主义者时，我的男性朋友们拒绝表达他们的感受。这对我而言，非常简单。但通过我最近的研究发现，女性主义却是一个非常不被接受的词语。很多女性也不愿意被定义为女权主义者。

⑦ 显然，我跻身于强烈表达自身想法的女性之间了，被认为"太嚣张了"，被认为

是孤立的，仇视男性，甚至没有吸引力。

⑧ 为什么这个词已变得那么令人不爽？

⑨ 我来自英国，我认为和男同事得到平等对待是正确的；我认为能够为自己的身体做决定是正确的；我认为(被掌声打断)……我认为女性能够代表我的利益、参与制定能影响到我的决策和决定是正确的。我认为，在社会层面上我能和男性们同样被尊重是正确的。但遗憾的是，我可以说，世界上没有一个国家的所有女性都可以指望得到这些权利。世界上也没有一个国家能说，他们已经实现了性别平等。

⑩ 这些权利，我认为是人权。但我是一个幸运的人。我的生命纯粹是一种特权，因为我的父母没有因为我是女孩儿而不爱我，我的学校没有因为我是一个女孩儿而限制我，我的导师没有因为我有一天可能会生孩子而认为我没有多大发展。他们是性别平等的大使，让我成为了今天的我。他们也许不知道，但他们无意间成为了改变着现今世界的女权主义者。我们需要更多的人参与其中。如果你还恨这个词，你要意识到这个词本身并不重要。它背后的思想更为重要。因为不是所有的女性都能享受到和我同样的权利。事实上，据统计，很少女性享有这样的权利。

⑪ 1997年，希拉里·克林顿在北京做了一场关于妇女权利的著名演讲。不幸的是，她想改变的许多事情在今天仍然存在着。站在我面前的听众中，男性还不到30%。如果只有那么少的男性愿意参与到我们的交流中，我们还谈何去改变世界？

⑫ 男性朋友们，我想借此机会向你们发出正式邀请。性别平等也是你们应该关心的议题。

■ 12.3.4　篇章口译[Passage Practice (C to E)]

1. Please interpret the following passage by using the techniques illustrated above. Please pay attention to the underlined sentences as they require special treatment during interpreting.

To Improve U.S.-China Relation with a Banjo
Abigail Washburn

① If you had caught me straight out of college in the halls of the Vermont State House where I was a lobbyist in training and asked me what I was going to do with my life, I would have told you that I'd just passed the Hanyu Shuiping Kaoshi, (the Chinese equivalency exam), and I was going to go study law in Beijing, and I was going to improve U.S.-China relations through top-down policy changes and judicial system reforms. I had a plan, and I never ever thought it would have anything to do with the banjo.

② Little did I know what a huge impact it would have on me one night, when I was at a party and I heard a sound coming out of a record player in the corner of room. And it was Doc Watson singing and playing "Shady Grove", "Shady Grove, my little love, Shady Grove, my darling, Shady Grove, my little love, Going back to Harlan." That sound was just so beautiful, the sound of Doc's voice and the rippling groove of banjo. And after being totally and completely obsessed with the mammoth richness and history of Chinese culture, it was like this total relief to hear something so truly American and so truly awesome. I knew I had to take a banjo with me to China. So before going to law school in China I bought a banjo, I threw it in my little red truck and I traveled down through Appalachia and I learned a bunch of old American songs, and I ended up in Kentucky at the International Bluegrass Music Association Convention. And I was sitting in a hallway one night and a couple girls came up to me. And they said, "Hey, do you want to jam?" And I was like, "Sure." So I picked up my banjo and I nervously played four songs that I actually knew with them. And a record executive walked up to me and invited me to Nashville, Tennessee to make a record.

③ It's been eight years, and I can tell you that I didn't go to China to become a lawyer. In fact, I went to Nashville. And after a few months I was writing songs. And the first song I wrote was in English, and the second one was in Chinese. "Outside your door the world is waiting." "Inside your heart a voice is calling." The four corners of the world are watching." "So travel daughter, travel." "Go get it, girl." It's really been eight years since that fates night in Kentucky. And I've played thousands of shows. And I've collaborated with so many incredible, inspirational musicians around the world. And I see the power of music. I see the power of music to connect cultures.

④ I see it when I stand on a stage in a bluegrass festival in east Virginia and I look out at the sea of lawn chairs and I burst out into a song in Chinese. And everybody's eyes just pop wide open like it's going to fall out of their heads. And they're like, "what's that girl doing?" And then they come to me after the show and they all have a story. They all come up and they're like, "You know, my aunt's sister's babysitter's dog's chicken went to China and adopted a girl." And I tell you what, it like everybody's got a story. It's just incredible.

⑤ And then I go to China and I stand on a stage at a university and I burst out into a song in Chinese and everybody sings along and they roar with delight at this girl with the hair and the instrument, and she's singing their music. And I see, even more importantly, the power of music to connect hearts. Like the time I was in Sichuan Province and I was singing for kids in relocation schools in the earthquake disaster zone. And this little girl comes up to me, Big sister Wong, Washburn, Wong, same difference. "Big sister Wong, can I sing you a song that my mom sang for me before she was swallowed in the earthquake?" And I sat down, she sat on my lap. She started singing her song. And the warmth of her body and the tears rolling down her rosy cheeks, and I started to cry. And the light that shone off of her eyes was place I could have stayed forever. And in that moment, we weren't our American selves, we weren't our Chinese selves, we were just mortals sitting together in that light that keeps us here. I want to dwell in that light with you and with everyone. And I know U.S.—China relations doesn't need another lawyer. Thank you.

2. Please interpret the following passage by using the techniques illustrated above. Please pay attention to the underlined sentences as they require special treatment during interpreting.

Steve Jobs' Legendary Speech at Stanford University

① And seventeen years later, I did go to college, but I naively chose a college that was almost as expensive as Stanford and all of my working-class parents' savings were being spent on my college tuition. After six months, I couldn't see the value in it. I had no idea what I wanted to do with my life, and no idea of how college was going to help me figure it out, and here I was, spending all the money my parents had saved their entire life. So I decided to drop out and trust that it would all work out OK. It was pretty scary at the time, but looking back, it was one of the best decisions I ever made. The minute I dropped out, I could stop taking the required classes that didn't interest me and begin dropping in on the ones that looked far more interesting.

② It wasn't all romantic. I didn't have a dorm room, so I slept on the floor in friends' rooms. I returned Coke bottles for the five-cent deposits to buy food with, and I would walk the seven miles across town every Sunday night to get one good meal a week at the Hare Krishna temple. I loved it. And much of what I stumbled into by following my curiosity and intuition turned out to be priceless later on. Let me give you one example. Reed College at that time offered perhaps the best calligraphy instruction in the country. Throughout the campus every poster, every label on every drawer was beautifully hand-calligraphed. Because I had dropped out and didn't have to take the normal classes, I decided to take a calligraphy class to learn how to do this. I learned about serif and sans-serif typefaces, about varying the amount of space between different letter combinations, about what makes great typography great. It was beautiful, historical, artistically subtle in a way that science can't capture, and I found it fascinating.

③ None of this had even a hope of any practical application in my life. But ten years later when we were designing the first Macintosh computer, it all came back to me, and we designed it all into the Mac. It was the first computer with beautiful typography. If I had never dropped in on that single course in college, the Mac would have never had multiple typefaces or proportionally spaced fonts, and since Windows just copied the Mac, it's likely that no personal computer would have them.

④ If I had never dropped out, I would have never dropped in on that calligraphy class and personal computers might not have the wonderful typography that they do.

⑤ Of course it was impossible to connect the dots looking forward when I was in college, but it was very, very clear looking backwards 10 years later. Again, you can't connect the dots looking forward. You can only connect them looking backwards, so you have to trust that the dots will somehow connect in your future. You have to trust in something — your gut, destiny, life, karma, whatever — because believing that the dots will connect down the road will give you the confidence to follow your heart, even when it leads you off the well-worn path, and that will make all the difference.

12.4　跨文化主题词汇汇总(Vocabulary Build-up)

exotic differences	外来差异
regional variations	地区差异
cultural diversity	文化差异
cultural barrier	文化障碍
official language	官方语言
non-verbal communication	非语言交际
play mahjong	打麻将
WeChat red envelope	微信红包
Spring Festival travel rush	春运
taboo	禁忌
get rid of the ill-fortune	去晦气
expat	侨民
asylum seeker	寻求庇护者
displaced people	流离失所者
country of origin	原住地
cultural diversification	文化多样性
cultural soft power	文化软实力
traditional cultural know-how	传统文化知识
international cultural trade	对外文化贸易
advance and enrich the fine cultural heritage of the nation	弘扬民族优秀文化
broad and profound	博大精深
folk culture	民间文化
traditional virtues	传统美德
cultural awareness	文化自觉
local conditions and customs	风土人情
cultural relics	文化遗迹
national pride	民族自豪
become increasingly prosperous	日益昌盛
realize national independence	实现民族独立
cultural reconstruction	文化重建
absorb what is advanced in other civilizations	吸收各国文明的先进成果
integration of cultural resources	文化资源整合
display one's vigor and vitality	展现生机和活力
major cultural industrial projects	重大文化产业项目

12.5　扩展练习(Enhancement Practice)

Making comments on a given topics.

Directions: Please read paragraph (1) and (2) carefully and then express your views on the given topics.

(1) Chinese rose with its strong resemblance means a lot in many traditional legends. Some people suggest taking it as the national flower, while others prefer pony. Which one do you think is the suitable choice?

　　Bearing a strong resemblance to other roses, yet with fewer thorns and larger petals, the plant originates from China, hence the name "Chinese rose". "Bloom or fade, the flower never cares about arrival of spring; Best peonies only appear in late spring and early summer, yet Chinese roses enjoy the four seasons with unceasing beauty," poet Su Shi from the Song Dynasties described the flower in his poem. Chinese people started to grow the rose about 2 000 years ago. In the Han Dynasty, Chinese roses were widely grown in royal gardens. And in the Tang Dynasty, the flowers found their way into most regions along the Yangtze River. Apart from being extracted to make perfume, the roots, leaves and flowers of Chinese roses are used in traditional Chinese medicine to cure menstruation disorders.

(2) Hollywood simply employs so many famous stars. But people believe that there are actually only 8 men in Hollywood because the handsome actors look so much alike each other. Do you agree or disagree?

　　Maybe there's a large cloning facility in the Hollywood Hills producing reliably compelling lead actors in gigantic spawning tanks. Because, honestly, this can't be nature's work. Do you think there's actually just a shortage of men so they're just using the same ones and hoping we won't notice? Or perhaps Hollywood simply only employs identical twins? Although triplets are acceptable too, clearly. Or are they just trying to make shape-shifters but they're not that advanced yet so they can only shapeshift ever so slightly? Whatever is going on though, they're clearly doing a sloppy job of keeping it secret. They didn't even bother giving these two different names! This is Chris Pine and Chris Hemsworth, but you can just call them The Chrises. We're on to you, Secret Hollywood Cloning Program. We're on to you.

12.6 延伸口译(Extended Interpreting)

习近平主席在塞尔维亚媒体发表署名文章

With a long history and a splendid culture, Serbia is an important country in Central and Eastern Europe (CEE) in general and the Balkans in particular. For centuries, Serbia has been a place where civilizations of the East and West meet, interact and together bring about major progress in human civilization. It is also on this land that the hard-working and brave Serbian people have left a heroic epic in their fight for national independence and freedom and written an inspiring chapter in pursuit of a happier life.

塞尔维亚是中东欧和巴尔干地区重要国家，拥有悠久历史和灿烂文化。千百年来，东西方文明在这里交融碰撞，激荡出人类文明发展的重要成果。在这一过程中，勤劳勇敢的塞尔维亚人民谱写了争取民族独立自由的英雄史诗和追求美好幸福生活的壮丽篇章。

In the 1940s, the Chinese and the Yugoslavians fought gallantly against Fascist aggression on the Eastern and Western fronts and went on to achieve national liberation and freedom. In the early 1950s, China and the Federal People's Republic of Yugoslavia established diplomatic relations, opening a new chapter of friendship and cooperation between the Chinese people and the Serbian people. The ancient Chinese philosopher Mencius said, one should befriend those with virtues. Over the past six decades and more, the profound friendship and special bond between our peoples have defied the passage of time and the long distance between us to become even stronger.

20世纪40年代，中国人民同南斯拉夫人民在东西方战场英勇抗击法西斯侵略，实现了民族解放和自由。50年代初，中国同南斯拉夫联邦人民共和国正式建交，掀开了中国人民同塞尔维亚人民友谊合作新的一页。中国古代思想家孟子说："友也者，友其德也。"60多年来，两国人民始终心手相连，彼此怀有特殊感情，跨越时空的真情厚谊历久弥新。

A Serbian proverb goes, "Prijatelj je plod vremena" (friends are the fruits of time). We will never forget this: Famous movies like Walter Defends Sarajevo and Bridge once inspired the patriotic ardor of many Chinese, and to this day, Bella ciao is still widely heard in China; and in the 1980s, when China was in a crucial period of reform and opening-up, the successful experience of the Serbian people served as valuable reference for China.

塞尔维亚有句俗语："朋友是时间的果实。"我们不会忘记，《瓦尔特保卫萨拉热窝》《桥》等著名影片曾经激发无数中国人的爱国热情，《啊，朋友再见》这首歌曲至今仍然在中国传唱。20世纪80年代，在中国实行改革开放政策的关键时期，塞尔维亚人民的成功实践和经验，为中国提供了宝贵借鉴。

Neither will we forget this: When the Chinese county of Wenchuan was hit by a massive earthquake in 2008, Serbia offered speedy assistance to China and provided a large amount of relief supplies to the people in the affected areas; and in September 2015, President Nikolic went to Beijing for the commemorative events marking the 70th anniversary of the victory of the Chinese People's War of Resistance against Japanese Aggression and the World Anti-Fascist War, sending a strong message of our two countries' commitment to upholding the post-war international order, safeguarding world peace and building a better future for mankind.

我们也不会忘记，2008年中国汶川发生特大地震灾害后，塞尔维亚第一时间向中国伸出援手，无私向灾区人民提供了大量救灾物资。2015年9月，尼科利奇总统赴北京出席中国人民抗日战争暨世界反法西斯战争胜利70周年纪念活动，更是发出了中塞两国携手维护战后国际秩序、捍卫世界和平、共建人类美好未来的最强音。

We will never forget that China-Serbia relations have been defined by mutual respect, mutual trust, mutual support and win-win cooperation. No matter how the international situation changes and how our countries develop and transform, we have always shown full understanding and respect for each other's choices of development path, given each other firm support on issues concerning core interests and major concerns, and remained committed to deepening our political trust and mutually beneficial cooperation.

我们更不会忘记，互尊互信、相互支持、合作共赢是中塞关系的真实写照。无论国际形势如何风云变幻、中塞两国各自如何发展变革，双方始终充分理解和尊重彼此选择的道路，坚定支持彼此核心利益和重大关切，致力于深化彼此政治互信和互利合作。

Today, our traditional friendship has gained fresh vitality, and the bilateral ties have grown in breadth and depth. In recent years, President Nikolic and I had a number of meetings and reached important agreement on consolidating traditional friendship, deepening political trust and advancing mutually beneficial cooperation. In 2009, our two countries established a strategic partnership, the first of its kind between a CEE country and China. In 2013, President Nikolic and I signed a joint statement on deepening China-Serbia strategic partnership, further enhancing the strategic significance of our relations.

当前，中塞传统友谊正在日益焕发出新的生机，两国关系的深度、广度不断提升。近年来，我同尼科利奇总统多次会晤，就巩固传统友谊、深化政治互信、推进互利合作达成重要共识。2009年，中塞建立战略伙伴关系，塞尔维亚成为第一个同中国建立战略伙伴关系的中东欧国家。2013年，我同尼科利奇总统一道签署《中塞关于深化战略伙伴关系的联合声明》，两国关系的战略重要性更加突出。

Both bilaterally and within the frameworks of the Belt and Road Initiative (the Initiative of the Silk Road Economic Belt and the 21st Century Maritime Silk Road) and China-CEEC cooperation, practical cooperation between our two countries is making breakthroughs and yielding more results than in other parts of Central and Eastern Europe. We have signed an MOU on jointly developing the Belt and Road. With the implementation of such major projects as the

Belgrade-Budapest Railway, the Mihajlo Pupin Bridge, the E763 Motorway, the expansion and upgrading of Kostolac Power Plant, and the acquisition of the Smederevo steel mill by Hebei Iron and Steel Group, our cooperation on major projects is making heartening and sweeping progress, delivering economic and social benefits and a positive impact on the entire Central and Eastern European region.

在双边关系、"一带一路"倡议、"16+1合作"等框架内，两国务实合作不断取得新突破，成果在中东欧地区最为突出。双方签署共同推进"一带一路"建设谅解备忘录。匈塞铁路、贝尔格莱德跨多瑙河大桥、E763高速公路、科斯托拉茨电站改扩建、河北钢铁集团收购塞尔维亚斯梅代雷沃钢厂等一批重大项目先后落地，形成了两国大项目合作整体推进的喜人局面，取得了良好的经济社会效益，在中东欧地区产生了积极影响。

There are closer exchanges between our peoples, sound cooperation in culture, education and science and technology, and regular inter-party and sub-national interactions. We have signed an agreement on setting up culture centers in each other's countries; the University of Belgrade and the University of Novi Sad have opened Confucius Institutes; the Chinese language is now taught on a pilot basis in more than 100 middle and primary schools in Serbia; and construction will soon start for the China Culture Center in Belgrade. All these represent new avenues of communication between our peoples.

两国人文交流日趋密切，文化、教育、科技等各领域合作良好，党际、地方交流频繁。双方签署了《关于互设文化中心的协议》，贝尔格莱德、诺维萨德大学已经开设孔子学院，塞尔维亚已经在全国100多所中小学启动汉语教学试点工作，贝尔格莱德中国文化中心即将启动建设，将为中塞两国人民心灵相通打开新渠道。

The Serbian people believe that "prvo skoci, pa reci hop" (walk the walk, then talk the talk) while the Chinese people believe that actions speak louder than words. China attaches great importance to its relations with Serbia and values the profound tradition of China-Serbia friendship. China is ready to tap the potential of win-win cooperation by utilizing our complementarity so as to achieve steady and sustained growth of our relations. The purpose of my upcoming visit to Serbia is to engage deeply and extensively with our Serbian friends to explore concrete actions that can bring our countries and peoples closer together and ensure a lasting friendship and true partnership.

塞尔维亚人讲："先跨越，再言语"，中国人常说"行胜于言"。中国高度重视发展同塞尔维亚的关系，珍视两国深厚的传统友谊，愿深入挖掘互利合作潜力，实现优势互补，推动两国关系行稳致远。我这次访问塞尔维亚，就是希望同塞方一道，通过深入交流和广泛协商，用实实在在的行动，把中塞两国和两国人民更加紧密联系在一起，做永远的朋友、真诚的伙伴。

We need to focus on the long term and always respect, trust and understand each other. We should firmly support each other on issues concerning our core interests and major concerns and work for a more strategic and comprehensive relationship. China respects the Serbian people's independent choice of development path as well as Serbia's sovereignty and territorial integrity, and understands Serbia's efforts toward EU membership.

我们要始终着眼长远，坚持相互尊重、相互信任、相互理解。双方要继续在涉及彼此核心利益和重大关切的问题上给予对方坚定的支持，不断提升两国关系的战略性和全面性。中国尊重塞尔维亚人民自己选择的发展道路，尊重塞尔维亚主权和领土完整，理解塞尔维亚致力于加入欧盟的努力。

We need to stay committed to pursuing win-win results and common development. China will share its development fruits and opportunities with Serbia, and work with Serbia to explore and strengthen alignment of our respective development strategies in a bid to expand converging interests, scale up trade and investment, especially in context of the Belt and Road Initiative and China-CEEC cooperation, further tap cooperation potential and facilitate greater cooperation on major projects in order to make China-Serbia cooperation a shining example for China-CEEC cooperation and bring real benefits to our two peoples.

我们要始终坚持互利共赢、携手共进、共同发展。中国愿同塞尔维亚分享发展成果和机遇，探索和加强双方发展战略对接，扩大利益融合，重点在"一带一路""16+1合作"等框架内扩大贸易和投资规模，不断挖掘合作潜力，打造更多大项目合作，使中塞合作成为"16+1合作"的标杆和典范，切实造福两国人民。

第13单元 口译应急技巧(Dealing with Unexpected Situations in Interpreting)

口译主题：食品安全

单元学习目的(Unit Goals) 💡

➢ 掌握本课程所讲授的口译应急技巧。
➢ 学习食品安全专题所涉及的常用词语和表达。

导入 (Lead -in)

1. 口译中遇到听不懂的词怎么办？
2. 如何翻译这句话：Things are different all the year round here.
3. 在口译现场如何纠正错误？
4. 口译表达中的应对技巧是什么？

13.1 技能讲解(Skill Introduction)

■ 13.1.1 口译中的常见困难(Common Difficulties in Interpreting)

(1) 现场口译时，译员会出现听不清或听不懂一个单词、句子或者一段话的情况。

(2) 初涉口译现场的译员因为经验不足、知识和翻译技能有限，再加上现场氛围造成的心理压力，也会出现听懂但是记不住或者翻译不出来的尴尬场面。

(3) 在某些专业翻译现场，由于没有足够的时间查字典或资料，也不能在现场仔细推敲或向有经验的同行求教，译员还有可能在翻译中出现差错。

▎13.1.2 可采用的补救策略(Recovery Tactics for Wrongly interpreting)

(1) 译前的准备工作需要做到全面而充分，针对翻译内容的语言和词汇收集相关资料。如果译员对翻译的领域不熟悉，还应该提前掌握该领域的专业术语，同时了解交流的双方人员概况、主题背景知识，会谈要点等相关内容。

(2) 译员在不能做到准确完整翻译时，可以通过比较模糊的表达，笼统概述。在听懂却一时找不到恰当的表达时，可以灵活处理，按照自己的理解进行解释，译出大意，传达主旨，保障交流的顺利进行。

(3) 对于源语中的人名、专业术语词汇，或不知道对应的译文表达时，可以模仿源语读音传递信息。有些缩略语在不清楚全称的情况下，可以重复缩略字母。

(4) 在遇到一时找不到适当的词语来表达说话者的意图时，译员可以利用填补词来增加思考的时间。

(5) 在讲话者言语啰唆、拖沓或重复、源语模糊、源语文化寓意微妙时，译员可以适当省略，对信息进行梳理重组，删繁就简，同义合并，合理简化，传达出原语的主要意思即可。

(6) 对于个别没有听懂的单词或片段，如果不影响对整体意思的理解，译员口译根据上下文对这些不太重要的内容进行合理猜测、调整和补充，使译文听上去即使不完全准确，也不至于出太大的问题。

▎13.1.3 口译表达中的应对技巧(Skills of Dealing with Unexpected Situation)

(1) 译员在遇到听不清或听不懂却需要翻译的重要词汇时，切忌慌乱或任意猜测，也不能删减遗漏，因为这样会给现场管理带来失误。此时，译员可以利用询问、手势、表情或眼神等间接方法示意讲话者做进一步解释，准确理解后再做出翻译。

(2) 译员可以依据语言语境和社交语境进行信息重构、联想和推断。社交语境中的各种信息可以为译员的联想和推断提供依据、开辟空间。

(3) 在某些专业性较强的口译现场，译员在遇到非常专业的词汇或技术术语时，可以借助现场实物、图片、参考手头文献或请教现场相关专家，沟通之后再做出翻译。

(4) 译员在遇到一些使用转化、派生、合成、压缩、混成和字母象形等方法构成的词汇时，可以利用平时掌握的构词法，合理猜测，大胆翻译。

(5) 口译现场遇到不能或不会准确表达的情况时，为了不影响信息的交流，可巧妙地绕开障碍，进行解释性翻译，这样的迂回释义口译帮助译员摆脱困境，顺利完成口译任务。

(6) 由于译员受到的现场关注多而产生的心理压力会导致胆怯情绪，影响口译的质量，这就要求译员能够调整心态，凭借翻译能力树立自信，做到临场不慌，从容应对。

13.2 主题口译(Topic Interpreting)

13.2.1 单句口译(Sentence Practice)

Please interpret the following sentences by using the techniques illustrated above. You may interpret to your partner first and then he/she comments on your performance.

(1) Many countries face challenges in terms of migration, poverty, food security, water management and climate change and we need to call attention to it.

(2) Coherent and holistic national food safety systems would not only improve health in countries with insecure food supplies — they would also help development and boost food trade.

(3) None of these problems — from food shortages and the spread of disease, to achieving sustainable economic growth — can be addressed without the use of science and technology.

(4) Experts recently met in Nairobi to discuss what to do about food shortages caused by drought.

(5) China produces more food for the same amount of water than other countries in Africa and Asia, researchers have found.

(6) 随着食品生产的工业化及其销售的全球化，努力确保食品安全的工作也同样具有国际意义。

(7) 在过去12个月期间，世界卫生组织和粮农组织平均每个月对高达200起食品安全事件展开调查，旨在确定其对公众健康造成的影响。

(8) 各级人民政府应当鼓励和支持改进食品加工工艺，促进提高食品卫生质量。

(9) 国务院卫生行政部门主管全国食品卫生监督管理工作。

(10) 食品卫生监督员必须秉公执法，忠于职守，不得利用职权谋取私利。

13.2.2 段落口译(Paragraph Practice)

1. Vocabulary Work: Study the following words and phrases and translate them into the target language.

遭到指责	specimen
泡沫聚苯乙烯	exclusivity
堕落	panelist
专家组长	sensory booth

2. Please interpret the following paragraphs by using the techniques illustrated above.

(1) 一回家就把从超市买的肉制品冷冻起来可以杀灭其中致命的病菌。冷冻的过程中可杀灭高达90%的弯曲杆菌细胞。弯曲杆菌病毒会诱发肠胃不适、呕吐、腹泻这些症状。11月17日，英国一位卫生部官员称，如果想要避免食物中毒，家庭在食用鸡肉前应该把鸡肉先冷冻再解冻。超市售卖的鸡肉当中，10只有6只都携带潜在的致命病菌——每年有50

万人因此染病。大约有100名受害者因呕吐和肠胃不适而丧命。几十年来，零售商和政府虽然知晓家禽农场里弯曲杆菌的猖獗，但依旧对此无能为力。然而，英国公共安全局的官员指出，在购买了鸡肉之后，顾客可以通过自行冷冻并在食用前完全解冻以免受其害。经过完全烹饪后的鸡肉已较为安全，但疾病仍然感染了很多人。英国每年在这一问题上的花费都接近900万英镑，同时也造成了大量的误工现象。对生肉进行冷冻的过程将食品的安全提升了一个层次。

(2) 研究发现，大多数英国人在烧烤时存在一些错误的卫生习惯，这些不卫生的习惯会给他们带来风险。因此，食品服务机构要求人们在烧烤之前先用烤箱预烹食物。食品标准机构表示，食物中毒在户外烹饪活动中确实存在，94%的人承认在烧烤时至少有一个坏习惯。在一项对2030名成年人的调查中，21%的人称曾因为食物而生病。近1/3的人承认没有检查食物是否烹饪得当。在晚夏周末休假的时候，人们喜欢到河岸边烧烤，在这个时候，当局会提前发布帮助人们避免食物中毒的提示。

(3) City'super, a supermarket chain in Hong Kong, has come under fire recently for selling what many have called "the most expensive strawberry in the world". Priced at HKD168 a piece, these Kotoka strawberries are apparently hand-picked to ensure that only the finest specimens hit the market, and flown in from Japan. They come individually packaged in plastic-covered paper boxes, complete with a straw nest and Styrofoam "sock", to emphasize their exclusivity. Photos of the ridiculously expensive "designer fruits" have been doing the rounds on social media in Hong Kong and the Chinese mainland, with most people declaring themselves appalled by the display of decadence.

(4) One of the world's leading chocolate brands is looking for a professional chocolate taster, who can provide honest feedback on their products. Mondelez, who own Cadbury's, Milka and Oreo, need someone they can trust to try out new products and tell them what they think. The job, with the official title of 'Chocolate and Cocoa Beverage Taster' requires seven and a half hours a week between Tuesdays and Thursdays from the lucky candidate. The professional sweet treat checker will be working with 11 panelists and a panel leader in the company's Reading office. The work will take place in sensory booths in the Consumer Science discussion rooms.

▌ 13.2.3 篇章口译[Passage Practice (E to C)]

1. Please interpret the following passage by using the techniques illustrated above. Please pay attention to the underlined sentences as they require special treatment during interpreting.

A Different Perspective on Genetic Modification (Excerpts)
Pamela Ronald

① I am a plant geneticist. I study genes that make plants resist disease and tolerant of stress.

In recent years, millions of people around the world have come to believe that there's something sinister about genetic modification. Today, I am going to provide a different perspective.

② First, let me introduce my husband, Raoul. He's an organic farmer. On his farm, he plants a variety of different crops. This is one of the many ecological farming practices he uses to keep his farms healthy. Imagine some of the reactions we get: Really? An organic farmer and a plant geneticist? Can you agree on anything?" Well, we can, it's not difficult, because we have the same goal. We want to help nourish the growing population without further destroying environment. I believe this is the greatest challenge of our time.

③ Now, genetic modification is not new; virtually everything we eat had been modified in some manner. Let me give you a few examples. On the left is an image of the ancient ancestor of modern corn. You see a single roll of grain that covered in a hard kits. Unless you have a hammer, teosinte isn't good for, making tortillas. Now, take a look at the ancient ancestor of banana. You can see the large seeds. And unappetizing Brussel sprouts, and eggplant, so beautiful.

④ Now, to create these varieties, breeders have used many different genetic techniques over there. <u>Some of them are quite creative, like mixing two different species together using a process called grafting to create – that half tomato, half potato.</u>[1] Breeders have also used other types of genetic techniques, such as random mutagenesis, which induces uncharacterized mutations into the plants. The rice in the cereal that are spent on our babies was developed using this approach. Now, today, breeders have even more options to choose from. Some of them are extraordinarily precise.

⑤ I want to give you a couple examples from my own work. I work on rice. Each year, 40% of the potential harvest is lost to pest and disease. For this reason, farmers plant rice varieties that carry genes for resistance. This approach has been used for nearly 100 years. Yet, when I started graduate school, no one knew what these genes were. It wasn't until the 1990s that scientists finally uncovered the genetic basis of resistance.

⑥ <u>In my laboratory, I isolated a gene from a unity to a very serious bacterial disease in Asia and Africa. We found we can engineer the gene into a conventional rice varieties that's normally susceptible, and you can see the two leaves on the bottom here are highly resistant to infection.</u>[2] Now, the same month my laboratory published our discovery on the rice immunity gene. My friend and colleague Dave Mackill stopped by my office. He said, "Seventy million rice farmers are having trouble growing rice." That's because their field are flooded, and these rice farmers are living on less than $2 a day.

⑦ Although rice grows well in standing water most rice varieties will die if they were submerged for more than 3 days. Flooding is expected to be increasingly problematic, as the climate changes. He told me that his graduate student Kenong Xu and himself were studying an ancient variety of rice that had an amazing property. It could withstand two weeks of complete submergence.

⑧ He asked if I would be willing to help them isolate this gene. I said "Yes", and I was excited, because I knew if we were successful. We could potentially help millions of farmers grow rice even when their fields were flooded. Kenong spent ten years looking for this gene. Then one day, he said, "come look at this experiment." I went to the greenhouse and I saw that the conventional variety that was flooded for 18 days had died, but the rice variety that we had genetically engineered with a new gene we had discovered called Sub 1 was alive.[3] Kenong and I were amazed and excited that a single gene could have this dramatic affect. But this is just a greenhouse experiment.

⑨ Would this work in the field? Now, I'm going to show you a video taken at the International Rice Resource Statue. Breeders there developed a rice variety carrying Sub 1 gene using another genetic technique called Precise Breeding. On the left, you can see the Sub 1 variety, and on the right is the conventional variety. Both varieties do very well at first, but then the field is flooded for 17 days. You can see the Sub1 variety does great. In fact, it produces three and a half times more grain than the conventional variety.[4] I love this video because it shows the power of plant geneticist to help farmers. Last year, with the help of the foundation three and a half million farmers raised Sub 1 rice. Thank you.

Notes on the text

(1) Some of them are quite creative, like mixing two different species together using a process called grafting to create – that half tomato, half potato.

其中一些是相当有创造性的，例如利用一个叫嫁接的程序把两种不同的品种结合在一起来创造一个一半是番茄、一半是土豆的植物。

(2) In my laboratory, I isolated a gene from a unity to a very serious bacterial disease in Asia and Africa. We found we can engineer the gene into a conventional rice varieties that's normally susceptible, and you can see the two leaves on the bottom here are highly resistant to infection.

在我的实验室里，我们分离了一个基因。发现我们可以把这个基因植入传统的大米品种里，而且你可以看到底下的两片叶子都抵抗了感染。

(3) I went to the greenhouse and I saw that the conventional variety that was flooded for 18 days had died, but the rice variety that we had genetically engineered with a new gene we had discovered called Sub 1 was alive.

我去到温室看到传统品种被淹18天后死了，但是被我们通过基因改造植入的、叫Sub 1 的新基因大米品种存活了。

(4) Both varieties do very well at first, but then the field is flooded for 17 days. You can see the Sub1 variety does great. In fact, it produces three and a half times more grain than the conventional variety.

两个品种开始都长得很好，但是接下来农田被淹了17天。你可以看到Sub1长得极好。实际上，它还可以生产比传统品种多3.5倍的谷物。

2. Please interpret the following passage by using the techniques illustrated above. Please pay attention to the underlined sentences as they require special treatment during interpreting.

A Different Perspective on Genetic Modification (Excerpts)
Pamela Ronald

① Now, many people don't mind genetic modification, when it comes to moving rice genes around, rice genes in rice plants, or even when it comes to making things' species together through grafting or random mutagenesis.[1] But when it comes to taking genes from viruses and bacteria and putting them into plants, a lot of people say."Yuck."Why would you do that? The reason is that sometimes is cheapest, safest and most effective technology for enhancing food security and inventing sustainable agriculture. I'm going to give you three examples. First, take a look at papaya, delicious right? But, now, look at this papaya. This papaya is infected with Papaya Ringspot virus. In the 1950s, this virus nearly wiped out the entire production of papaya on the island of Oahu in Hawaii. Many people thought that Hawaii papaya was doomed, but then, a local Hawaiian, a plant pathologist Danes decided to try to fight this disease using genetic engineering. He took a snippet of viral DNA and inserted it into the papaya genome. He took a snippet of viral DNA and inserted it into the papaya genome. Now, take a look at his field trial. You can see the genetically engineer papaya in the center. It's immune to infection.[2] The conventional papaya around the outside is seriously infected with the virus. Danes pioneering works is credited with the rescuing the papaya industry.

② Today, 20 years later, there is still no other method to control this disease. There's no organic method. There is no conventional method. 80% of Hawaiian papaya is genetically engineered. Now, some of you may still look crazy about engineering food, but consider this. That genetically engineered papaya carries just a trace amount of the virus. If you bite into an organic or conventional papaya that is infected with the virus, you will be chewing on tenfold more virus protein.

③ Now, take a look at this pest feasting on the eggplant. The brown you see is frass, what comes out of in the back of the insect. To control this serious pest, which can devastate the entire eggplant crop in Bangladesh, Bangladeshi farmers spray insecticides two to three times a week, sometimes twice a day when pest pressure was high.[3] But we know that some insecticides were very harmful to human health especially when farmers and their families cannot afford proper protection, like these children. In less developed countries, it is estimated that 300,000 people die every year because of the pesticide misuse and exposure.

④ Cornell and Bangladeshi scientists decided to fight this disease using a genetic technique that builds on an organic farming approach. Organic farmers like my husband Raoul sprays a pesticide call B.T. which is based on a bacteria. This pesticide is very specific to caterpillar pest and in fact, it's nontoxic to human, fish and birds. It's less toxic than table salt. But this approach doesn't work in Bangladesh. That's because these insecticide sprays are difficult to find, they're expensive, and they don't prevent the insect from peeling inside the plants. In the genetic approach, scientists cut a gene out of bacteria and insert it directly into eggplant genome. Will this work to reduce insecticide sprays in Bangladesh? Definitely. Last season, farmers reported they were able to reduce insecticide use by a huge amount, almost down to zero. They're able to harvest the plant for next season.

⑤ Now, I have given you a couple of examples how the genetic engineering can be used to fight pest and disease and to reduce the amount of insecticides. My final example is an example where genetic engineering can be used to reduce malnutrition. In less developed countries, 500 000 children go blind every year because lack of vitamin A. More than half will die. For this reason, scientists supported by Rockfeller Foundation genetically engineered a golden rice to produce beta-carotene, which is the precursor of the Vitamin A.[4]

⑥ This is the same pigment that we find in carrots. Researchers estimate that just one cup of golden rice per day will save the lives of thousands of children. But golden rice is virulently opposed by activists who are against genetic modification. Just last year, activists invaded and destroyed a field trial in the Philippines. When I heard about the destruction, I wondered if they knew that they were destroying much more than the scientific research project that they were destroying medicines that children desperately needed to save their sight and their lives. Some of my friends and family still worry: How do you know genes in the food are safe to eat? I explained the genetic engineering; the process of moving genes between species has been used for more than 40 years, in wines, in medicine, in plants, in cheeses. In all that time, there hasn't been a single case serving harm to human health or the environment. But I say, look, I'm not asking you to believe me. Science is not a belief system. My opinion doesn't matter. Let's look at the evidence.

⑦ After 20 years of careful study and rigorous peer review by thousands of independent scientists, every major scientific organization in the world has concluded that the crops currently on the market are safe to eat, and that the process of genetic engineering is no more risky than older methods of genetic modification.[5] These are precisely the same organizations that most of us trust when it comes to other important scientific issues such as global climate change or the safety of vaccines. Raoul and I believe that, instead of worrying the genes in our food, we must focus on how we can help children grow up healthy. We must ask if farmers in rural communities can thrive, and if every can afford the food. We must try to minimize environmental degeneration.

⑧ What scares me most about loud controversy and mistaken information the about plant genetics is that the poorest people who most needed this technology maybe denied access because of the vague fierce prejudices of those who have enough to eat. We have a huge challenge in front of us. Let's celebrate scientific innovation and use it. It's our responsibility to do everything we can to help alleviate human suffering and safeguard the environment. Thank you.

Notes on the text

(1) Now, many people don't mind genetic modification, when it comes to moving rice genes around, rice genes in rice plants, or even when it comes to making things' species together through grafting or random mutagenesis.

现在，很多人不在意转基因，比如我们在别处使用大米基因，把大米基因用在大米农作物上，或者甚至通过移植把不同物种结合在一起，再或者采用随机变异公式。

(2) He took a snippet of viral DNA and inserted it into the papaya genome. He took a snippet of viral DNA and inserted it into the papaya genome. Now, take a look at his field trial. You can see the genetically engineer papaya in the center. It's immune to infection.

他提取了一小瓶病毒DNA，然后把它插入木瓜的基因组中。这就像人类接种疫苗。现在，看一下他的农场试验。你可以看到被基因改造了的木瓜在中间。它不受感染的影响。

(3) To control this serious pest, which can devastate the entire eggplant crop in Bangladesh, Bangladeshi farmers spray insecticides two to three times a week, sometimes twice a day when pest pressure was high.

为了控制这种可以摧毁孟加拉国所有茄子作物的严重害虫，孟加拉国的农民每个星期喷射两至三次的杀虫剂，有时候当虫害严重时一天两次。

(4) In less developed countries, 500 000 children go blind every year because lack of vitamin A. More than half will die. For this reason, scientists supported by Rockfelle Foundation genetically engineered a golden rice to produce beta-carotene, which is the precursor of the Vitamin A.

在欠发达国家，每年有50万儿童因缺乏维生素A而失明，一半以上会死亡。基于这个原因，科学家在洛克菲勒基金的支持下，从基因上设计了一种能够生产β-胡萝卜素的维生素A的黄金大米。

(5) After 20 years of careful study and rigorous peer review by thousands of independent scientists, every major scientific organization in the world has concluded that the crops currently on the market are safe to eat, and that the process of genetic engineering is no more risky than older methods of genetic modification.

经过20多年由成千上万独立的科学家谨慎的研究和严格的同业互查，世界上每一个主要的科学机构已经断定市场上的所有庄稼都是可安全食用的，而且转基因的方法没有比传统基因改造方法更危险。

▌13.2.4 篇章口译[Passage Practice (C to E)]

1. Please interpret the following passage by using the techniques illustrated above. Please pay attention to the underlined sentences as they require special treatment during interpreting.

改变孩子和食物之间的关系(一)
安·库珀

① 我们应该怎样做才能改变孩子和食物之间的关系？我想说的不仅仅是为什么我们需要去改变，而是我们必须要去改变。我逐渐意识到，我们有责任给孩子们灌输健康的地球、有益于健康的食物和健康的孩子这三者之间的共生关系。如果我们不那么做的话，人类将会灭绝，因为我们的喂养方式会使孩子们一步步走向死亡。

② 这就是我的前提。我们看到，身体差的孩子变得越来越虚弱。<u>造成这种现象的原因总的来说是因为我们的食品体系和食品商品化过程中政府采取的方式，政府监管食品的手段，和美国农业部设定的食物进入孩子们餐盘的流通渠道都是不健康的，并且这直接导致那些对身体有害的食物进入学校。</u>

③ 我们大家都心照不宣地把子女、孙子、侄女、侄子送去学校，并且告诉他们学校教什么就学什么。而当你给孩子们提供劣质的食物时，也是孩子们在学校里学到的一部分。这才是关键问题之所在。我们走到这一步要拜那些农业综合企业巨头们所赐。我们如今在一个大多数人没有权利决定吃什么的国家里。那些生产落叶剂和耐污地毯的大财团，如孟山都和杜邦，他们掌握全美国90%的商业化种子。仅仅十家公司，就掌控着零售店里出售的大部分商品和食品，这不能不说是个问题。

④ 因此，当我开始思考这些问题以及思考怎样才能改变孩子们所摄入的食物时，注意力集中在这样一个问题上，即我们应该给孩子们灌输什么。首先我们要灌输给孩子们的是区域性食品，即尝试食用本地出产的食物。毋庸置疑，随着化石燃料的不断消耗和油价的持续飙升，是时候开始思考我们把食物从1500英里以外运送过来的这种做法是否是可行的。因此，我们和孩子们交流探讨这种现象，并且开始让孩子们食用本地出产的食物。

⑤ 现在，我们来谈一谈有机食品。<u>目前，大部分校区负担不起有机食品，但我们，作为一个国家，必须开始考虑把消费、种植和给孩子们提供不含有化学物质的食品摆上我们的议事日程。</u>我们不能让孩子们再继续摄入杀虫剂、除草剂、抗生素和激素了。我们不能再那样做。这样做是行不通的。这样做的结果是孩子们的身体将会变得越来越糟糕。

⑥ 现在我想着重谈一谈抗生素。在美国，70%的抗生素用于畜牧业。孩子们每天都从牛肉和其他动物蛋白中摄取抗生素。70%，不可思议的数字，其结果是将导致疾病。我们面临着像大肠杆菌这样无法攻克的难题，当孩子们生病感染时，我们却束手无策。

⑦ 抗生素的滥用不仅仅是医学界的现象，同时也是食品供应中出现的问题。我可以举一个很好的例子，美国农业每年要消耗12亿磅的杀虫剂。这就意味着我们每个人以及我们的孩子要消耗大约5磅重的袋装农药，平时家里用的袋子那么大，假设我现在手头有这

样的口袋，并且把它撕开，把里面的东西摊在地上，这就是我们自己和我们的孩子们每年摄入的农药量，导致这一切的原因是因为流入我们食品供应环节中的农产品以及我们摄取农产品的方式。美国农业部为我们食品供应环节中流入的抗生素、激素和杀虫剂开了绿灯，并且还为时代杂志上的这则广告买单。

Notes on the text

(1) 造成这种现象的原因总的来说是因为我们的食品体系和食品商品化过程中政府采取的方式，政府监管食品的手段，和美国农业部设定的食物进入孩子们餐盘的流通渠道都是不健康的，并且这直接导致了那些对身体有害的食物进入学校。

The reason this is happening, by and large, is because of our food system and the way the government commodifies food, the way the government oversees our food, the way the USDA put food on kids' plates, that's unhealthy, and allows unhealthy food into schools.

(2) 目前，大部分校区负担不起有机食品，但我们，作为一个国家，必须开始考虑把消费、种植和给孩子们提供不含有化学物质的食品摆上我们的议事日程。

No, most school districts can't really afford organic food, but we, as a nation, have to start thinking about consuming, growing and feeding our children food that's not chock-full of chemicals.

2. Please interpret the following passage by using the techniques illustrated above. Please pay attention to the underlined sentences as they require special treatment during interpreting.

改变孩子和食物之间的关系(二)

安·库珀

① 好，那我们现在来谈谈雷切尔·卡逊和滴滴涕，我们知道，滴滴涕对我们每个人都是有害的。但这却是美国农业部在食品供应中允许的物质。这点必须要改变。我们再也不能把美国农业部的相关规定视为我们给孩子们吃什么以及哪些物质被允许摄入的权威。我们不相信他们的心里存有我们的最大利益。与之相反的是可持续的食物。这也是我试图让人们了解的。

② 我想把它灌输给孩子们，我认为这是最重要的一点。在这种可持续性食物的作用下，我们的地球不会消亡，孩子们将健康成长，并且能够缓解我们所遭受的一切负面的影响。这完全是一个全新的理念。我的意思是人们总是谈论可能性，但是我们必须搞清楚可持续性到底是什么。

③ 在不到200年的时间里，仅仅几代人的时间，我们农民的比例数从100%下降到95%，直到不足2%。现在我们生活在一个囚徒比农民的数量还要多的国家，210万囚徒，190万农民。平均一年我们花在狱中一个囚徒身上的钱达到35 000美元，而校区每年却只花费500美元给一个孩子提供膳食，也难怪犯罪分子层出不穷了。随之而来的是，我们的身

体越来越差，我们和我们的孩子都将被疾病所困扰。这和我们为孩子们提供的食物有关。

④ 我们摄入的食物是什么样我们就会变成什么样。摄入的食物和我们休戚相关。如果我们继续沿着这条老路走下去，如果我们继续为我们的孩子提供劣质食物，如果我们不教给他们什么是对健康有益的食物，将会发生什么呢？你们知道将会发生什么呢？我们的整个医疗系统将会受到什么样的影响？

⑤ 随之而来的是，我们的下一代的寿命将会比我们这一代更短。据疾病防控中心的统计数据显示，在2000年出生的新生儿人群中，(这些孩子现在大多7~8岁左右)每三个白种人，每两个非洲裔美国人和西班牙裔美国人中就会有一个孩子患上糖尿病。如果这还不足以引起警惕的话，疾病防控中心进一步表明，糖尿病多出现在这些孩子们高中毕业之前。这就意味着40%或45%的学龄儿童将会在未来的十年间对胰岛素产生依赖。

⑥ 将会发生些什么呢？疾病防控中心说，那些2000年出生的孩子可能会成为我们国家历史上首代寿命短于他们父辈的一代人。这都要归功于我们提供给他们的食物。因为八岁大的孩子还没有决定权，如果他们有决定权的话，他们会送你去看心理医生。我们有责任去决定孩子们该吃些什么。

⑦ 但是现在，这或许成了这些大财团们的事，大财团们每年要花掉200亿美元投入在给孩子们吃的垃圾食品的广告费上。200亿美元，能使大多数孩子一年看到10 000个垃圾食品广告。这样做的结果是让孩子们认为不吃鸡块就会死。大家都觉得孩子应该尽可能多地多吃。

⑧ 为什么我们可以买到售价29美分的大杯饮料和99美分的双层汉堡呢？原因是政府在食品商品化过程中所采取的手段，以及流入我们食品供应环节中的廉价玉米和大豆，正是这些原因，使得这些垃圾食品的价格非常低廉。这就是为什么在一开始我把这称之为一件关乎社会公平的大事。

Notes on the text

(1) 在这种可持续性食物的作用下，我们的地球不会消亡，孩子们将健康成长，并且能够缓解我们所遭受的一切负面的影响。这完全是一个全新的理念。

It's consuming food in a way in which we'll still have a planet, in which kids will grow up to be healthy, and which really try to mitigate all the negative impacts we're seeing. It really is just a new idea.

(2) 如果这还不足以引起警惕的话，疾病防控中心进一步表明，糖尿病多出现在这些孩子们高中毕业之前。这就意味着40%或45%的学龄儿童将会在未来的十年间对胰岛素产生依赖。

And if that's not enough, they're gone on to say, most before they graduate high school. This means that 40 or 45% of all school—aged children could be insulin-dependent within a decade.

(3) 大财团们每年要花掉200亿美元投入在给孩子们吃的垃圾食品的广告费上。200亿美元，能使大多数孩子一年看到10 000个垃圾食品广告。这样做的结果是让孩子们认为不吃鸡块就会死。

Big companies spend 20 billion dollars a year marketing non-nutrient foods to kids. 20

billion dollars a year. 10 000 ads most kids see. The result of which is kids think they're going to die if they don't have chicken nuggets.

13.3　参考译文(Reference Version)

▌13.3.1　单句口译(Sentence Practice)

Please interpret the following sentences by using the techniques illustrated above. You may interpret to your partner first and then he/she comments on your performance.

(1) 许多国家面临人口流动、贫困、食品安全、水资源管理和气候变化带来的挑战，我们需要呼吁各方注意。

(2) 连贯而全面的国家食品安全体系不仅会改善食品供应不足的国家的卫生——它们也会帮助发展和促进食品贸易。

(3) 这些问题——从粮食短缺和疾病传播到实现可持续的经济增长——没有一个能够在不使用科学技术的情况下解决。

(4) 专家们最近在内罗毕举行会议，讨论如何面对干旱造成的粮食短缺。

(5) 研究人员发现，中国用同样数量的水生产出了比非洲和亚洲其他国家更多的粮食。

(6) With the industrialization of food production and the globalization of its marketing, efforts to ensure food safety likewise take on an international dimension.

(7) During the last 12 months, an average of up to 200 food safety incidents per month have been investigated by WHO and FAO to determine their public health impact.

(8) The people's governments at various levels shall encourage and support efforts to improve food processing technology so as to promote the improvement of hygienic quality of food.

(9) The administrative department of public health under the State Council shall be in charge of supervision and control of food hygiene throughout the country.

(10) Food hygiene supervisors shall enforce laws impartially, be loyal to their duties and may not seek personal gain by taking advantage of their office.

▌13.3.2　段落口译(Paragraph Practice)

1. Vocabulary Work: Study the following words and phrases and translate them into the target language.

under fire	样本
Styrofoam	独占权
decadence	专家组成员
panel leader	感官试验棚

2. Please interpret the following paragraphs by using the techniques illustrated above.

(1) Freezing meat once it is home from the supermarket could kill deadly bugs. The process of freezing meat kills up to 90 percent of campylobacter cells. Campylobacter bugs can cause stomach upsets, vomiting and diarrhea. Families should freeze and defrost chicken if they want to avoid food poisoning, a health chief said yesterday. Six in every 10 chickens sold by supermarkets contain potentially lethal bugs that infect half a million people a year. Around 100 of the victims die from vomiting and stomach upsets. For decades, retailers and officials have known that campylobacter is rife on poultry farms but have failed to take action. Instead an official at Public Health England suggests consumers can help protect themselves by freezing chicken after purchase and thoroughly defrosting it before cooking. Thoroughly cooking poultry makes it safe but the disease still infects a huge number of people, costing the British economy an estimated £9million a year in health costs and missed work hours. The freezing process adds an extra level of security in the event of undercooked meat.

(2) People are being urged to pre-cook food in the oven before barbecuing it after research found most Britons make risky hygiene mistakes at the grill. The Food Standards Agency said food poisoning was a real danger of outdoor cooking, with 94% of people admitting to at least one bad barbecue habit. In a survey of 2 030 adults, 21% said they believed they had been ill due to something they ate. And nearly a third admitted to not checking if food was properly cooked. The FSA warned that food hygiene risks could lead to illnesses like campylobacter, which affects more than a quarter of a million people every year. Ahead of the late summer bank holiday weekend — a popular time for barbecues — the government body issued tips to help people avoid food poisoning.

(3) 近日，香港连锁超市超生活因出售被许多人称为"世界上最贵的草莓"而遭到指责。这种日本进口的科托卡草莓一颗售价168港币，据说为了保证供应品相最优的草莓，它们都是经过精挑细选的。为了彰显它们的尊贵，这些套着泡沫网的草莓被单独放在裹着塑料的纸盒子里，盒子里面还铺着稻草。这种贵得离谱的"名牌水果"的照片在香港和大陆的社交媒体上流传，很多人对这样奢侈腐化的产品感到震惊。

(4) 世界顶级巧克力品牌正在寻找一名专业巧克力试吃员，为他们的产品提供忠实的反馈。旗下拥有吉百利、妙卡和奥利奥等品牌的亿滋国际公司需要一名可以信任的人来试吃他们的新产品并告知试吃感受。这一职位的官方名称叫"巧克力及可可饮料品尝员"，幸运的当选者每周周二到周四间将需要花费七个半小时来从事这份工作。专业的甜食试吃员将在该公司的Reading office和11名专家及1名专家组长共事。试吃将在消费者科学讨论室的感官试验棚内进行。

■ 13.3.3　篇章口译[Passage Practice (E to C)]

1. Please interpret the following passage by using the techniques illustrated above. Please pay attention to the underlined sentences as they require special treatment during interpreting.

重新看待转基因食品(节选)
帕梅拉·罗纳德

① 我是一个植物遗传学家。我研究一些能抵抗疾病和耐抗压的基因。最近几年来，世界上成千上万的人相信转基因改造存在灾害性。今天，我将要提出一个不同的观点。

② 首先，请让我介绍我的丈夫，拉乌尔，他是一个有机农民。在他的农田里，他种着各种不同的农作物。这是许多生态农业试验的其中一个，即用来保持他的农田健康的实践。试想一些我们会得到的反应：“真的吗？一个有机农民和一个植物遗传学家？你们能达成什么共识？”恩，我们可以，而且这并不困难，因为我们有共同的目标。我们想帮助滋养不断增长的人口而不进一步破坏环境。我相信这是我们时代的巨大挑战。

③ 如今，基因改造不是新事物，事实上我们吃的所有食物都在一定程度上被基因改造了。让我来给你举几个例子。左边的图片是现代玉米的古老祖先。你看到一行覆盖着硬壳的玉米粒。除非你有一个锤子，墨西哥类蜀黍不适合用于制作墨西哥饼。现在，看一下古老的香蕉祖先。你能看到巨大的种子，以及引不起食欲的芽甘蓝和茄子，如此美丽。

④ 如今，为了创造这些变种，多年来培育者应用了很多不同的基因技术。其中一些是相当有创造性的，例如利用一个叫嫁接的程序把两种不同的品种结合在一起来创造一个一半是番茄、一半是土豆的植物。培育者还使用其他种类的基因技术，例如随机突变，能让植物产生非典型的基因突变。许多人用来喂婴儿的谷物大米，就是用上述的方法改造的。今天，培育者甚至有更多的选择。其中很多是非常精确的。

⑤ 我想从我的工作中给大家举几个例子。我研究大米。每一年，有40%的潜在粮食产量都损失于虫害和疾病。为此，农民种植携带耐抗性基因的大米品种。这种方法已经被用了将近100年。但是，当我在研究院时，还没有人知道这些基因是什么。直到20世纪90年代才有科学家最终发现耐抗性的基因基础。

⑥ 在我的实验室里，我们分离了一个基因。我们发现，可以把这个基因植入传统的大米品种里，而且你可以看到底下的两片叶子都抵抗了感染。现在，同一个月里我的研究室发布了我们对大米免疫基因的发现。我的朋友也是同事Dave Mackill探访了我的办公室。他说：“7000万的大米农民正在面临种植大米的困难。”那是因为他们的农民都被洪水淹没了，那些农民每天靠着不到2美元来生活。

⑦ 虽然大米能很好地在积水里生长，但如果被淹3天以上，大多数种类的大米会淹死。随着天气的改变，洪灾发生越来越不确定。他告诉我他的研究生Kenong Xu 和他本人正在研究一种拥有惊人性能的古老大米品种，它能够在被完全淹没的情况下生存两周。

⑧ 他问我是否愿意帮他们分离这个基因。我答应了他，我非常激动。我们可能可以帮助无数的农民种植大米，即使他们的农田被淹没。Kenong花了10年来寻找这个基因。然

后有一天，他说："请来看看这个实验，你一定要来看。"我去到温室看到传统品种被淹18天后死了，但是被我们通过基因改造植入的、叫Sub 1的新基因大米品种存活了。Kenong和我都很惊讶和兴奋，一个基因能够有如此大的影响。但是这只是一个温室实验。

⑨ 这在田地中是否也能成功呢？现在，我将要给大家展示一个在国际大米研究所拍摄时长4个月定时拍摄的视频。那里的培育着利用另一种叫精准培育的基因技术。在左边，你可以看到Sub 1，在右边的是传统品种。两个品种开始都长得很好，但是接下来农田被淹了17天。你可以看到Sub1长得极好。实际上，它还可以生产比传统品种多3.5倍的谷物。我很喜欢这个视频，因为它展示了植物遗传学帮助农民的力量。上一年，350万农民种植了Sub 1大米。谢谢。

2. Please interpret the following passage by using the techniques illustrated above. Please pay attention to the underlined sentences as they require special treatment during interpreting.

重新看待转基因食品 (节选)
帕梅拉·罗纳德

① 现在，很多人不在意转基因，当我们在别处使用大米基因，把大米基因用在大米农作物上，或者甚至通过移植，很多人都不会反对基因改造。但是当我们从病毒或者细菌上提取基因然后植入到农作物上，很多人都说："不好。"大家为什么会这样呢？原因有时候就是最便宜、最安全和最有效率的科技才能提高食物的安全性和改进可持续农业。我会给大家三个例子。首先，看一下木瓜，很美味，是吗？但是现在，看一下这个木瓜。这个木瓜被感染了木瓜环斑病病毒。20世纪50年代，这种病毒几乎感染了夏威夷欧胡岛的全部木瓜作物。许多人认为夏威夷木瓜肯定完了，然而，一个夏威夷本地人，一个叫丹尼斯·贡萨斐斯的植物病理学家决定尝试利用基因工程来对抗这种疾病。他提取了一小瓶病毒DNA，然后把它插入木瓜的基因组中。这就像人类接种疫苗。现在，看一下他的农场试验。你可以看到被基因改造了的木瓜在中间。它不受感染的影响。环绕在外的传统木瓜则被病毒严重感染了。丹尼斯的先驱性工作救援了木瓜行业。

② 20年之后，仍然没有其他方法来控制这种疾病，没有有机的方法，也没有传统的方法。80% 的夏威夷木瓜都是基因改造过的。如今，可能有些人对基因食物感到狂热。但想一想：被基因改造的木瓜只是携带了微量的病毒。如果你咬一口被病毒感染的有机的或传统的木瓜，你会嚼多于十倍的病毒蛋白质。

③ 现在，看一下这只正在吃茄子的害虫。你看到的棕色物质是虫粪，它是从害虫子的后端出来的。为了控制这种可以摧毁孟加拉国所有茄子作物的严重害虫，孟加拉国的农民每个星期喷射两至三次的杀虫剂，有时候当虫害严重时一天两次。但是我们知道虫害对人类健康非常有害，尤其是当农民和他们的家人负担不起恰当的安全措施时。在欠发达国家里，据估计每年有30万人死于杀虫剂的滥用和暴露。

④ 康奈尔和孟加拉国的科学家决定使用一种建立在有机农业方法的基因技术，有机农民，如我的丈夫乌拉尔，喷洒一种以细菌为基础的叫做B.T.的杀虫剂。这种杀虫剂对

毛虫很特别，实际上，它对人类、鱼和鸟都没有毒性。它比食盐的毒性更小。但这种方法在孟加拉国作用不大，因为这种杀虫剂很难得到，它们很贵，而且它们不能阻止害虫进入植物里。在基因方法里，科学家从细菌里切除一个基因，然后把它直接放进茄子的基因组里这个方法能不能够减低杀虫剂在孟加拉国的使用呢？当然可以。上一个季节，农民回应他们已经可以大大减少杀虫剂的使用，几乎不需要使用。他们能够收割庄稼和为下一季重新种植。

⑤ 现在我已经给大家举了几个例子，即基因工程是如何被用来抵抗害虫和疾病，以及用来减少杀虫剂的使用量。我最后的例子是关于基因工程能够被用来降低营养不良的人数。在欠发达国家，每年有50万儿童因缺乏维生素A而失明。一半以上会死亡。基于这个原因，科学家在洛克菲勒基金的支持下，从基因上设计了一种能够生产β-胡萝卜素的维生素A的黄金大米。

⑥ 这是我们在胡萝卜里找到的同样的色素。研究人员估计每天只要一杯黄金大米就可以拯救上千的儿童。但是黄金大米被反基因工程的积极分子大力反对。就在上一年，积极分子们侵入和毁坏了在菲律宾的一片试验田。当我听到试验田被毁坏时，我在想他们是否知道他们毁坏的不只是一个科学研究项目，他们毁坏的是孩子们迫切需要的用来挽救他们视力和生命的药物。我的一些朋友和家人仍然很担心：你怎么知道食物里的基因是安全可吃的？我解释了基因工程，在物种间移取基因的方法已经在酒中，在药物中，在植物中，在芝士中，一直以来，都没有一个对人类健康或者环境造成伤害的个案。但是，我并不是要求你要相信我。科学不是一个信仰体系。我的观点不重要。我们相信的是证据。

⑦ 经过20多年由成千上万独立的科学家谨慎的研究和严格的同业互查，世界上每一个主要的科学机构已经断定市场上的所有庄稼都是可安全实用的，而且转基因的方法没有比传统基因改造方法更危险。这些机构恰好是大部分人在其他重要科学问题上，例如在全球气候改变或者疫苗安全问题上，都会相信的机构。乌拉尔和我相信，与其担心食物中的基因，我们更需要关注如何帮助儿童健康成长。我们必须问一问农村社区的农民是否能够营生，和每个人是否都能买得起食物。我们必须努力将环境退化最小化。

⑧ 关于对植物基因激烈的争论和错误的信息，令我最害怕的是那些最需要这种科技的最贫穷的人否认这种方法，正是因为一些有足够食物的人的不明忧虑和见解给我们巨大的挑战。让我们庆祝和利用科学的创新。这是我们的责任，去做任何我们可以做的事情来帮助减轻人类遭受的磨难和保卫环境。谢谢。

▌13.3.4 篇章口译[Passage Practice (C to E)]

1. Please interpret the following passage by using the techniques illustrated above. Please pay attention to the underlined sentences as they require special treatment during interpreting.

To Change Children's Relationship to Food
Ann Cooper

① How do we really change children's relationship to food? And I'll tell you why we need to change it, but we absolutely have to change it. And what I came to understand is we needed to teach children the symbiotic relationship between a healthy planet, healthy food and healthy kids. And that if we don't do that we're really going to become extinct, because we're feeding our children to death.

② That's my premise. We're seeing sick kids get sicker and sicker. The reason this is happening, by and large, is because of our food system and the way the government commodifies food, the way the government oversees our food, the way the USDA put food on kids' plates, that's unhealthy, and allows unhealthy food into schools.

③ And by tacitly, all of us send our kids or grandchildren, or nieces, or nephews, to school and tell them to learn, you know, learn what's in those schools. And when you feed these kids bad food, that's what they're learning. So that's really what this is all about. The way we got here is because of big agribusiness. We now live in a country where most of us don't decide, by and large, what we eat. We see big businesses, Monsanto and DuPont, who brought out Agent Orange and stain resistant carpet. They control 90% of the commercially produced seeds in our country. These are 10 companies control much of what's in our grocery stores, much of what people eat. And that's really, really a problem.

④ So when I started thinking about these issues and how I was going to change what kids ate, I really started focusing on what we would teach them. And the very first thing was about regional food, trying to eat food from within our region. And clearly, with what's going on with fossil fuel usage, or when, as the fossil fuels going away, as oil hits its peak oil, you know, we really have to start thinking about whether or not we should or could, be moving food 1,500 miles before we eat it. So we talked to kids about that, and we really start to feed kids regional food.

⑤ And then we talk about organic food. Now, most school districts can't really afford organic food, but we, as a nation, have to start thinking about consuming, growing and feeding our children food that's not chock-full of chemicals. We can't keep feeding our kids pesticides and herbicides and antibiotics and hormones. We can't keep doing that. You know, it doesn't work. And the results of that are kids getting sick.

⑥ One of my big soapboxes right now is antibiotics. Seventy percent of all antibiotics consumed in America is consumed in animal husbandry. We are feeding our kids antibiotics in beef and other animal protein every day. Seventy percent, it's unbelievable. And the result of it is we have diseases. We have things like E. Coli that we can't fix, that we can't make kids better when they get sick.

⑦ And, you know, certainly antibiotics have been over-prescribed, but it's an issue in the food supply. One of my favorite facts is that U.S. agriculture uses 1.2 billion pounds of pesticides every year. That means every one of us, and our children, consumes what would equal a five-pound bag, those bags you have at home. If I had one here and ripped it open, and that pile I would have on the floor is what we consume and feed our children every year because of what goes into our food supply, because of the way we consume produce in America. The USDA allows these antibiotics, these hormones and these pesticides in our food supply, and the USDA paid for this ad in Time magazine.

2. Please interpret the following passage by using the techniques illustrated above. Please pay attention to the underlined sentences as they require special treatment during interpreting.

To Change Children's Relationship to Food
Ann Cooper

① Okay, we could talk about Rachel Carson and DDT, but we know it wasn't good for you and me. And that is what the USDA allows in our food supply. And that has to change, you know, the USDA cannot be seen as the be-all and end-all of what we feed our kids and what's allowed. We cannot believe that they have our best interest's heart. The antithesis of this whole thing is sustainable food. That's what I really try and get people to understand.

② I really try and teach it to kids. I think it's the most important. It's consuming food in a way in which we'll still have a planet, in which kids will grow up to be healthy, and which really try to mitigate all the negative impacts we're seeing. It really is just a new idea. I mean, people toss around sustainability, but we have to figure out what sustainability is.

③ In less than 200 years, you know, just in a few generations, we've gone from being 200, being 100%, 95% farmers to less than 2% of farmers. We now live in a country that has more prisoners than farmers, 2.1million prisoners, 1.9 million farmers. And we spend 35 000 dollars on average a year keeping a prisoner in prison, and school districts spend 500 dollars a year feeding a child. It's no wonder, you know, we have criminals. And what's happening is, we're getting sick. We're getting sick and our kids are getting sick. It is about what we feed them.

④ What goes in is what we are. We really are what we eat. And if we continue down this path, if we continue to feed kids bad food, if we continue not to teach them what good food is what's going to happen? You know, what is going to happen? What's going to happen to our whole medical system?

⑤ What's going to happen is, we're going to have kids that have a life less long than our own. The CDC, the Center for Disease Control, has said, of the children born in the year 2000, those seven, and eight-year-old today, one out of every three Caucasians, one out of every two African-Americans and Hispanics are going to have diabetes in their life time. And if that's not enough, they're gone on to say, most before they graduate high school. This means that 40 or 45% of all school—aged children could be insulin-dependent within a decade.

⑥ What's going to happen? The CDC has gone further to say that those children born in the year 2000 could be the first generation in our country's history to die at a younger age than their parents. And it's because of what we feed them. Because eight-year-old doesn't get to decide, and if they do, you should be in therapy. You know, we are responsible for what kids eat.

⑦ But oops, maybe they're responsible for what kids eat. Big companies spend 20 billion dollars a year marketing non-nutrient foods to kids. 20 billion dollars a year. 10 000 ads most kids see. The result of which are kids think they're going to die if they don't have chicken nuggets. You know that everybody thinks they should be eating more, and more, and more.

⑧ Why can we have 29-cent Big Gulps and 99-cent double burgers? It's because of the way the government commodifies food, and the cheap corn and cheap soy that are pushed into our food supply that makes these non-nutrient foods really, really cheap. This is why I say it's a social justice issue.

13.4 食品主题词汇汇总(Vocabulary Build-up)

delicacy	美食
palatable	美味的
protein	蛋白质
vegetarian	素食者
reduce food wastes	减少食物浪费
nutritious	有营养的
entomophagy	食用昆虫
sustainable consumption	可持续消费
radiation-affected area	核辐射地区
illegal additive	非法添加剂
the State Food and Drug Administration	国家食品药品监督管理局
insoluble fiber	不可溶性纤维
sell-by date	保质期
fatty seafood	高脂海鲜
crunchy	松脆的
monosodium glutamate	味精
biodegrade	生物降解
fast	禁食，斋戒
carbohydrate	碳水化合物

13.5 扩展练习(Enhancement Practice)

Making comments on a given topics.

Directions: Please read paragraph (1) and (2) carefully and then express your views on the given topics.

(1) German ministry is under fire for meat-free buffets. The decision makers believed that take meat and fish off the menu will satisfy vegetarians. Do you agree or disagree?

Politicians stormed out of a buffet at a German government symposium on "exporting green technology" in Berlin this month when meat was not served, a media report said on Saturday. Instead of the salami rolls, cocktail sausages or goulash soups one would ordinarily expect at similar functions in the German capital, the lunchtime menu offered Belgian endives with caramelized apple and a soya vegetable lasagne, the Guardian reported. The vegetarian spread was the first manifestation of the German Environment Ministry's decision this month to became the first government agency to take meat and fish off the menu at official functions, citing a need to lead by example when it comes to environmentally sustainable consumption and the "consequences of consuming meat".

(2) The bug-eating kit may help humanity survive future global food shortages because insects take up less room but provide enough protein. Do you agree or disagree on eating bugs?

There are health benefits to tucking into creepy crawlies. There are around 27g of protein per 100 grams, but between 35 to 48g in chapuline grasshoppers. And insects take up a lot less room than bigger livestock, like chicken, cows and pigs. In addition, most countries have access to or can import edible insects, with countries including Australia, China, and Mexico having a particularly large variety already available. Designer Kobayashi Wataru is offering a small solution to the problem of making insects seem palatable for cultures where they aren't yet widely eaten which his creation BugBug utensils. The range, which isn't available in shops, includes especially designed chopsticks, a pork for picking up bugs, and a set of claws which slide over the fingers and help when eating bugs like crisps. He won UCL's Institute of Making 'Cutlery Design Challenge' with his design last year.

13.6 延伸口译(Extended Interpreting)

习近平主席在波兰媒体发表的署名文章

I visited Poland in the 1990s, which left me a deep impression. The Polish people are diligent, intelligent and courageous, and the country has a proud history and brilliant culture. Nicolaus Copernicus, exploring the vast universe, pioneered the theory of "the Sun rather than the Earth at the center of the Universe," transforming mankind's understanding of the Universe. Madam Curie, studying the micro world, discovered the two isotopes of Polonium and Radium, which paved the way for the development and application of the theory of radioactivity. Like music lovers all over the world, the Chinese people are fond of F.F. Chopin, a towering musician of Poland. The melodious tunes of Chopin's piano compositions, in particular, have a powerful resonance in our hearts.

20世纪90年代，我到过波兰，那次访问给我留下了深刻的印象。波兰人民勤劳、勇敢、智慧，历史文化底蕴深厚。哥白尼探索宇宙之无限大，创立"日心说"，改变了人类的宇宙观。居里夫人认识微观世界之无限小，发现钋和镭两种新元素，促进了放射性理论发展和应用。同世界上所有音乐爱好者一样，中国人民喜爱音乐大师肖邦的作品，特别是肖邦钢琴曲的优美旋律始终回荡我们心间。

In recent years, China-Poland relations have enjoyed fast growth. President Duda and I reached extensive agreement on increasing high-level interactions, deepening strategic mutual trust and expanding practical cooperation across the board during his successful visit to China at the end of last year. And the two sides signed an MOU on jointly building the "Belt and Road." All these have laid a solid foundation for exchanges and cooperation between the two countries in all fields. Poland became one of the first countries in Central and Eastern Europe to establish a strategic partnership with China and was the first CEE country to join the Asian Infrastructure Investment Bank (AIIB).

近年来，中波关系快速发展。去年年底，杜达总统成功访华，我们就加强两国高层交往、深化战略互信、推动各领域务实合作达成广泛共识。双方签署关于共同推进"一带一路"建设的政府间谅解备忘录，为两国各领域交流合作奠定了坚实基础。波兰是中东欧地区较早同中国建立战略伙伴关系、第一个加入亚洲基础设施投资银行的国家。

In recent years, China and Poland have achieved stable economic growth and remained each other's biggest trading partner in their respective regions for consecutive years. In 2015, two-way trade reached 17.09 billion U.S. dollars. Mutual investment grew steadily. And the two sides continued to expand and enhance cooperation in mining, infrastructure, transportation and logistics, finance, aerospace, science and technology and agriculture.

近年来，中波两国经济保持稳定增长，连续多年互为对方在各自地区的最大贸易伙伴。2015年，中波双边贸易额达到170.9亿美元，双向投资稳步增长，双方采矿、基础设施建设、交通物流、金融、航天、科技、农业等领域合作规模不断扩大，水平不断提高。

We also maintained dynamic people-to-people exchanges. "Happy Chinese New Year in Poland" has been held for six years, while such events as Polish culture season and Polish cultural festival are gaining popularity in China. Five Confucius Institutes have been established in Poland. More and more Chinese universities have started to offer Polish language programs. The China-Poland Regional Forum has been held successfully for three sessions, providing a platform for sub-national interactions. Our people-to-people exchange has grown more diverse in form and rich in content, injecting fresh vigor into our traditional friendship.

中波人文交流日益活跃。"欢乐春节·波兰行"已经连续举行6届，波兰文化季、波兰文化节等活动在华开展得有声有色。5所孔子学院相继在波兰落地生根，越来越多的中国高校开设波兰语教学。中波地方论坛成功举办3届，为两国地方交往提供了平台。双方人文交流形式多样、内涵丰富，两国传统友谊薪火相传，不断焕发出新的光彩。

Central and Eastern Europe as a sub-region boasts the greatest potential for growth in all of Europe. China and Central and Eastern European countries (CEECs) share a profound traditional friendship, sincere desire for cooperation and strong economic complementarity. This is the source of the vitality and great potential for cooperation between China and the CEECs (16+1 cooperation). Over the past four years, guided by the spirit of mutual respect, mutual benefit, openness and inclusiveness, the 16+1 cooperation has maintained strong momentum, expanded and deepened, and has become more mature and ready for harvest. We should promote the 16+1 cooperation with a forward-looking and people-oriented approach, and aim to make greater contribution to the prosperity of Europe and the growth of China-Europe relations.

中东欧是欧洲最有发展潜力的地区，中国和中东欧国家有着深厚传统友谊、真诚合作意愿，经济互补性强，这为中国—中东欧国家合作("16+1合作")提供了充沛动力和巨大空间。4年多来，有关各方相互尊重、互利共赢、包容开放，"16+1合作"保持快速发展势头，合作广度和深度不断扩大，已经进入成熟期和收获期。我们要本着面向未来、造福人民的精神，务实推进"16+1合作"，为欧洲繁荣和中欧关系发展作出更大贡献。

As comprehensive strategic partners, China and the EU have maintained strong relations which hold out great promise for further development. In 2014, during my visit to the EU headquarters, the EU leaders and I agreed to develop China-Europe partnerships for peace, growth, reform and progress of civilizations, identifying the strategic direction for China-Europe cooperation in the new era. Progress has been made concerning the five platforms we agreed to build, i.e. co-investment vehicle, connectivity platform, legal affairs dialogue, digital cooperation and mobility of the people.

中国同欧盟是全面战略伙伴。中欧关系发展顺利，面临良好历史机遇。2014年，我访问欧盟总部期间，同欧盟领导人一道决定打造中欧和平、增长、改革、文明四大伙伴关系，确立了新时期中欧合作的战略方向。双方共同决定推进的中欧共同投资基金、互联互通平台、法律事务对话、数字化合作、便利人员往来等五大平台建设取得积极进展。

Both China and Europe are now carrying out structural reforms to boost economic and social development. China is acting on its new vision of innovative, coordinated, green, open and shared development. It is upgrading its growth model and economic structure to maintain medium-high speed of growth and move to medium and upper ends of the industrial chain. The EU is implementing the investment plan for Europe, and has rolled out a combination of policy measures to sustain the growth momentum in Europe. As the world's two major forces, two big markets and two celebrated civilizations, China and Europe have every reason to enhance synergy in their development strategies, deepen shared interests, promote common growth and contribute to world peace and development.

当前，中欧双方都在推进结构性改革，促进经济社会发展。中国提出创新、协调、绿色、开放、共享的发展理念，致力于转方式调结构，推动经济保持中高速增长、产业迈向中高端水平。欧盟正在保持经济发展势头，实施欧洲投资计划，推出一系列组合措施。中欧作为全球两大力量、两大市场、两大文明，完全可以深度对接各自发展战略，深化利益融合，促进共同增长，为世界和平与发展作出积极贡献。

The 16+1 cooperation and China-Europe relations cannot go far without the growth of bilateral ties between China and countries of this region. China-Poland relations are now facing great opportunities. Madam Curie once said, one never notices what has been done; one can only see what remains to be done. I hope that this visit will be a good occasion for me to work with Polish leaders to enhance cooperation between our two countries across the board and achieve a higher level of development and broader and deeper growth for the 16+1 cooperation and China-Europe relations.

"16+1合作"和中欧关系发展离不开中国同地区国家双边关系发展。当前，中波关系面临良好发展机遇。贵国科学家居里夫人曾经说过："人不要总看做过什么，而应关注还有什么要做。"我期待通过这次访问，同波兰领导人一道，加强两国各领域合作，推动"16+1合作"以及中欧关系向着更高水平、更宽领域、更深层次发展。

We should treat each other as equals, build up mutual trust, and jointly meet the challenges of our times. Over the past 67 years, China and Poland have made remarkable achievements along their own path of development in keeping with their national conditions. Confucius, the great philosopher in ancient China, once observed that "a gentleman upholds high principles in all his pursuits and fulfills his mission with good faith." In the same spirit, our two countries should view bilateral relations from a strategic and long-term perspective, accord each other understanding and support on issues of core interests and major concern, and ensure steady and sound growth of China-Poland relations in the coming years.

我们要坚持平等互信、共对时代挑战。67年来，中波两国立足本国国情，坚持走符合自身国情的发展道路，取得巨大成就。中国古代思想家孔子说"义以为质""信以成之"。双方应该从战略高度和长远角度看待双边关系，相互理解和支持对方的核心利益和重大关切，确保中波关系长期稳定健康发展。

We should align development strategies and jointly explore ways of development. Poland is at the heartland of Europe. It is also where the Amber Road and the Silk Road meet. Several China Railway Express trains to Europe pass through Poland or are bound for Poland. Based on the MOU signed between the two governments on joint building of the Belt and Road, the two sides should speed up the formulation of cooperation plans, identify and prepare for major projects and work for early harvest.

我们要加强战略对接、共商发展大计。波兰是欧洲的"十字路口"，也是"琥珀之路"和"丝绸之路"的交汇点。目前，有多条中欧班列途经波兰或以波兰为目的地。双方应该以签署共同推进"一带一路"建设政府间谅解备忘录为基础，加紧完成两国规划纲要编制，充分梳理和筹备重大合作项目，争取早期收获。

We should deepen practical cooperation and jointly boost economic development. Poland is pursuing reindustrialization, while China is seeking international cooperation on production capacity. China is ready to join the Polish reindustrialization drive through cooperation on production capacity. China is also keen to cooperate more closely with Poland in such sectors as energy, infrastructure, transportation and logistics, communications and aerospace, with a view to raising the quality and level of bilateral cooperation.

我们要深化务实合作、共促经济发展。波兰正在致力于再工业化，中国正在大力推进国际产能合作。中方愿同波方一道，通过产能合作参与波兰再工业化进程，深化能源、基础设施建设、交通物流、通信、航天等各领域合作，提高双边合作含金量。

We must expand people-to-people ties and consolidate traditional friendship. Both China and Poland have great historical and cultural heritages. We should learn from each other and expand cooperation on culture, education, tourism, sports and at sub-national levels. We should encourage the younger generation to take the baton of friendship and do their part in deepening and renewing our traditional friendship.

我们要扩大人文交流、巩固传统友谊。中波两国都拥有丰富优秀的历史和文化传统。我们要互学互鉴，扩大文化、教育、地方、旅游、体育等领域交流合作，让两国青年接好中波友好的接力棒，为巩固两国传统友谊作出积极贡献。

We must make good use of existing platforms and jointly promote regional cooperation. Poland was the first proponent of 16+1 cooperation and hosted the first Meeting of Heads of Government of China and Central and Eastern European countries. It has actively supported and participated in 16+1 cooperation, and has played an important role in boosting investment and commerce within this framework. We are ready to work with Poland and all other Central and Eastern European countries to make good use of the 16+1 mechanism for regional cooperation and deliver more benefits to the people of our 17 countries.

我们要用好现有平台、共谋区域合作。波兰是"16+1合作"首倡国，是首届"16+1"领导人会晤举办国，始终积极支持和参与"16+1合作"，在投资、商务等领域发挥了重要促进作用。我们愿同包括波兰在内的中东欧国家一道，用好这一区域合作平台，造福十七国人民。

第14单元　口译表达及综述技巧
(Delivery Skills in Interpreting)

口译主题：科学技术

单元学习目的(Unit Goals) ☀

➤ 掌握本课程所讲授的口译综合表达技巧。
➤ 学习科学技术专题所涉及的常用词语和表达。

导入 (Lead -in)

1. 口译表达的重要性是什么？
2. 口译综述有哪些原则？
3. 口译综述有哪些环节？
4. 逻辑主线常见的类型有哪些？

14.1　技能讲解(Skill Introduction)

■ 14.1.1　口译综合表达的原则(Principles of Delivery in Interpreting)

　　口译表达是口译的最后一个环节，它直接影响着说话方和听话方之间的交流，也会影响到交际双方对译员的信任程度。译员应当摆脱原文本身的束缚，将源语的词语和意思分离。最重要的是让口译员开口讲话，忠实地表达原文的意思。另外，译员在表达过程中可能碰到一些具体的问题，译员可以运用其他口译技巧，如询问、重复或者根据自己的理解运用迂回的表达源语含义，等等，尽量表达理解了的内容，而且强调表达的内在逻辑和关联性，可懂程度和准确度以及流畅性。

　　(1) 内容简明扼要。综述以迅速掌握源语内容梗概为目的，要求简明准确地表达源语的重要内容。综述必须涵盖源语的有效信息，不得有重大遗漏，也不能添加任何主观评论和解释。综述就是保留源语的主干，去除源语的枝节。

(2) 抓取逻辑主线。综述必须把握源语的逻辑主线，抓主要的信息点，并体现信息的转换。

(3) 语言用词准确。综述的语言要求言简意赅，避免拖沓啰唆。

(4) 长度控制得当。综述的长度一般不超过源语的1/3。

■ 14.1.2　质量标准(Criteria of Delivery in Interpreting)

(1) 可信度。译文信息转达完整、准确、忠实于原文内容。

(2) 可接受度。译语表达层次分明、逻辑清晰、确切到位、遣词造句贴切、发音清楚，听众容易接受。

(3) 简明度。发言人的风格、说话方式能在译语中准确反映，译语简洁明了。

(4) 多样性。译员适应不同口音，明晰不同题材，了解不同专题的发言，并且表达清晰自如。

(5) 迅捷度。译员能在很短的时间内应付难题，即使转达交流双方的信息，也能综合发言人的思路，概述或简译源语发言。

(6) 技术性。译员必须掌握相关技巧，必须熟悉有关设备技术。

■ 14.1.3　口译综合表达的环节(Steps of Delivery in Interpreting)

(1) 听辨理解。口译实战中，译员首先要理解大意，其次要抓逻辑主线和主要信息点。理解大意，就是对源语的主题、主要观点进行整体的把握，而不是拘泥于单句，甚至是单个单词，那样只会对听辨形成干扰，影响听辨效果。逻辑主线常见的类型有：时间和空间、归纳或演绎、问题分析、情节叙述和新闻模式。

(2) 信息整理。译员的笔记记录伴随听辨过程。笔记应用纵线记录源语信息主线，动词的时态要格外注意。综述应该尽量遵循源语的逻辑顺序。

(3) 综述表达。综述的语言要求简练准确、客观公正、通顺流畅、全面完整；时态须与源语保持一致；大多数情况下译员需要自己构造句子，把要点串联起来。综述里的有效信息要均匀分配。

■ 14.1.4　训练方法及技巧(Skills of Delivery in Interpreting)

(1) 信息。听懂什么记什么，记下什么译什么，能直译就直译，不能直译就意译。

(2) 连贯。译完该译的内容后，译员要注意口译表达的连贯性，注重句子之间或段落之间的连贯。

(3) 节奏。译员在口译时要把握自己说话的节奏，说话不要时快时慢。译员应该保持一个稳定的速度，每个意群结束时做一个停顿。停顿时，译员可以从笔记本上抬起头来，与听众目光接触。这样能增强听众对讲话的兴趣和理解。另外，译员一定要在讲话人讲完两秒钟之内开始口译。

(4) 声音。口译时译员不能只顾传达文字，而不顾自己的声音、声调对观众的影响。针对讲话人不同的发言风格，译员应适当调整自己的声音和声调。

14.2　主题口译(Topic Interpreting)

▌14.2.1　单句口译(Sentence Practice)

Please interpret the following sentences by using the techniques illustrated above. You may interpret to your partner first and then he/she comments on your performance.

(1) "Industry 4.0" was first introduced in Germany and denotes the fourth stage of the industrial revolution. The focus is now on the convergence of the classical manufacturing space with internet technologies and the increasing intelligence of devices.

(2) Data has become a raw material of business, a vital economic input, used to create a new form of economic value. In fact, with the right mind, data can be cleverly reused to become a fountain of innovation and new services.

(3) It has also detected nine small planets within so-called habitable zones, where conditions are favorable for liquid water and potentially life. NASA said it was the biggest single announcement of new exoplanets.

(4) In today's world, no one company and no one country can hope to keep abreast of technology development alone. Access to new ideas and new technology from across the globe is therefore critical to success.

(5) Currently, more and more countries, including developing ones, are making the development of space activities an important strategic choice. Thus, space activities around the world are flourishing.

(6) 中华文明对人类文明做出了巨大的贡献。我们在2300年前发明了指南针，在公元105年发明了造纸，比欧洲早1000年。公元808年，我们又发明了火药。

(7) 屠呦呦，中国中医科学院研究员，同爱尔兰科学家威廉·坎贝尔和日本科学家大村智一起获得了2015年诺贝尔生理学或医学奖，以表彰他们在寄生虫疾病治疗研究方面取得的开创性成就。

(8) 航天是当今世界最具挑战性和广泛带动性的高科技领域之一，航天活动深刻改变了人类对宇宙的认知，为人类社会进步提供了重要动力。

(9) 中国首次月球探测工程的圆满成功，是继人造地球卫星、载人航天飞行取得成功之后，我国航天事业发展的又一里程碑，是我国科技自主创新取得的标志性成果。

(10) 中国政府于设定了在"十三五"期间(2016—2020)推进建设100个智慧城市的目标。为了实现这一目标，国家发展和改革委员会与其他几个部委携手，承诺进一步开放和分享数据，网络安全也将在这一过程中得到加强。

■ 14.2.2 段落口译(Paragraph Practice)

1. Vocabulary Work: Study the following words and phrases and translate them into the target language.

潮汐	hacker
阿司匹林	be compelled to
消炎	non-invasively
血小板	MRI

2. Please interpret the following paragraphs by using the techniques illustrated above.

(1) 科学以多种方式帮助人类。科学发明为我们的生活带来了许许多多的改变。世界的文明因科学而产生飞跃式的进步。因为科技，我们的生活变得更加舒适。我们可以用多种多样的交通工具来完成我们的旅行和运输。电的发明也在方方面面帮助着我们。今天，夜晚不再黑暗无光，冬天不再寒冷，夏天也不再炎热。电视机的发明帮助我们获取发生在世界各地的新闻、娱乐和电视直播，而我们足不出户就能纵观天下之事。在大气层上方轨道中运行的通信卫星可以为我们预报天气、飓风以及海洋中的潮汐变化，等等。电脑和互联网帮助人类大大延伸了信息技术的范畴。今天的生活如果没有科学，将无法想象。

总之，我们可以说科学是今天的魔法精灵，如果能够认真加以利用，它将为我们创造奇迹。

(2) 阿司匹林一直以来都是一种被用来抑制疼痛、治疗发烧和炎症的药物，但是最近一项研究表明每天服用阿司匹林还能预防癌症。早先一些研究已经发现阿司匹林可以降低患上某些癌症的风险，但是科学家们对于这种药物到底是如何预防癌症困惑了很多年，许多人都认为原因是阿司匹林可以消炎。据这项最新研究显示，德州退伍军人事务局的科学家们表示称，这种药物和血小板(血小板可以凝固血液)相互作用，可以防止肿瘤生长。通常情况下，受伤血管阻塞之后，血小板可以帮助形成新的血管，但是这一功能也能帮助肿瘤增殖和生存。

(3) For the past three decades, hackers have done a lot of things, but they have also impacted civil liberties, innovation and Internet freedom, so I think it's time we take a good look at how we choose to portray them, because if we keep expecting them to be the bad guys, how can they be the heroes too? My years in the hacker world have made me realize both the problem and the beauty about hackers: They just can't see something broken in the world and leave it be. They are compelled to either exploit it or try and change it, and so they find the vulnerable aspects in our rapidly changing world. They make us, they force us to fix things or demand something better, and I think we need them to do just that, because after all, it is not information that wants to be

free, it's us.

(4) We're going to fly into my colleague Peter's brain. We're going to do it non-invasively using MRI. We don't have to inject anything. We don't need radiation. We will be able to fly into the anatomy of Peter's brain—literally, fly into his body—but more importantly, we can look into his mind. When Peter moves his arm, that yellow spot you see there is the interface to the functioning of Peter's mind taking place. Now you've seen before that with electrodes you can control robotic arms, that brain imaging and scanners can show you the insides of brains. What's new is that that process has typically taken days or months of analysis. We've collapsed that through technology to milliseconds, and that allows us to let Peter to look at his brain in real time as he's inside the scanner. He can look at these 65 000 points of activation per second. If he can see this pattern in his own brain, he can learn how to control it.

▌ 14.2.3　篇章口译[Passage Practice (E to C)]

1. Please interpret the following passage by using the techniques illustrated above. Please pay attention to the underlined sentences as they require special treatment during interpreting.

The Future of the Car

① People love their automobiles. They allow us to go where we want to when we want to. They're a form of entertainment, they're a form of art, a pride of ownership. Songs are written about cars. Prince wrote a great song: "Little Red Corvette." He didn't write "Little Red Laptop Computer" or "Little Red Dirt Devil". He wrote about a car.

② The fact is, when we do our market research around the world, we see that there's nearly a universal aspiration on the part of people to own an automobile. And 750 million people in the world today own a car. And you say, boy, that's a lot. But you know what? That's just 12 percent of the population. We really have to ask the question: Can the world sustain that number of automobiles? And if you look at projections over the next 10 to 15 to 20 years, it looks like the world car park could grow to on the order of 1.1 billion vehicles. Now, if you parked those end to end and wrapped them around the Earth, that would stretch around the Earth 125 times.

③ Now, we've made great progress with automobile technology over the last 100 years. Cars are dramatically cleaner, dramatically safer, more efficient and radically more affordable than they were 100 years ago. But the fact remains: the fundamental DNA of the automobile has stayed pretty much the same. <u>If we are going to reinvent the automobile today, rather than 100 years ago, knowing what we know about the issues associated with our product and about the technologies that exist today, what would we do?</u>⁽¹⁾

④ We wanted something that was really affordable. The fuel cell looked great: one-tenth as many moving parts and a fuel-cell propulsion system as an internal combustion engine — and it emits just water. And we wanted to take advantage of Moore's Law with electronic controls and software, and we absolutely wanted our car to be connected. So we embarked upon the reinvention around an electrochemical engine, the fuel cell, hydrogen as the energy carrier. First was Autonomy. Autonomy really set the vision for where we wanted to head. We embodied all of the key components of a fuel cell propulsion system. We then had Autonomy drivable with Hy-Wire, and we showed Hy-Wire here at this conference last year. Hy-Wire is the world's first drivable fuel cell, and we have followed up that now with Sequel. And Sequel truly is a real car.[2] So if we would run the video —

⑤ But the real key question I'm sure that's on your mind: where's the hydrogen going to come from? And secondly, when are these kinds of cars going to be available? So let me talk about hydrogen first. The beauty of hydrogen is it can come from so many different sources: it can come from fossil fuels, it can come from any way that you can create electricity, including renewables. And it can come from biofuels. And that's quite exciting. The vision here is to have each local community play to its natural strength in creating the hydrogen. A lot of hydrogen's produced today in the world. It's produced to get sulfur out of gasoline — which I find is somewhat ironic. It's produced in the fertilizer industry; it's produced in the chemical manufacturing industry. That hydrogen's being made because there's a good business reason for its use. But it tells us that we know how to create it, we know how to create it cost effectively, we know how to handle it safely.

⑥ We did an analysis where you would have a station in each city with each of the 100 largest cities in the United States, and located the stations so you'd be no more than two miles from a station at any time. We put one every 25 miles on the freeway, and it turns out that translates into about 12 000 stations. And at a million dollars each, that would be about 12 billion dollars. Now that's a lot of money. But if you built the Alaskan pipeline today, that's half of what the Alaskan pipeline would cost. But the real exciting vision that we see truly is home refueling, much like recharging your laptop or recharging your cellphone. So we're pretty excited about the future of hydrogen. We think it's a question of not whether, but a question of when.

⑦ What we've targeted for ourselves — and we're making great progress for this goal— is to have a propulsion system based on hydrogen and fuel cells, designed and validated, that can go head-to-head with the internal combustion engine — we're talking about obsoleting the internal combustion engine — and do it in terms of its affordability, add skill volumes, its performance and its durability. So that's what we're driving to for 2010. We haven't seen anything yet in our development work that says that isn't possible. We actually think the future's going to be event-driven. So since we can't predict the future, we want to spend a lot of our time trying to create that future.

⑧ I'm very, very intrigued by the fact that our cars and trucks sit idle 90 percent of the time: they're parked, they're parked all around us. They're usually parked within 100 feet of the people that own them. Now, if you take the power-generating capability of an automobile and you compare that to the electric grid in the United States, it turns out that four percent of the automobiles, the power in four percent of the automobiles, equals that of the electric grid of the US. That's a huge power-generating capability, a mobile power-generating capability. And hydrogen and fuel cells give us that opportunity to actually use our cars and trucks when they're parked to generate electricity for the grid.

⑨ And we talked about swarm networks earlier. And talking about the ultimate swarm, about having all of the processors and all of the cars when they're sitting idle being part of a global grid for computing capability. We find that premise quite exciting. The automobile becomes, then, an appliance, not in a commodity sense, but an appliance, mobile power, mobile platform for information and computing and communication, as well as a form of transportation.

⑩ And the key to all of this is to make it affordable, to make it exciting, to get it on a pathway where there's a way to make money doing it. And again, this is a pretty big march to take here. And a lot of people say, how do you sleep at night when you're rustling with a problem of that magnitude? And I tell them I sleep like a baby: I wake up crying every two hours. Actually the theme of this conference, I think, has hit on really one of the major keys to pull that off—and that's relationships and working together. Thank you very much. (Applause).

Notes on the text

(1) If we are going to reinvent the automobile today, rather than 100 years ago, knowing what we know about the issues associated with our product and about the technologies that exist today, what would we do?

如果我们今天来重新发明汽车，而不是在100年前，在已经知道汽车的各种缺陷之后，结合现在的各种先进技术，我们会如何制造汽车？

(2) First was Autonomy. Autonomy really set the vision for where we wanted to head. We embodied all of the key components of a fuel cell propulsion system. We then had Autonomy drivable with Hy-Wire, and we showed Hy-Wire here at this conference last year. Hy-Wire is the world's first drivable fuel cell, and we have followed up that now with Sequel. And Sequel truly is a real car.

最初，通用汽车研发出的是一款名为Autonomy的概念车。它奠定了通用汽车之后的环保车发展方向。对于燃料电池推进系统的设计，我们整合了所有关键性的元素之后，我们在Autonomy中融入氢燃料电池-线传操控技术。去年的这个研讨会上曾展出过Hy-Wire概念车。它是世界上第一款可驾驶的燃料电池汽车。在Autonomy和Hy-Wire之后，现在我们又带来最新一代的氢燃料电池车Sequel。Sequel是一辆真正意义上的汽车，而非概念车。

2. Please interpret the following passage by using the techniques illustrated above. Please pay attention to the underlined sentences as they require special treatment during interpreting.

Barack Obama' Parting Shot for his Successor Donald Trump

① Barack Obama had a parting shot for his successor this week. A day before Donald Trump predicted he would be "the greatest jobs producer that God ever created", the outgoing US president appeared like the ghost at the feast, warning of "the relentless pace of automation that will make many jobs obsolete".[1]

② It is at least possible that both will be proved right. Automation has been a constant for decades, and the latest advances in robotics and artificial intelligence all but guarantee that the pace will accelerate. But timing is all. For companies and their investors — no less than for politicians — the key question is not "whether", but "when".

③ For society at large, the pace of automation will determine how easily the displacement of workers can be handled — and whether the political backlash grows worse. The pace is equally important for the companies trying to push the latest robots and smart machines into the real world, and their investors. Few are in the position of Google parent Alphabet, which has taken the long view on bets like driverless cars — and even Alphabet these days has a new sense of impatience about when it will see returns from "moonshots" like this.

④ The variables that will affect the rate of adoption are huge. In a new report on automation this week, Mckinsey estimates that half of all the tasks people perform at work could be automated using technologies that have already been proven. But this estimate gives no clue about how long it will take.

⑤ Given the uncertainties about everything from regulation to the ability of companies to change their processes, the consultants estimate it could take anything from 20 to 60 years.[2] Try building an investment model with that level of variability. Take the case for autonomous cars and trucks. Much of the technology has already been demonstrated, and the potential markets — for both vehicle makers and tech suppliers — are vast. But will it take five, 10 or 30 years for this to become a significant market?

⑥ Car companies are already spending hundreds of millions of dollars on building driverless car platforms. At this month's Consumer Electronics Show and Detroit Auto Show, it was clear that driverless technology has graduated from the experimental: carmakers are now racing to bring this technology to the roads.[3] The biggest companies are able to amortise this cost over a large vehicle fleet, but the increasing level of technology in vehicles will challenge many of the industry's smaller players.

⑦ Companies like Audi talk of autonomy as a progression. It says 60 per cent of new car buyers already opt to pay $3 000—$6 000 for features like automated acceleration and braking.

Those customers might reasonably be expected to keep paying up for additional levels of safety and convenience. The shift from cars that stay in their lanes automatically to hands-off-the-wheel driving might turn out to be a smooth — and profitable — evolution.

⑧ But the strongest business case for driverless cars comes from the more radical, all-or-nothing step of eradicating the need for human drivers. In a report on automation's impact on the economy late last month, the White House said that most of today's 1.7m drivers of heavy trucks in the US are likely to be replaced — though it added that "it may take years or decades" for this to happen.

⑨ There are some very practical considerations. As Michael Cui, a partner at McKinsey, points out it is vastly expensive to replace the estimated 2m heavy trucks on US roads, with an average lifespan of 20 years. Even without new driverless technology, McKinsey estimates it would cost $320bn. But there are likely to be specific investment cases for speedier adoption. Long-haul routes are the low-hanging fruit of trucking. Platooning, in which trucks form a convoy behind a lead truck driven by a human, could bring a form of supervised automation. Although the long tail of automation may take decades, the market for early adopters could still be vast.(4)

⑩ Rather than wiping out jobs immediately, progressive automation might make the lives of today's truckers more comfortable and then make up for an expected driver shortage in the mid term, before eliminating jobs eventually. This prospect represents the rosy scenario for the companies leading the AI and robotics charge. But as today's turbulent political climate shows, they would be foolish to count on such a smooth transition.

Notes on the text

(1) Barack Obama had a parting shot for his successor this week. A day before Donald Trump predicted he would be "the greatest jobs producer that God ever created", the outgoing US president appeared like the ghost at the feast, warning of "the relentless pace of automation that will make many jobs obsolete."

巴拉克·奥巴马(Barack Obama)给他的继任者留下了一句临别赠语。在唐纳德·特朗普(Donald Trump)预言自己将成为"上帝创造的最伟大的就业制造者"一天前，离任的美国总统似乎像是宴会上的幽灵，警告称"自动化的无情步伐将淘汰很多就业岗位"。

宴席上的骷髅/幽灵(源自古埃及人，他们在重大宴席上都要放一具骷髅，以提醒人们居安思危，不忘苦难和死亡)，现在用来表示令人扫兴的事或人。

(2) it could take anything from 20 to 60 years

这可能需要20年至60年

(3) At this month's Consumer Electronics Show and Detroit Auto Show, it was clear that driverless technology has graduated from the experimental: carmakers are now racing to bring this technology to the roads.

在本月的拉斯维加斯消费电子展(Consumer Electronics Show)和底特律车展(Detroit Auto Show)上，无人驾驶技术显然已摆脱实验阶段：汽车制造商正竞相把这项技术推向道路。

(4) Platooning, in which trucks form a convoy behind a lead truck driven by a human, could bring a form of supervised automation. Although the long tail of automation may take decades, the market for early adopters could still be vast.

车辆结队(Platooning, 多辆卡车在由人类驾驶的领头卡车后面组成一个车队)可能带来一种受到监控的自动化形式。尽管自动化的长尾效应可能耗时几十年，但早期采用者的市场仍可能巨大。

14.2.4　篇章口译[Passage Practice (C to E)]

1. Please interpret the following passage by using the techniques illustrated above. Please pay attention to the underlined sentences as they require special treatment during interpreting.

《2016中国的航天》白皮书

① 航天是当今世界最具挑战性和广泛带动性的高科技领域之一，航天活动深刻改变了人类对宇宙的认知，为人类社会进步提供了重要动力。当前，越来越多的国家，包括广大发展中国家将发展航天作为重要战略选择，世界航天活动呈现蓬勃发展的景象。

② 中国政府把发展航天事业作为国家整体发展战略的重要组成部分，始终坚持为和平目的的探索和利用外层空间。中国航天事业自1956年创建以来，已走过60年光辉历程，创造了以"两弹一星"、载人航天、月球探测为代表的辉煌成就，走出了一条自力更生、自主创新的发展道路，积淀了深厚博大的航天精神。(1)为传承航天精神、激发创新热情，中国政府决定，自2016年起，将每年4月24日设立为"中国航天日"。

③ "探索浩瀚宇宙，发展航天事业，建设航天强国，是我们不懈追求的航天梦。"未来五年及今后一个时期，中国将坚持创新、协调、绿色、开放、共享的发展理念，推动空间科学、空间技术、空间应用全面发展，为服务国家发展大局和增进人类福祉作出更大贡献。

④ 为进一步增进国际社会对中国航天事业的了解，特发表《2016中国的航天》白皮书，介绍2011年以来中国航天活动的主要进展、未来五年的主要任务以及国际交流与合作等情况。(2)

Notes on the text

(1) 中国航天事业自1956年创建以来，已走过60年光辉历程，创造了以"两弹一星"、载人航天、月球探测为代表的辉煌成就，走出了一条自力更生、自主创新的发展道路，积淀了深厚博大的航天精神。

Over the past 60 years of remarkable development since its space industry was established in 1956, China has made great achievements in this sphere, including the development of atomic and hydrogen bombs, missiles, man-made satellites, manned spaceflight and lunar probe.

(2) 为进一步增进国际社会对中国航天事业的了解，特发表《2016中国的航天》白皮书，介绍2011年以来中国航天活动的主要进展、未来五年的主要任务以及国际交流与合作等情况。

To enable the world community to better understand China's space industry, we are publishing this white paper to offer a brief introduction to the major achievements China has made in this field since 2011, its main tasks in the next five years, and its international exchanges and cooperation efforts.

2. Please interpret the following passage by using the techniques illustrated above. Please pay attention to the underlined sentences as they require special treatment during interpreting.

中医介绍

① 已有两千至三千年历史的中医(TCM)有其独特的诊断与治疗疾病的方法。⁽¹⁾不同于西医，中医对人体的认识基于道教对宇宙的整体性的认识，对疾病治疗的基础主要是诊断与辨别病症。

② 中医学的基本特点是之一就是整体观念。整体就是指统一性和完整性。中医学非常重视人体本身的统一性、完整性以及与自然界的相互关系。人体本身是一个有机的整体，构成人体的各个组成部分是相互协调、相互影响的。同时，人体与外界自然环境有着密切的、不可分割的关系。这种内外环境的统一性、机体自身整体性的思想，称之为整体观念。

③ 人体是有机的整体，人体是由若干脏器和组织器官组成的，它们都有各自不同的功能，这些不同的功能又都是整体活动的一个组成部分，决定了机体的整体统一性，因而在生理上相互联系、相互协调，在病理上则相互影响。

④ 人类生活在自然界，自然界存在着人类赖以生存的必要条件。因此，自然界的运动变化可以直接或间接地影响着人体，而人体也必然相应地产生生理或病理上的反映。

⑤ 另一中医学的基本特点就是辩证论治。它是中医认识和治疗疾病的基本原则，是中医学对疾病的一种特殊的研究和处理方法，也是中医学的基本特点之一。⁽²⁾所谓辩证，就是分析、辨别、认识疾病的症候。论治就是辩证的结果，确立相应的治疗法则。辩证是决定治疗的前提和依据；论治是治疗疾病的手段和方法，也是对辩证是否正确的检验。辩证和论治，是诊治疾病过程中相互联系不可分割的两部分，是理论和实践相结合的体现。辨证论治之所以是中医学的一个特点，是因为它既不同于一般的对症治疗，也不同于现代医学的辨病治疗。一个病的不同阶段，可以出现不同的症候，不同的疾病，其发展过程中可能出现同样的证候。因此，同一疾病的不同证候，治疗方法就不同，而不同疾病只要证

候相同，就可以运用同一治疗方法。由此可见，辩证的证，是疾病的原因、部位、性质、以及致病因素和抗病能力相互斗争的概括。

⑥ 中医认为脏腑为人体的核心。人体器官和组织通过经络和血管组成的网络相连接。气承担信息载体的功能，通过经络得以表达。从病理学的角度讲，脏腑的功能障碍可能通过网络反映到人体表面。同样，身体表面的疾病也可能影响相关的脏或腑。受到感染的脏和腑也可能通过内在的连接网互相影响。中医的诊治由分析人体的整体系统开始，然后通过调节脏腑器官的功能纠正病态变化。评估症状不仅包括寻找病因、病理、病灶及疾病的性质，还包括致病因素与身体抗性之间的冲突。对疾病的治疗不仅仅以症状为基础，还以区别症状为基础。因此，对有相同疾病的患者的治疗有多种方式。此外，不同的疾病可能症状是相同的，所以治疗方法也是相似的。中医的临床诊断和治疗的基础是阴阳五行学说。阴阳五行学说将自然现象与规律运用于人的生理活动和病理变化以及这两者之间的内在联系之中。典型的中医治疗手段包括针刺疗法、中药和气功锻炼。[3]针刺疗法的治疗是刺激人的外在体，中药作用于内在的脏腑器官，而气功通过对气的调节，用于恢复网络中有序的信息流。这些治疗方法看上去非常不同，但对人体的性质及其在宇宙中的位置的假定与理解都是相同的。一些科学家将中药、针刺疗法和气功的治疗方式称为 "信息治疗法"。

⑦ 阴阳学说

中医的哲学基础来自于道家学说。大部分的道家思想是基于观察自然世界及其运行的方式，因此中医系统广泛地借鉴自然界的象征这点并不奇怪。在中医里，在观察自然基础上得来的、象征性地理解人体的观点在阴阳五行学说理论中得到了完全表达。在中文里，阴阳概念的本义是一个物体的阳面和阴面。中国哲学用阴阳的概念来代表更宽泛的宇宙中物质的属性：冷与热、快与慢、静与动、雌与雄、低与高等。一般而言，任何运动的、上升的、光亮的、发展的、过度活跃的，包括人体的机能性疾病都属于阳性；带有静止、递减、阴郁的、退化的、不够活跃的，包括人体器官性疾病都属于阴性。阴阳的功能受到辨证对立统一法则的指引。[4]换句话说，阴阳是对立的，但同时也是互相依存的。阴阳的性质是相对的，两者都不能单独存在。没有 "冷" 就没有 "热"，没有 "动" 就没有 "静"，没有 "阴" 也就没有 "阳"。最能说明阴阳相互依赖的例子就是物质和功能的内在联系。人体必须拥有充足的物质才能健康运转，同时，只有当运转处于健康的过程之中，人体的基本物质才能适当地更新。

⑧ 一切物质和现象的对立永远处于不变的运动与变化之中：一方的增加、增长、前进意味着另一方的减少、下降、后退。例如白天是阳，而夜晚是阴，但清晨被理解成为阳中之阳，下午是阳中之阴，午夜之前的晚间是阴中之阴，午夜之后的时间为阴中之阳。种子是阴，植物是阳，土壤是阴。种子长成植物，植物枯萎回土壤，这个过程发生在季节的变化之中。冬季是阴，冬季通过春季转变到夏季。夏季是阳，又通过秋季转回到冬季，又变成阴。因为自然现象在持续的阴阳互换中保持平衡，阴阳互换或相互转化便被认为是普遍的法则。

中医认为人的生命是一个处于运动和变化之中的生理过程。在正常的条件下，阴阳的消长保持于某种范围，反映了生理学上的动态平衡。当平衡被打破，疾病便来袭。<u>与疾病有关的失衡现象的典型例子包括阴盛、阳盛、阴衰、阳衰。</u>⁽⁵⁾

Notes on the text

(1) <u>已有两千至三千年历史的中医(TCM)有其独特的诊断与治疗疾病的方法。</u>

With a history of 2000 to 3000 years, Traditional Chinese Medicine (TCM) has formed a unique system to diagnose and cure illness.

(2) <u>另一中医学的基本特点就是辨证论治。它是中医认识和治疗疾病的基本原则，是中医学对疾病的一种特殊的研究和处理方法，也是中医学的基本特点之一。</u>

The other essential characteristics of TCM is treatment determination based on syndrome differentiation. It is an essential principle in TCM in understanding and treating disease. It is a specific research and treatment method of disease in TCM, and also one of the essential characteristics of TCM."

(3) <u>中医的临床诊断和治疗的基础是阴阳五行学说。阴阳五行学说将自然现象与规律运用于人的生理活动和病理变化以及这两者之间的内在联系之中。典型的中医治疗手段包括针刺疗法、中药和气功锻炼。</u>

The clinical diagnosis and treatment in Traditional Chinese Medicine are mainly based on the yin-yang and five elements theories. These theories apply the phenomena and laws of nature to the study of the physiological activities and pathological changes of the human body and its interrelationships. The typical TCM therapies include acupuncture, herbal medicine, and qigong exercises."

(4) <u>在中文里，阴阳概念的本义是一个物体的阳面和阴面。中国哲学用阴阳的概念来代表更宽泛的宇宙中物质的属性：冷与热、快与慢、静与动、雌与雄、低与高等。一般而言，任何运动的、上升的、光亮的、发展的、过度活跃的，包括人体的机能性疾病都属于阳性；带有静止的、递减的、阴郁的、退化的、不够活跃的，包括人体器官性疾病都属于阴性。阴阳的功能受到辨证对立统一法则的指引。</u>

The direct meanings of yin and yang in Chinese are bright and dark sides of an object. Chinese philosophy uses yin and yang to represent a wider range of opposite properties in the universe: cold and hot, slow and fast, still and moving, masculine and feminine, lower and upper, etc. In general, anything that is moving, ascending, bright, progressing, hyperactive, including functional disease of the body, pertains to yang. The characteristics of stillness, descending, darkness, degeneration, hypo-activity, including organic disease, pertain to yin. The function of yin and yang is guided by the law of unity of the opposites."

(5) <u>与疾病有关的失衡现象的典型例子包括阴盛、阳盛、阴衰、阳衰。</u>

Typical cases of disease-related imbalance include excess of yin, excess of yang, deficiency of yin, and deficiency of yang.

14.3 参考译文(Reference Version)

■ 14.3.1 单句口译(Sentence Practice)

Please interpret the following sentences by using the techniques illustrated above. You may interpret to your partner first and then he/she comments on your performance.

(1) 工业 "4" 首次在德国引入，是工业革命的第四个阶段。现在关注的是经典制造业空间的收缩、互联网技术和设备越来越多的智能性。

(2) 数据已经成为一种商业资本，一项重要的经济投入，可以用来创造新的经济利益。事实上，只要思路正确，人们就可以巧妙地使用数据以开发新产品，提供新服务。

(3) NASA还在所谓的 "可居住带" 内发现了9颗较小的行星，就这些行星的空间位置来看，很有可能存在液态水和生命。NASA说这是有史以来最大的太阳系外星系发现报告。

(4) 在当今世界，没有哪个企业或国家能够指望凭自身的实力，保持技术发展的领先势头。因此，能够从全球各地获得新的思想和技术对成功非常关键。

(5) 当前，越来越多的国家，包括广大发展中国家将发展航天作为重要战略选择，世界航天活动呈现蓬勃发展的景象。

(6) Chinese civilization has made great contributions to human civilization. We invented the compass 2 300 years ago, and paper-making in 105AD, 1 000 years ahead of Europe. In 808 AD, we invented gunpowder.

(7) Tu Youyou, a researcher at the China Academy of Traditional Chinese Medicine, shared the 2015 Nobel Prize for Medicine with Irish-born William Campbell and Satoshi Omura of Japan for unlocking revolutionary treatments for parasitic diseases.

(8) Space activities make up one of the most challenging hi-tech fields which exert enormous impact on other fields. Space activities have greatly improved man's knowledge of space, and provide an important driving force for social progress.

(9) The complete success of China's first lunar exploration project is another milestone in the development of China's space industry following the successes made in man-made satellite and manned space flight, and also a landmark achievement resulted from China's independent scientific and technical innovation.

(10) Chinese authorities set a goal of moving ahead on construction of 100 smart cities during the 13th Five-Year Plan period (2016—2020). In order to meet the target, the National Development and Reform Commission has joined hands with several other ministries, promising to further open up and share data, and cyber security will also be strengthened during the process.

■ 14.3.2　段落口译(Paragraph Practice)

1. Vocabulary Work: Study the following words and phrases and translate them into the target language.

tidal	黑客
Aspirin	被迫
inflammation-lowering	非侵入性的
platelets	核磁共振成像(Magnetic Resonance Imaging)

2. Please interpret the following paragraphs by using the techniques illustrated above.

(1) Science helped mankind in innumerable ways. The scientific inventions have brought about many changes in our lives. The civilizations of the world have progressed by leap and bounds. It has helped us in countless ways to make our everyday life comfortable. For traveling or transportation we have many types of vehicles. The invention of electricity has helped us in many ways. Today nights are not dark, winters are not so cold and summers are not so hot. The invention of TV sets has helped us in getting news, entertainment, live telecasts of distant events around the world. We need not go out of our houses to witness those events. Communication satellites moving in their orbits above the earth's atmosphere can forecast weather reports, cyclones, tidal changes in the sea etc. Computers and the Internet have helped mankind dramatically extend the scope of information technology. Today's life without science is unthinkable. To conclude we can say that science is the magic wizard of today. It can do wonders for us if it is used carefully.

(2) Aspirin has been used as a medication to treat pain, fever and inflammation, but a new study shows that daily doses of aspirin could also help ward off cancer. Earlier studies have discovered that aspirin may decrease the risk of certain types of cancer, but scientists remain puzzled for years over how exactly the drug works to prevent the deadly disease, with many attributing it to the drug's inflammation-lowering properties. According to the new study, scientists from Veterans Affairs in Texas suggested that the pain-relief medication's interaction with platelets, the blood cells that form clots to stop bleeding, could stop tumors from growing. Normally, platelets can help form new blood vessels when a clot forms after a wound, but the same action can help tumors proliferate and survive.

(3) 过去的30年以来，黑客做过很多事，他们也影响过公民自由、创新和网络自由，所以现在是时候让我们来看看，我们应该选择如何看待他们，因为如果我们一直觉得他们是坏人，他们又如何同时成为英雄呢？我在黑客世界的这些年让我意识到黑客的问题和美好两方面：他们就是不能看到这个世界上有缺陷的东西而置之不顾。他们被迫开发或者尝试改变它，所以他们在我们这样一个日益巨变的世界找到脆弱的地方。他们强迫我们去修复东西，或者要求更好的东西，我想我们需要他们做这些事，因为毕竟不是信息需要自由，是我们需要它。

(4) 我们将要进入我同事彼得的脑中，且是用非侵入性的方法，那就是使用核磁共振造影。不必注入任何东西进入体内，不需要冒着辐射的危害，就能够进入彼得的脑部的解剖结构中，确确实实地飞入他的体内。但更重要的是，我们可以观察他的心智运作。当彼得挥动他的手臂，你可以看那个黄色的点，是彼得脑中对应功能发生运作的地方。你们之前已经看过了，你可以透过电极控制机械手臂，脑部成像及扫描器可以显示出大脑内部。最新的进展是原本这个程序一般需经过几天甚至是几个月的分析。我们现在用最新技术可将时间缩短至几毫秒钟，且彼德在扫描器中可以同时看到自己的脑部运作。他可以看到这些每秒内激发的65 000点。如果他可以看到在他自己脑袋中运作的模式，他便可以学习如何控制它。

14.3.3 篇章口译[Passage Practice (E to C)]

1. Please interpret the following passage by using the techniques illustrated above. Please pay attention to the underlined sentences as they require special treatment during interpreting.

汽车的未来

① 人人都爱车。有了车，我们就能随时随地前往我们想去的地方。车是一种娱乐形式，是一种艺术形式，是一种因为所有权而产生的骄傲。有许多关于汽车的歌曲。王子(Prince)写了一首很棒的《小小红色雪佛兰》。他写的不是《小红笔记本电脑》，也不是《小红吸尘器》，而是关于一辆车的歌曲。

② 实际上，我们在做世界范围的市场调研时发现，人们都是对车充满渴望的。现在全球有7.5亿人拥有汽车。你可能觉得，哇，这么多！但你们知道吗，这个数字仅仅占全球人口的12%。我们不得不产生这样的疑问：地球经受得了这么多车吗？如果你注意到对未来10年、15年至20年的预测。你会发现世界上停车场的数量将会增长到能容纳下11亿车辆。如果将这些车首尾相连绕地球停放，那么其长度将是地球周长的125倍。

③ 在过去的100年里，汽车技术飞速发展。汽车变得更加清洁、安全、高效。比起100年前，现在汽车已成为大众消费品，而不是让我们望而兴叹的东西。但实际上，汽车的基本构造功能没变。如果我们今天来重新发明汽车，而不是在100年前，在已经知道汽车的各种缺陷之后，结合现在的各种先进技术，我们会如何制造汽车？

④ 我们需要的是人们能够买得起的汽车。燃料电池似乎不错。只有其他许多移动部件的1/10大，并且燃料电池推进系统作为内燃机，仅仅释放出水而已。我们想通过摩尔定律来解释电子控制系统和软件方面的更新。同时我们也希望车辆之间能互通联系。所以我们开始着手改造电化学发动机里的燃料电池，使氢作为能源载体。最初，通用汽车研发出的是一款名为Autonomy的概念车。它奠定了通用汽车之后的环保车发展方向。对于燃料电池推进系统的设计，我们整合了所有关键性的元素之后，我们在Autonomy中融入氢燃

料电池-线传操控技术。去年的这个研讨会上曾展出过Hy-Wire概念车。它是世界上第一款可驾驶的燃料电池汽车。在Autonomy和Hy-Wire之后，现在我们又带来最新一代的氢燃料电池车Sequel。Sequel是一辆真正意义上的汽车，而非概念车。让我们看看这个视频短片吧。

⑤ 你们肯定都有这样一个关键的疑问：氢气从何而来？这种燃料电池汽车什么时候能真正面世？我先谈谈氢气吧！氢气的奇妙之处在于它可以从许多资源中获得：石油，任何能产生电能的方式：包括可再生能源；生物燃料，也能产生氢气。这很棒吧，我们的愿景是：每一个社区内都能够稀松平常地获得氢气。当今世界热衷于生产氢气，因为氢气能减少汽油的消耗。这让我觉得有点讽刺意味。化肥工业生产氢气，化学工业生产氢气，而生产氢气是因为它具有良好的经济效益。但关键是，我们要知道如何生产氢气，如何降低生产氢气的成本，以及如何进行安全生产。

⑥ 我们做了个分析，在全美100个最大的城市里设定一个车站，将车站设定在无论何时你都距其不到2英里的范围内，我们在高速公路上每隔25英里设一个车站，那么大约有1.2万个车站。如果一个车站需要花费100万美元，那么就需要花费120亿美元。这可是一大笔钱，但如果现在开建阿拉斯加输油管，120亿美元仅是铺设输油管的所花费的一半而已。我们认为最激动人心的前景是在家加油，就像在家里给笔记本或手机充电一样，我们都看好氢气在未来的应用前景。这不是是否应该应用氢气的问题，而是何时能够应用的问题。

⑦ 对于我们的目标，其正在进展中并且不断得到改进。这个目标就是制造一个以氢燃料电池为基础的推进系统。经过设计及验证后，这个推进系统将能与内燃机媲美。我们打算淘汰内燃机，在提高可购性、增加技能卷、提高性能和耐用性方面努力。这就是2010年我们要做的工作。目前还没发现在研发过程中，有任何迹象表明我们的想法不可行。我们相信未来将为事件所驱动。虽然我们无法预测未来，但是我们会努力创造未来。

⑧ 我们的汽车以及卡车有90%的时间是停着的，我对如何挖掘这段时间内车子的潜能很感兴趣。这些车就停在我们周围，停在距离他们的所有者不到100英尺的范围内。比较汽车和美国电网的发电能力，汽车电力的1/4，相当于美国电网的供电能力。由此，可看出汽车发电能力的强大，而且还是可移动的发电，氢燃料电池让我们能够充分利用资源，即使汽车和卡车停着的时候也能发电，为电网所用。

⑨ 之前我们谈到群网络，最强大的群是将所有的处理器，所有未处于使用状态的汽车集合起来，作为具有计算能力的全球电网的一部分。这个假想让我们振奋不已，汽车能够成为一种电器，不是作为商品意义上的电器，而是作为一种能够提供信息、计算、通信的电器、移动电源、移动平台，当然也是一种交通工具。

⑩ 但最重要的是，我们要让汽车价廉物美和令人兴奋，并且有足够的资金进行研发。要实现我们的设想，还有很长的路要走。许多人担心如果考虑这样一个巨大的工程，晚上怎么睡得着。我告诉他们我的睡眠就像小婴儿一样。每两个小时就醒来哭一次，我认为这次研讨会的主题，实际上就是策划出关键要素，并予以实现，那就是关系网的建立与相互合作。

谢谢！(掌声)

2. Please interpret the following passage by using the techniques illustrated above. Please pay attention to the underlined sentences as they require special treatment during interpreting.

巴拉克·奥巴马留给其继任者唐纳德·特朗普的临别赠言

① 巴拉克·奥巴马(Barack Obama)给他的继任者留下了一句临别赠语。在唐纳德·特朗普(Donald Trump)预言自己将成为"上帝创造的最伟大的就业制造者"一天前，离任的美国总统似乎像是宴会上的幽灵，警告称"自动化的无情步伐将淘汰很多就业岗位"。

② 这两种说法至少都可能被证明为正确。几十年来，自动化一直是个常数，而机器人和人工智能领域的最新进展基本上确保了其应用速度将加快，但关键在于时机。对于公司及其投资者(对于政治人士也是如此)而言，关键问题不是"是否"，而是"何时"。

③ 对于整个社会而言，自动化的步伐将决定应对工人失业的难度有多大，以及政治反弹是否会加剧。对于那些试图将最新机器人和智能设备推向真实世界的公司及其投资者而言，自动化的步伐同样重要。几乎无人处在谷歌(Google)母公司Alphabet那样的位置上，该公司对押注于自动驾驶汽车等领域持长远眼光，但如今就连Alphabet也开始对这样的"登月式项目"何时带来回报感到不耐烦。

④ 影响普及速度的变量很多。在有关自动化的一份最新报告中，麦肯锡(McKinsey)估计，在人们从事的所有工作中，有一半可以通过已得到验证的技术被自动化。但这个估计没有说明整个过程需要多长时间。

⑤ 考虑到各种不确定性(从监管到企业改变流程的能力)，咨询顾问们估计，这可能需要20~60年。试着根据那种程度的变异性来构建一个投资模型吧！以自动驾驶汽车和卡车为例，很多技术已得到验证，而潜在市场(对于汽车制造商和科技供应商而言)是巨大的。但是，要让它变成一个可观的市场，需要5年、10年还是30年？

⑥ 汽车制造商已投入数亿美元打造无人驾驶汽车平台。在本月的拉斯维加斯消费电子展(Consumer Electronics Show)和底特律车展(Detroit Auto Show)上，无人驾驶技术显然已摆脱实验阶段：汽车制造商正竞相把这项技术推向道路。最大的公司有能力将研发成本分摊在较大的车辆保有量上，但汽车的技术含量越来越高，将让该行业很多规模较小的参与者面临挑战。

⑦ 奥迪(Audi)等公司将自动化称为一种进展。该公司表示，60%的新车买家已选择支付3000~6000美元添加自动加速和刹车功能。可以合理地指望这些消费者会为更高水平的安全和便利付出更高价格。从汽车自动保持在自己的车道上，到开车不用手握方向盘，这一转变可能会是一场平稳(且有利可图)的演变。

⑧ 但无人驾驶汽车的最强大商业理由来自于更为彻底的、要么全有要么全无的一步：消除对人类驾驶员的需要。在上月末一份有关自动化对经济影响的报告中，白宫表示，目前美国的170万重型卡车司机中，多数人很可能会被取代，尽管该报告补充称，这"可能需要几年甚至几十年"才会发生。

⑨ 有一些非常实际的考量。正如麦肯锡合伙人迈克尔·崔(Michael Cui)指出的那样，

更换目前在美国道路上行驶的大约200万辆重型卡车的成本极其高昂，这些卡车的平均寿命为20年。麦肯锡估计，即便没有新的无人驾驶技术，更换成本也将高达3200亿美元。但很可能会有加快采用新技术的特定投资理由。长途路线是卡车运输领域最容易摘取的果实。车辆结队(Platooning，多辆卡车在由人类驾驶的领头卡车后面组成一个车队)可能带来一种受到监控的自动化形式。尽管自动化的长尾效应可能耗时几十年，但早期采用者的市场仍可能巨大。

⑩ 渐进自动化不会立即消灭就业岗位，而是可能会先让卡车司机的日子更舒适，然后在中期弥补司机数量的短缺，最终才会消除这些就业岗位。这种前景为那些引领人工智能和机器人潮流的公司描绘了一幅美好的愿景。但就像当今动荡不安的政治气候所显示的那样，指望如此平稳地过渡将是愚蠢的。

14.3.4　篇章口译[Passage Practice (C to E)]

1. Please interpret the following passage by using the techniques illustrated above. Please pay attention to the underlined sentences as they require special treatment during interpreting.

China's Space Activities in 2016

① Space activities make up one of the most challenging hi-tech fields which exert enormous impact on other fields. Space activities have greatly improved man's knowledge of space, and provide an important driving force for social progress. Currently, more and more countries, including developing ones, are making the development of space activities an important strategic choice. Thus, space activities around the world are flourishing.

② The Chinese government takes the space industry as an important part of the nation's overall development strategy, and adheres to the principle of exploration and utilization of outer space for peaceful purposes. Over the past 60 years of remarkable development since its space industry was established in 1956, China has made great achievements in this sphere, including the development of atomic and hydrogen bombs, missiles, man-made satellites, manned spaceflight and lunar probe. It has opened up a path of self-reliance and independent innovation, and has created the spirit of China's space industry. To carry forward this spirit and stimulate enthusiasm for innovation, the Chinese government set April 24 as China's Space Day in 2016.

③ "To explore the vast cosmos, develop the space industry and build China into a space power is dream we pursue unremittingly." In the next five years and beyond China will uphold the concepts of innovative, balanced, green, open and shared development, and promote the comprehensive development of space science, space technology and space applications, so as to contribute more to both serving national development and improving the well-being of mankind.

④ To enable the world community to better understand China's space industry, we are publishing this white paper to offer a brief introduction to the major achievements China has made in this field since 2011, its main tasks in the next five years, and its international exchanges and cooperation efforts.

2. Please interpret the following passage by using the techniques illustrated above. Please pay attention to the underlined sentences as they require special treatment during interpreting.

Introduction to TCM

① With a history of 2000 to 3000 years, Traditional Chinese Medicine (TCM) has formed a unique system to diagnose and cure illness. The TCM approach is fundamentally different from that of Western medicine. In TCM, the understanding of the human body is based on the holistic understanding of the universe as described in Daoism, and the treatment of illness is based primarily on the diagnosis and differentiation of syndromes.

② One of the essential characteristics of TCM is the concept of wholism. Wholeness means unity and integrity. TCM pays attention to the unity and integrity of the body, and interrelation between the human body and nature. The human body itself is seen an organic whole. Every part composing the body is inter-cooperative and inter-influenced. The human body is also closely related to external natural surroundings. This idea of unity between interior and exterior conditions, and wholeness of the body itself is called the "concept of whole".

③ The human body as an organic whole, the human body is composed of a number of viscera, organs and tissues, which have their own respective functions. Every functions, however, is a component of the general activity, and inter-influence pathologically.

④ Humans are tied to nature, and there is in nature an essential condition for people to live. Changes in nature, therefore, may directly or indirectly influence the body, and accordingly cause physiological or pathological reactions.

⑤ The other essential characteristics of TCM is Treatment determination based on syndrome differentiation. It is an essential principle in TCM in understanding and treating disease. It is a specific research and treatment method of disease in TCM, and also one of the essential characteristics of TCM. Syndrome differentiation includes analyzing, differentiating and recognizing syndrome of disease. Treatment determination includes deciding in an appropriate therapeutic measure according to syndrome differentiation. Syndrome differentiation is the prerequisite and basis for determining treatment. Treatment determination is the means to treat disease, and also involves examination of whether syndrome differentiation is correct or not. Syndrome differentiation and treatment determination are inseparable in the process of diagnosis and treatment of disease, and embody the combination of theory and practice. Treatment determination base on syndrome different both from common symptomatic treatment and treatment according to different disease in modern medicine. In different stages if a disease, there may appear different syndromes; and in different diseases, the same syndrome may appear. So different syndromes in one disease should be treat by different treatments; while different disease, as long as they express the same syndrome, can be treated with the same treatment. It should be noted that syndrome is a summary of the cause, place, and nature of a disease, and a situation of mutual conflict between the pathology factors and resistance.

⑥ The TCM approach treats zang—fu organs as the core of the human body. Tissue and organs are connected through a network of channels and blood vessels inside human body. Qi (or Chi) acts as some kind of carrier of information that is expressed externally through jingluo system. Pathologically, a dysfunction of the zang-fu organs may be reflected on the body surface through the network, and meanwhile, diseases of body surface tissues may also affect their related zang or fu organs. Affected zang or fu organs may also influence each other through internal connections. Traditional Chinese medicine treatment starts with the analysis of the entire system, then focuses on the correction of pathological changes through readjusting the functions of the zang-fu organs. Evaluation of a syndrome not only includes the cause, mechanism, location, and nature of the disease, but also the confrontation between the pathogenic factor and body resistance. Treatment is not based only on the symptoms, but differentiation of syndromes. Therefore, those with an identical disease may be treated in different ways, and on the other hand, different diseases may result in the same syndrome and are treated in similar ways. The clinical diagnosis and treatment in Traditional Chinese Medicine are mainly based on the yin-yang and five elements theories. These theories apply the phenomena and laws of nature to the study of the physiological activities and pathological changes of the human body and its interrelationships. The typical TCM therapies include acupuncture, herbal medicine, and qigong exercises. With acupuncture, treatment is accomplished by stimulating certain areas of the external body. Herbal medicine acts on zang-fu organs internally, while qigong tries to restore the orderly information flow inside the network through the regulation of Qi. These therapies appear very different in approach yet they all share the same underlying sets of assumptions and insights in the nature of the human body and its place in the universe. Some scientists describe the treatment of diseases through herbal medication, acupuncture, and qigong as an "information therapy."

⑦ The Theory of Yin-Yang

The philosophical origins of Chinese medicine have grown out of the tenets of Daoism (also known as Taoism). Daoism bases much of its thinking on observing the natural world and manner in which it operates, so it is no surprise to find that the Chinese medical system draws extensively on natural metaphors. In Chinese medicine, the metaphoric views of the human body based on observations of nature are fully articulated in the theory of Yin-Yang and the system of Five Elements. The direct meanings of yin and yang in Chinese are bright and dark sides of an object. Chinese philosophy uses yin and yang to represent a wider range of opposite properties in the universe: cold and hot, slow and fast, still and moving, masculine and feminine, lower and upper, etc. In general, anything that is moving, ascending, bright, progressing, hyperactive, including functional disease of the body, pertains to yang. The characteristics of stillness, descending, darkness, degeneration, hypo-activity, including organic disease, pertain to yin. The function of yin and yang is guided by the law of unity of the opposites. In other words, yin and yang are in conflict but at the same time mutually dependent. The nature of yin and yang is relative, with neither being able to exist in isolation. Without "cold" there would be no "hot" without "moving" there would be no "still"; without "dark", there would be no "light". The most illustrative example of yin-yang interdependence is the interrelationship between substance and function. Only with ample substance can the human body function in a healthy way; and only when the functional processes are in good condition, can the essential substances be appropriately refreshed.

⑧ The opposites in all objects and phenomena are in constant motion and change: The gain, growth and advance of the one mean the loss, decline and retreat of the other. For example, day is yang and night is yin, but morning is understood as being yang within yang, afternoon is yin within yang, evening before midnight is yin within yin and the time after midnight is yang within yin. The seed (Yin) grows into the plan (Yang), which itself dies back to the earth (Yin). This takes place within the changes of the seasons. Winter (Yin) transforms through the Spring into Summer (Yang), which in turn transforms through Autumn into Winter again. Because natural phenomena are balanced in the constant flux of alternating yin and yang, the change and transformation of yin-yang has been taken as a universal law. Traditional Chinese medicine holds that human life is a physiological process in constant motion and change. Under normal conditions, the waxing and waning of yin and yang are kept within certain bounds, reflecting a dynamic equilibrium of the physiological processes. When the balance is broken, disease occurs. Typical cases of disease-related imbalance include excess of yin, excess of yang, deficiency of yin, and deficiency of yang.

14.4　科学技术主题词汇汇总(Vocabulary Build-up)

astronomy	天文学
meteorology	气象学
geonomy	地球学
geology	地质学
seismology	地震学
oceanography	海洋学
quantum mechanics	量子力学

(续表)

high energy physics	高能物理学
astrophysics	天体物理学
aerothermo-dynamics	空气热动力学
genetic engineering	遗传工程
microbiology	微生物学
botany	植物学
zoology	动物学
ecology	生态学
biochemistry	生物化学
archaeology	考古学
environmental science	环境科学
virtual reality technology	虚拟现实技术
broadband technology	宽带网技术
netizen	网民
cyberspace	网络空间
the web; world wide web(www)	万维网
genetically modified food	转基因食品
recombinant DNA technology	重组DNA技术
recreational agriculture	休闲农业
solar storm	太阳风暴
acid rain	酸雨
network database	网络数据库
genetic screening	遗传筛查
nutrition immunology	营养免疫
bioinformatics	生物信息学
chromosome	染色体
food chain	食物链

14.5 扩展练习(Enhancement Practice)

Making comments on a given topics.

Directions: Please read paragraph (1) and (2) carefully and then express your views on the given topics.

(1) Computers do not help children learn more efficiently; on the contrary, computers used in schools have negative effects on children's physical and mental development. Do you agree or disagree?

　　Some people hold the view that computes used to teach children fail to enhance youngsters' learning while exerting undesirable effects on the development of their mind and physique. I agree with this idea. Computers negatively impact children's minds. General features of children determine that they are not keen on using computers as a way of acquiring knowledge and accumulating information. Rather, they are mainly in to diverse computer games and the illusive but intriguing world in the game. Thus, it is imaginable that if teenagers are immersed in an "academic" environment like that, a comprehensive mental education is not the direction where computers point children to. Children's obsession with the Internet serves as another example of computers' bad influence on the young mind. Hordes of pornographic entertainment materials are available for consumption by innocent minds. A premature contact with such information will definitely trouble children a lot and might, in some cases, lead them astray. On the basis of children's infatuation with computer games and the Internet, it can be concluded that computer using can be addictive. One immediate aftermath of such an addiction is children's sacrificing their time of playing outside for sitting in front of the computer screen for hours one time in a roll. Under such circumstances, no one is entitled to pronounce that such a practice is beneficial to the advancement of children's physique. In short, the incorporation of computers into children's school education does not bear the pleasant results preconceived by some people. Quite the opposite, it has fathered many disagreeable outcomes.

(2) Motorized flight is the greatest invention in the modern world. No other invention has had a more significant impact on our lives. Do you agree or disagree?

It is certainly true that in the battle against environmental problems, cooperation at the international level is highly desirable. But I cannot fully agree with the claim that international joint efforts are the only way to protect environment. Individual countries and individual persons also have an important part to play in combating environmental problems. In a sense, the advent of motorized flight has brought dramatic changes to public as well as cargo transportation. For one thing, it is by far the fastest means of transportation. What used to be a good ten-hour ride by car can now be easily covered in one hour and a half by air. For another, it is as safe as it is fast. The number of deaths from airplane crash is much less than that of any other means of mass-transportation. On the strengths of these two advantages, motorized flight is widely used for industrial, commercial, military and other purposes, and is gradually changing the way business is conducted, travel plans are made, and wars are fought. I am definitely not suggesting that it is the most important invention ever. It is only one of many which have greatly transformed the modern would. The invention of the internet is a good case in point. To some degree, it is even more important than the transportation revolution in that it has reshaped the way we study, the way we entertain, the way we work, or even the way we socialize, by putting a large part of human activities online. Of course there are quite a few other inventions such as genetic engineering, breakthroughs in medical science, etc., which are as important as the two inventions mentioned above. Human progress results from the combined efforts of various forces and it is improper to attribute it to any single invention.

14.6　延伸口译(Extended Interpreting)

习近平主席在二十国集团领导人汉堡峰会上关于世界经济形势的讲话

各位同事：

Dear colleagues,

汉堡被誉为"世界桥城"。很高兴同大家在这里相聚，共商架设合作之桥、促进共同繁荣大计。首先，我谨对默克尔总理及德方的热情周到接待，表示衷心感谢。

It is a great pleasure to be with you in Hamburg, the City of Bridges, to discuss ways of building a bridge of cooperation to advance our shared prosperity. First of all, I express heartfelt appreciation to you, Chancellor Merkel, and the German government for your warm hospitality.

当前，世界经济出现向好势头，有关国际组织预计，今年世界经济有望增长3.5%。这是近年来最好的经济形势。有这样的局面，同二十国集团的努力分不开。同时，世界经济中的深层次问题尚未解决，仍然面临诸多不稳定、不确定的因素。

The global economy is showing signs of moving in the right direction. The related international organizations forecast that it will grow by 3.5 percent this year, the best performance that we have seen in several years. This would not be possible without the efforts of the G20. On the other hand, the global economy is still plagued by deep-seated problems and faces many uncertainties and destabilizing factors.

面对挑战，杭州峰会提出了二十国集团方案：建设创新、活力、联动、包容的世界经济。汉堡峰会把"塑造联动世界"作为主题，同杭州峰会一脉相承。我们要共同努力，把这些理念化为行动。这里，我愿谈几点意见。

Facing such challenges, the G20 agreed in Hangzhou last year on the path forward: building an innovative, invigorated, interconnected and inclusive world economy. This year, building on the theme of the Hangzhou Summit, the Hamburg Summit has made "Shaping an Interconnected World" its theme. What we need to do now is to work together to translate our vision into action. With this in mind, I wish to state the following:

第一，我们要坚持建设开放型世界经济大方向。这是二十国集团应对国际金融危机的重要经验，也是推动世界经济增长的重要路径。国际组织当前调高世界经济增长预期，一个重要原因就是预计国际贸易增长2.4%、全球投资增加5%。我们要坚持走开放发展、互利共赢之路，共同做大世界经济的蛋糕。作为世界主要经济体，我们应该也能够发挥领导作用，支持多边贸易体制，按照共同制定的规则办事，通过协商为应对共同挑战找到共赢的解决方案。

Firstly, we should stay committed to building an open global economy. This commitment of the G20 to build open economies saw us through the global financial crisis, and this commitment is vital to reenergizing the global economy. Various international organizations have revised upward forecast for this year's global growth, mainly because of a projected 2.4 percent growth for global trade and 5 percent growth for global investment. We must remain committed to openness and mutual benefit for all so as to increase the size of the global economic "pie". As the world's major economies, we should and must lead the way, support the multilateral trading system, observe the jointly established rules and, through consultation, seek all-win solutions to common challenges we face.

第二，我们要共同为世界经济增长发掘新动力。这个动力首先来自创新。研究表明，全球95%的工商业同互联网密切相关，世界经济正在向数字化转型。我们要在数字经济和新工业革命领域加强合作，共同打造新技术、新产业、新模式、新产品。这个动力也来自更好地解决发展问题，落实2030年可持续发展议程。这对发展中国家有利，也将为发达国家带来市场和投资机遇，大家都是赢家。杭州峰会就创新和发展达成重要共识，有关合作势头在德国年得以延续，下一步要不断走深、走实。

Secondly, we should foster new sources of growth for the global economy. Innovation, more than anything else, is such a new source of growth. Research shows that 95 percent of the world's businesses are now closely linked with the Internet, and the global economy is transitioning toward a digital economy. This means we should boost cooperation in digital economy and the new industrial revolution and jointly develop new technologies, new industries, new business models and new products. Another source of growth derives from making greater efforts to address the issue of development and implement the 2030 Agenda for Sustainable Development, and such efforts will both benefit developing countries and generate business and investment opportunities for developed countries. In other words, this will be a win-win game for all. At the Hangzhou Summit last year, we reached important consensus on innovation and development. This momentum of cooperation created has been sustained this year under the German chairmanship of G20. Going forward, we should see that more substantial and concrete outcomes are delivered.

第三，我们要携手使世界经济增长更加包容。当前，世界经济发展仍不平衡，技术进步对就业的挑战日益突出。世界经济论坛预计，到2020年，人工智能将取代全球逾500万个工作岗位。二十国集团的一项重要使命，就是本着杭州峰会确定的包容增长理念，处理好公平和效率、资本和劳动、技术和就业的矛盾。要继续把经济政策和社会政策有机结合起来，解决产业升级、知识和技能错配带来的挑战，使收入分配更加公平合理。二十国集团应该更加重视在教育培训、就业创业、分配机制上交流合作。这些工作做好了，也有利于经济全球化健康发展。

Thirdly, we should work together to achieve more inclusive global growth. Currently, global economic growth is not balanced, and technological advances work against job creation. According to the projection of the World Economic Forum, artificial intelligence will take away more than 5 million jobs in the world by 2020. The G20 has an important mission, which is to reaffirm the vision of pursuing inclusive growth agreed upon at the Hangzhou Summit last year, and strike a balance between fairness and efficiency, between capital and labor, and between technology and employment. To achieve this goal, we must ensure synergy between economic and social policies, address the mismatch between industrial upgrading and knowledge and skills, and ensure more equitable income distribution. The G20 needs to place more importance on cooperation in education, training, employment, business start-up and wealth distribution-related mechanisms, as progress on these fronts will make economic globalization work better.

第四，我们要继续完善全球经济治理。国际金融危机爆发以来，二十国集团在加强宏观政策协调、改革国际金融机构、完善国际金融监管、打击避税等方面取得了积极成果，为稳定金融市场、促进经济复苏作出了重要贡献。下一步，我们要在上述领域继续努力，特别是要加强宏观政策沟通，防范金融市场风险，发展普惠金融、绿色金融，推动金融业更好地服务实体经济发展。

Fourthly, we should continue improving global economic governance. In the wake of the global financial crisis, the G20 has done a lot to improve macroeconomic policy coordination, reform international financial institutions, tighten international financial regulation and combat tax avoidance, thus ensuring financial market stability and recovery. We should build on these achievements. In particular, we should strengthen coordination of macroeconomic policies, forestall risks in financial markets and develop financial inclusion and green finance to make the financial sector truly drive the development of the real economy.

不久前，中国成功举办"一带一路"国际合作高峰论坛。与会各方本着共商、共建、共享精神，在促进政策沟通、设施联通、贸易畅通、资金融通、民心相通上取得丰硕成果，努力打造治理新理念、合作新平台、发展新动力。这同二十国集团的宗旨高度契合。

China recently hosted a successful Belt and Road Forum for International Cooperation. Acting in the spirit of extensive consultation, joint contribution and shared benefits, the forum participants achieved fruitful outcomes in terms of boosting the connectivity of policies, infrastructure, trade, finance and people. Guided by a new vision of governance, we built a new platform of cooperation to tap into new sources of growth. The commitment of the Belt and Road Forum is highly compatible with the goal of the G20.

德国谚语说，一个人的努力是加法，一个团队的努力是乘法。让我们携手合作，推动联动增长，促进共同繁荣，不断向着构建人类命运共同体的目标迈进！

A German saying goes to the effect that, "Those who work alone, add; those who work together, multiply." In this spirit, let us work together to promote interconnected growth for shared prosperity and build toward a global community with a shared future.

谢谢大家。

Thank you.

——2017年7月7日，汉堡

—Hamburg, 7 July 2017

参考文献

[1] 梅德明. 高级口译教程. 上海：上海外语教育出版社，2002

[2] 雷天放，陈菁. 上海：上海外语教育出版社，2008

[3] 吴钟明. 英语口译笔记法实战指导. 武汉：武汉大学出版社，2005

[4] 仲伟合，王斌华. 基础口译. 北京：外语教学与研究出版社，2009

[5] 彭萍. 实用旅游英语翻译. 北京：对外经济贸易大学出版社，2010

[6] 金正昆. 涉外礼仪教程. 北京：中国人民大学出版社，2005

[7] 林超伦. 实战口译. 北京：外语教学与研究出版社，2005

[8] 邬姝丽. 实用英语高级口译教程. 北京：外语教学与研究出版社，2012

[9] 卢信朝. 英汉口译技能教程听辨. 北京：北京语言大学出版社，2012

[10] 梅德明. 口译进阶教程专业交传. 北京：北京大学出版社，2008

[11] 任文. 英汉口译教程. 北京：外语教学与研究出版社，2016

[12] 梅德明. 口译进阶教程联络陪同. 北京：北京大学出版社，2011

参考网址：

[1] http://www.people.com.cn

[2] http://www.fmprc.gov.cn/web

[3] http://www.xinhuanet.com

[4] http://www.kekenet.com

[5] http://www.huanqiu.com

[6] http://learning.sohu.com

[7] http://cpc.people.com.cn

[8] http://wenku.baidu.com

[9] http://www.chinadaily.com.cn

[10] http://www.hjenglish.com

[11] http://www.en8848.com.cn

[12] http://blog.sina.com.cn/s/blog_4b901a8601009p4o.html~type=v5_one&label=rela_nextarticle

参考文献

[1] 胡锦涛. 《论口译教程》. 上海：上海外语教育出版社，2002.
[2] 梅德明. 吴冰，主编. 北京：中国对外翻译出版社，2008.
[3] 仲伟明，杨柳燕. 口译基础理论，北京，北京大学出版社，2005.
[4] 仲伟合，王斌华. 基础口译，北京：外语教学与研究出版社，2009.
[5] 雷天. 实用英汉口译教程，北京：对外经济贸易大学出版社，2010.
[6] 金正昆. 商务礼仪教程，北京：中国人民大学出版社，2005.
[7] 林超伦. 实战口译，北京：外语教学与研究出版社，2005.
[8] 鲍刚，实用英汉互译技巧，北京：外语教学与研究出版社，2012.
[9] 方凡泉. 新汉口译实用技巧，广州：北京语言大学出版社，2012.
[10] 陈德鸿. 口译理论与技巧，北京：北京大学出版社，2008.
[11] 刘宓庆. 口译论，北京：中国对外翻译出版公司，2010.
[12] 杨承淑. 口译教学研究理论与实践，北京：中国对外翻译，2011.

参考网址：
[1] http://www.people.com.cn
[2] http://www.fmprc.gov.cn/web
[3] http://www.xinhuanet.com
[4] http://www.kekenet.com
[5] http://www.hjenglish.com
[6] http://learning.sohu.com
[7] http://cpc.people.com.cn
[8] http://en.chinagate.com
[9] http://www.chinadaily.com.cn
[10] http://www.chinaspeak.com
[11] http://www.cctv.com.cn
[12] http://blog.sina.com.cn/blog_48b07a550100p9e6.html?type=v5_once_label=rela